Theoretical Morphology

Edited by

Michael Hammond
Department of Linguistics
University of Wisconsin-Milwaukee
Milwaukee, Wisconsin

Michael Noonan
Department of English
University of Wisconsin-Milwaukee
Milwaukee, Wisconsin

Theoretical Morphology

Approaches in Modern Linguistics

Academic Press, Inc.
Harcourt Brace Jovanovich, Publishers
San Diego   New York   Berkeley   Boston
London   Sydney   Tokyo   Toronto

ACADEMIC PRESS, INC.
1250 Sixth Avenue
San Diego, California 92101

United Kingdom Edition published by
ACADEMIC PRESS INC. (LONDON) LTD.
24-28 Oval Road, London NW1 7DX

Library of Congress Cataloging-in-Publication Data

Theoretical morphology : approaches in modern linguistics / edited by
    Michael Hammond, Michael Noonan.
        p.   cm.
    Includes index.
    ISBN 0-12-322045-9 (alk. paper). ISBN 0-12-322046-7 (pbk. : alk.
paper)
    1. Grammar, Comparative and general—Morphology.   I. Hammond,
Michael (Michael T.) II. Noonan, Michael (Michael P.)
P241.T54   1988
415—dc19   88-19287
                                                                    CIP

PRINTED IN THE UNITED STATES OF AMERICA
    89 90 91   9 8 7 6 5 4 3 2

Contents

Contributors

STEPHEN R. ANDERSON Department of Linguistics, University of California, Los Angeles, California 90024

MARK ARONOFF Program in Linguistics, State University of New York, Stony Brook, New York 11794

JOSEF BAYER Max-Planck-Institut für Psycholinguistik, NL-6525 XD Nijmegen, The Netherlands

RIA DE BLESER Forschergruppe "Aphasie und kognitive Störungen", Abteilung Neurologie, RWTH Aachen, Pauwelsstr, D-5100 Aachen, Federal Republic of Germany

JOAN L. BYBEE Department of Linguistics, State University of New York, Buffalo, New York 14261

ANDREW CARSTAIRS Department of English, University of Canterbury, Christchurch 1, New Zealand

STUART DAVIS Speech Research Laboratory, University of Indiana, Bloomington, Indiana 47405

WOLFGANG U. DRESSLER Institut für Sprachwissenschaft, Universität Wien, Vienna A-1090 Austria

MICHAEL HAMMOND Department of Linguistics, University of Wisconsin-Milwaukee, Milwaukee, Wisconsin 53201

GREGORY K. IVERSON   Department of Linguistics, University of Iowa, Iowa City, Iowa 52242

RICHARD D. JANDA   Department of Linguistics, University of New Mexico, Albuquerque, New Mexico 87131

BRIAN D. JOSEPH   Department of Linguistics, Ohio State University, Columbus, Ohio 43210-1229

JULIETTE LEVIN   Department of Linguistics, University of Texas, Austin, Texas 78712

BRIAN MACWHINNEY   Department of Psychology, Carnegie-Mellon University, Pittsburgh, Pennsylvania 15213

ALEC MARANTZ   Department of English, University of North Carolina, Chapel Hill, North Carolina 27514

MARIANNE MITHUN   Department of Linguistics, University of California, Santa Barbara, California 93106

MICHAEL NOONAN   Department of English, University of Wisconsin-Milwaukee, Milwaukee, Wisconsin 53201

DAVID M. PERLMUTTER   Department of Linguistics, University of California, San Diego, La Jolla, California 92093

DOUGLAS PULLEYBLANK   Department of Linguistics, University of Southern California, Los Angeles, California 90089-1693

KEREN RICE   Department of Linguistics, University of Toronto, Toronto, Ontario M5S 1A1 Canada

JERROLD M. SADOCK   Department of Linguistics, University of Chicago, Chicago, Illinois 60637

GERALD SANDERS   Department of Linguistics, University of Minnesota, Minneapolis, Minnesota 55455

RICHARD SPROAT   AT&T Bell Laboratories, MH 2D-443, Murray Hill, New Jersey 07974

S. N. SRIDHAR   Program in Linguistics, State University of New York, Stony Brook, New York 11794

DIETER STEIN   Institut for Anglistik und Americanistik, Universität Giessen, D-6300 Giessen, Federal Republic of Germany

JOSEPH PAUL STEMBERGER   Department of Linguistics, University of Minnesota, Minneapolis, Minnesota 55455

DEIRDRE W. WHEELER   Department of English, University of New Hampshire, Durham, New Hamshire 03824

Preface

Until recently, morphology was something of a stepchild of linguistics, accorded far less attention by researchers than syntax and phonology, as witnessed by the relative scarcity of books and university courses devoted to the topic. In the last few years the situation has changed a good deal, and indeed some issues in morphology have assumed the status of "hot topics" in the field.

The goal of this volume is to bring together a collection of studies representative of both the approaches to morphology in contemporary linguistics and the issues currently being debated within these approaches. The core of the volume consists of a selection of the papers presented at the *Milwaukee Morphology Meeting*, the Fifteenth Annual Linguistics Symposium of the University of Wisconsin-Milwaukee. The volume also contains several invited chapters that make the volume more representative of work currently done in the field.

The first chapter in the collection is an introductory article by the editors, which attempts to place current work in a historical perspective and to outline some of the theories and issues. The remainder of the collection is divided into five parts: "Inflection," "Rules and Representations," "Historical/Areal Studies," "Mapping to Other Components," and "Morpho-phonology."

The first part, "Inflection," contains chapters by Stephen R. Anderson, Ria de Bleser and Josef Bayer, Andrew Carstairs, David M. Perlmutter, and Joseph Paul Stemberger and Brian MacWhinney. Anderson outlines the Extended Word-and-Paradigm theory of inflection and attempts to treat cliticization in the context of this theory. De Bleser and Bayer argue that data from agrammatic aphasics can be accounted for in terms of theories of lexical morphology, theories in which inflection is added in the lexicon. Carstairs investigates the question of what constitutes distinct inflectional paradigms.

He suggests that apparent differences based solely on stem allomorphy do not count as separate. Perlmutter treats a class of apparent counterexamples from Yiddish to what he terms the "split morphology hypothesis," the idea that inflection occurs outside the lexicon. Stemberger and MacWhinney investigate the question of what forms are stored in the lexicon. In particular, they provide psycholinguistic evidence bearing on whether all members of inflectional paradigms should be listed separately in the lexicon.

The second part, "Rules and Representations," includes chapters by Joan L. Bybee, Wolfgang U. Dressler, and Gerald Sanders. Bybee proposes a theory of morphology containing only a lexicon whereby the relationships between lexical entries are captured in terms of direct connections between entries and the relative strengths of those entries. Dressler proposes that strict universals be replaced with preferences on basis of the "word-based hypothesis," the idea that words are the input to morphology. In an investigation of the issue of zero derivation, Sanders argues the inadequacy of an overt analog as a criterion and suggests that nonformal principles be invoked instead.

The third part, "Historical/Areal Studies," includes studies by Mark Aronoff and S. N. Sridhar, Brian D. Joseph and Richard D. Janda, Marianne Mithun, and Dieter Stein. Aronoff and Sridhar demonstrate the existence of prefixes in Kannada and argue for a structural difference between them and compounding. Joseph and Janda investigate putative cases of historical demorphologization and argue that their rarity follows from the "morphocentricity" of grammar. Mithun investigates the evolution of number marking in a number of Native American languages. Stein deals with the motivations and mechanisms of the change of *-th* to *-s* in marking the third person singular in English.

The fourth part, "Mapping to Other Components," contains chapters by Alec Marantz, Jerrold M. Sadock, and Richard Sproat. Marantz argues for a treatment of cliticization in terms of principles independently required to effect the mapping from syntax to phonology. Sadock outlines the Autolexical Theory of morphology and shows how it provides for a useful classification of lexemes. Sproat argues that anaphoric islands follow from independently required principles of syntax and that they therefore provide no evidence for separating morphology from syntax.

The last part, "Morphophonology," contains chapters by Stuart Davis, Gregory K. Iverson and Deirdre W. Wheeler, Juliette Levin, Douglas Pulleyblank, and Keren Rice. Davis argues against transfer-based analyses of internal reduplication in favor of a more traditional analysis using direct association. Iverson and Wheeler argue against the Elsewhere Condition in phonology and morphology in favor of the earlier Revised Alternation Condition. Levin argues that all cases of lexical bidirectional foot assignment involve multiple lexical strata. Pulleyblank demonstrates that the Morphemic Tier Hypothesis can be extended into the tonal domain. Finally, Rice argues against allowing the phonology access to notions like c-command, showing that voicing alternations in Slave can be reanalyzed in terms of underspecification.

We would like to acknowledge financial support for the conference from the following units at the University of Wisconsin-Milwaukee: Department of Communication, Department of Comparative Literature, Department of Curriculum and Instruction, Department of German, Department of Linguistics, Department of Philosophy, Department of Slavic Languages, Department of Spanish and Portuguese, Department of Speech Pathology and Audiology, the Center for Twentieth Century Studies, the College of Letters and Science, the Language Resource Center, the Master of Arts in Foreign Language and Literature Program, and Wisconsin Teachers of English to Speakers of Other Languages.

We would also like to thank the others on the conference organizing and program committees: Ashley Hastings, Diane Highland, Gary Krukar, Peter Lee, Edith Moravcsik, Rita Rutkowski Weber, and Jessica Wirth.

Thanks also to Sue Cronce for preparing the indices.

Finally, we would like to thank Tshim Kadima-Kolombo and Bernice Rothenberg for administrative assistance and the staff at Academic Press for editorial assistance.

Chapter 1

Morphology in
the Generative Paradigm

Michael Hammond & Michael Noonan

1.

One of the more striking developments in the history of the generative paradigm has been the resurrection and subsequent elaboration of a separate morphological component. It is true that, for the most part, this development
did not come about because of any special concern for morphological problems per se; on the contrary, it was motivated primarily by concerns internal
to the syntax and phonology. Nonetheless, we have now come full circle, from
the elimination of an autonomous morphology in the earliest generative
model, *Syntactic Structures*, to a position similar to that of the traditional
and the pre-Chomskyan structuralist models in recognizing morphology as
a central, independent component of the grammar.

In this chapter, we review the recent history of morphological theorizing.
Our goal is not to provide a detailed or systematic survey; rather, we intend
only to provide a sketch of major developments. (Scalise, 1984, gives a detailed
history of generative morphology through the early 1980s.) Further, our sketch
is not organized in a strictly chronological manner: We first survey models
developed within the "orthodox" tradition of generative linguistics, after which
we turn our attention to the more functionally oriented "natural" approaches.

2.

In *Syntactic Structures* and in works based on the model presented there [such
as Lees (1960)], there was not only no autonomous morphology, there was

not even an independent lexicon. Lexical items were inserted into phrase markers by means of a set of context-free rewriting rules that did not differ in any formal way from ordinary phrase structures rules. Morphological operations, for example, affixation and compounding, were handled by transformation.

There were a number of unfortunate consequences of this approach to morphology that became apparent fairly quickly. For example, it resulted in a proliferation of categorial nodes in order to accommodate the selectional idiosyncrasies of lexical items. The VP expansion rule, for instance, would have to allow for numerous classes of verbs—transitive, intransitive, ditransitive, copular, and so on—which required the use of categorial symbols such as V_{tr}, V_{intr}, V_{cop}. This meant that, in the absence of special conventions, there was no simple way to generalize over the class of verbs without making a long list, and thus even relatively simple transformations like subject–verb agreement were cumbersome to state formally.

It was obvious, then, that if the syntax were to be maximally simple and general, it would have to rid itself of this lexical baggage. This was done in Chomsky (1965). In *Aspects*, the lexicon was given its autonomy, albeit as a subcomponent of the base. Idiosyncratic information about lexical items now resided within the lexicon. Lexical insertion was accomplished by a special transformation which replaced a terminal node, indicated by $\triangle$, with a lexical item, matching the information in the selectional and strict-subcategorization features of the latter with the tree structure into which the lexical item was to be inserted.

While morphology had been resurrected in the sense that there were now some aspects of a morphology that were independent of syntax and phonology, most of the traditional purview of morphology still lay within these domains. Affixation and compounding, that is, the combining of morphemes, were still a function of the syntax. And the interpretation of the strings of morphemes and accompanying syntactic features that resulted from the application of syntactic rules was done in the phonological component.

Two general problems resulted from this partitioning of morphology. First, it led to rather complex and powerful theories of phonology and syntax. In phonology, it necessitated a theory in which information about morphological conditioning could be formalized in a purely phonological manner, which in turn resulted in a rather problematic theory of boundaries. It had the further consequence of encouraging very abstract analyses: Since the phonology took as input the product of the word-formation rules of the transformational component, and these, especially in the early days, were likely to consist of agglutinated strings of abstract morphemes, an abstract analysis was made almost inevitable (see, e.g., Lightner, 1965, and Foley, 1965 as examplars of this sort of abstract analysis). Further, there was in any case a strong temptation to deal with morphologically conditioned alternations as though they were phonologically conditioned, since the model provided no other convenient (or intuitively satisfying) location for the expression of such alternations. In syntax, the inclusion of affixation and compounding rules meant that otherwise valid generalizations, such as the fact that syntactic rules cannot refer to the internal structure of words, could not be stated.

A second problem resulting from the bifurcation of morphology was the restatement of morphological generalizations in both the syntax and the phonology. For example, it is well known that phonological rules applying in the shallower areas of the morphology, for example, inflection, are generally more productive than rules applying in the deeper zones of the morphology. On the other hand, it is also clear that syntactic rules sensitive to shallower inflectional facts exist, while there are, some have maintained, no syntactic rules sensitive to deeper derivational morphology. These two facts are most likely instantiations of the same underlying morphological principle: Deeper levels in the morphology are less transparent to external manipulation. As long as there is no morphological component, this generalization must be stated twice—in the syntax and in the phonology. In fact, the problem may be even more serious, since semantic interpretation also seems to be sensitive to morphological depth. For example, as noted by Allen (1978), the interpretation of the level-ordered affixes *non-*, *un-*, and *in-* varies in accordance with their relative depth in the morphology. Thus, the problem of no independent morphology is magnified by every domain it interacts with.

But perhaps the most serious consequence of the lack of an independent morphology related to formal problems encountered in trying to elaborate a theory of word formation totally within the syntax. The earliest proposals, those made in Lees (1960), ran afoul of the prohibition handed down by Chomsky in *Aspects* that transformations not be allowed to change meaning. For example, Lees proposed that compounds be generated from fully specified Ss via a device similar to that needed independently for relative clauses and, in his model, attributive adjectives. Thus, *manservant* would be derived from a structure like *servant* [*man* pres *be servant*]. The problem is that many compounds are ambiguous, which in Lees's model meant that they would have more than one deep structure. So, *rat poison* can mean either 'poison for rats' or 'poison made from rats'; since the surface structure is ambiguous and a unique deep structure cannot be determined, we are confronted with an instance of nonrecoverable deletion, which is disallowed in the *Aspects* model. There were other, more substantive problems with Lees's model as well. For example, treating the derivation of compounds identically with the derivation of attributive adjectives resulted in paradoxes like the following: *a white blackboard* is a grammatical (and pragmatically possible) utterance, whereas its source within Lees's model, *a board* [*which is black*] [*which is white*], is not (see Allen, 1978, for further discussion and exemplification).

Another problem was noted by Chomsky (1970) in formulating his lexicalist hypothesis. Chomsky noted that the meanings of nominalizations like *revolution, construction, reference*, and *referral* are not necessarily predictable from the meanings of their corresponding verbs and therefore cannot be derived transformationally. In fact, the problem is much more general than Chomsky indicated, affecting all manner of derivational morphology. Just to take one example, the fact that there now exist *white blackboards, green blackboards*, and so on clearly shows that the meanings of compounds like *blackboard* cannot be derived from the meanings of their component parts.

3.

By the early 1970s there was considerable evidence that the transformational approach to word formation was misguided, though not all linguists found the evidence convincing. In particular, the generative semanticists took the transformational approach to word formation to its logical conclusion, deriving even monomorphemic forms like *kill* from complexes of more primitive predicates like *cause [become [not [alive]]]*. Despite the many (eventually overwhelming) problems that such a program entails for them, the transformationalist approach was for the generative semanticists entirely consistent with their 'logicist' goal of creating a sort of universal base, which would contain only semantic primitives, variables, and proper names, and from which not only the sentence patterns, but also the vocabulary of the world's languages would be derived.

Within more orthodox approaches—termed then "interpretive semanticist" because of the presence within the model of an interpretive (as opposed to a generative) semantic component—the role of the syntax in word formation was being greatly curtailed. Jackendoff (1972) proposed his extended lexical hypothesis whereby transformations were prevented from operating on purely morphological material, which instead came under the domain of morphological rules, though the nature of these rules was not fully specified. Even so, Jackendoff's proposal laid the groundwork for the elaboration of a uniquely morphological component, a task that was taken up, though only in the form of a programmatic outline, by Halle (1973).

Halle proposed that the model include an autonomous morphological component that would be given complete responsibility for the creation of words, thus removing the syntax from word formation entirely. The new component would consist of a dictionary, which contain all and only the words of a language; a list of morphemes, understood as being distinct from the dictionary; a list of word-formation rules; and a filter, which specifies exceptions and adds any idiosyncratic information, such as the fact that *reference* and *referral* have semantic idiosyncrasies vis à vis the verb refer.

There were a number of problems with Halle's 1973 model that were brought out in the literature during the next few years, for example, Siegel (1974), Jackendoff (1975), and, most important, Aronoff (1976). One problem concerned the redundant specification of forms in both a list of morphemes and a dictionary. Another concerned the apparently unrestricted formal power of the word-formation rules. And yet another concerned the fact that Halle continued the tradition, inherited from the pregenerative structuralist approaches to morphology, of regarding the morpheme as the basic unit of the lexicon—though in this regard Halle did make use of the generative innovation of considering words to have internal structure, that is, as not consisting of a simple unbracketed string of morphemes, such as *un + remark + able*, but rather as a labeled bracketing: [*un*[[*remark*]$_V$*able*]$_A$]$_A$.

Aronoff (1976) provided the first comprehensive model of word formation within the generative paradigm. Purely formal matters aside, his main innovation was to replace the morpheme with the word as the minimal unit of a generative morphology. (Postal, 1969, had provided evidence that the word is the minimal unit in the syntax also.) His argument ran as follows: Words do seem to be analyzable in terms of morphemes; that is given words like *huckleberry, transmit,* or *antidisestablishmentarianism,* we can decompose them into strings of component elements—*huckle + berry, trans + mit, anti + dis + establish + ment + arian + ism*—elements which often help us to understand the sense of new words. But if we try to reverse the process, to construct words and their senses from lists of morphemes given in a lexicon, we run into significant, perhaps insuperable, difficulties. No doubt the component *-berry* contributes to the sense of *huckleberry,* but what does *huckle*-mean? We know what *straw* means, but what component of the sense of *straw* do we find in *strawberry*? Similarly, *transmit* shares the stem *mit* with a series of other words—*commit, remit, submit, admit, permit,* and so on. When the nominalizing suffix *-ion* is added to these words, *mit* undergoes a morphophonemic rule converts it to *miss*—*transmission, commission, remission, submission.* But what does *mit* mean? Apart from the fact that all are active verbs, these *mit* words seem to have nothing in common semantically, no semantic content that we could attribute to *mit,* even though the words have something in common morphologically.

Aranoff's model was formally simpler than Halle's, consisting only of a dictionary in which were stored words, not morphemes, and a set of word-formation rules. The rules were more restricted than Halle's since they could not have access to syntactic or phonological information.

4.

Halle and Aranoff's proposals for an autonomous morphology were consistent with the general tenor of developments within the new government and binding (GB) syntax, which was developing a theory of independent MODULES having their own sets of principles and interacting with the other modules in the course of a derivation. It was now clear that the morphology, like the modules within the syntax, had its own principles. What had not been worked out yet was how the morphology interacted with the other components of the grammar, particularly the phonology.

Some suggestions about how the phonology and the morphology might interact had been made in some of the earliest work on an independent morphology. Siegel (1974) had suggested that the morphological component of the grammar consisted of a set of levels and that the cyclic rules of word stress in English applied within these levels. Pesetsky (1979) extended the idea to include other sorts of rules as well and, further, suggested ways to access morphological information without recourse to the familiar boundary symbols (e.g., + and #) of *The Sound Pattern of English* (Chomsky and Halle, 1968). This work led to the development of lexical phonology (LP), the principles of which were spelled out in Mohanan (1982) and Kiparsky (1982). (See Mohanan (1986) for an updated and expanded discussion of the theory of LP.)

LP is, without doubt, the dominant morphological theory in North America today. Central to its claims is the notion that a subset of phonological rule applications takes place within the morphological component, referred to within the theory of LP as the LEXICON. In the lexicon, the application of phonological rules alternates with the application of morphological rules in such a way that each operates on the output of the other.

Another important claim of this theory is that phonological rules can be indexed to the morphological strata. In this way, LP theory allows the phonology to be sensitive to morphological constituency and obviates the need for the traditional boundary symbols.

A further important claim within the theory of LP includes the notion that morphological processes are level ordered; that is, that morphological affixation processes are organized à la Siegel, into a series of levels, or STRATA. Affixes are divided into classes, which in turn are matched with a given stratum. The theory claims that the affixes of any particular stratum may occur in any order with respect to other affixes of the same stratum. Since the strata are ordered relative to each other, the affixes on earlier strata are necessarily inside affixes of later strata. That is, the affixes of the first stratum would be the innermost affixes, while those of the last stratum would be the outermost.

Consider an example. In English, compounding precedes productive inflectional morphology, but irregular morphology precedes compounding. Thus we find irregular, unproductive inflection within compounds, but not regular inflectional morphology. Kiparsky (1982) cites the following pairs:

(1)   teeth marks   lice-infested
          *claws marks   *rats-infested

A level-ordered morphology could account for this by positing three levels in the English lexicon; the first containing irregular inflection, the second compounding and the third regular inflection:

(2) Stratum 1   irregular inflection
     Stratum 2   compounding
     Stratum 3   regular inflection

This would account for the facts in (1).

Problems arise within simple models of LP like the one presented above which have led various researchers to propose additional strata, a different arrangement of strata, and various restrictions on rule application (e.g., Halle and Mohanan, 1985). For example, suffixes like *-like* and *-hood* (i.e., Siegel's Class II suffixes) would, in the model presented above, be inserted in Stratum 3 along with regular inflection. The simple version of the model predicts that such suffixes should occur outside Stratum 1 suffixes and should be freely ordered relative to other Stratum 3 suffixes. The examples in (3) and (4) show that neither prediction necessarily results in grammatical forms.

(3) *licelike   louselike
     *teethlike   toothlike
     *licehood   lousehood
     *teethhood   toothhood

(4) *ratslike   ratlike
     *clawslike   clawlike
     *ratshood   rathood
     *clawshood   clawhood

One conclusion that might be drawn from facts like those above is that level-ordered morphology must be supplemented by taking into account the special role of inflection in morphology, that is, recognizing that inflection must be treated differently from derivation. (For example, Hammond, 1984, claims essentially that to be interpreted by the syntax, inflection in English must be word peripheral.)

One model, a current alternative to LP, does just that: The extended word paradigm theory (EWP) does indeed accord special status to inflection. EWP was developed in a series of papers by Anderson (1977, 1982, this volume). The theory makes the following claims: First, inflection is distinct from derivational morphology, being a distinct component with its own principles. Second, inflection is transparent to the syntax, that is, syntactic rules may look at and manipulate inflection, but not derivation. Third, inflectional affixation is accomplished by rule. Fourth, phonological rules may be interspersed with morphological rules.

There are certainly similarities between LP and EWP. Both allow phonological rules to apply within the morphological component, and both introduce elements of modularity into the morphology. The differences, however, are considerable, at least in their formal aspects. In LP, phonological rules are organized into strata which may be cyclic or noncyclic, while in EWP phonological rules can be interspersed among the inflectional rules and are taken to apply noncyclically. While both theories introduce modularity into the morphology, in LP there are any number of strata and inflection can appear on any one of them, while in EWP there is an inflectional component that follows the derivational component.

In comparing these theories, a number of interesting questions arise, the answers to which might help decide between them. One such question is whether inflectional strata are cyclic. In English, derivational morphology in Stratum 1 is unarguably cyclic: The associated phonological rules obey the strict cyclic condition. On the other hand, there is no evidence that inflectional morphology at Stratum 1, or at any other stratum, is necessarily cyclic, which lends support to the EWP model since the noncyclicity of phonological rules with regard to inflection is a given within the theory. The situation, however, is not quite as straightforward as this, since the question itself supposes a clear-cut distinction between inflectional and derivational morphology. Any such distinction must in turn hinge on the properties of the syntactic model to which the morphology is paired, since in the EWP model, for instance, inflection is defined as morphology relevant to the syntax. This is obviously an issue that requires much more careful investigation in inflectional systems more complex than English.

Another question concerns the relation between inflectional and derivational morphology with regard to morphological processes like reduplication. In the LP model, there is no formal difference between inflection and derivation, whereas in the EWP model there is. If it turns out that inflection and derivation behave differently with regard to reduplication, this would constitute evidence in favor of EWP against LP. If, on the other hand, there is no evidence for differentiating the two sorts of morphology with regard to processes like reduplication, the LP position would be vindicated (if not necessarily proven correct) .

Within the formal tradition, there is yet a third approach to morphology, rather different in a number of respects from the models discussed above. This model is incorporated into a theory of grammar referred to as autolexical syntax (AS), a theory proposed in recent work by Sadock (1985, 1987, this volume). The central claim of this theory is that the requirements of the morphology, syntax, and semantics are satisfied in different components and then mapped onto each other by a theory of intermodular mapping: An expression must satisfy the requirements of each of the modules in order to count as a sentence. The theory differs from the standard GB model and its antecedents in not assigning a central role to the syntax; rather, each module has the power to generate an infinite number of representations quite independently of the other modules.

In AS, unlike LP or EWP, the morphological module is viewed as being distinct from the lexicon. The lexicon contains the basic vocabulary for each of the modules, including information about the structural properties of each item with respect to each of the modules. For example, the word *dog* would be entered in the lexicon as (5) (from Sadock, this volume).

(5)　*dog*:
　　　syntax: N[0]
　　　semantics: PROP
　　　morphology: N[−0]

Dog is thus a noun in the syntax, a property expression in the semantics, and a noun stem in the morphology. Within this model, it is quite possible for some lexeme to have properties in some subset of the modules, but not in others. For example, the lexeme *-s* in German, found in words like *leben + s + versicherung* 'life insurance,' would have a lexical entry like (6) (Sadock, this volume):

(6)　*-s*
　　　syntax: nil
　　　semantics: nil
　　　morphology: N[M2, CF]/N[F]

Details aside, this entry indicates that this lexeme has only morphological properties.

Morphological rules in AS describe morphological processes like affixation, compounding, and the creation of superwords, that is, words containing clitics. Like the EWP model, AS distinguishes between inflection and derivation, but interestingly, not in the morphology per se: The syntax recognizes and brackets inflectional morphology but not derivational morphology. (The idea that morphology and syntax impose independent bracketings has also been suggested recently in Marantz, 1984 and Sproat, 1985.) This feature of the model might provide a sort of explanation for the observation that inflectional morphology is word peripheral. Certain formal difficulties would arise if one tried to provide a bracketing for inflection that occurred between stems and derivational affixes in a model where derivational affixes receive no syntactic bracketing.

It should be noted that the character of the morphology proposed by Sadock is at least partially independent of the AS theory of intermodular mapping. Thus one might imagine a hybrid version of AS where the morphological bracketing is provided by a theory like LP or EWP. This is not to say that Sadock's morphological proposals are not potentially interesting, but he has yet to say how phonological rules would be integrated into his morphology and how he would deal with morphological processes which are not essentially concatenative in nature.

5.

In sections 3 and 4 we have discussed the development of morphological theory within what we have termed the "orthodox" generative tradition. We now turn our attention to a pair of traditions that, like the orthodox, or mainstream, tradition, trace their origins back to *Aspects* and *The Sound Pattern of English* (SPE) (Chomsky and Halle, 1968). One of these traditions in particular represents a radical departure from the methods and concerns of the North American generative mainstream. Purely morphological problems were not at issue in the early stages of the development of these approaches but were to assume considerable importance later on.

The publication in 1968 of SPE constitutes a landmark in the history of North American phonological theory because here, for the first time, the principles of the emerging generative phonology were laid out in sufficient depth and detail to be subjected to thorough scrutiny. Two aspects of the theory raised important theoretical questions almost immediately. The first concerned the problem of evaluating the "naturalness" of phonological rules, the second concerned the nature of the relation between surface and underlying representations, that is, the question of phonological abstractness.

The issue of the naturalness of rules begins with the problem of evaluation of alternate solutions: In principle, for any given phonological alternation, there are an infinite number of possible descriptions of that alternation that can be constructed within the system of formal notation provided by SPE. So, for example, an alternation involving intervocalic voicing of obstruents which could be stated with a single rule, could also, if one were willing to introduce a sufficiency of irrelevant features, environments, and so on, be stated with 5 rules, 17 rules, or 379 rules. In order to deal with this sort of problem, SPE theory provided an evaluation metric, a method of counting the features and notational devices so as to select, among the alternate solutions, the simplest in this formal sense. General considerations of economy apart, the simplest solution was valued because it was believed that only by means of it could one express the true generalizations of the language. It was also believed that, in the process of language acquisition, the child, confronted with the monstrous complexity of human language, would always select the simplest solution since this was naturally the easiest to learn, store, and use.

In this way, the SPE model was designed to capture what is possible in a phonological system by means of the set of notations and the accompanying evaluation metric. The model, however, did not succeed in providing an adequate evaluation of the naturalness of phonological systems; it was incapable of distinguishing normal, expected, "natural" phonological systems from bizarre, unexpected, "unnatural" ones. Given a set of unnatural rules with the same formal complexity as a set of natural rules, the SPE model would predict that a child would learn both sets with equal ease. This result is intuitively unsatisfying.

The problem was recognized in SPE itself. The proposal there was to incorporate within the model a theory of phonological markedness which could be used to evaluate the naturalness of rules. But the SPE markedness theory ran into a number of formal and substantive problems and, despite some initial interest, sank into oblivion, with a phonologist occasionally paying lip service to it, but without it being incorporated in any serious way into phonological descriptions and theorizing. (See Lass, 1972 and Anderson, 1982 for a discussion of problems arising from the SPE theory of markedness.) The issue of rule naturalness, however, did not disappear along with the SPE proposal to deal with it, as we see below.

The second problem, that of phonological abstractness, occupied center stage in phonological theory in the late 1960s and into the 1970s. The issue was raised initially by Kiparsky (1968, 1973), who pointed out that, among other things, the SPE model allowed, one might even say encouraged via the evaluation metric, what Kiparsky referred to as the "diacritic use of phonological features," that is, marking as a difference in phonological feature composition a distinction which does not reflect the surface phonetic realizations of some segments but rather their behavior vis à vis some rule(s). To eliminate this sort of thing, Kiparsky proposed the alternation condition, which has the effect of prohibiting the assignment of a feature value to an underlying segment that is not associated with some phonetic realization of that segment.

Kiparsky's proposal stirred a hornet's nest of criticism, with numerous apparent counterexamples offered to his alternation condition. Almost all of these counterexamples themselves rested ultimately on the SPE version of the evaluation metric and so were not really valid counterexamples, though some of Kiparsky's critics—Hyman (1970), for example—recognized that Kiparsky had changed the rules of the game somewhat by introducing historical data as part of his argument and not relying exclusively on synchronic distributional data. Kiparsky's proposal stirred controversy and helped define issues within the orthodox tradition. But it was outside the orthodox approaches that Kiparsky's proposals were to have the most profound effect.

6.

The two approaches that we discuss in this section originated as responses to the two perceived problems with the SPE model noted above: The problem of the naturalness of rules and the problem of abstractness. The two approaches share a functional bias and both have incorporated the term "natural" into their labels, but they differ in a number of respects, some superficial, some fundamental.

The first of these approaches derives from the work of Stampe (1969, 1972; Donegan and Stampe, 1979). Since Stampe's initial proposal concerned only phonology, his model was referred to as "natural phonology." Recently Dressler (1985a) has added the term "natural morphology" for the extension of the model into things morphological, so it seems only a natural extension of the existing terminology to refer to the approach as a whole as "natural grammar" (NG).

Stampe was concerned with the problem of rule naturalness. He began by rejecting markedness theory since this, from his point of view, did nothing more than provide a way to evaluate notations. Instead, Stampe proposed to stand the problem on its head: Rather than supposing that a child enters upon language acquisition with a sort of *tabula rasa*, knowing no rules at the outset and gradually learning rules in the course of acquisition, Stampe proposed that a child begins by knowing all phonetic rules (N.B., not morphophonemic ones) and applying them all at the outset. In the course of language acquisition, a child learns not to apply certain rules, that is, to inhibit their application, while other rules continue to apply given the lack of negative evidence for the application.

The attraction of Stampe's theory is that it appears to unite description with explanation, synchronic phonology with language acquisition and history, the particular with the universal. It also appears to provide a natural way to deal with the problem of different phonological rules operating at different tempi: Fewer rules are inhibited in faster speech. Various authors have pointed out problems with the approach, however, both of a general and a specific nature (see, e.g., Dressler, 1974; Anderson, 1975).

NG has not attracted many converts in North America, though most linguists interested in phonology are familiar with the general outlines of its program. It is in Europe, where functionalist approaches have never gone out of fashion, that NG has had its major impact. It is there also that NG has moved away from Stampe's exclusive concern with phonology to encompass morphology as well.

The attraction of Stampe's theory to linguists of a functional persuasion is that it provides a model for why phonological systems are the way they are: They exist to make speech pronounceable and perceptible. Phonological rules exist to make words easier to pronounce, but their application must be inhibited in order to make words easier to distinguish from one another, that is, to make them maximally perceptible. This tension between production and perception was interpreted within a Peircean semiotic model by Dressler and his associates (e.g., Dressler, 1985a,b, this volume), Mayerthaler, 1981, Wurzel, 1984, and extended into morphophonology and morphology. The continuity between Stampe and Dressler lies in their common interest in motivating rules in terms of communicative needs: While Stampe, whose interests lie mainly in phonology, evoked phonetics as his explanatory medium, Dressler, who extends the model to morphology, evokes semiotic principles.

Consider the following example of how Dressler extends the NG model into morphology: Dressler (1985a) attempts to define a number of functional parameters, each with a semiotic basis, along which he can define degrees of naturalness. The most natural phenomena along each parameter should be most frequent; conversely, the most unnatural phenomena should be extremely infrequent or should not occur at all. When conflicts along parameters arise, as they inevitably will, Dressler tries to limit the possible outcomes. In this way, he hopes to create a predictive theory that can ultimately be made into an explanatory model.

As a simple example of how this might work in morphology, consider the following purportedly universal scale of morphotactic transparency (from Dressler, 1985a). (PR indicates a phonological rule; MPR a morphophonemic rule; MR a morphological rule.)

(7)

I	II	III	IV
Intrinsic Allophonic PRs	PRs interfere, e.g., resylla-bification	Neutralizing PRs, e.g., flapping (AmE)	MPRs (no fusion), velar softening
excite + ment	*exis^s + tence*	*rid + er*	*electric + ity*
excite	*exist*	*ride*	*electric*

V	VI	VII	VIII
MPRs with fusion	MRs intervene, e.g., Great Vowel Shift	Weak supple-tion, no rules	Strong Supple-tion, no rules
conclusion	*decision*	*childr + en*	*be, am, are*
conclude	*decide*	*child*	*is, was were*

The scale in (7) constitutes a parameter of the sort characterized above, representing the performance of a communicative function, namely morpheme combination, and having a basis in the semiotic principle of transparency, ultimately connected with the semiotic principles of biuniqueness and iconicity (Dressler, 1985a, p. 323). About the scale, Dressler maintains that word formation is best served at Level I, the most transparent level, being consistent with the principle of transparency; it is badly served at Levels IV and V, and is worst served at Level VIII. Further, Dressler makes several probabilistic predictions from (7): Morphotactically transparent derived words are more frequent than opaque ones (Dressler, 1982), children should acquire rules which do not affect morphotactic transparency earlier (Dressler *et al.*, 1985) and aphasics should retain them better (Dressler and Stark, 1986).

It should be clear from the example given above that the program of NG is considerably different from that of LP and EWP. Speaking very grossly, while the latter are concerned primarily with the development of descriptive mechanisms that will lead to explanatory principles, the former begins with a set of explanatory principles (semiotics and phonetics) and is concerned with developing descriptive mechanisms that are compatible with them. The next functional approach we consider, natural generative grammar (NGG), is likewise primarily concerned with explanation, but differs considerably from NG in its basic preoccupations and its methodology.

NGG has its origins in the natural generative phonology of Vennemann (1971, 1974) and Bybee [(Bybee) Hooper, 1976]. Just as NG developed from SPE phonology out of a concern for rule naturalness, NGG developed from the SPE model out of a concern with the problem of abstractness, which in turn relates to the more general problem of representations.

From the beginning, NGG evidenced a more empiricist orientation than the other, rationalistically oriented approaches discussed in this Chapter. As a result, the proponents of NGG have been loath to posit formal mechanisms and representations that exceed the absolute minimum required by the data. Further, they make no appeals to an evaluation metric à la SPE and therefore no appeals to formal simplicity as a criterion for setting up representations. They have therefore staked out an extreme "concrete" position relative to the extreme "abstract" position staked out in SPE.[1]

A further difference between NGG and models in the orthodox tradition is the range of data allowed in formulating hypotheses about grammars. The orthodox tradition, true to its structuralist origins, concerns itself primarily with distributional data. Other sorts of data—from language acquisition, language history, speech errors, and so on—are at best of only secondary interest. For NGG, synchronic distributional data alone cannot suffice since, lacking an evaluation metric, there would be no way to evaluate alternate solutions. From the beginning, therefore, NGG has admitted historical and acquisition data on a par with distributional data, and the research program of Bybee has involved psycholinguistic experimentation (e.g., Bybee and Pardo, 1981; Bybee and Slobin, 1982). In many respects, Bybee's method more closely resembles that of the scholars investigating first language acquisition with whom she has been associated than the standard practice of linguistics.

Bybee has recently (Bybee, 1985) articulated a theory of morphology within the NGG framework. The model she presents is not completely new. It is,

[1]In the early 1970s there was an interesting tendency for those who advocated very concrete analyses in phonology to advocate very abstract analyses in syntax. Vennemann is a case in point. Bartsch and Vennemann (1972) present an analysis of adverbs that is quite in keeping with the most extreme logicist position of the generative semanticists. This pairing of the concrete and the abstract is not as paradoxical as it might seem. The empiricist assumptions of the NGG program would necessarily lead one to base one's analyses on the hardest data around, and this, they assume, included phonetic data—a comparatively uncontroversial assumption—and meaning—perhaps a somewhat more controversial assumption.

to a certain extent, a summary of work presented over a period of some years, and in any case the general outlines of the NGG position on morphology were largely implicit in the earliest NGG work on phonology. Nonetheless, it is here that the specifics of the position and their implications are most fully developed.

Bybee draws together data from a variety of sources—cross-linguistic, experimental, diachronic—in an attempt to explain the recurrent properties of morphological systems in terms of the dynamic processes that create them. A major inssue is the interaction of rules and rote processing, that is, the relationship between derived and basic forms. As an illustration of Bybee's approach to this problem, we consider Dressler's scale of morphotactic transparency presented as (7) above. Dressler, and a long tradition of linguists before him, consider the state of affairs represented by Level I as good and natural and those represented by Levels IV through VIII, involving allomorphy and suppletion, as unnatural and undesirable. Yet allomorphy and suppletion are well attested in natural language. Bybee notes (1985, p. 208) that if we expand our horizons beyond morphology and consider all modes of linguistic expression, we discover that morphotactic transparency, the one meaning–one form principle, is in fact used rather sparingly. If the principle were applied rigorously in language, we would have few monomorphemicx words, for nearly every concept that is named by a word can be broken down into more primitive units, each of which can be given independent formal expression; consider, in this regard, the generative semantic decomposition of *kill* into [*cause*[*become*[*not*[*alive*]]]]. Clearly, languages are not structured according to this principle in any simple sense. In its place, Bybee proposes the notion of RELEVANCE: The more relevant semantic units are to each other, the more likely they will be coded as a single, unanalyzable form. Morphological fusion is thus expected in cases where affixes can be interpreted as highly relevant to the stem. The principle can be extended to derivational and inflectional morphology, which Bybee views as points along a continuum with lexical expression on one end and syntactic expression, that is, expression by means of autonomous units, on the other. The greater degree of fusion found in derivational morphology (as opposed to inflectional morphology) is a result of the greater relevance of the derivational affix to the stem. From this principle, one can predict which sorts of affixes (tense, aspect, mood, valence, etc.) are more likely to be inflectional and which derivational.[2]

Another determinant of allomorphy and suppletion within Bybee's model is FREQUENCY, which is involved both in the maintenance of morphological irregularities and in their creation. Highly frequent and salient combinations of semantic units, as a mere consequence of their frequency, will be highly

---

[2]Dressler (1985a, p. 333) notes that conflicts may arise among parameters and that this might result in forms that are disfavored along one parameter being commonly encountered nonetheless.

distinguishable cognitively and therefore treated by the grammar as unanalyzed wholes. Thus the suppletion found in the paradigms of *be, have,* and the modal auxiliaries, is just as natural in Bybee's model as regular expression.

NGG, at least in Bybee's version, differs both from NG and the orthodox approaches in adopting a nonclassical, Roschian approach to categorization, which manifests clearly in her conception of the lexicon. Forms are AUTONOMOUS, that is, have their own lexical entry, by degree, and indeed are related to each other by degree. This applies within paradigms, where suppletive forms are autonomous, but regular forms, those whose morphological shapes are predictable by rule, may also be autonomous if they are sufficiently frequent and/or if the categories the form contains are highly relevant to the stem and thus affect or change its meaning. Low frequency items are thus analyzed and understood in terms of other items, especially if the categories they contain are less relevant to the stem. Lexical items within paradigms are related, but the more autonomous forms are related less to each other than to the other forms for which they serve as the base in basic/derived relationships. Even forms within different paradigms can be shown to be lexically related (*lend/loan, seat/sit*), a fact which can help account for the combination of historically different paradigms into a single paradigm, as in English *be* and *go.* Bybee adduces several sorts of evidence for this from language change, language acquisition, and psycholinguistic experimentation.

7.

Because of their different methodologies, principles, and short-term goals, it is often difficult to compare work done in the orthodox approaches with that done in one of the natural frameworks. In a few cases, direct comparison is possible. One such case involves the inflection—derivation distinction. A central feature of Anderson's EWP approach is the assumption that inflectional and derivational processes are organized into separate components. LP and Sadock's and Bybee's models make no such formal distinction. Bybee in particular asserts that what have traditionally been considered inflectional and derivational phenomena are really just points along a continuum which ranges from loosely joined, syntactic expression on the one hand to thoroughly fused, lexical expression on the other:

(8)   Lexical—Derivational—Inflectional—Free grammatical—Syntactic

        <——

        greater degree of fusion

Therefore, we should not, according to Bybee, expect there to be any well-defined boundary between inflectional and derivational expression; they are merely convenient descriptive labels without theoretical import.

There are a few other direct points of comparison, for example, the nature of lexical entries, and the number (and character) of distinct modules posited in the arena of phonology and morphology, but at this stage, with their different assumptions and foci of interest, direct comparison is often a pointless exercise. It is primarily on the larger, metatheoretical plane that comparison yields much of interest. We summarize a few of these differences below:

1. Rationalist/empiricist: LP, EWP, AS, and NG share a fundamentally rationalist approach to science, while NGG is more empirically oriented. The empiricism of the latter is manifested in, for instance, Bybee's reluctance to admit formal devices beyond those (she believes) confirmed by experimental data, while for the former (with the possible exception of NG) a formal device is admitted if it allows for a "simpler" description of the synchronic distributional corpus.

2. Functionalism: NG and NGG have a functionalist orientation. (Note the curious, implicit equation of "natural" and "functional" in the coincidence of the theories' names.) These models then make few appeals to innateness; rather, they try to locate constructs, explanations, and so forth in the communicative situation. LP, EWP, and AS, the "orthodox" approaches, are clearly nonfunctionalist in this sense.

3. Historical and experimental data: NG and NGG admit historical and experimental data, while for the orthodox approaches such data are not immediately relevant. For NGG in particular, such data are not only relevant, but are crucial in formulating hypotheses about language structure.

These remarks provide only the barest sketch of the deep differences between these models; a thorough discussion of the metatheoretical differences has yet to be written.

8.

There is no doubt that the period from the mid-1970s through the 1980s has seen a renaissance of morphological theory. The autonomy of morphology as a distinct area of study and focus of theorizing is no longer at issue. There is also no doubt that the work of this period has increased our understanding of morphological phenomena considerably. While it is clear that there is an enormous amount of work yet to be done, it is equally clear that any serious contender for the "linguistic theory of the 1990s" must take morphology very seriously.

References and Suggested Readings

Allen, M. (1978). *Morphological Investigations*. Doctoral dissertation, University of Connecticut.
Anderson, S. (1977). On the formal description of inflection. *CLS* **13**, 15–44.

18   *Michael Hammond and Michael Noonan*

Anderson, S. (1982). Where's Morphology? *Linguistic Inquiry* **13**, 571–612.

Anderson, S. (1985). "Phonology in the Twentieth Century" Univ. of Chicago Press, Chicago.

Aronoff, M. (1976). "Word Formation in Generative Grammar." MIT Press, Cambridge, MA.

Bartsch, R., T. Vennemann, T. (1972). "Semantic Structures." MIT Press, Cambridge, MA.

Bybee, J. (1985). "Morphology." Benjamins, Amsterdam.

Bybee, J., and Pardo, E. (1981). Morphology and lexical conditioning of rules: Experimental evidence from Spanish. *Linguistics* **19**, 937–968.

Bybee, J., and Slobin, D. (1982). Rules and schemas in the development and use of the English past tense. *Language* **58**, 265–289.

Chomsky, N. (1957). "Syntactic Structures." Mouton, The Hague.

Chomsky, N. (1965). "Aspects of the Theory of Syntax." MIT Press, Cambridge, MA.

Chomsky, N. (1970). Remarks on nominalization. *In* "'Readings in English Transformational Grammar," (R. Jacobs and P. Rosenbaum, eds.). Ginn, Waltham, MA.

Chomsky, N., and Halle, M. (1968). "The Sound Pattern of English." Harper, New York.

Donegan, P., and Stampe, D. (1979). The study of natural phonology. *In* (D. Dinnsen, ed.) "Current Aproaches to Phonological Theory" Indiana Univ. Press, Bloomington.

Dressler, W. (1974). Some diachronic puzzles for natural phonology. *In* "Natural Phonology Parasession." CLS.

Dressler, W. (1982). Zur semiotischen Begründung einer natürlichen Wortbindungslehre. *Klangenfurter Beiträge zur Sprachwissenschaft* **8**, 72–87.

Dressler, W. (1985a). On the predictiveness of natural morphology. JL **21**, 321–37.

Dressler, W. (1985a). "Morphonology: The Dynamics of Derivation." Karoma, Ann Arbor, Michigan.

Dressler, W., and Stark, J. (1986). On the acquisition of morphology in normal children and Down's Syndrome. *Studie Grammatyczne*.

Dressler, W., Shaner-Wolles, Ch. and Grossman, W. (1985). "Linguistic Studies in Aphasia." Academic Press, New York.

Foley, J. (1965). *Spanish Phonology*. Doctoral dissertation, MIT.

Halle, M. (1973). Prolegomena to a theory of word formation. *Linguistic Inquiry* **4**, 3–16.

Halle, M., and Mohanan, K. (1985). The segmental phonology of Modern English. *Linguistic Inquiry* **16**, 57–116.

Hammond, M. (1984). Level ordering, inflection, and the righthand head rule. *MIT Working Papers in Linguistics* **7**, 33–52.

[Bybee] Hooper, J. (1976). "An Introduction to Natural Generative Phonology." Academic Press, New York.

Hyman, L. (1970). How concrete is phonology? *Language* **48**, 58–76.

Jackendoff, R. (1972). "Semantic Interpretation in Generative Grammar" MIT Press, Cambridge, MA.

Jackendoff, R. (1975). Morphological and semantic regularities in the Lexicon. *Language* **51**, 639–671.

Kiparsky, P. (1968, 1973). How abstract is phonology? *In* "Three Dimensions of Phonological Theory" (O. Fujimura, ed.). TEC, Tokyo.

Kiparsky, P. (1982). Lexical phonology and morphology. *In* "Linguistics in the Morning Calm" (I.S. Yange, ed.). Linguistic Society of Korea, Seoul.

Lass, R. (1972). How intrinsic is content? markedness, sound change, and "Family Resmblances." *In* "Essays on the Sound Pattern of English" (D. Goyvaerts and G. Pullum, eds.). Story-Scientia, Ghent.

Lees, R. (1960). "The Grammar of English Nominalizations" Mouton, The Hague.

Lightener, T. (1965) . *The Segmental Phonology of Modern Standard Russian*. Doctoral dissertation, MIT.

Marantz, A. (1984). "On the Nature of Grammatical Relations" MIT Press, Cambridge, MA.

Mayerthaler, W. (1981). "Morphologische Natürlichkeit." Athenaion, Wiesbaden.

Mohanan, K. (1982). *Lexical Phonology.* Doctoral dissertation, MIT.

Mohanan, K. (1986). "The Theory of Lexical Phonology." Reidel, Dordrecht.

Pesetsky, D. (1979). "Russian Morphology and Lexical Theory." Ms, MIT.

Postal, P. (1969). Anaphoric Islands. *CLS* **5**, 205-39.

Sadock, J. (1985). Autolexical syntax: A theory of noun incorporation and similar phenomena. *NLLT* **3**, 379-440

Sadock, J. (1988). *Autolexical syntax: A Theory of Parallel Grammatical Representations,* in press.

Scalise, S. (1984). "Generative Morphology." Foris, Dordrecht.

Siegel, D. (1974). *Topics in English Morphology.* Doctoral dissertation, MIT.

Sproat, R. (1985). *On Deriving the Lexicon.* Doctoral dissertation, MIT.

Stampe, D. (1969). On the acquisition of phonetic representation. *CLS* **5**.

Stampe, D. (1972). *A Dissertation on Natural Phonology.* Doctoral dissertation, University of Chicago.

Vennemann, T. (1971). *Natural Generative Phonology.* Paper read at the Annual Meeting of the Linguistic Society of America.

Vennemann, T. (1974). Words and syllables in natural generative grammar. *Natural Phonology Parasession* **CLS**.

Wurzel, W. (1984). Flexionsmorphologie und Natürlichkeit. *Studia Grammatica* **21**.

Part I

Inflection

Chapter 2

Inflection

Stephen R. Anderson

The problems addressed in this chapter originate with the question of what must be done to maintain the lexical hypothesis. Originally formulated in much more modest terms by Chomsky (1970), this is usually understood today as something like the claim in (1):

(1)   LEXICALIST HYPOTHESIS: The syntax neither manipulates nor has access to the internal form of words.

I assume in general that the syntax is organized more or less along the lines of government and binding theory both for the sake of concreteness and because it imposes a useful organization on the task. The things I have to say could be translated into, say, lexical functional grammar, generalized phrase structure grammar, or other current formal frameworks without any essential differences.

The point is that there are a number of areas in which the rather strong claim in (1) is apparently at odds with the facts, and our aim is to examine the extent to which they really show that it cannot be maintained.

The first kind of problem is that posed by clitics. These look like syntactically significant elements, but ones which form parts of a word with other items that are syntactically quite distinct. Following the spirit of a distinction originally due to Zwicky (1977), we can distinguish two sorts of clitics: simple and special. The former we take to be elements corresponding to members of other syntactic classes; they appear in positions relative to the rest of the clause where they would (or at least could) be put by the normal rules of the syntax, but they happen to form a phonological unit with some other part of the structure. An example is the English form — 's in (2), where it represents a reduced form of the verb *is* or *has*:

(2)   a.   *L.A.'s the place.*
      b.   *L.A.'s got a lot of great Albanian restaurants.*

One might well take these clitics, which are clearly manipulated by the syntax, to falsify (1); but an alternative view would be that they simply make it evident that phonological criteria alone do not suffice to settle the question of what a word is. The notoriously labored traditional literature on how to define a word leads to the conclusion that there are several distinct kinds of "word": phonological, syntactic, lexical, and so on. Often, but not always, these overlap. What simple clitics tell us is that (1) must refer, if it is true, not to the phonologically defined word, but to some other unit.

Accordingly, we might simply say that simple clitics have a particular lexical peculiarity, which we could characterize as follows: Ordinary lexical words have not only segmental structure, but also prosodic structure, in the form of an organization of segments into syllables, feet, and ultimately phonological words. A simple clitic differs from other lexical items in lacking the prosodic status of "word": it has segmental, and possibly syllabic and even foot structure, but it is not a word. Since something can only be pronounced if it is part of a word (and perhaps beyond that, part of a phonological phrase and maybe other prosodic categories), such items have to be incorporated into a neighboring prosodic word by rule (which might, on a language-particular basis, attach them either to the right or to the left). There might in principle be particular rules of the grammar that turn nonclitics into clitics under certain conditions; the stuctural change performed by these rules would then be precisely the removal of the appropriate prosodic category.

The other class of clitics, the special clitics, we take to be those which appear in a position where the syntax would not regularly put them. Like the simple clitics, they form part of a phonological word with something else; but their location must be due to something other than the language's normal sentential syntax. The best-known such principle is probably the tendency of clitics in many languages to appear in second position within some constitutent (where the notion of "second position" may be somewhat idiosyncratic). The literature on special clitics is of course vast, but it seems fair to say that a certain amount of consensus has been achieved due to the work of Zwicky (1977), Klavans (1980, 1985), Kaisse (1985) and others, including a dissertation by Nevis (1985). According to these works, the set of parameters in (3) is adequate to specify clitic placement:

(3)   a.   The clitic is located by reference to the {beginning vs. end vs. head} of the constituent in which it appears.
      b.   The clitic {precedes vs. follows} the reference point.
      c.   The clitic forms part of a phonological word with material on its {right vs. left}.

As a threat to the lexicalist hypothesis, special clitics are not notably more serious than simple ones; they form part of a word with other material (with (3c) reducing to the direction in which a language-particular rule of "stray adjunction" operates); but we might take that to be for uninterestingly phonological reasons. Of course, we still need some sort of principles to put them where they belong, but that would appear to be the problem of the syntax, not of the morphology. As a result, we leave them aside for the moment, but come back to them later.

The most serious challenge to the lexicalist hypothesis comes not from the study of clitics, but rather from the domain of inflectional morphology. Here there is a real issue: There does not seem to be any interestingly noncircular notion of "word" that would be completely impervious to the effects of structures in which words appear. In Anderson (1982), I cite several sorts of properties that appear to call for a non-null interaction of syntax and word structure, which I repeat (slightly augmented) in (4):

(4) a. CONFIGURATIONAL PROPERTIES: assigned on the basis of the larger structure a word appears in (e.g., case in NP; special forms of verbs in relative clauses)
     b. AGREEMENT PROPERTIES: aspects of the exact form of a word which are determined by reference to the properties of some other word in the same structure.
     c. INHERENT PROPERTIES: properties of a word which must be accessible to whatever rule assigns agreement properties to other words in agreement with it (e.g., gender of noun)
     d. PHRASAL PROPERTIES: properties of larger phrasal domains which determine the way these domains behave syntactically but which are realized on particular words within the structure (e.g., the effect of tense in defining the scope of binding relations)

All of these fall under (an appropriate interpretation of) the notion of inflectional morphology, when this is construed as exactly what is relevant to the syntax. An alternative way of putting this has been advocated by Borer (1984), who suggests that a morphological rule is inflectional insofar as it obeys the projection principle, which licenses it to apply in the syntax. I personally do not think this is the right way to formulate the distinction, but it is clear that Borer and I are talking about essentially the same basis for recognizing inflection as the area in which syntax and morphology overlap. Obviously, the recognition of such an area is exactly the recognition that (1) is not absolute—and a theory of inflectional morphology is exactly a theory of just how much interpenetration of the morphology by the syntax (and vice versa) there is.

A question that immediately arises is whether there is any point to distinguishing inflection (the morphology that involves interaction with the syntax) from derivation (the morphology that does not). A number of theories have at least proclaimed, in fact, that this distinction is illusory. Sadock's notion of autolexical syntax (Sadock, 1985), to take one kind of example, argues that because there is some interaction between word structure and syntax, we ought simply to assign the responsibility for morpheme positioning, including intraword morphotactics as well as standard syntax, to the syntax; this effectively confines the morphology to specifying the shapes of morphemes and their grouping into larger units (words). The problem with this point of view (aside from the sort of argument that was originally raised years ago as the motivation for lexicalist syntax in the first place; see, e.g., Chomsky, 1970, and Jackendoff, 1975), is that the syntax often is incompetent to get the morphemes in the right place. It is beyond the scope of the present chapter to demonstrate this rigorously, but in a language Kʷakʷ'ala (see Anderson, 1985b), a rather rigid phrasal syntax is systematically contradicted at every turn by the principles that locate formatives with respect to one another within the word. I conclude that letting the syntax have free rein over the morphology (as in the halcyon days of generative semantics) is ultimately not the answer.

Most claims that there is no distinction between inflection and derivation have been quite different from the suggestion that virtually all of morphotactics is part of the syntax, though. Lapointe, for example, in his thesis (1980), assigns all word structure to the lexicon and allows the syntax to have no say whatsoever. At least in that work, the grammar ensured that inflectionally proper choices of word forms were made through an enrichment of the semantics: Agreement, in particular, was handled by assigning purely formal but semantically operative features to words which mirror their agreement properties, and then requiring that, for example, verbs and the subject NPs they agree with must be semantically compatible. It is not clear that this approach can be extended to such domains as the configurational and phrasal properties mentioned above; but even if it could, one might want to protest that properties like arbitrary gender (which often function in agreement systems) are exactly the sort of thing that has only an accidental, perhaps historical, connection with meaning, and thus ought to be exorcised from the semantics.

A slightly less a priori argument against the program which puts all of inflection into the semantics can perhaps be derived from external evidence, specifically the evidence of aphasia studies. The much-discussed phenomenon of agrammatism in (some) Broca's aphasics is now widely (if not universally) considered to reflect a deficiency in the patient's ability to manipulate syntactic structures. A standard diagnostic for this condition is the subject's omission or inappropriate use of function words and inflectional morphology. Now in fact, most studies of this problem do not carefully distinguish between inflection and derivation, and simply talk about problems with "little words" and "affixes"; and the patients involved, being very sick, are not easy to test for their fluency with words like *antidisestablishmentarianism*; but there is at least some reason to believe that this syntactic deficit is associated primarily with inflectional, not derivational, difficulties. Caramazza and his colleagues (see Micelli and Caramazza, 1987; Caramazza *et al*, 1987) have studied Italian patients for whom syntactic loss in aggrammatism goes along with a loss of ability to control inflection, but derivation remains relatively intact. If true, this would suggest that at least in a performance model there is some morphology (namely, inflection) which is integrated with the syntax in a crucial way; while other aspects of morphology (derivation) are primarily tied up with meaning.

A less extreme way to reject the inflection–derivation distinction is to admit that there are, indeed, syntactically manipulated properties which affect choice of word from within a paradigm, but to argue that all actual word formation takes place within a unitary lexicon that cannot be interestingly divided between an inflectional and derivational part. On this view, some of the operations of word formation specify properties that are syntactically relevant, but these are simply part and parcel of a general set of morphological operations. It is only at the level of choosing a specific lexical form that the inflectional properties are relevant per se: The demands of the syntax have to be satisfied by the properties of the actual form chosen, but the syntax takes complete, fully inflected words out of the lexicon (just as it surely takes fully derived ones, on any theory even a little bit like lexicalism).

The main argument that seems to be offered for this view is the observation that inflectional and derivational operations are not formally distinct in the kind of structural change they perform. Affixes of all kinds (prefixes, suffixes, infixes, and even circumfixes), as well as other nonconcatenative operations like ablaut, reduplication, subtraction, and metathesis, have both inflectional and derivational uses. This is certainly a valid point, though I think it is unusual that some of the same people who argue that a single rule "move-α" applies all over the lot, in the syntax, in logical form, and even in the phonology, then go on to argue that in morphology such a similarity of structural changes shows there is no component-like difference between inflection and derivation! Even granting this point, though, the argument does not appear to show much. In particular, we could perfectly well accept the observation that both kinds of rule make similar structural changes in the shape of word forms without that requiring that there be no other interesting differences between them. Minimally, the two kinds of rule differ in the extent to which they refer to or affect the information available to the syntax about words. It remains an empirical question to determine whether this difference has any other basis or consequences.

Rather surprisingly to some, perhaps, there do seem to be reasons to claim that the inflectional rules are not simply a part of the same apparatus that does derivation. One motivation for separating the two is that this seems indicated if we are to maintain a plausible version of the notion that word-formation rules are "word-based": that it is words, as they exist in the lexicon of a language (whether they are internally complex or not), and not morphemes which serve as the input to such rules.[1] If the relevant notion of "word" for a word-based morphology is in fact an existing surface word, it is not hard to find abundant counterexamples to such a principle. Consider, for example, formation of adjectives from nouns in Latin according to the sort of pattern illustrated by the pair *vir* 'man,' *virīlis* 'manly.' In this case, the suffix meaning roughly 'belonging or pertaining to (noun)' can be added directly to the nominative singular of the noun to form the adjective. But what of other pairs, such as those in (5)?

(5) a. *vulgus* 'common people'; *vulg-āris* 'commonplace'
    b. *rēx* 'king'; *rēg-ius* 'royal'
    c. *mors* 'death'; *mort-ālis* 'mortal'

In these cases, the base from which the adjective is derived never shows up as a word by itself; in every occurrence, it is followed by some ending marking case and number. Of course, the correct move here is to say that it is not words but stems that function as the base of word-formation rules. An appropriately constrained notion of stem, in turn, seems to be "word minus (productive) inflectional affixation." If correct, this provides at least the skeleton of an argument to the effect that the class of (possibly complex) forms representing the output of rules of derivation but prior to the operation of productive inflection has a special status in the grammar: Essentially, these are the lexical items that are entered in the dictionary of a language. But this in turn implies that inflectional rules are separable from derivation, in that the latter apply to form lexical items, while the former apply to convert these into surface inflected words.

An interesting argument for the separation of inflection from derivation was suggested by David Perlmutter (personal communication). His point is based on the fact that inflectional systems often display "portmanteau" morphs. These are formatives that realize, in a single and unanalyzable unit, values of two or more linguistic categories. Inflectional portmanteaux are things like an agreement marker that indicates simultaneously the person and number of the subject and of the object. One language in which this sort of thing seems prominent is Yuma (see Halpern, 1946), part of whose verbal inflection is shown in the partial paradigm of the verb 'see' with the nonfuture suffix -*k* in (6). A consideration of these forms will convince the reader that while there are some tantalizing similarities among the verbal markers, it is not possible to decompose them into a subject marker and an object marker.

---

[1] This position is proposed and argued for in Aronoff (1976). Further discussion of the inappropriateness of morphemes (as opposed to words) as the basic units of lexical structure can be found in Anderson (1983), among other references.

(6)   Yuma agreement markers

Subject	Object (singular)		
	1st person	2nd person	3rd person
1st person	—	nʸ-ayú·-k	ʔayú·-k
2nd person	ʔanʸm-ayú·-k	—	m-ayú·-k
3rd person	nʸ-ayú·-k	m-ayú·-k	ayú·-k

Perlmutter pointed out that portmanteaux are much rarer in derivation (if indeed any such elements exist at all) and, what is most relevant here, that there never seem to be elements which combine inflectional and derivational categories in the same portmanteau. If there were, there might be an element which represented, say, "causative with 2pl object." If the two sorts of operation are performed in the same component, why should they display this unwillingness to combine with one another?

An argument tending in the same direction, which is stronger perhaps because it has a positive rather than a negative character, is due to Bat-El (1986). She argues that in Modern Hebrew, many words are derived by a process of extraction from other existing words. This process consists in the association of the consonants present in the first word (preserving order) with an independently existing word-structure template (somewhat along the lines of the analysis of Arabic morphology in McCarthy, 1981). The interesting property of this extraction operation which shows it is not simply reducible to the use of an underlying root made up solely of consonants is the fact that some of the extracted consonants may represent affixal, not root, elements. Consider the forms in (7):

(7)   a.   *t*V- + *kicer* 'to shorten' → *takcir* 'summary' → *tikcer* 'to summarize'
      b.   *xišev* 'to calculate' + *-on* → *xešbon* 'calculation' → *xišben* 'to calculate'
      c.   /hit-sakel/ → *histakel* 'to observe' + *-an* 'agent' → *staklan* 'observer'

In (7a), a consonant which originates as part of a prefix appears in the final derived form, while in (7b), a consonant from a suffix is extracted. Finally, in (7c), the sequence of consonants in the form derived by extraction reflects the operation of a rule of metathesis on the /t + s/ sequence which is underlying in this "hitpa'el" form of the root $\sqrt{s.k.l.}$

What is interesting about this process (besides the substantial evidence it provides for the claim that at least some word formation has the character of a "parasitic derivation" of one surface word from another) is the fact that, as Bat-El shows, only material from derivational affixes is ever extracted. Insofar as we have reason to describe an affix as inflectional [in the terms of (4)], its consonants are never extracted. Clearly, derivational material must be available to word-formation processes in a way that differentiates it from inflectional material.

Another argument for this claim can probably be derived from the frequent observation that inflection appears "outside of" derivation. We return to the precise content of this claim below, but for now we can note simply that it seems quite generally to be the case that when functionally inflectional material is introduced by a productive rule, it is added to a form which is already complete in terms of its derivational content, and not vice versa. This sort of ordering relation would be quite unexpected if the rules of inflection and derivation are part of the same unitary lexical component. In the framework of lexical phonology, for example (see Kiparsky, 1982), it would amount to a stipulation that productive inflectional rules are always on the last level, while derivational rules are on earlier levels. Given the apparent generality of the observation, we would like it to follow as a theorem from the organization of the grammar, rather than as a stipulation. This would only seem to be possible, however, if we recognize that inflection and derivation constitute separate parts of the morphology in some interesting sense.

Let us agree then, if only for the sake of argument, that there might be a distinguishable component of inflectional morphology which is responsible for specifying properties like those referred to in (4). This theory is concerned precisely with the interface between the syntax and the structure of words. What would such a theory consist of? It appears that we need to provide substantive subtheories at least for all of the domains in (8):

(8) a. A theory of MORPHOSYNTACTIC REPRESENTATION (the representation of the inflectional properties of a word, including an account of the way this is constructed and manipulated by the syntax, on the one hand and referred to in inflectional word formation, on the other)
     b. A theory of CONFIGURATIONAL ASSIGNMENT for the properties called "configurational" in (4a)
     c. A theory of AGREEMENT
     d. A theory of PHRASAL PROPERTY REALIZATION, including in particular a theory of INFL (what it is, where it is, how it gets there, and how it affects binding relations)
     e. A theory of the PHONOLOGICAL REALIZATION of inflectional properties

Given this logical organization of the problem, it becomes clear that many presentations of the issue of whether inflection is in the lexicon, in the syntax, in the phonology, and so on (as in, e.g., Scalise, 1984, Chap. 6) are fundamentally misguided. That is, we can identify two general aspects of the inflection of words: The (syntactically relevant) categories they bear, and the formal ways in which those categories are realized. In views of morphology based on the morpheme as a minimal sign, a word bears signification (of any sort) exactly insofar as it contains a morpheme with that signification. Since the attachment of such morphemes is presumably a unitary process, it must be the case that a word acquires both its form and its sense at some determinate point in the grammar, as supposed by accounts like that of Scalise. If we separate questions of what features a word bears from questions of how those features are reflected, however, as non-morpheme-based views do, it becomes clear that more than one part of the grammar may jointly contribute to the overall domain of inflection.

Needless to say, it is impossible to provide full accounts of all of the domains in (8) here. I simply sketch an approach, with particular attention to the claim that these problems are in fact intimately related to the notion of inflectional morphology as what is relevant to the syntax.

Starting with (8a), we might say that a minimal theory of the inflectionally relevant representation of words would be simply an analysis of them into their constituent morphemes. Indeed, this is often taken as so obvious that the issue of what such a representation would look like is not even raised. But the point I make here is that even if we ignore the problem of how to locate those problematic nonconcatenational "morphemes" in such a structure, the decomposition of a word into morphemes is both too strong and too weak to serve as a valid analysis of it for inflectional puposes.

It is too strong in the sense that it may well include information that I claim could never in principle be inflectionally relevant, such as the actual linear order of formatives. In Muskogean languages like Choctaw, for example, the first person singular active subject marker is a suffix /-li/ [as in (9a)], while the first person plural active subject marker (as well as all of the other markers of this set, in fact) is a prefix [as in the other forms in (9)].

(9)   Choctaw active subject markers
    a.   *hilha-li-h* 'I danced'
    b.   *ii-hilha-h* 'We danced'
    c.   *ish-hilha-h* 'You (sg) danced'

Of course, the difference between prefixed and suffixed markers is relevant only to word structure, and is not something which is manipulated by or accessible to the syntax.

A similar point comes from the observation that the same category may be reflected in more than one place in a single word. In this connection, consider the inflection of adjectives in the Kubachi dialect of the Northeast Caucasian language Dargwa (see, Magometov, 1976, for further information). In this dialect arguments are classified as referring either to males, females, or nonhumans (as well as first, second, or third person), and as singular or plural. The set of class markers is shown in (10).

(10)   (Kubachi) Dargwa class-agreement markers

	Male	Female	Nonhuman
Singular	/w/	/j/	/b/
3 plural	/b/		/d/
1, 2 plural		/d/	

Now consider the agreement pattern in the adjective noun NPs in (11).

(11)   a.   *b-īk'a-zi-b qalče* 'little bird'
        b.   *d-īk'a-žu-d qulč'-ne* 'little birds'
        c.   *w-īk'a-zi-w gal* 'little child'
        d.   *b-īk'a-žu-b gul-e* 'little children'

Each of the adjectives in (11) contains three distinct agreement markers: (a) an initial marker that agrees with the gender/number class of the noun; (b) a final marker that also agrees with the noun's gender/number class; and (c) a penultimate marker that agrees only with the number of the noun. Despite this richness of agreement marking, the inflectionally relevant property of the NP as a whole (and presumably of the adjective) is simply the gender and number of the head noun. The syntax does not (and presumably could not, in principle) pay attention to the presence of three separate markers. One does not, for example, find that an intransitive verb that has one of the NPs in (11) as subject is inflected for more than one argument, as if it were transitive or ditransitive.

Just as the structure provided by a literal analysis of the formatives in a complex word may prove to be substantially richer than what the syntax must or can refer to, it may also prove insufficient for this purpose. There are at least two senses in which this may be true. One is perhaps trivial in appearance: A single formative may provide information about more than one structurally relevant property of the form. Thus, in Yuma, as we saw in (6), many of the verbal agreement markers are portmanteaux and provide information about both subject and object in a single formative. As far as the syntax is concerned, such forms include information about both the person and number of the subject and the properties of the object. A structural analysis of the morphemes contained in the form, however, does not provide this information without further interpretation: It gives us only a single element from which two structural constituents can be inferred.

The second sense in which a structural analysis of the composition of a form may prove inadequate might be called the argument from "the dog that did not bark in the night." Sometimes essential properties of a form are to be inferred not from elements that are present in it, but rather from elements that are absent. Consider the Georgian form in (12), for example.

(12)   *mo-g-k'lav* 'I will kill you'
         preverb–2obj–kill

Ignoring the way in which the form in (12) indicates the future, the point is that it is quite unambiguous in its indication of the person and number of both subject and object despite the fact that it contains only one agreement marker. The /g-/ in the form indicates that the object is second person, and we can easily determine that the number of the object is singular, since there would otherwise be a final suffix *-t* to mark plurality. But how do we know that the subject is first person singular? Again, the number follows from the absence of a final *-t*, but the person follows from a more circuitous line of reasoning. The subject could not be second person, since the object is second person, and if both were the same, the object would have to be reflexive, and in Georgian, reflexives are formally third person. Further, if the subject were third person, the verb would have a final suffix *-s*. The only remaining possibility is first person. First person subjects normally call for a prefix *v-* on the verb, but in the present case this prefix cannot show up, because both *v-* 'first person sbj' and *g-* 'second person obj' occur in the same "slot" in the verbal morphology, with *g-* taking precedence. An analysis often offered in the traditional literature suggests that both *v-* and *g-* are underlyingly present, with the combination simplified for phonological reasons; but since both [vg] and [gv] are perfectly acceptable clusters (and also possible as parts of more complex clusters), such a simplification would have to be restricted to these specific morphological elements. A morpheme-specific deletion rule, of course, would be equivalent to the analysis offered here, on which the appearance of only one of the two motivated markers is a fact about the morphology of inflected verb forms in Georgian. We can thus infer unambiguously that the form in (12) has a first person subject, but only from a consideration of what is not there.

We conclude, then, that it is not the morphology per se that the syntax cares about, but rather a distinct, possibly more abstract, but certainly differently structured representation of the inflectional categories that a particular form indicates. A minimal theory of this MORPHOSYNTACTIC REPRESENTATION would be that it consists simply of an unordered bundle of features, including all and only those feature values that (in a particular language) are referred to, introduced, or manipulated by the syntax. This is essentially the line Chomsky took in *Aspects* (Chomsky, 1965), where the complex symbols that constitute the terminal nodes of phrase markers play the same role as our morphosyntactic representations. Unfortunately, however, this minimal sort of picture is not adequate, since a given morphosyntactic representation may in some languages have to contain more than one specification for the same paradigmatic dimension. When that happens, we need some way to keep them separate. This is the case, for instance, when a language has agreement with both subject and object (and also, a fortiori, when there are three or even more potentially agreeing NPs) or when an NP that is itself 3sg for the purposes of agreement also has to be inflected for the presence of, say, a 2pl possessor. In such cases we need some way of structuring the morphosyntactic representation so that the rules of the morphology can tell what's what.

Apparently, it is sufficient to allow for limited hierarchical structure in morphosyntactic representations as it is imposed by the layering convention proposed in (13).

(13)   LAYERING PRINCIPLE: When a rule assigns features from a paradigmatic dimension D to a morphosyntactic representation R that already contains values from D, the result is that the previous values are made hierarchically subordinate to the new values.

For example, if a language has both subject and object agreement, this could be represented by two rules: first copy the relevant features from an object NP (if there is one), and then copy the relevant features from the subject NP. The result is that a transitive verb will be given a morphosyntactic representation like (14a), and an intransitive one like (14b).

(14)   a.   Transitive [tense, etc., F_i [F_j]]
       b.   Intransitive: [tense, etc., F_i]

In these representations, the features F_i and F_j represent the features of agreement with the subject and object NPs, respectively. Importantly, the inflectional rules can tell from looking at (14a) which features (if any) ought to be reflected by an object marker (the "inner" ones), and which by a subject marker. A rule introducing a portmanteau, of course, would just look at both layers together.

An alternative to this sort of representation would be to tag each feature directly with the grammatical position from which it was copied, as in the representations in (15). A view similar to this has been advocated by Zwicky (1986).

(15)   a.   Transitive: [tense, etc., sbj: F_i, obj: F_j]
       b.   Intransitive: [tense, etc., sbj: F_i]

On that view, the morphosyntactic representation actually encodes a certain amount of the structure of the phrase marker, while in the view represented by (14) the relation is less direct. There are various other alternatives one could consider, but there is some reason to prefer something along the lines of (14) over (15) as a way of representing multiple instances of the same feature set. Notice that a rule operating on the representations in (14) might refer to the values of the "outermost" features in a representation, in which case it would examine exactly the features that correspond to subjects of both transitive and intransitive verbs. Alternatively, it might refer to the "innermost" feature values present, in which case it would operate on the features corresponding to the object in (14a), but the subject in (14b). Such a rule would in effect be applying to the absolute NP, but in a way that does not necessitate our recognizing absolutive as a structural relation in the syntax. This seems exactly the right result, since as far as we know (with the usual exception made for Dyirbal and its friends), the use of ergative/absolutive categories is a fact about morphology, not syntax.

Interestingly, the fact that it is not the syntactic structure which is referenced directly is suggested by the fact that the same language may refer in effectively simultaneous ways to both absolutives and subjects. Consider the verbal agreement system in Kubachi Dawgwa (Magometov, 1976), as illustrated in (16).

(16) Kubachi Dargwa verbal agreement
    a. Transitive verb *iddi id gap wāqʼaj* 'he praised him'

	Object class			
Subject	3sg male	1pl	2pl	3pl
1sg	*w-āqʼa-d*	*d-āqʼa-d*	*d-āqʼa-d*	*b-āqʼa-d*
2sg	*w-āqʼa-t:e*	*d-āqʼa-t:e*	*d-āqʼa-t:e*	*b-āqʼa-t:e*
3sg	*w-āqʼaj*	*d-āqʼaj*	*d-āqʼaj*	*b-āqʼaj*

    b. Intransitive verb *id liw* 'he is'

	Subject class		
Subject	Male	Female	Nonhuman
1sg	*li-w-da*	*li-j-da*	*li-b-da*
2sg	*li-w-de*	*li-j-de*	*li-b-de*
3sg	*li-w*	*li-j*	*li-b*

In these forms we see that Kubachi Dargwa has two distinct kinds of agreement: a class marker (/w/, /d/, /b/, or /j/, prefixed to the verb in (16a) and suffixed in (16b)) that agrees with the absolute NP, and a suffixed marker which depends on the tense and agrees with the subject NP in person and number. A representation like that in (14) allows us to treat these as simply two different rules that look at different aspects of the same representation, while a representation along the lines of (15) makes it less obvious how this might be done.

We can also observe that representations like (14) allow us to treat at least some cases of apparent inversion of grammatical relations as morphological rather than syntactic facts—a picture that has much to recommend it, as I argued for Georgian (Anderson, 1984b). It appears that (14) is on the right track, therefore. On that basis, our theory of morphosyntactic representations is essentially that these are unordered feature complexes, whose only internal structure is that which results from principle (13). This suggests a rather restricted picture of just how the syntax interacts with these objects: In fact, we can propose that the only effect of the syntax on the morphosyntactic representation is limited by the constraint in (17).

(17)   The only operation a syntactic rule can perform on a morphosyntactic representation is to add features to it.

In addition to this constraint on the effect syntactic operations can have on morphosyntactic representations, we would clearly like to constrain the accessibility of these latter to the syntax. Ideally, something like (18) might be maintained.

(18)   Only a rule that adds features to one morphosyntactic representation can examine the content of another.

On the present view, lexical insertion (which must of course examine morphosyntactic representations) is not actually a rule of the syntax, but a process of interpretation of the terminal nodes of phrase markers to yield a phonological form; it is thus not relevant that it violates (18). Unfortunately, in addition to the core of cases accommodated by (18), we also have to allow the binding theory to look at the content of INFL in order to identify domains corresponding to "tensed clauses" or whatever the relevant notion is. Assuming that this exception can be incorporated directly into the principles of the binding theory, we are left with a narrowly constrained view of the syntax-morphology interface, but one that is apparently adequate to deal with the facts of inflection.

The next task for a theory of inflection is the formulation of a theory of the assignment of configurational properties (4a), such as case in NP, and special relative clause forms of verbs (see Anderson, 1982, 1985a for further exemplification of the range of such properties across languages). A comprehensive account of the relevant notions would clearly exceed the scope of this chapter, but the issues seem to break down into two classes.

First, there are instances in which a configurational property is assigned on the basis of structural considerations alone, for example, mechanical assignment of "accusative" to any NP directly dominated by the VP in some languages. This, I would assume, is the proper domain of the aptly yclept "theory of case" in government and binding theory. Much of the existing literature on the theory of case assumes that "case" is a largely abstract property which is only mediately (if at all) related to overt morphological categories. I suggest that this view is largely an artifact of the focus of much relevant syntactic work on languages like English, where the system of overt case is seriously impoverished or even completely absent. For such languages, the notion of abstract case may well have a role to play, but I am personally a believer in the proposition that abstract case is only present (if at all) to the extent a language is lacking in morphological case. You would be surprised what you can do with overt case, if you take it seriously. I have attempted to demonstrate elsewhere [for Kʷakʷʼala in Anderson (1984a) and for Georgian in Anderson (1984b)] the extent to which a serious and explicit account of overt case-marking in languages with such a system can render an appeal to abstract case unnecessarily redundant.

The second variety of configurational assignment is found when such assignment is sensitive not simply to structural position, but also to the requirements of other lexical items in the structure. Thus, in German, the verb *helfen* 'help' takes a dative rather than an accusative object, a property that cannot apparently be deduced from the structure in which the object NP appears. Such behavior often goes by the unfortunate name of "quirky" case, especially in the literature on Germanic languages such as Icelandic in which it is particularly richly attested. I suggest that rather than being an instance of lexically governed assignment of case, this situation actually involves the free assignment of case as a property of NPs in certain positions, together with lexical subcategorization of argument-taking items for certain properties of their arguments. The theory of quirky case, then, would fall under the domain of the theory of subcategorization.

The theory of agreement also breaks down into two subcases. The first of these is agreement of modifiers with their heads. This, I think, is a matter of the inheritance by subordinate (nonhead) elements within an $\overline{X}$ of features that have been assigned to the phrasal node itself. These features may, in turn, either be imposed from outside by a configurational assignment rule, or project features of the head of the phrase upwards. This part of the theory would be the responsibility of an $\overline{X}$ theory, if, as Pullum (1985) quite appropriately points out, we had such a thing. In any event, the relevant notions have probably been most extensively studied by syntacticians working within the framework of generalized phrase structure grammar (and its derivatives), where they play a more obvious and important role in syntactic description than in other frameworks.

The second subcase of agreement is the agreement of predicates with their arguments. There is obviously a lot to be said here, and again I lack space in which to say it. Two important points, however, can be mentioned. First, such agreement seems always to be "local" to a clause. Apparent instances of long-distance agreement can always be reduced to a chain of individually local agreements. Second, predicate-argument agreement appears to involve not only the copying of features, but also the establishment of a co-indexing relation. The feature [3sg] on a verb does not simply record the presence of a third person singular argument, but relates to a particular 3sg NP. There are a number of arguments from several languages that show that verbal agreement plays a role somewhat similar to a sort of pronominal element, rather than just registering the fact that a certain formal kind of NP is present in the clause. As a result, much of the theory of predicate–argument agreement turns out to fall within the domain of the binding theory, as various people have claimed for quite independent reasons.

We turn now to the theory of how phrasal properties are to be realized. This, in turn, brings us back to the problem of special clitics raised earlier, for several influential works on clitics have suggested that special clitics are really a kind of phrasal affix, that is, elements that encode properties of phrases in a way analogous to the way affixes record properties of words. If we were to accept that analogy, what would it entail? On the line taken here, one expectation we might have would be that there could be two sorts of phrasal affix, corresponding to the difference between derivational and inflectional morphology. One set of special clitics (the derivational ones) would correspond to the introduction of changes in the semantic properties of the phrases they occur in. These are the elements usually lumped together as particles, often quite obscure and discourse related, but not neutral in meaning. The other set (the inflectional ones) would then consist of auxiliaries, tense markers, and clitic pronouns that represent the arguments of the clause, or the corresponding elements like determiners and possessors within NPs. The extent to which systematic analogs of the distinction between derivation and inflection can be found in the domain of clitics seems an interesting topic for future investigation; so far as I know, this possibility has not previously been raised. Other aspects of the parallel between affixes (within words) and clitics (as affixes on phrases) are noted below.

First, however, I would like to sketch the outlines of a theory of INFL. This is the set of features assigned to the clause as a whole, including tense and agreement (with various arguments), and which are relevant to determining the scope of a domain such as tensed (or finite) clause which may be relevant to the binding and/or bounding theory. On the present view, these features (which are fundamentally asigned to the clause node itself) are then realized by a rule of special cliticization which assigns them either directly to the verb (considered as the head of S), or to another special-clitic position (typically, second position; recall that location with respect to the head is also a possible position for special clitics).

The famous verb-second phenomenon results when the features of INFL are assigned to second position but not directly to a lexical item. When that happens, the verb (or rather, the only verb not already inflected as past or present participle, and so on, as a result of the requirements of some auxiliary element) must move to the position of these inflectional features without lexical content, both so that it can be inflected and also so that the features of INFL can be realized. This basically encodes the original claim of Wacker-nagel (1892) that the finite verb in a certain stage of Indo-European was a second position (special) clitic.

Now let us note that if the equation of special clitics with phrasal affixes is correct, we would expect to find properties that are common to inflection/derivation and cliticization. Obviously, clitics share with affixes the properties that neither are phonologically autonomous. In fact, though, there are more interesting parallels, some of which we can adduce here. (See Anderson, 1986a, for additional discussion of these points.)

Interestingly, the range of places affixes can be put by a morphological rule can probably be reduced to the same parameters that govern clitic placement (see (3)). Thus, the most common kinds of affixes are of course prefixes (parallel to clitics preceding the phrase-initial element) and suffixes (parallel to clitics following the phrase-final elements). Infixes such as Tagalog -*um*- in *gumabi* 'get on toward nighttime' (cf. *gabi* 'night') are analogous to second-position clitics: They are located with respect to the beginning of the phonological phrase within which they appear (namely, its initial C-slot or syllabic onset), but they follow this anchor point. Other affixes are located with respect to the head of the word in which they appear, in one of two senses. The relevant notion of "head" may be the head of the prosodic structure (i.e., the main stress), as in the Samoan infixed reduplication in *faʻamalolosi* 'encourage, force (pl)' (cf. *faʻamalosi* 'encourage, force (sg)'; Samoan stress falls on the syllable containing the penultimate mora of the word). Alternatively, the notion of head may be a nonphonological one. Thus, languages like Georgian and Icelandic have internally complex words, with a nonhead constituent (initial preverbs in Georgian, a final middle marker in Icelandic) and rules that assign affixes as prefixes or suffixes to the head stem rather than the whole word. We thus appear to find exactly the same range of degrees of freedom in affix placement within words as in clitic placement within phrases.

The extent to which clitics constitute a close phrasal analog to affixes within words can be further extended in the area of the formal apparatus required to describe them. Just as word-level morphology includes both affixation and nonaffixal changes (vowel changes, consonant mutation, metathesis, deletion, etc.), phrasal morphology is sometimes affixal (e.g., English -*'s* in *I once knew that guy you're talking about's brother-in-law*) and sometimes nonaffixal. Examples of nonconcatenative clitics are not widely cited as such, but once we look for them, they turn up. For example, in Tongan (as described by Churchward, 1953; the analysis here follows Poser, 1985), the normal location of stress is on (the syllable containing) the penultimate mora. A sort of definiteness is marked by a stress shift from this position to the final mora, affecting only the final word of the entire NP. The location of this effect is completely insensitive to the word class and other attributes of the word it occurs on, exactly parallel to the insensitivity of English -*'s* to the category of its host. Some representative Tongan examples are cited in (19).

(19) a. *kuo maumau 'a   e   sālioté*
          past broke   abs art cart-def
          'The cart is broken.'

      b. *kuo maumau 'a   e   sāliote 'a   Feletí*
          past broke   abs art cart   gen Fred-def
          'Fred's cart is broken.'

      c. *kuo maumau 'a   e   sāliote 'a   Feleti mo Sioné*
          past broke   abs art cart   gen Fred and John-def
          'Fred and John's cart is broken.'

      d. *te u 'alu ki he fale   kuo nau fakataha aí*
          fut I go to art house past they assemble in-it-def
          'I will go to the house in which they have assembled.'

      e. *na'a ke 'alu ki he fakataha lahí   aneafi*
          Q   you go to art meeting big-def yesterday
          'Did you go to the big meeting yesterday?'

Phrasal morphology may also involve affixes that are incompletely specified with respect to their phonological content. For example, Rotuman (as described by Churchward, 1940) uses the difference between the complete phase and the incomplete phase in a way parallel to the Tongan definitive accent discussed above. Within an NP, all words are in the incomplete-phase form except the last, which is either complete or incomplete depending on the definiteness of the entire NP. As is well known, the surface manifestation of the difference between complete and incomplete phase in Rotuman involves a combination of vowel deletion, vowel change, and metathesis. Examples are given in (20), with the complete-phase forms in boldface.

(20) a. *'oris **siva*** 'their fans'
      b. *siav **riri'i*** 'the little fans'
      c. *siav riri' ne **tore*** 'the little fans that are left'

In fact, it can be shown that the alternations in question result from the suffixation of an affix consisting of exactly one (otherwise unspecified) vocalic position to the lexical form in order to make the complete-phase form, with no such position appearing in the incomplete phase. Lexically present vocalic material which thus lacks its own vocalic position in the incomplete phase either reassociates to a preceding vowel slot (as in the alternation *siva/siav*) or is lost (as in *riri'i/riri'*).[2] The complete phase is thus represented by a phrasal

---

[2] The analysis of Rotuman here, on which the incomplete phase reflects the lexical form while the complete phase is constructed by affixing a vowel slot to this, was apparently first suggested in an unpublished paper by Mamoro Saito in 1981. McCarthy (1986) adopts it from that source, though without justifying his choice of this account over the alternative of forming the incomplete phase by a rule truncating a vowel slot from a lexical form more-or-less identical to the complete phase. In fact, however, it can be shown from the rest of the morphology that the lexical form must resemble the incomplete-phase form, as McCarthy assumes, rather than the complete-phase form.

affix consisting only of skeletal material, unspecified for melodic content, much as current accounts of reduplication treat this as a word affix made up of skeletal material only.

The analogies between clitic introduction into phrases and morphology as an operation on words, then, appear to be quite intimate.

The final domain in which we need a theory concerns the way inflectional specifications are introduced into words to reflect the properties of their morphosyntactic representation. Much of the literature on the "extended word-and-paradigm" theory of morphology addresses this area in particular. The formal realizations of inflectionally relevant properties seem to have two distinguishable loci in the grammar. Insofar as they are idiosyncratic to specific lexical items, they must be present in the lexical representation of the corresponding stems. Thus, *mice* must be lexically present as the [+plural] member of the paradigm of *mouse*. Furthermore, *left* must be listed, as the [+past] member of the paradigm of *leave*. Even though there is probably a rule of English by which *left* is formed, it is a lexically idiosyncratic rule, and there is no way to tell from other properties of *leave* that it applies—so *left* goes in the lexicon. A principle of disjunctive ordering governs the choice among such lexically related forms, and also between lexical stems and inflectional rules. Some discussion of the principle and its effects in morphology is found in Anderson (1986b).

Other properties are introduced into forms by rules of inflectional morphology, operating on a pair consisting of a stem chosen from the lexicon (and perhaps already modified by the operation of other rules) and the morphosyntactic representation. These rules are in principle productive, but again disjunctive ordering may intervene to prevent their application in particular cases, either as a consequence of the prior applicability of more specific inflectional rules or because the stem is already characterized for the features marked by the rule in question. The references cited above, as well as papers by several writers in Thomas-Flinders (1981), give examples of how this works.

Notice now that the picture developed above gives a more precise form to the theorem claiming that inflection is outside of derivation, which can now be stated as in (21).

(21)   INFLECTION FOLLOWS DERIVATION: Material introduced by inflectional rule (not lexically) on the basis of properties assigned in the syntax to the morphosyntactic representation of the word presupposes, but is not presupposed by, material that is present in the lexical form.

In particular, nonregular (hence lexical) morphology is not constrained by the organization proposed in (21), and may appear in derivational forms or compounds because it is in the lexicon; so may material which is introduced not in response to the requirements of the syntax but for semantic or purely formal derivational reasons, even when it is homophonous with elements that are otherwise markers of inflection. This rather precise claim follows as a theorem from this proposed organization of the grammar, and as far as I can see it is a correct one.

While there are obviously lots of details that remain to be worked out on this picture, and many things that are not just details, I hope to have made it plausible that there is something about inflection worth studying from a theoretical point of view. Once you take inflection seriously, not much of the grammar remains unaffected by the way things work out. Inflection is sort of the Times Square of natural language.

Acknowledgment

This research was supported in part by Grant #BNS-84-18277 from the National Science Foundation.

References

Anderson, S.R. (1982). Where's morphology? *Linguistic Inquiry*, **13**, 571–612.

Anderson, S.R. (1983). Rules as 'morphemes' in a theory of inflection. *Proceedings of the 1983 Mid-America Linguistics Conference*, pg. 3–21.

Anderson, S.R. (1984a). Kwakwala syntax and the Government-Binding theory. *In* The Syntax of Native American Languages (Eu.-D. Cook and D.B. Gerdts, eds.) pp. 21–75. Academic Press, New York.

Anderson, S.R. (1984b). On representations in morphology: Case, agreement and inversion in Georgian. *Natural Language and Linguistic Theory* **2**, 157–218.

Anderson, S.R. (1985a). Inflectional morphology. *In* "Language Typology and Syntactic Description" (T. Shopen, ed.), Vol. 3, pp. 150–201. Cambridge Univ. Press, Cambridge.

Anderson, S.R. (1985b). *Kʷakʷala morphology.* Paper read at Conference on Canadian Native Languages in Theoretical Perspective, SUNY Buffalo.

Anderson, S.R. (1986a). *Clitics are phrasal affixes.* Paper read at 2nd International Conference on Word Formation, Veszprém, Hungary.

Anderson, S.R. (1986b). Disjunctive ordering in inflectional morphology. *Natural Language and Linguistic Theory* **4**, 1–32.

Aronoff, M. (1976). "Word Formation in Generative Grammar." MIT Press, Cambridge, MA.

Bat-El, O. (1986). *Extraction in Modern Hebrew morphology.* Master's thesis, UCLA.

Borer, H. (1984). The projection principle and rules of morphology. *Proceedings of the North Eastern Linguistics Society* **14**, 16–33.

Caramazza, A., Laudanna, A., and Romani, C. (1987). *Lexical access and inflectional morphology.* Reports of the Cognitive Neuropsychology Laboratory, Johns Hopkins University.

Chomsky, N. (1965). "Aspects of the Theory of Syntax." MIT Press, Cambridge, MA.

Chomsky, N. (1970). Remarks on nominalizations. *In* "Readings in English Transformational Grammar" (R.A. Jacobs and P.S. Rosenbaum, eds.), pp. 184–221. Ginn, Waltham, MA.

Churchward, C.M. (1940). "Rotuman Grammar and Dictionary." Australasian Medical Publ., Sydney.

Churchward, C.M. (1953). "Tongan Grammar." Oxford Univ. Press, London.

Halpern, A.M. (1946). Yuma. *In* "Linguistic Structures of Native America," pp. 249–88. Viking Fund, New York.

Jackendoff, R.S. (1975). Morphological and semantic regularities in the lexicon. *Language* **51**, 639–71.

Kaisse, E. (1985). "Connected Speech." Academic Press, New York.

Kiparsky, P. (1982). Lexical morphology and phonology. *In* "Linguistics in the Morning Calm," pp. 3–91. Hanshin Publ., Seoul.

Klavans, J.L. (1980). "Some Problems in a Theory of Clitics." Indiana University Linguistics Club.

Klavans, J.L. (1985). The independence of syntax and phonology in cliticization. *Language* **61**, 95–120.

Lapointe, S. (1980). *A theory of grammatical agreement*. PhD thesis, University of Massachusetts.

McCarthy, J.J. (1981). A prosodic theory of non-concatenative morphology. *Linguistic Inquiry* **12**, 373–418.

McCarthy, J. (1986). OCP effects: Gemination and antigemination. *Linguistic Inquiry* **17**, 207–263.

Magometox, A. (1976). Sub'jektno-ob'jektnoje soglasovanije glagola v lakskom i darginskom jazikax ["Coordination of the subject and object of the verb in Lak and Dargwa"]. *Iberiul-ḳavḳasiuri enatmecnierebis çeliçdeuli* **3**, 203–18.

Micelli, G., and Caramazza, A. (1987). *Dissociation of inflectional and derivational morphology*. Reports of the Cognitive Neuropsychology Laboratory, Johns Hopkins University.

Nevis, J.A. (1985). *Finnish particle clitics and general clitic theory*. PhD thesis, Ohio State University.

Poser, W. (1985). Cliticization to NP and lexical phonology. *West Coast Conference on Formal Linguistics* **4**.

Pullum, G.K. (1985). Assuming some version of X-bar theory. *Proceedings of the Chicago Linguistic Society* **21**, 323–353.

Sadock, J. (1985). Autolexical syntax: a proposal for the treatment of noun incorporation and similar phenomena. *Natural Language and Linguistic Theory* **3**, 379–439.

Scalise, S. (1984). "Generative Morphology." Foris, Dordrecht.

Thomas-Flinders, T. (1981). *Inflectional morphology: Introduction to the extended word and paradigm theory.* Occasional Papers in Linguistics 4, UCLA Dept. of Linguistics.

Wackernagel, J. (1892). Über ein Gesetz der indogermanische Worstellung. *Indogermanische Forschungen* **1**, 333–436.

Zwicky, A. (1977). "On Clitics." Indiana University Linguistics Club.

Zwicky, A. (1986). *Imposed vs. inherent feature specifications, and other multiple feature markings*. To appear in Indiana University Linguistic's Club Twentieth Anniversary Volume.

Chapter 3

On the Role of Inflectional
Morphology in Agrammatism

Ria de Bleser & Josef Bayer

1. Introduction

There is an ongoing debate in generative linguistics as to the place of morphology, and in particular of inflection, in a model of grammar. We have
argued in de Bleser and Bayer (1986) that lexical morphology is an appropriate
framework to explain data from certain aphasic patients who show dissociations between a retained morphophonological lexicon and a disrupted syntactic and semantic system. Our purpose here is to show how lexical
morphology can also explain data from argrammatic aphasics in an elegant
and consistent way. The performance of three German-speaking agrammatics
in various experimental tasks demonstrates a surprisingly good command over
inflected forms in addition to other aspects of morphology in the face of
a relatively impoverished syntax. The elicited data are incompatible with those
accounts of agrammatism which assume a total abolition of morphosyntax
or a deficit in accessing bound morphemes. The data also contradict explanations which take agrammatism to be a processing disorder, while syntactic
representations are largely preserved. Retention of a rich lexicon by agrammatics may account for both their morphosyntactic abilities and their deficit(s)
in syntax proper.

2. Two Ways of Locating Morphology in Generative Grammar

For the purpose of this chapter, we make a simplified distinction between
two classes of generative theories, (a) the split morphology theories (SMT)
and (b) the lexical morphology theories (LMT). With SMT, we refer to models

which locate inflectional morphology outside of the lexicon and in a component of grammar different from other word-formation processes such as derivational morphology and compounding. Some prominent examples are Aronoff (1976), Anderson (1982), and a more radically syntax-oriented example, Fabb (1984). With LMT, we refer to models which argue in favor of a unified word-formation component which comprises all morphological operations including inflection and which is distinct from phrase-level syntax. Examples are Lieber (1980), Lapointe (1983), and Kiparsky (1982), and with more emphasis on phonology, Halle and Mohanan (1985).

Naturally, what should be captured descriptively by both is that across languages of the world inflectional affixes tend to occur "outside" of noninflectional affixes and that they follow other word-formation rules.[1] SMT and LMT account for this tendency in different ways, the former by making a distinction in terms of components (lexicon versus syntax), the latter by separating levels within one component ("late" inflection level in the lexicon). By making this distinction between lexical and syntactic affixation, SMT emphasizes the syntax relevance of inflection as in agreement and case. However, in LMT the syntax-orientedness of inflection does not necessitate the generation of inflected forms within the syntax.

While SMT has certain problems in explaining cases where syntax-relevant morphology precedes noninflectional morphology,[2] LMT can solve such cases because any morphological process is in principle open to interaction with another one, everything being in one component. This was one of the reasons for Lieber to emphasize LMT.

Free interaction, however, would overgenerate in an unprincipled way. One would not be in a position to explain why, for example, case affixes never appear in nonheads of compounds.[3] Layered conceptions of the lexicon, such as Kiparsky's, can cope with this problem by locating inflection in a late level of the lexicon.

In de Bleser and Bayer (1986) we argued that both language-internal aspects of German word structure and external data from language pathology favor

---

[1]Exceptions to this are dealt with later.

[2]For example, in German, the plural can precede the diminutives *-chen* and *-lein*, as in

(i)   *Kind - er - lein*
        child pl   dim
(ii)   *Lied - er - chen*
        song pl   dim

[3]*Helfen* 'to help' and *ähnlich* 'similar' both subcategorize for a dative and govern to the left in German. Thus, if case were available in compounding, one would expect the forms in (ii) but not in (i).

(i)   *Ärzte - helferin*   (ii)   **Ärzte - n - helferin*
        doctors she-helper   dat
        rinder - ähnlich   **rinder - n - ähnlich*
        oxen   similar   dat

LMT as a theoretical account. Patients who were shown to have hardly any access to syntactic and semantic representations could be shown to successfully manipulate all kinds of morphological forms, including such clearly syntax-relevant types as gender, number, and case. This cannot easily be reconciled with the assumption made by SMT. For these reasons we continue to use LMT as a linguistic framework to account for data from other aphasic disorders, such as agrammatism.

3. Lexical and Syntactic Morphological Abilities in Agrammatism

3.1. What is Agrammatism?

Present-day clinical definitions of AGRAMMATISM (in Broca's aphasia) are essentially the same as those given by K. Kleist in 1914 for AGRAMMATIC PRODUCTION and in 1916 for AGRAMMATIC COMPREHENSION. Especially with respect to agrammatism in the English language, the leading symptom is the patient's omission of the so-called closed-class vocabulary. Utterances are only of highly simplified syntactic structures, consisting mostly of simple predications, given that the patient can communicate in multiple-word utterances at all.

A parallel disturbance in comprehension, though usually hypothesized, cannot so easily be assessed by clinical observations only.

In the 1970s, the clinical picture led to psycholinguistic investigations which resulted in the strong claim that agrammatism is a disruption of the central syntactic parser (see Caramazza and Berndt, 1978; Berndt and Caramazza, 1980, for surveys of studies within this paradigm). While comprehension and production should be affected to the same extent, certain extralinguistic strategies (semantic and pragmatic heuristics) may cover up the deficit on the comprehension side. Closely parallel with this, another line of research interpreted agrammatism mainly as a disordered system of lexical access. The normal retrieval of the closed-class vocabulary which is a precondition for building syntactic frames on-line does not function any longer in agrammatism (see Bradley *et al.*, 1980).

Another proposal stands in strong contrast to these accounts. It is based on a certain discrepancy between actual performance and tacit linguistic abilities in agrammatics. Linebarger *et al.* (1983) gave evidence that patients who have clear agrammatic comprehension and production disorders nevertheless show high sensitivity to grammatical ill-formedness. They conclude that agrammatics, whose syntactic abilities are largely preserved, are unable to process syntax and semantics simultaneously, as is required in most tasks, including spontaneous speech.

Together with other researchers we feel that it may be premature to characterize agrammatism along these lines, as long as global concepts like "syntax" or "semantics" are being used in the reasoning about the disorder. (See Caplan, 1985; Grodzinsky, 1986.) Modern generative linguistic theories offer fractionations of these pretheoretical concepts which may lead to a more principled characterization of linguistic deficits like agrammatism.

Using the cover-term "agrammatism" might give the impression that we are dealing with a unitary category. This was indeed the underlying assumption in the group-study paradigm of the 1960s and 1970s, a point of view which is being questioned (Badecker and Caramazza, 1985). It might well be that in-depth single case studies will reveal asymmetries of various kinds, for example, between intact syntactic comprehension and agrammatic production, or between free and bound morphemes. We are concerned only indirectly with such issues in the present study.

3.2. Subjects

Three agrammatic patients (C.B., M.H., and H.R.), quite similar on the basis of clinical examination, are reported. All three had a left hemisphere lesion due to a cardiovascular accident. According to the Aachen Aphasia Test (Huber *et al.*, 1984) they were classified as clear cases of Broca's aphasia with outspoken agrammatism in spontaneous speech. One criterion among others for the selection of these patients was the absence of articulatory disorders due to dysarthria.[4] The experiments reported were conducted 28, 9, and 2 years post onset for C.B., M.H., and H.R. respectively. Thus the patients presented a stable picture of their language deficit.

We give examples of spontaneous speech and the description of action pictures in the appendix. The examples illustrate that in the latter, more restrictive task, speech is less disturbed with respect to morphosyntactic characteristics. For lack of space we are unable to give a detailed analysis of the material.

However, even a superficial analysis reveals that in spontaneous speech, in contrast to the description task, infinitives and past participles are more frequently used, while the functor vocabulary is more often omitted. One may well expect these patients to have command over even more morphological and syntactic structure if the tasks which elicit performance are still more constrained.

Four questions are answered, at least tentatively:

[4]Case endings, e.g., nasals, often cannot be distinguished in the presence of dysarthria.

1. Is there a dissociation between "early" morphology (derivation, compounding, irregular inflection) and "late" morphology (regular inflection)?
2. If late morphology tends to be available, can it be exploited for syntactic purposes?
3. If 2 is answered affirmatively, is there a distinction to be drawn between domains of application?
4. What do the patterns of relative preservation versus disturbance teach us about the nature of the deficit in certain cases of agrammatism?

3.3. Morphological Abilities

3.3.1. *Linguistic structures and materials*   In order to understand the tasks the patients had to perform, it is necessary to say a few words about German gender, number, and case morphology.

German has three genders; masculine, feminine, and neuter, which show up in the definite articles *der, die,* and *das,* respectively. Gender is largely grammatically determined. Formal cues, if present at all, are usually weak and unreliable (e.g., two-syllable nouns ending in *-e* are often feminine, but see *der Käse* 'the cheese', *das Auge* 'the eye').

In compound words (nominal derivations and compounding), the right-hand head of the word determines its gender. For instance, the derivational suffix [$_N$ *-er*] is masculine and [$_N$ *-ung*] is feminine. *Erfinder* 'inventor,' which is analyzed as [$_N$ [$_V$*erfind*] *-er*] is masculine, whereas *Erfindung* 'invention,' [$_N$ [$_V$ *erfind*] *-ung*] is feminine. In the same way, in compounding the right-hand noun determines the gender of the compound, for example, [$_N$ [$_N$*Hut*$_{masc}$] [$_N$ *Schachtel*$_{fem}$]] 'hatbox' is feminine.

One could argue that highly frequent compounds and, naturally, derived forms like *Umgebung* 'surrounding' and *Frechheit* 'cheekiness' are stored in the lexicon as atomic expressions. Therefore, a crucial test to investigate word-syntactic abilities seems to be the assignment of gender (e.g., by supplying the definite article *der, die, das*) to pseudocompounds and nonword derivations. Examples are creations like *Sterngans* 'star-goose,' *Hautglas* 'skin-glass,' or *Stippung* and *Mielheit*, where neither *stipp-* nor *miel-* are existing stems of the German lexicon.

Let us now turn to number. Ignoring learned and Latinate words, German has at least nine distinct plural forms:

(1)
Plural forms	Singular	Plural
—ø	*Esel*	*Esel*
¨—ø	*Vogel*	*Vögel*
—ə	*Bein*	*Beine*

⸚ə	*Zug*	*Züge*
⸚ər	*Blatt*	*Blätter*
—n	*Flasche*	*Flaschen*
—ən	*Frau*	*Frauen*
—s	*Auto*	*Autos*
—ər	*Kind*	*Kinder*

In spite of the various attempts to reduce the plural forms to a smaller number of morphemes, it would be rather unconvincing to ascribe these kinds of word formations to the active competence system of present-day speakers, at least if we do not want to assume access to historical facts about German by ordinary speakers. The only clearly predictable form is the plural *-s* for foreign words ending in an unreduced vowel or in a consonant. While one may argue that plural is syntactically relevant and should thus arise in syntax, it is far from clear how this would work. Given the fact that for virtually each German count noun there exists a rather idiosyncratic plural form, syntax-oriented rules of pluralization seem to be out of place. This unpredictability also disallows locating the German plural uniquely at the latest level of a lexical morphology model.

A third variable which plays a role in our investigation is case, since German is a case-inflecting language. In the masculine singular paradigm, the four cases are morphologically distinct, as shown by the inflections of the definite article.

(2) Nominative *der*
     Genitive   *des*
     Dative   *dem*
     Accusative *den*

The left-hand column of (3) gives an example of the paradigm of definite article–adjective–noun; the right-hand column shows the corresponding indefinite article–adjective–noun.

(3) Nominative *der dreckige Schuh*   *ein dreckiger Schuh*
                 'the dirty shoe'
     Genitive   *des dreckigen Schuhs*   *eines dreckigen Schuhs*
     Dative   *dem dreckigen Schuh*   *einem dreckigen Schuh*
     Accusative *den dreckigen Schuh*   *einen dreckigen Schuh*

It is useful to distinguish two mechanisms of case assignment: structural case and lexical case. There are lexical case assigners like verb, adjective, preposition assigning case to an NP which they govern. Notice that each lexical entry has an associated case; for example, the adjective *treu* 'faithful, loyal' governs a dative, *fähig* 'capable' governs a genitive. Verbs which differ only minimally in their semantics often govern different cases; for example, *lauschen* 'listen to, spy' governs a dative, while *belauschen* 'spy on' (like all *be*-verbs) governs an accusative; *gedenken* 'be mindful of' governs a genitive. These are examples of lexical case. Structural case, on the other hand, is intimately connected with a specific syntactic configuration. Thus, the external argument of a V-projection will usually be nominative if the head of this V-projection is a +tense V/INFL. Another example of structural case is the configuration in (4), where NP_j will always be genitive.

(4) $[_{NP_i}NP_i [_{NP_j} \text{——}]]$ or $[_{N_i'} N_i' [_{NP_j} \text{——}]]$

It could be argued that V-governed accusative is also structural and that the lexicon only specifies case if V is subcategorized for a nonaccusative. Accusative then would be a kind of objective case by default. Since this is highly theory dependent, we rather continue to assume that all V-governed cases are lexical cases. It can be expected that the default case would be the nominative, because this is the form used for citation.

Referring back to SMT and LMT, they would make different predictions for German gender, number, and case morphology. Gender is idiosyncratic in German. Thus it must be encoded with each gender-bearing lexical element. On the other hand, gender morphology is regular; for example, the genitive of a masculine is always *-(e)s*. LMT generates forms like *Mann-es* in the morphological component of the lexicon, while SMT spells out *-(e)s* after a full syntactic phrase has been completed.

With respect to number, things are less clear-cut, considering the irregularity of the various paradigms. Lexical specifications would probably be necessary for both theories, except for the *-s* plural, which SMT should treat in the same way as the English regular plural, that is, postsyntactically.

As far as case is concerned, its morphological realization is regular in German, and it is of course syntax relevant. Thus SMT would spell out case morphemes postsyntactically by rule. LMT, on the other hand, generates these forms at a late but presyntactic level of a lexical morphology component.

3.3.2. Tasks and results   In order to investigate their command over gender, the patients were tested with 30 pictures of objects which had to be named together with the appropriate definite article. Target names were simple nouns throughout. The same 30 (concrete) nouns and an additional 30 uncomposed abstract nouns were used in a repetition task in which the patient had to provide the article while repeating the noun. The same 60 nouns were also used in a test for auditory decision: Of 120 article-plus-noun sequences, half were well-formed and half ill-formed with respect to gender. Similar tasks were performed with nominal compounds. There were 60 such compounds, which had to be repeated while adding the definite article. These 60 items were used for auditory decision also. Notice that 15 items were pseudocompounds as described in 3.3.1.[5] Each item was given with all three articles, only one of which was appropriate. This made 180 stimuli.

Patients were given 120 derived words and 120 nonwords derived by existing German suffixes in order to check their ability to assign gender to derived nouns. Half of the suffixes in each set were native and half non-native (Latinate or Greek). The patients had to provide the definite article while repeating the stimuli. Finally, they were asked to provide a properly inflected adjective and a sequence of indefinite article plus adjective to the 30 concrete nouns previously used in naming. The results are given in Table I.

If the leading symptom of agrammatism is the loss of the closed class vocabulary, the results for gender assignment given in Table I constitute remarkable counterevidence. The data show at least the following three things: (a) Information about gender can be retrieved from the mental lexicon, both in recognition and production; (b) gender information can be used creatively for the purpose of agreement in NPs,[6] and (c) both in compounding and in derivation, the gender features of the (right-hand) head can in principle be used for assigning gender to the complex expression, that is, the patients have intuitions about word structure and silent features sitting in bound morphemes. It should be noticed that the higher error rates in derivation may be due to frequency differences between the affixes, which we were unable to control for. An explanation along these lines is viable since certain suffixes attract almost no errors. Thus, even in nonwords affixed by -*ist*, -*ner*, and -*in*, for example, *Salmist, Luppner, Rühlerin*, no error was committed at all.

The next area for checking morphological abilities in agrammatism is number. Recall that in German there are eight quite irregular forms of the plural and one quite regular form (for nonnative nouns ending in an unreduced vowel or a consonant). The patients were given 90 singulars which they had to pluralize, 10 of each class. The results are as follows. C.B. had 79% correct responses. The major part (42%) of his errors were confined to the ø-plural class, where singular and plural have identical forms. Obviously, the patient was puzzled by this fact, as he did not respond most of the time to these items. M.H. had 86% correct responses; errors were distributed over different classes, not showing any interesting pattern. H.R. had 77% correct responses. Her errors involved two classes: -ə tended to become -ər and -ən tended to become -ə. We do not know what conclusions can be derived from this. In addition to this task, 20 plural nouns had to be singularized. C.B. seemed to expect a change in form in this task also, and he therefore failed in every case where plural and singular were identical. Still, his overall performance was very

---

[5]These items were controlled in many ways. Reporting the details seems unimportant, since the variables built in did not show any effects.

[6]Notice that, out of context, German NPs always carry nominative inflection. We return to other cases below.

Table I   Gender Assignment (Percentage Correct)

	Number of items	C.B.	M.H.	H.R.
Simple nouns				
Nouns in naming pictures	30[a]	0.83[b]	0.83[b]	1.00[b]
Article in naming pictures	30	0.90[b,c]	1.00[b,c]	0.97[b,c]
Production of article in repetition	60	0.93[b,c]	0.93[b,c]	0.83[b,c]
Auditory decision of article	120	0.97[b,c]	0.98[b,c]	0.91[b,c]
Compound nouns				
Production of article in repetition	60	0.80[c]	0.73[c]	0.67[c]
Auditory decision of article	180	0.86[b,c]	0.92[b,c]	0.82[c]
Derived nouns				
Production of article to				
Real stem + affix	120	—[d]	0.66[c]	0.77[c]
Neologistic stem + affix	120	—[d]	0.53[c]	0.69[c]
Agreement in NPs				
Adjective agreement	30[a]	—[d]	0.83[b]	0.87[b]
Indefinite article + adjective				
agreement	30[a]	—[d]	0.77[b]	0.90[b]

[a]Due to indeterminable response possibilities, chance level cannot be fixed.

[b]P-value compatible with a pc (criterion probability) of .90, according to the binomial model; for tasks with more than 100 items the normal approximation to the exact binomial distribution is used.

[c]P-value significantly above chance.

[d]In these tasks, the patient showed perseveratory tendencies at the time of testing. Retesting at a later date was impossible due to the patient's death.

good (85% correct). M.H. made no errors at all; H.R. had 95% correct responses. One may plausibly argue that German plurals are largely unpredictable and have to be listed in the lexicon in an early layer of lexical morphology; this, however, is not true for the -*s* plural. Since the three patients did not have major problems in either of these tasks, one can safely assume that they have command over both irregular and regular number inflection.

Finally, we report the agrammatics' abilities for case inflection. The patients had to substitute the missing endings in complex NPs like *ein. . . klug. . . Minister* 'a wise minister' which appeared in a sentential context.[7] In this section, we only report their performance with respect to NP-internal agreement, not with respect to the syntactic appropriateness of the case assigned. (Agreement here depends on gender, number, and case.) Since masculine nouns were used throughout, all possible case inflections of the paradigm could be expected: nominative, genitive, dative, and accusative. Among the 80 NPs to be inflected, all three patients used all possible forms, although with rather different frequencies. Internal agreement was defective for C.B. in 19% of the cases, for M.H. in 8%, and for H.R. in 16%. This shows that, as in the

[7]For the functional role of case in this task see Section 3.4.2. The substitution was performed while the patient read the sentences, if necessary with the help of the examiner.

task where only the unmarked nominative case (default case) was required, the patients had good command over oblique case forms as well.[8]

The results in all three areas of morphology—gender, number, and case—are impressive and unexpected if agrammatism is predominantly seen as a loss of closed-class elements (free as well as bound morphemes).

What can linguistic theories like SMT and LMT say about these results? Assuming that the agrammatic language production of these patients is indicative of a syntax deficit, their largely retained command over inflectional morphology may be seen as a problem for SMT. Recall that SMT requires this morphology to be a by-product of some syntactic representation. LMT, on the other hand, would be compatible with these results, because the inflected forms can be drawn from the lexicon, that is, the syntax does not crucially interfere with the form side of the inflection vocabulary. A counterargument could be that agrammatic production may not be a reliable reflection of the patients' actual syntactic competence, given that many poorly understood factors or linguistic performance could conceal it. Therefore, the next step is to investigate the patients' ability to associate inflections with their functional role in syntax. The most promising area to do this is case assignment in various syntactic environments. In addition, grammaticality judgments should provide further information about the patients' syntactic intuitions.

3.4. Syntactic Abilities

3.4.1. *Linguistic structures and materials* Basic facts about German NP-internal agreemment as well as the distinction between structural and lexical case were introduced in Section 3.3.1. Some further aspects which are relevant to the syntactic tasks are described here.

German is most consistently described as an SOV language. Word order, however, is mixed, because root sentences observe the V-SECOND RULE. There is complete complementary distribution between the presence of an overt complementizer and V-end on the one hand and the absence of such a complementizer and V-second on the other. It is always the finite verb which moves to the second position. In the V-second cases, the preverbal position can be occupied by any X-projection, although a nominative NP in this position is felt to be the canonical option if ordinary transitive verbs are involved. Thus, even on the basis of surface parsing it is often required that the preverbal NP be linked to the main verb in order to satisfy its argument structure, as, for example, in (5).

---

[8] Recall that C.B.'s responses were characterized by perseverations in the nominative case task. Notice that again in this task he showed a perseveratory tendency by overusing the accusative case. However, all case forms were produced even by C.B.

(5)   [$_{NP}$ *dem Mann*]$_j$ [*hat$_i$* [$_S$ [$_{NP}$ *der Arzt*] *e$_j$ geholfen e$_i$*]]
       the man-dat   has   the doctor-nom   helped

'It is the man (who) the doctor has helped.'

In (5), the past participle *geholfen* assigns dative case to its complement NP, which, however, appears in a position that would be occupied by the nominative NP in the unmarked case.

To see how agrammatics can cope with the interaction of case marking and syntactic environment, the results reported in Section 3.3.2 had to be further evaluated. Uninflected NPs appears in the following constellations (the NP to be completed by the patients is in boldface):

(6)   Canonical   Noncanonical

NP$_{nom}$	V	NP	NP	V	**NP**$_{nom}$	(structural)
NP	V	**NP**$_{acc}$	**NP**$_{acc}$	V	NP	
NP	V	**NP**$_{dat}$	**NP**$_{dat}$	V	NP	(lexical)

(7)
NP	V	P	**NP**$_{acc}$	(lexical)
NP	V	P	**NP**$_{dat}$	
NP	V	NP	**NP**$_{gen}$	(structural)

Consider the following three views on agrammatism: (a) Syntactic abilities are almost completely abolished. This was the predominant view in the 1970s (see, e.g., von Stockert and Bader, 1976; Berndt and Caramazza, 1980). (b) Syntactic abilities are basically preserved; difficulties in syntax would result from disturbed processing mechanisms unrelated to the architecture of grammar (see Linebarger *et al.*, 1983). (c) Syntactic abilities are not lost/retained across the board, but specific syntactic representations are inaccessible (see, e.g., Grodzinsky, 1986; Caplan and Hildebrandt, 1986).

In a grammatical framework including a lexical morphology component, (a) would predict that at best lexically assigned case is retained, while structural case should be lost; (b) would predict that there is no principled distinction, thus either everything works well or disturbances are pervasive; (c) would predict that there are losses which can at least partially be derived from patterns of the grammar.

In addition to these materials, we also tested the patients for their ability to judge grammaticality with a number of other constructions. Samples of both grammatical and ungrammatical test sentences are given in (8).

(8) a.   Agreement
         i.   *Die Männer haben Zucker gekauft.*
              The men   have   sugar   bought
              'The men have bought sugar.'
         ii. * *Die Männer hat Zucker gekauft.*

    b.   WH-questions (resumptive pronouns ungrammatical)
        i. *Wen habt ihr gesehen?*
           'Who have you seen?'
        ii. * *Wen habt ihr ihn gesehen?*
    c.   Subjecthood (pro-drop ungrammatical)
        i. *Wir fragten, wann es etwas   zu Essen gibt.*
           We asked   when it something to eat   is
           'We asked when there will be something to eat.'
        ii. * *Wir fragten, wann etwas zu Essen gibt.*
    d.   Reflexive verbs (agreement with subject obligatory)
        i. *Du freust dich   über das Lied*
           you enjoy yourself over the song
           'You are enjoying the song.'
        ii. * *Du freust ihn über das Lied*
    e.   Verb-second (no complementizer)
        i. *Wir glauben, die Erde ist rund.*
           'We believe the earth is round.'
        ii. * *Wir glauben, die Erde rund ist.*
    f.   Verb-end (with complementizer)
        i. *Sie fragt, ob   die Vase auf dem Tisch steht.*
           She asks whether the vase on the table   stands
           'She asks whether the vase stands on the table.'
        ii. * *Sie fragt, ob die Vase steht auf dem Tisch.*
    g.   Prefix verbs
        i. *Der Junge packt den Koffer schnell aus.*
           the boy   packs the suitcase quickly out
           'The boy quickly unpacks the suitcase.'
        ii. * *Der Junge auspackt den Koffer schnell.*

As in English, German observes person and number agreement between subjects and finite verbs (8a). In the same vein, resumptive pronouns are not allowed in ordinary cases of *wh*-movement (8b). In contrast to English, German occasionally allows for subjectless sentences (see Haider, 1985); however, we used sentences which require the presence of either an expletive or a referential *es* 'it' (8c). A fairly large class of verbs is obligatorily reflexive in German, like in Romance and many other languages. Naturally, the reflexive has to agree in gender and number with the subject NP (8d). The examples in (8e) and (8f) illustrate the complementary distribution between the absence of a complementizer and verb second. Connected to the verb-second phenomenon is also the fact that stress-bearing prefixes to the verb must be left in situ when verb movement takes place (8g).

3.4.2. *Tasks and results* With respect to case assignment, the task of the patients was the same as reported in 3.3.2., that is, sentences had to be completed while reading them. In each of these sentences, one NP appeared uninflected. Thus, the patients were given examples as in (9a) which they had to make into something like (9b).

(9) a. *Ein__ alt__ Zauberer sieht einen bösen Zwerg$_{acc}$*
       An   old   sorcerer sees a   wicked dwarf
    b. Ein alter Zauberer$_{nom}$ sieht einen bösen Zwerg

Thirty semantically reversible sentences with this canonical order had to be completed, 10 with nominative, 10 with accusative, and 10 with dative. The same 30 sentences reappeared in noncanonical order, as in (10).

(10) a. *Einen alten Zauberer$_{acc}$ sieht ein__ bös__ Zwerg*
     b. Einen alten Zauberer   sieht ein   böser Zwerg$_{nom}$

Another 10 sentences had to be completed in which an NP followed a preposition that subcategorizes either for dative or for accusative. Finally, there were 10 sentences in which a genitive NP had to appear after an NP. In this structural case assignment, there was always a clear possession relation between the two NPs.

The results for C.B., M.H., and H.R. are given in Table II. The defective agreement category is to be understood as follows: Despite there being an agreement morpheme lacking, the NP in question can unambiguously be interpreted as a specific case form, for example, *ein klein-en$_{acc}$ Fuchs* instead of *ein-en$_{acc}$ klein-en$_{acc}$ Fuchs* 'a small fox.' The category "uninterpretable" covers reactions which were blends of different case forms, for example, *ein-en$_{acc}$ klein-er$_{nom}$ Fuchs*.

Let us begin with case-assignment by preposition. The first thing to be noticed here is that none of the patients selects the default case (nominative) here. Subcategorization for both accusative and dative seems to be preserved only for C.B., while M.H. and H.R. tend to apply a single objective case in both environments: M.H. selects accusative, H.R., dative. Structurally assigned genitive is possible for all three patients. Turning to case-assignment in the canonical condition, we observe that only H.R. shows a systematic pattern. She basically selects nominative for the preverbal and oblique case for the postverbal position. (In the noncanonical condition, she seems to select dative and accusative at random for the postverbal position.) C.B. and M.H. predominantly use one particular case, irrespective of environment. C.B.'s constant use of the accusative indicates that his "correct" responses come about by chance. M.H. shows somewhat more variation, but in general she tends to apply the nominative. Interestingly, she occasionally manipulates the given case form in such a way that a canonical structure results, that is, she strongly

Table II Case Assignment (in Percentage)ᵃ

Target		Nominative			Accusative			Dative			Genitive			Defective Agreement			Uninterpretable		
		CB	MH	HR	CB	MH	HR	CB	MH	HR	CB	MH	HR	CB	MH	HR	CB	MH	HR
Canonical	Nom	—	**80**	**100**	100	20	—	—	—	—	—	—	—	40	—	—	—	—	—
	Acc	—	70	—	**100**	**30**	**70**	—	—	30	—	—	—	20	10	10	—	—	—
	Dat	—	30	10	90	50	50	**10**	**10**	**20**	—	—	—	10	10	10	—	10	20
Non-canonical	Nom	—	**50**	**10**	100	40	50	—	—	40	—	—	—	—	10	—	—	10	—
	Acc	—	70	100	**100**	**30**	—	—	—	—	—	—	—	10	—	—	—	—	—
	Dat	20	70	90	60	30	—	**20**	—	—	—	—	—	30	—	—	—	—	10
After P	Acc	—	—	—	**100**	**100**	**20**	—	—	80	—	—	—	—	—	—	—	—	—
	Dat	—	—	—	—	100	—	**80**	—	**80**	—	—	—	—	—	—	20	—	20
After NP	Gen	—	—	—	—	20	10	—	—	—	**90**	**80**	**70**	10	20	40	10	—	20

ᵃCorrect reactions are in boldface.

adheres to a nominative < accusative pattern. In the noncanonical condition, H.R. adheres to the strategy of applying nominative preverbally and an oblique case postverbally. The resulting ungrammaticality (e.g., two identical cases in a simple transitive sentence) does not seem to inhibit her behavior.

The common core of the results given in Table II is that both lexical and structural case seem to be available in principle in this production task. Although the distinction between accusative and dative is captured only by C.B. in the preposition task, there is a general awareness that nominative must be out in this context.[9] Most remarkable are the results of the genitive task. The patients seem to be able to use two sources of linguistic knowledge here: (a) they notice the semantic relation that holds between the referents of the two adjacent NPs, for example, possession, and (b) they know how many arguments can be bound by the transitive verb involved, that is, they do not confuse simple transitive constructions with ditransitive ones. All the syntactic work to be done is the selection of one NP as the head and the (local) assignment of genitive case to the other.

On the other hand, case assignment in the canonical condition seems to be more difficult than it looks. Given that the preverbal position in German can be occupied by nonsubjects [in fact by almost any single X^n phrase $(n \geq 0)$], if a full syntactic parse of the sentence cannot be accomplished, there are two ways for the patient to cope with the task: (a) stick to a canonical—and in fact quite frequent—sentence pattern, namely NP_{+nom} V NP_{-nom}, or (b) provide some default form (as a reflex of the variable word order in German). Both types of responses are documented by our patients: H.R. follows strategy (a); as a consequence, she is fairly successful in the canonical condition, but fails completely in the noncanonical condition.

[9]A reviewer of this article wondered why the assignment of accusative and dative case by verbs should be any different from assignment by prepositions. It is argued that the better performance might be due to the high frequency of prepositions. If this were true, however, one would expect other differences as well. Since every tensed sentence requires a nominative subject but not necessarily another case, nominatives should be overused due to frequency effects. As the data in Table II show, this prediction does not hold. Other data contradict the frequency argument even more severely: While genitive is almost completely abandoned in colloquial speech, it appears well preserved in our patients (see Table II).

Another reason for the difference might be that prepositions are always string adjacent to a nonnominative while verbs are not, a result of the verb-second rule and other word order possibilities in German. We have evidence from another agrammatic patient which shows that the nonlinguistic cues do not seem to be involved. His performance on SVO and OVS sentences was basically like C.B.'s, i.e., he used the accusative by default. Given, however, OV items, i.e., VPs like *d. . . Frau helfen* 'help the woman', *d. . . Mann suchen* 'seek the man,' his performance was almost as good as with prepositions as case assigners. It should be noticed that case assignment by P and V is maximally similar here. If inflected verbs come into play, the task might be more complex due to the fact that (a) the verb can assign two cases: The stem assigns lexical (oblique) case and the tense morpheme assigns nominative, and (b) the verb moves to second position in the sentence. This suggests that the greater difficulty patients face in the processing of inflected transitive sentence derives from the enhanced linguistic complexity.

C.B. and M.H. represent (b) by overusing accusative and nominative respectively.

We briefly return to the three views on agrammatism stated at the beginning of Section 3.4.1. The results on case assignment together with the results on NP-internal agreement clearly dismiss view (a), that morphosyntax is almost completely abolished. View (b) in its extreme form is falsified as well, because the asymmetry in our results does relate to the architecture of the grammar. Notice that this asymmetry follows from specific properties of the grammar, that is, while case assignment by a preposition or in the domain of an NP is strictly local, case assignment by a verb or by INFL may be nonlocal, due to movement rules, the use of slash categories, or some equivalent device.

Given the agrammatics' performance, a processing account would have to closely reflect the underlying grammar. This leads, of course, to an adoption of view (c). Notice that this argumentation extends immediately to the well-preserved NP-internal agreement produced by our subjects.

In order to deepen the empirical basis for view (c), the patients were asked to judge the sentences given in (8) for grammaticality.

The results for C.B. and M.H. are given in Table III. H.R. was left out, because she followed a "yes strategy," that is, she basically accepted everything.

The data show that C.B. and M.H. seem to have an awareness of grammatical well formedness, because they tend not to reject the grammatical sentences. On the other hand, they do not consistently reject the ungrammatical sentences either. Strikingly, C.B. and M.H. show a very similar pattern. This indicates that their responses to ungrammaticality were not random. Since it is not entirely clear which sources of linguistic knowledge are tapped by judgments, the results are difficult to evaluate. An explanation, however, has

Table III   Grammaticality Judgments[a]

	Ungrammatical sentences				Grammatical sentences			
	C.B.		M.H.		C.B.		M.H.	
	Hit	Fail	Hit	Fail	Hit	Fail	Hit	Fail
Agreement	5	5	6	4	10	—	10	—
Wh-question	5	5	6	4	10	—	9	1
Subjecthood	1	9	1	9	10	—	9	1
Reflexive verb	4	6	4	6	10	—	10	—
V-second	1	9	2	8	10	—	10	—
V-end	7	3	6	4	10	—	8	2
Prefix verb	8	2	7	3	10	—	9	1

[a]Each sentence type occurred ten times; the numbers given are absolute values.

to be given at least for the fact that both patients fail especially in detecting missing subject pronouns (subjecthood) and the ungrammaticality of sentences like *Sie fragt, ob die Vase steht auf dem Tisch* (V-second). An account should also be given of the patients' relative success in detecting verb prefixes in the wrong position. According to an exact test for a 4-fold table (Fisher Test, see Hays, 1963), the following pairs were significantly different where indicated by an asterisk. The *p*-values in parentheses are close to significance.

		V-end	Prefix verbs
Subjecthood	C.B.	$p = .020^*$	$p = .006^*$
	M.H.	$(p = .057)$	$p = .020^*$
V-second	C.B.	$p = .020^*$	$p = .006^*$
	M.H.	$p = .170$	$(p = .070)$

Turning first to the difference between V-second and V-end sentences, it should be kept in mind that agrammatics analyze the input semantically. If they have access to a full-fledged lexical entry, they detect that complements introduced by a complementizer like *ob* 'whether' and *daß* 'that' fulfill an obligatory argument place of the verb. The complements in question receive a semantic interpretation to the same extent that a V-second root sentence may receive one.[10] What the patients seem to lack is a sensitivity to the complementary distribution between the presence of an overt complementizer and the V-end position. Why then is their performance slightly better with respect to ungrammatical V-end sentences? Notice that despite their ungrammaticality, these sentences could still get an interpretation.

Let us assume that agrammatics know the subcategorization properties of verbs which take sentential complements. Thus, they would know that *glauben* 'believe' selects either *that*-type complements or root sentences. Furthermore, we can safely assume that even patients with severe agrammatism know that in root sentences the finite verb has to be in second position. From this it follows immediately that they will be puzzled about examples like *Wir glauben [die Erde rund ist]*. The bracketed phrase is not a possible root sentence of German. What about their inability to detect the ill formedness of *Wir glauben [daß die Erde ist rund]*? The lexical template can detect that *glauben daß* is a licit string. The knowledge about the structure of root sentences guarantees that the following sentence can pass also. What the patients seem to lack is the ability to build a global syntactic representation which would show that *daß* and *ist* are in complementary distribution. Our tentative explanation of the results is that, like normals, agrammatics strive for semantic interpretation, while they are sensitive to formal violations only as long as

[10]Notice that V-second sentences are very frequent in German and that they persist even in agrammatism, mostly when finite verb forms are used.

the sentence violates lexical templates. These assumptions also cover the results on "subjecthood," that is, that C.B. and M.H. seem to be insensitive to missing subject pronouns: Semantic interpretation is guaranteed and the lexicon does not provide a filter.

As far as the prefix verbs are concerned, ungrammaticality is detected more easily than in cases where a clitic subject is missing or where V-second is inappropriate. Separability of the verbal prefix is a property that has to be specified in the lexical entry of the verb. Given that the patients have intuitions about the V-second constraint, it is plausible that they tend to notice violations of prefix stranding.[11]

The most difficult question with respect to the judgment data is on what basis C.B. and M.H. judge the well-formed sentences. It seems as if they have a sensitivity for grammatical sentences, but not for most of the ungrammatical ones. Notice that a yes-bias in performing the task, as suggested by a reviewer, would neither account for the difference between grammatical and ungrammatical sentences nor for the different response patterns within the set of ungrammatical sentences, as seen in Table III. As a working hypothesis we propose the following: Assume that speakers of a language have some kind of "familiarity" with possible frequent sentence types of the language. These sentence types may well be stored as a finite set. This latter aspect indicates immediately that such a finite set must be different from the usual linguistic capacity which speakers have to assign representations to an infinite number of strings. It should be noticed that the grammatical sentences offered in our judgement task were all of a highly frequent and rather simple pattern. If our explanation in terms of familiarity should have any content, it should follow that unfamiliar but fully grammatical sentences should also be judged at random. Since we do not have data that can address this hypothesis, we leave it as a speculation.

To summarize the results on syntax testing of C.B., M.H., and H.R., the main finding is that the linguistic abilities of these patients are far beyond what they exhibit in unsolicited free speech. It was noted in Section 3.2 that they show more linguistic structure in picture descriptions. In tasks which force them to use inflected categories, they show even more structure. This,

---

[11]C.B., who never uses tensed verbs in free speech, produces prefixed verbs in their underlying lexical form, as shown in examples like *nieder + gelegt* 'put down,' *mit + gefahren* 'rode along,' and *ein + kaufen* 'shop.' M.H., in addition, sometimes uses tensed prefix verbs. In such cases she strands the prefix correctly, e.g., *frißt auf* 'eats up.' The same holds for H.R.'s spontaneous speech. As a matter of fact, the distance between the verb and the prefix is kept at a minimum. The patients extrapose intervening phrases rather than having the prefix in the distant end position. When H.R. used the verb *auf + stehen* 'get up,' she said *Ich stehe auf um 9 Uhr* 'I get up at 9 o'clock' rather than *Ich stehe um 9 Uhr auf.* This strategy, which seems to be quite consistent across milder cases of agrammatism in German, points to a processing deficit which does not allow the patient to construct full-fledged syntactic structures on-line, while manipulations in small domains are well possible.

however, does not mean that they have a tacit full command of morphosyntax. The data provide evidence that while lexically triggered gender, number, and case agreement in NPs, case assignment by lexical categories, and close structural assigners are quite well preserved, the functional role of case (abstract case in the sense of Vergnaud, Chomsky, and others) seems to be accessible to a limited extent only. Thus, in simple transitive sentences, the patients were quite unable to assign case to one NP in dependence of another, that is, if the correct assignment of case presupposed the successful processing of another case-marked NP. There seems to be a contradiction between the claim that lexicon-induced case (including oblique case assigned by the verb) is relatively well preserved and the patients' rather poor performance as shown in Table II (canonical and noncanonical condition). It should be kept in mind, however, that the use of tensed transitive sentences in this task requires other processes in addition to lexical case assignment, as we have argued above.

The data on grammaticality judgments remain problematic due to the poorly understood nature of the task. Some patterns which arise from the data indicate that the two patients studied have intuitions about the basic word-order properties of their language. A case in point is the intuition about the placement of the tensed verb in root sentences, which seems to be quite stable in most aphasic patients. They overgeneralize this V-second pattern, however, as shown by their acceptance of V-second sentences after a complementizer. On the other hand, their rather high rejection rate of prefix verbs in second position follows if one assumes that they have access to elaborate lexical representations, that is, to representations which specify separability of a given prefix. While it would be difficult to derive from these results that they reflect a totally disturbed syntax (see the good intuitions about the grammatical sentences), it cannot be maintained either that syntactic intuitions are intact (see the poor intuitions about many of the ungrammatical sentences).

4. Implications for the Linguistic Interpretation of Agrammatism

The four questions asked in Section 3.2 can now be answered as follows with respect to the three patients under investigation:

1. No dissociation could be found between "early" and "late" morphology. The patients could produce regular as well as irregular plurals and they have (regular) case forms in their repertoires. Also, the intermediate levels of morphology including derivation and compounding were shown to be accessible. (We do not exclude the possibility that other agrammatic patients show dissociations within the lexicon.)

2. "Late" morphology (inflection) can in principle be exploited for syntactic purposes. This was shown in the case of NP-internal agreement, in the

use of oblique case after prepositions, and in the use of (structurally triggered) genitive case.

3. The ability to use inflectional morphology for syntactic purposes seems to be limited to strictly local domains. This was shown insofar as a proper case can be inserted in the immediate neighborhood of an assigner, but not if assignment presupposes the processing of trace binding.

4. Given such patterns of relative preservation versus disturbance in our patients, we give the following explanation of the agrammatic deficit: The patients are unable to build phrase structures which pass a certain threshold of complexity. We keep this deliberately vague, because the threshold may vary from one patient to the next, possibly depending on the severity of the brain damage. For the patients in this study, it seems that local syntactic phrases can be processed, given that they do not go beyond the limits of a possibly reduced working memory. "Locality" must be understood as adjacency between head and specifier/complement. This allows for the processing of NPs, VPs, PPs, but not for the processing of, say, unbounded dependencies or other kinds of discontinuous elements.[12]

In contrast to this defective system of phrase structure building, agrammatics have a relatively intact lexicon. According to LMT, this lexicon has a component in which morphologically complex words are formed, including inflected words. The lexical entries contain rich information about syntactic and semantic selection. In a purely linguistic sense, they fulfill the role of filtering templates which rule out cases of overgeneration in the syntax.[13] As long as the syntactic structures to be processed do not leave the threshold mentioned above, lexical insertion can project syntax relevant information in the phrase. Thus, what agrammatics (of this kind) ideally can achieve are syntactic chunks which are well formed in all respects. Up to this point, their linguistic capacity may really not be much different from that of a normal person. The deficit comes into play as soon as these chunks have to be inserted into a more global syntactic plan. As we showed in Section 3, some of our data are suggestive in this respect: While the patients can form genitive NPs in dependence of a given (adjacent) NP, they are almost unable to assign an NP oblique case if the case of the given NP has to be checked first. The same

---

[12]An account of agrammatism along these lines is given in Grodzinsky, 1986. Grodzinsky claims that agrammatics do not have access to S-structures which contain traces, i.e., abstract categories which are bound by a distant antecedent. He supports his theory with data showing among other things that English-speaking agrammatics fail to comprehend semantically reversible passive sentences.

[13]This would explain the ease with which agrammatics can detect so-called syntactic violations, e.g., *He came my house yesterday* (Linebarger *et al.*, 1983). Mapping the VP onto the template for *come* would rule out this sentence, because *come* optionally takes a PP complement, not an NP complement.

holds for some of the judgment data. Highly suggestive for our explanation of agrammatism is the following incident (see Bayer *et al.*, 1987): C.B. was asked to provide the case-inflected definite article for the two object NPs in ditransitive sentences like *Der Aufseher schenkt d(en)*$_{acc}$*Hamster d(em)*$_{dat}$*Gärtner* 'The foreman gives the hamster (to) the gardener.' Notice that this task goes beyond the locality constraint insofar as the dative NP *dem Gärtner* is not adjacent to the case-assigning verb. Given his classical agrammatism, C.B. solved the task in his own way: *Der Aufseher schenkt ein*$_{nom}$*Hamster des*$_{gen}$*Gärtners* 'The foreman gives a hamster of the gardener.' What C.B. did was reduce the syntactic processing load by segmenting the setence into a subject–predicate phrase (*Der Aufseher schenkt*) and a complex NP (*ein Hamster des Gärtners*). Obviously it is not the inflectional morphology that creates trouble,[14] it is the global syntactic structure.

Although the data presented here are not totally conclusive with respect to the question of which theory of inflectional morphology is the appropriate one, we feel that much speaks in favor of the lexical theory: First, the agrammatics in this study do have access to elaborate lexical structures and word-formation rules. It would be surprising to see that they manipulate a subset of word structures only via a disrupted syntactic processor. Second, if inflectional affixation is inextricably tied to the phrase-building module, one would expect to see a certain breakdown of correlation between the two. As we have shown, the contrary seems to be the case. The phrase-building module is severely limited, while the morphological component manipulates sophisticated word structures across the board. Third, if word formation and phrase formation were intimately linked, we would like to observe a correlation between frequent phrase types and frequent word types, for example, SVO sentences and nominative case. What we actually observe, however, is that the most frequent syntactic structures can hardly be processed, while case inflections (e.g., genitive) are used which are almost extinct in colloquial German.

Together with the findings of de Bleser and Bayer, 1986, these aspects clearly favor LMT over SMT.

It still remains an important question why agrammatics speak in one- or two-word utterances if they have considerable morpholexical abilities and some syntactic abilities at their disposal. An answer to this would require knowing exactly what kind of a task free speech is and what resources it necessitates. Of course, a theory of spontaneous language production still remains to be formulated. As a first approach, however, let us assume that the patient attempts to use propositional speech. He is thus under the pressure to use predications, that is, he cannot confine himself to selecting appropriate forms

---

[14]Notice that the dative form would have required only an article, while the actually chosen genitive required the affixation of *-s* to the noun in addition to the article *des*.

from the lexicon, but must project these forms into phrases which are beyond his capacities. Given that in communication exactly those forms have to be used which are most unstable (EXOCENTRIC constructions), the preserved abilities to form local (ENDOCENTRIC) constructions are neutralized. As a consequence, the system as a whole, including the access to available lexical forms, collapses. If the patient's syntactic capacities are already exhausted by the pressure to produce a simplified predication, the least demanding thing to do is certainly to select a form from the lexicon which does not itself presuppose an elaborate syntactic phrase. To give an example, a patient may well produce the verb form *ge-schlag-en* 'beaten' but not the adjectival participle in an NP like *der ge-schlag-en-e Hund* 'the beaten dog,' although, as we have shown, he may have enough linguistic knowledge to use such inflections correctly. It is clear that under these assumptions spontaneous speech is not seen as a direct reflection of the underlying deficit, but rather as the outcome of a trade-off between a set of more-or-less preserved linguistic abilities and the requirements of communicative success. We would thus take clinical definitions of agrammatism (based on the frequent omission of function words and inflection in spontaneous speech) merely as a guideline for selecting patients. However, given the heterogeneity of the phenomena governing spontaneous speech, we would try to capture the common core of the deficit in different linguistic performances by psycholinguistic investigation and with reference to representations which promise to have far-reaching explanatory power.

The relation between linguistics and aphasiology, as we see it, arises predominantly from the need to integrate data from different domains of language behavior into a unified theory of language and language processing. We believe that such data cannot be fully accounted for in a linguistics-free procedural framework, since it is necessary to ultimately state what the objects of processing are. In our conception, they must be linguistic representations at some point. Thus, taking linguistic concepts to account for data of language pathology seems to be a reasonable consequence, even in the absence of a full-fledged processing theory. This holds especially for off-line investigations like those reported here. A case in point that calls for "linguistic aphasiology" (Caplan, 1987) is the Chomskyan distinction between concrete and abstract case. As we have shown, a patient may well have all possible case forms of a given language, while not being able to relate these forms to their abstract role in syntax.

The beneficial influence between two fields of research like linguistics and aphasiology does not have to be one way such that linguistic concepts feed into aphasiology. In principle it is possible that linguistic aphasiology will lead to results which can be decisive for the evaluation of competing linguistic theories.

Acknowledgments

The research on which this chapter is based was partially supported by Grant P. 41/16-2 of the Deutsche Forschungsgemeinschaft. We thank an anonymous reviewer for suggestions and Klaus Willmes for assistance with the statistical analyses.

References

Anderson, S.R. (1982). Where's morphology? *Linguistic Inquiry* 13, 571–613.

Aronoff, M. (1976). "Word Formation in Generative Grammar." MIT Press, Cambridge, Mass.

Badecker, W., and Caramazza, A. (1985). On considerations of method and theory governing the use of clinical categories in neurolinguistics and cognitive neuropsychology: The case against agrammatism. *Cognition* 20, 207–220.

Bayer, J., de Bleser, R., and Dronsek, C. (1987). Form und Funktion von Kasus bei Agrammatismus. *In* "Grammatik und Kognition" (J. Bayer, ed.). Westdeutscher Verlag, Wiesbaden.

Berndt, R.S., and Caramazza, A. (1980). A redefinition of Broca's aphasia: Implications for a neuropsychological model of language. *Applied Psycholinguistics* 1, 225–278.

de Bleser, R., and Bayer, J. (1986). German word formation and aphasia, *The Linguistic Review*, 6, 1–40.

Bradley, D.C., Garrett, M.E., and Zurif, E.B. (1980). Syntactic deficits in Broca's aphasia. *In* "Biological Studies of Mental Processes" (D. Caplan, ed.). MIT Press, Cambridge, Mass.

Caplan, D. (1985). Syntactic and semantic structures in agrammatism. *In* "Agrammatism" (M.L. Kean, ed.). Academic Press, New York.

Caplan, D. (1987). "Neurolinguistics and Linguistic Aphasiology: An Introduction." Cambridge Univ. Press, London.

Caplan, D., and Hildebrandt, N. (1986). Language deficits and the theory of syntax: A reply to Grodzinsky. *Brain and Language* 27, 168–178.

Caramazza, A., and Berndt, R.S. (1978). Semantic and syntactic processes in aphasia: A review of the literature. *Psychological Bulletin* 85, 898–918.

Fabb, N. (1984). *Syntactic affixation*, Doctoral dissertation, MIT, Cambridge, Mass.

Grodzinsky, Y. (1986). Linguistic theory and aphasic deficits. *Brain and Language* 27, 135–159.

Haider, H. (1985). The case of German. *In* "Studies in German Grammar" (J. Toman, ed.). Foris, Dordrecht.

Halle, M., and Mohanan, K.P. (1985). Segmental phonology of modern English. *Linguistic Inquiry* 16, 57–116.

Hays, W.L. (1963). "Statistics." Holt, London.

Huber, W., Poeck, K., and Willmes, K. (1984). The Aachen aphasia test. *Advances in Neurology* 42, 291–305.

Kiparsky, P. (1982). From cyclic phonology to lexical phonology. *In* "The Structure of Phonological Representations" (H. van der Hulst and N. Smith, eds.). Foris, Dordrecht.

Kleist, K. (1914). Aphasie und Geisteskrankheiten, *Münchener Medizinische Wochenschrift* **61**, 8–12.

Kleist, K. (1916). Über Leitungsaphasie und grammatische Störungen. *Zeitschrift für Psychiatrie und Neurologie* **40**, 118–199.

Lapointe, S.G. (1983). Some issues in the linguistic description of agrammatism. *Cognition* **14**, 1–39.

Lieber, R. (1980). *On the organisation of the lexicon*. Doctoral dissertation, MIT, Cambridge, Mass.

Linebarger, M.C., Schwartz, M.F., and Saffran, E.M. (1983). Sensitivity to grammatical structure in so-called agrammatic aphasics. *Cognition* **13**, 361–392.

von Stockert, T.R., and Bader, L. (1976). Some relations of grammar and lexicon in aphasia. *Cortex* **12**, 49–60.

Appendix

C.B.

Spontaneous speech

Question: *What did you do on vacation?*

Answer: ...*lang schlafen und äh*...*Kaffee getrunken*...*spazieren gehen.*
        'late sleep   and uh   coffee drank   walk take
        und dann. essen. und äh Stunde niedergelegt. dann Kaffee getrunken
        and then eat   and uh hour lay down   then coffee drank.'

Description of action pictures

Target: *Der Junge weint, weil er ein Glas zerbrochen hat.*
        'The boy is crying because he has broken a glass.'

Reaction: *Das ist äh äh der zerbrochene Krug oder was und äh äh*...
        'This is uh uh the broken jug   or what and uh uh...

        Kind äh weint   [adjective]
        child uh cries.'   ← [no progressive used]

Target: *Der Mann liegt auf der Couch, raucht Pfeife und liest die Zeitung.*
        'The man is lying on the couch, smoking a pipe and reading the
        newspaper.'

Reaction: *Pfei*...*der Mann raucht*...*die Zeitung lesen*
        'Pipe..the man smokes... newspaper read.'   [No aspect]

M.H.

Spontaneous speech

Question: *Could you tell me the story of the Little Red Riding Hood* (LRRH)?

Answer: *Der Wolf hat das Rotkäppchen*..*gesucht und*...*äh*...
        'The wolf has the LRRH   searched and   uh

        Wald. Wald und die Flasche...*und*..*äh*...*ja und äh wuh-wuh.*
        forest. forest and the bottle   and   uh   yes and uh woh-woh

        und der der Wolf Großmutter gut... *nein gefressen und*...
        and the the wolf grandmother good...no eaten   and...

äh Häubchen da...äh...das Häubchen. und.äh das.
uh little-hat   there uh   the little-hat   and uh the

äh und Reg...äh Rotkäppchen...äh...schlimm das Rotkäppchen
uh and   uh LRRH   uh   bad   the LRRH

äh...frißt auf...und der Jäger
uh   eats up   and the hunter.

Description of action pictures
Target: *Der Mann bettelt.*
           'The man is begging.'
Reaction: *Der...Mann...Bettler*
           'the man beggar'
Target: *Die beiden Männer schreien sich an.*
           'The two men are shouting at each other.'
Reaction: *Der Mann. und. der Mann. schreit sich an*
           'the man and the man shouts each-other at'

H.R.
Spontaneous speech
Question: *Tell me what you do on a normal day.*
Answer: *Ja ich. stehe auf um neun Uhr. ungefähr   und. dann*
          'yes I. get up at nine o'clock. approximately and then

          wasche mich oder. ja. und. ziehe um.   ziehe   ich.
          wash myself or. yes.   and. change (clothes). change I

          ziehe   ich dann äh sehe ich das Was. sehe ich das Wetter.
          change I   then uh see I   the   see I the   weather.

          dann äh ich äh brummig und gehe hinunter im Wohnzimmer
          then uh I   uh grumpy and go   down   in the living room

          und. trinke Kaffee. mit Papa und essen so. Brot   oder Brötchen
          and. drink coffee. with daddy and eat   so. bread or   roll(s)'

Description of action pictures
Target: Same as for C.B.
Reaction: *Das Kind weint. Die Vase ist kaputt*
           'The child cries. The vase is broken.'
Target: Same as for C.B.
Reaction: *Die La. der Mann liegt auf dem Sofa und liest die Zeitung*
           'The ? the man   lies on the sofa and reads the newspaper.'

Chapter 4

Nonconcatenative Inflection and Paradigm Economy

Andrew Carstairs

Nineteenth-century linguists, whose staple diet was Indo-European historical phonology and morphology, took the inflectional paradigm for granted as an indispensable descriptive tool. The new preoccupations of twentieth-century linguistics, however, resulted for various reasons in the relegation of the paradigm to a marginal status, of little or no theoretical interest—a fact commented on with surprise by Seiler (1966). But, in the years since Seiler wrote, the new seriousness with which morphological phenomena have been studied has inevitably led to a reawakening of interest in the paradigm and the allied notions of declension class and conjugation class, most notably on the part of Wurzel (1984; cf Carstairs, 1985b). At the same time as this revival of interest in the paradigm, though largely independent of it, there has arisen a new interest in the distinctions between the different sorts of morphological process (affixation, ablaut, infixation, etc.) whose characteristics were so lucidly summarized by Sapir (1921, Chap. 4). Indeed, an interest in the contrast between affixation and other morphological processes is a common element linking some superficially quite diverse studies, for example, Mayerthaler (1981) and Dressler (1985) on the semiotic appropriateness of different morphological processes to different inflectional or derivational functions, Lieber (1981) on their respective roles within the generative lexicon, and McCarthy (1981) on the formal representation of certain nonconcatenative processes.

In this chapter I propose a solution to a problem which involves both the nature of the paradigm and the distinction between morphological processes. At first sight, the problem may seem rather unimportant, perhaps trivially terminological, in fact. But it turns out to have an empirical aspect which can be readily investigated, and the outcome is both a useful refinement of the paradigm concept and a further example of the difference in behavior between concatenative and nonconcatenative inflection. The problem thus derives its importance from the fact that in its solution two independent morphological issues converge in an unexpected and satisfying fashion. I conclude with a caveat: The fact that two word forms count as inflectionally similar for one purpose does not imply that they count as similar for all purposes.

Consider two lexical items belonging to the same word class, each with a range of inflected forms, whose inflectional behavior is identical so far as affixes are concerned but different in some nonaffixal respect (for example, stress pattern or ablaut). Do these lexical items conform to the same paradigm or not? Examples of this kind of inflectional contrast are given in (1)–(5), where the forms (a) and (b) [or (a), (b), and (c)] are identical affixally but distinct in some other respect.1

(1) English

	(a)	(b)
	speak	*give*
	speak-s	*give-s*
	speak-ing	*giv-ing*
	spoke	*gave*
	spok-en	*giv-en*

(2) German

	(a)		(b)	
Sg Nom/Acc	*Tag*	'day'	*Gast*	'guest'
Gen	*Tag-es*		*Gast-es*	
Dat	*Tag(-e)*		*Gast(-e)*	
Pl NAG	*Tag-e*		*Gäst-e*	
Dat	*Tag-en*		*Gäst-en*	

(3) Hungarian

	(a)		(b)	
Sg 1	*hív-t-am*	'I called'	*it-t-am*	'I drank'
2	*hív-t-ál*		*it-t-ál*	
3	*hív-ott*		*iv-ott*	
Pl 1	*hív-t-unk*		*it-t-unk*	
2	*hív-t-atok*		*it-t-atok*	
3	*hív-t-ak*		*it-t-ak*	

1All forms are in ordinary orthography or a transcription thereof. The acute accent in (5) indicates stress; in (3) it indicates vowel length. In (4c), *sc* represents a palato-alveolar fricative before *i* or *e*, and [sk] elsewhere.

(4) Italian

	(a)		(b)		(c)	
Sg 1	*part-o*	'I leave'	*salg-o*	'I go up'	*esc-o*	'I go out'
2	*part-i*		*sal-i*		*esc-i*	
3	*part-e*		*sal-e*		*esc-e*	
Pl 1	*part-iamo*		*sal-iamo*		*usc-iamo*	
2	*part-ite*		*sal-ite*		*usc-ite*	
3	*part-ono*		*salg-ono*		*esc-ono*	

(5) Russian

	(a)		(b)	
Sg Nom	*vxod*	'entrance'	*stol*	'table'
Gen	*vxód-a*		*stol-á*	
Dat	*vxód-u*		*stol-ú*	
Pl Nom	*vxód-y*		*stol-ý*	
Gen	*vxód-ov*		*stol-óv*	
Dat	*vxód-am*		*stol-ám*	
	etc.		etc.	

In the English and German examples the differences between the (a) and (b) columns reside in the vowels of the stem; for example, in (1a) the past participle form has the same vowel as the past tense form, whereas in (1b) it does not. In (3) the difference involves stem consonants: The (a) verb *hív-* has the same alternant throughout the past indefinite tense, whereas the (b) verb has two alternants, *it-* and *iv-*. In the Italian examples in (4) the differences involve both consonantism and vocalism. Finally, in (5) there is a difference in stress pattern: In the declension of *stol* the stress is always carried by the inflectional suffix, whereas in *vxod* it is carried by the stem.

At first sight, little seems to hinge on our decision here. But quite a lot hinges on it when we consider its implications for paradigm economy. The notion of PARADIGM ECONOMY arises from consideration of the following question: Is there any constraint on the number of distinct inflectional paradigms (declensions or conjugations) into which the inflectional resources of any language may be organized? Consider a language with, say, eight case–number combinations for nouns (four singular and four plural cases), each of which can be realized in one of two distinct (and phonologically unpredictable) fashions. Evidently this language must have a minimum of two distinct noun declensions. It is also possible to calculate a maximum for the number of distinct declensions, namely 28 = 256. Is it possible to predict an actual, as opposed to a mathematical, maximum? Various studies suggest that the answer is yes, and that (subject to certain specifiable conditions) the actual maximum is as low as it could possibly be (Carstairs, 1983, 1984a,b, 1985a, 1986, 1987). Formulating this constraint precisely requires a considerable amount of preliminary definition and discussion (for which see Carstairs, 1987); for present purposes, we can make do with an informal (and overstrong) statement of the central principle:

(6) PARADIGM ECONOMY PRINCIPLE (informal version)
The inflectional resources for any word class in any language must be organized into as few paradigms (declensions or conjugations) as possible, that is, as few as is necessary to put all the inflections to work.

Clearly, if a claim as strong as this is anywhere near the truth, it restricts morphological theory in a highly desirable fashion; so it is of interest to look carefully at prima facie counterexamples to the principle to see whether they indeed suggest that it is fundamentally wrong or whether they point to natural modifications or refinements which still preserve its spirit.

A corollary of the principle is that there can be no "mixed" paradigms, that is, paradigms in which no inflection is unique, every inflection being shared with some other paradigm for the same word class in the same language. Yet mixed paradigms do exist. Examples are (7) and (8), where inflectional identity is highlighted by equality signs.

(7)   Russian [cf. (5)]

		Stem stress		Mixed stress		Ending stress
Nom/Acc		*vxód-y*	=	*zúb-y* 'teeth'		*stol-ý*
Gen		*vxód-ov*		*zub-óv*	=	*stol-óv*
Dat		*vxód-am*		*zub-ám*	=	*stol-ám*
Instr		*vxód-ami*		*zub-ámi*	=	*stol-ámi*
Loc		*vxód-ax*		*zub-áx*	=	*stol-áx*

(8)   Sanskrit

		n-stem		Mixed stem		*i*-stem
Sg NVA		*nāma* 'name'		*asthi* 'bone'	=	*vāri* 'water'
Instr, etc.		*nāmn-ā*, etc.	=	*asthn-ā*, etc.		*vāriṇ-ā*, etc.
Du NVA		*nām(a)n-ī*	=	*asth(a)n-ī*		*vāriṇ-ī*
DAb		*nāma-bhyām*		*asthi-bhyām*	=	*vāri-bhyām*
GL		*nāmn-oh*	=	*asthn-oh*		*vāriṇ-oh*
Pl NVA		*nāmān-i*	=	*asthān-i*		*vārīṇ-i*
Instr		*nāma-bhih*		*asthi-bhih*	=	*vāri-bhih*
DAb		*nāma-bhyah*		*asthi-bhyah*	=	*vāri-bhyah*
Gen		*nāmn-ām*	=	*asthn-ām*		*vārīṇ-ām*
Loc		*nāma-su*		*asthi-ṣu*	=	*vāri-ṣu*

There are apparently two nominative plural inflections illustrated in the Russian forms in (7), namely -*y* and -*ý*, and similarly two inflections for each of the other cases (genitive -*ov* and -*óv*, etc.), so the paradigm economy principle predicts that the words exhibiting these inflections ought to be organized into only two declension types. Yet we seem to find three declension types: two unmixed ones (illustrated by *vxod* and *stol*) and a mixed type illustrated by *zub*, which "goes like" *vxod* in the nominative plural (as well as throughout the singular, not illustrated here) but like *stol* in the other plural cases. In (8), similarly, if we regard each case–number combination as being realized jointly by both the suffix and the stem alternant (a reasonable assumption, since the choice of stem alternant may in Sanskrit discriminate between identically suffixed forms, e.g., nominative plural *rājān-aḥ* versus accusative plural *rājñ-aḥ* "kings"), we find three apparently distinct paradigms despite the fact that there are only two distinct inflections for each case–number combination.

Notice, however, that the analysis under which (7) and (8) exhibit breaches of paradigm economy presupposes the answer "no" to our earlier question about affixal and nonaffixal inflection; that is, it presupposes that we recognize differences in nonaffixal inflection as sufficient ground for setting up distinct paradigms. If we do not allow this, the number of distinct paradigms exhibited in each of (7) and (8) shrinks to one, since the affixal inflection (ignoring stress and stem alternations) is identical in the three columns. With this analysis, then, the apparent breach of the paradigm economy principle presented by (7) and (8) disappears. Consequently, if we think the principle worth maintaining as a hypothesis, we have a reason for choosing what we might call the "affixes-only" answer to our question about paradigm identity.

The affixes-only answer has another, less obvious, advantage. In (1), (2), (3), and (4) there is no suggestion of paradigm mixture and no prima facie conflict with the paradigm economy principle. But why, then, are none of the inflectional differences between columns (a), (b), and (c) located in the affixes? For example, if what we see in the Italian verb forms in (4) are three distinct paradigms, why does none of them take the opportunity (as it were) to differ from the other two at least partly in affixal inflection as well as in stem allomorphy? Why, for example, does none of these offspring of the Latin fourth conjugation take the opportunity to retain as first plural suffix the form *-*imo* that would have resulted from the Latin ending *-imus* by regular phonological developments, instead of replacing it with the ending *-iamo*, which has become generalized in all modern Italian present tense inflection, both indicative and subjunctive? We are presented here with almost the opposite problem to that of (7) and (8): unexpectedly little inflectional diversity, rather than too much. One could answer that much of the affixal uniformity is a historical accident, which need not inhibit us from recognizing synchronically distinct paradigms. One could add, too, that there is nothing in the paradigm economy principle to require distinct paradigms to maximize their distinctness, and that among the other principles governing the paradigmatic organization of inflections there may well be ones encouraging paradigm convergence. Even so, it is an advantage of the single-paradigm analysis that neither of these excuses needs to be resorted to; the affixal uniformity in (1)–(4) is due simply to the fact that each illustrates only one paradigm, not two or three. The combination here of affixal uniformity with divergence in nonconcatenative inflection is just what we expect, if inflectional paradigms are properly defined by reference to affixal (concatenative) inflection only.

As already mentioned, morphologists in both North America and Europe have recently highlighted the distinction between concatenative and nonconcatenative morphology from a variety of different angles. None of them, however, has been concerned with paradigm economy. The fact that the paradigm economy principle, too, requires us to pay attention to the distinction therefore independently confirms the distinction's importance. At the same time, it is gratifying to find that the way to deal with the class of apparent counterexamples to the principle exemplified in Russian and Sanskrit in (7) and (8) turns out to involve not some otherwise-unmotivated complication of the principle itself but rather a quite natural refinement of our understanding of what constitutes an inflectional paradigm. This outcome clearly adds weight to the view that the paradigm deserves to be recognized as a central notion of morphological theory, not a mere expository device in old-fashioned pedagogical grammar books.

The main argument of this chapter is now complete. However, one can envisage an objection, one which is quite easily answered, but whose answer usefully emphasizes the diversity of factors which influence inflectional behavior. If differences in stem alternation and other such nonconcatenative goings-on are not indicators of distinctness in declension type or conjugation type, why do we not find much more such variation within paradigms than we actually do? For example (the objection continues), if stem alternation is so innocuous, why does not Sanskrit have far more nouns of the mixed type illustrated by *asthi* in (8), rather than just four (see Whitney, 1889)? The answer is that, even though nonconcatenative inflection does not "count" for paradigm-economy purposes, that does not mean that it has no realizational function or that it can safely be ignored by inflectional theorists. Consider the German forms in (2). Even though *Tag* and *Gast* belong to the same paradigm (in our terms), the umlaut that appears in some inflected forms of *Gast* is certainly not mere random decoration, since in all modern German nouns where it appears it correlates exactly with the morphosyntactic property plural. This is in fact perhaps the most frequently cited example of an alternation that was once phonologically conditioned acquiring a morphological function instead. So *Tag* and *Gast*, while they belong to the same paradigm, are certainly not identical from the point of view of how the property plural is realized. Similarly, the nouns *Tag* and *Garten* 'garden' (pl *Gärten*) can be construed as belonging to the same paradigm (or "macroparadigm," in the terminology of Carstairs (1986)), since the absence of overt plural suffixes in the latter is predictable phonologically; yet, from the point of view of the distinction drawn in natural morphology between additive and modificatory inflection, the two words fall on opposite sides of the fence (see Mayerthaler, 1981; Wurzel, 1984; Carstairs, 1985b). But the fact that two words which are the same for paradigm-economy purposes may be different for other morphological purposes is no embarrassment; it simply illustrates the increasingly evident variety of distinct organizational principles and constraints of a purely morphological kind to which inflection is subject. The complexity of the interaction of these principles constitutes the main challenge for the inflectional theorist, as well as the main reason for the widespread but mistaken assumption, current until quite recently, that inflectional morphology is just a hodgepodge of language-particular idiosyncrasies.

References

Carstairs, A. (1983). Paradigm economy. *Journal of Linguistics* **19**, 115–28.

Carstairs, A. (1984a). "Constraints on Allomorphy in Inflexion," Bloomington, Indiana University Linguistics Club.

Carstairs, A. (1984b). Paradigm economy in the Latin third declension. *Transactions of the Philological Society* 117–37.

Carstairs, A. (1985a). *Paradigm economy in Latin*. 6th International Conference on Historical Linguistics, pp. 57–70.

Carstairs, A. (1985b). Review of Wurzel 1984. *Journal of Linguistics* **21**, 487–93.

Carstairs, A. (1986). Macroclasses and paradigm economy in German nouns. *Zeitschrift für Phonetik, Sprachwissenschaft und Kommunikationsforschung* **39**, 3–11.

Carstairs, A. (1987). "Allomorphy in Inflexion." Croom Helm, London.

Dressler, W.U. (1985). "Morphonology: The Dynamics of Derivation." Karoma, Ann Arbor, Michigan.

Lieber, R. (1981). "The Organization of the Lexicon." Bloomington, Indiana University Linguistics Club.

McCarthy, J.J. (1981). A prosodic theory of nonconcatenative morphology. *Linguistic Inquiry* **12**, 373–418.

Mayerthaler, W. (1981). "Morphologische Natürlichkeit." Athenaion, Wiesbaden.

Sapir, E. (1921). "Language." Harcourt Brace, New York.

Seiler, H.J. (1966). Das Paradigma in alter und neuer Sicht. *Kratylos* **11**, 190–205.

Whitney, W.D. (1889). "Sanskrit Grammar," 2nd Ed. Harvard Univ. Press, Cambridge, MA.

Wurzel, W.U. (1984). "Flexionsmorphologie und Natürlichkeit." Akademie-Verlag, Berlin.

Chapter 5

The Split Morphology Hypothesis: Evidence from Yiddish

David M. Perlmutter

1. The Problem

This paper focuses on what I call the "split morphology hypothesis"—the idea that some morphological rules are in the lexicon and some are extralexical. Anderson (1982) has proposed a version of this hypothesis positing some morphological rules that refer to the internal structure of lexical entries and others that refer to the morphosyntactic representations in syntactic structures. The former apply before lexical insertion in syntactic structures. Since the latter refer to morphosyntactic representations unavailable in the lexicon but present in syntactic structures, they can apply only after lexical insertion.[1] This distinction in terms of the operations performed by rules correlates in an interesting way with the distinction between derivational and inflectional morphology. Since rules of derivational morphology refer to lexical entries' internal structure independently of morphosyntactic representations, they are predicted to be lexical. Since rules of inflectional morphology concern syntactically relevant morphosyntactic representations, they cannot apply until after lexical insertion. Anderson makes one consequence of his hypothesis explicit:

(1) It represents the fact, often noted but never really explained, that (with certain well-defined exceptions) inflectional morphology appears "outside of" derivational morphology. For instance, if a morphologically complex form contains both derivational and inflectional suffixes, the inflectional ones will follow the derivational ones. (p. 609)

This chapter examines two aspects of Yiddish noun morphology—the

[1]To avoid confusion with the term "postlexical," which has acquired a specific meaning in the tradition of lexical phonology inaugurated by Kiparsky (1982), I call such rules "extralexical."

Theoretical Morphology Copyright © 1988 by Academic Press, Inc.

formation of plurals and diminutives—because their interaction provides apparent counterexamples to this prediction. Because attributive adjectives and articles agree with the head noun and verbs agree with their subjects in number in Yiddish, number is syntactically relevant, that is, it figures in morphosyntactic representations. Diminutives, on the other hand, are syntactically irrelevant; they belong to the derivational morphology. The split morphology hypothesis would thus predict that plural inflection will appear "outside" the diminutive morphology. However, there are several classes of cases where just the opposite appears to be true:[2]

(2)

	Sg	pl	1st dim sg	1st dim pl	2d dim sg	2d dim pl
braid	*cop*	*cep*	*cepl*	*ceplex*	*cepele*	*cepelex*
shoe	*šux*	*šix*	*šixl*	*šixlex*	*šixele*	*šixelex*

(3)

	Sg	pl	Dim pl
child	*kind*	*kinder*	*kinderlex*
thorn	*dorn*	*derner*	*dernerlex*

(4)

	Sg	pl	Dim pl
body	*guf*	*gufim*	*gufimlex*
pupil	*talmid*	*talmidim*	*talmidimlex*

In (2) the plural is formed by ablaut, and the diminutives (both singular and plural) are apparently formed on the plural form of the noun. This is also the case in (3), where the plural form exhibits the suffix −*er* (in addition to ablaut in *derner*). The examples in (4) are Hebrew/Aramaic loan words with plurals in −*im*, where the diminutive plural −*lex* occurs suffixed to the plural form. (2–4) all appear to counterexemplify the prediction of the split morphology hypothesis.

We examine these cases in detail, concluding that Yiddish does not disconfirm the split morphology hypothesis, but actually supports it.

2. Plural Formation in Yiddish

2.1 Traditional Classifications

Traditional Yiddish grammars generally distinguish a large number of noun classes according to whether they form their plurals with −*s*, −*en*, −*er*, ø,

---

[2] Yiddish has several distinct diminutive forms, of which only two are relevant here: the first diminutive, marked by the suffixes −*l* (sg) and −*lex* (pl), and the second diminutive, marked by −*ele* and −*elex*. I use *o* to represent [ɔ] and *e* to represent the unstressed vowel that appears as [ɛ] in an open syllable and as schwa in a closed one. Stress is on the initial syllable in Germanic words and on the penultimate syllable in Hebrew/Aramaic words. Loan words from other languages may have stress on a different syllable, in which case I indicate it explicitly. The diminutive suffixes do not affect stress.

ablaut, ablaut + *er*, −*ex*, or −*im*, plus a class with irregular plurals.[3] This picture can be simplified considerably.

2.2 The Regular Plural Rules

The largest class of Yiddish nouns form their plurals with the suffix −*en*, which is reduced to syllabic *n* after a nonnasal, nonsyllabic consonant by a regular phonological process (Sapir, 1915).[4]

(5)		Sg	Pl
	newspaper	*caytung*	*caytungn*
	language	*šprax*	*špraxn*
	notebook	*heft*	*heftn*
	ear	*oyer*	*oyern*
	door	*tir*	*tirn*
	engineer	*inženír*	*inženírn*
	sea	*yam*	*yamen*
	blackboard	*tovl*	*tovlen*
	heaven, sky	*himl*	*himlen*
	ideal	*ideál*	*ideáln*
	magazine	*žurnál*	*žurnáln*

Nouns ending in an unstressed vowel form their plurals in −*s*:

(6)			Sg	Pl
	a.	gift	*matone*	*matones*
		war	*milxome*	*milxomes*
		joyous occasion	*simxe*	*simxes*
		tombstone	*maceyve*	*maceyves*
		bride	*kale*	*kales*
		wedding	*xásene*	*xásenes*
		kingdom	*meluxe*	*meluxes*
		piece of advice	*eyce*	*eyces*
		family	*mišpoxe*	*mišpoxes*

[3] I have especially benefited from consulting Weinreich (1965, 1968) and Zarecki (1929). There is also a class of plurals in −*es*, used primarily for Slavic loans, especially those ending in −*ik*. These plurals do not concern us here.

[4] That −*en* is reduced to syllabic *n* (rather than an underlying −*n* being converted to −*en* by epenthesis) can be seen from the dative forms of nouns ending in unstressed −*e*, e.g., *tate* 'father,' dative (*dem*) *tatn*, *zeyde* 'grandfather,' dative (*dem*) *zeydn*.

	biography	*biográfiye*	*biográfiyes*
	revolution	*revolúciye*	*revolúciyes*
	father	*tate*	*tates*
	grandfather	*zeyde*	*zeydes*
	piano	*piane*	*pianes*
	form	*forme*	*formes*
	group	*grupe*	*grupes*
b.	question	*frage*	*frages*
	task	*oyfgabe*	*oyfgabes*
	legend	*legende*	*legendes*
c.	ghetto	*geto*	*getos*
	Nazi	*naci*	*nacis*

(6a) shows this pattern in a variety of nouns, including Hebrew/Aramaic and Slavic loans. (6b) shows it in words of Germanic origin. While most words ending in an unstressed vowel end in $-e$, (6c) shows the same pattern in loan words ending in other unstressed vowels.

These data are accounted for by the rules in (7).

(7)   PLURAL INFLECTION

    a. $[\text{ X V }]_N \rightarrow [\quad]_N + s$
         [−str]

    b. $[\quad]_N \rightarrow [\quad]_N + en$

By the principle of disjunctive ordering tracing back to Panini, and incorporated into generative theory in different forms by Chomsky (1967), Chomsky and Halle (1968), Anderson (1969), and Kiparsky (1973), these rules apply disjunctively. (7a), having a more specific environment, applies first, making the forms to which it applies ineligible to undergo (7b). Nouns ending in an unstressed vowel are thus assigned the plural suffix $-s$, the rest getting $-en$.[5]

[5] A class of nouns ending in a resonant have plurals in $-s$:

	Sg	Pl
rain	*regn*	*regns*
life	*lebn*	*lebns*
cemetery	*beysoylem*	*beysoylems*
feather	*feder*	*feders*
theater	*teater*	*teaters*
clock	*zeyger*	*zeygers*

These plurals can be accounted for by a lexical rule. The deverbal agentive suffix $-er$ should be marked for membership in this class: *šraybers* 'writers,' *arbeters* 'workers,' etc. The suffix $-er$ that forms nouns denoting nationalities, residents of cities, etc. is in the class with zero plurals: *xinezer* 'Chinese,' *italyener* 'Italians,' *roymer* 'Romans,' *parizer* 'Parisians,' etc.

Under both Anderson's hypothesis and Lieber's idea that regular inflection is extralexical, the rules in (7) are extralexical.

2.3 The Prediction of the Split Morphology Hypothesis

The regular plural suffixes derived by (7) never appear in diminutives.

(8)

		Sg	Sg dim	Pl	Pl dim	
	ear	*oyer*	*oyerl*	*oyern*	*oyerlex*	**oyernlex*
	piece of advice	*eyce*	*eycele*	*eyces*	*eycelex*	**eyceslex*
	gift	*matone*	*matonele*	*matones*	*matonelex*	**matoneslex*

In plural diminutives we find −*lex*; −*en* and −*s* never appear. This is exactly what the split morphology hypothesis predicts. Diminutives, an aspect of derivational morphology, are derived in the lexicon. Since inflectional rules like (7) are extralexical, they cannot feed rules of derivational morphology. This accounts for the starred forms in (8). Further, following Aronoff's (1976), Kiparsky's (1983), and Anderson's (1986) interpretation of the disjunctive ordering principle, the existence of plural forms like *matonelex* in the lexicon blocks application of (7), thus blocking forms like **matonelexn*.

In brief, the data in (8) strongly support the split morphology hypothesis, which explains them. The apparent counterexamples to the split morphology hypothesis differ from the examples in (8): They either do not involve plural affixation or involve lexically restricted types of plural affixation that occur in the lexicon. This explains their occurrence "inside" diminutive suffixes.

2.4 Two Restricted Classes of Plurals

(9) illustrates two restricted classes of nouns: those with no plural inflection (often called ZERO PLURALS) and those with plurals in −*er*.

(9)

			Sg	Pl
	a.	letter	*briv*	*briv*
		fish	*fiš*	*fiš*
		star	*štern*	*štern*
		friend	*fraynd*	*fraynd*
		window	*fenster*	*fenster*
		sister	*švester*	*švester*
		time	*mol*	*mol*
	b.	picture	*bild*	*bilder*
		child	*kind*	*kinder*
		song	*lid*	*lider*
		wife	*vayb*	*vayber*

hundred	*hundert*	*hunderter*
thousand	*toyznt*	*toyznter*
stone	*šteyn*	*šteyner*

These two classes have a restricted membership that is not phonologically predictable. Zero and −*er* plurals are therefore listed in the lexicon, the singular–plural correspondences accounted for by lexical rules. Under the disjunctive ordering principle, the existence of these lexical plural forms blocks application of (7).

3. Plurals with Ablaut

3.1 The Phenomenon

Some nouns form plurals with ablaut:

(10)

			Sg	Pl
	a.	wall	*vant*	*vent*
		night	*naxt*	*next*
		mountain	*barg*	*berg*
	b.	name	*nomen*	*nemen*
		pot	*top*	*tep*
		daughter	*toxter*	*texter*
	c.	· foot	*fus*	*fis*
		brother	*bruder*	*brider*
	d.	mouse	*moyz*	*mayz*
	e.	bird	*foygl*	*feygl*

(11)

			Sg	Pl
	a.	leaf, page	*blat*	*bleter*
		forest	*vald*	*velder*
	b.	people	*folk*	*felker*
		word	*vort*	*verter*
		castle	*šlos*	*šleser*
	c.	book	*bux*	*bixer*
		room	*štub*	*štiber*
	d.	belly	*boyx*	*bayxer*
	e.	tree	*boym*	*beymer*

The examples in (10) form their plurals by ablaut alone, those in (11) by ablaut plus the −*er* suffix. As the breakdown into (a–e) indicates, the vowel alternations in the two classes are the same.

Whether or not a stem ablauts is not phonologically predictable:

(12)

		Sg	Pl
a.	plan	*plan*	*plener*
	airplane	*aeroplán*	*aeroplánen*
b.	man	*man*	*mener*
	husband	*man*	*manen*
c.	son	*zun*	*zin*
	sun	*zun*	*zunen*
d.	square, place	*plac*	*plecer*
	crack	*plac*	*placn*
e.	he-goat	*bak*	*bek*
	cheek	*bak*	*bakn*
f.	mouse	*moyz*	*mayz*
	Frenchman	*francoyz*	*francoyzn*

3.2 The Stem Suppletion Analysis

A theory of the lexicon under which the lexicon contains both uninflected stems and irregularly inflected forms provides the basis for a theory of suppletion that distinguishes two types of suppletion—stem suppletion and full suppletion—according to whether the suppletive items are uninflected stems or inflected forms. We find examples of both types of suppletion in Yiddish noun morphology.

Generative treatments of ablaut—especially of German umlaut, which, like Yiddish ablaut, is the residue of a Middle High German phonological rule—have posited vowel-changing rules, sometimes combined with affixation rules, to produce the ablaut (umlaut) forms.[6] I call this the "rule analysis." I propose instead that ablaut be treated as a case of stem suppletion, with both stems listed in the lexicon. There are two reasons for positing these stems (rather than positing only inflected singular and plural forms). First, as pointed out in Section 3.4, this makes it possible to account for singular–plural alternations by the same lexical rules needed for certain nonablaut stems. Second, the ablaut stems serve as input to the rules that derive diminutives, discussed in the appendix. Since these rules operate only on the ablaut stems of ablaut/nonablaut pairs, a feature [ablaut] can be used to distinguish them. As is made clear in Section 5, the ablaut stems must be unmarked for number.

---

[6] I use the term "umlaut" for a phonological phenomenon, "ablaut" for a morphological one that is not phonologically conditioned. Although modern German has ablaut, not umlaut, by this criterion, most scholars speak of it as "umlaut." Some recent treatments of German ablaut are briefly discussed in Section 6.

I give several arguments for the stem suppletion analysis before turning to its consequences for the split morphology hypothesis.

3.3 Argument One: The Nonpredictability of Ablaut Alternations

The examples in (10) and (11) show that under the rule analysis, neither the ablaut nor the nonablaut stem can be taken as basic, with the other derived from it. If the nonablaut stem is basic, there is no way to predict whether the rule should change *oy* to *ay* or to *ey*. If the ablaut stem is basic, on the other hand, there is no way to predict whether the rule should change *e* to *a* or to *o*. Under the stem suppletion analysis, however, there is no problem; both stems are listed in the lexicon. To capture the regularities in stem alternations, well-formedness conditions can be stated on pairs of stems in terms of the stressed vowel:

(13) Well-formed pairs of stems:

[−ablaut]	[+ablaut]
a	*e*
o	*e*
u	*i*
oy	*ay*
oy	*ey*

3.4 Argument Two: Parallels between Ablaut and Nonablaut Plural Classes

The second argument for the stem suppletion analysis comes from the fact that the ablaut plurals divide into two classes: those with the suffix −*er* and those with no ("zero") plural suffix. These two classes of ablaut plurals, displayed in (10) and (11), exactly parallel the two classes of nonablaut plurals in (9). Under the rule analysis, the rules accounting for ablaut plurals and the plurals in (9) would be distinct; it would not be possible to take advantage of their partial similarity. Under the stem suppletion analysis, with the two stems listed in the lexicon, the plural forms of the ablaut stems can be accounted for by lexical rules in the same way as the plural forms in (9). For this to be possible, the ablaut stems must be listed in the lexicon alongside the inflected forms, so that the lexical rules can relate them in the same way they relate the pairs in (9). Under the stem suppletion analysis, then, the plurals of ablaut stems are just a special case of the plural types in (9). By the disjunctive ordering principle, the existence of these lexical plurals will block application of (7).

3.5 The Relevance of Disjunctive Ordering

The plural of many nouns differs from the singular in two ways: ablaut and suffixation with −*er*. The fact that ablaut and suffixation are not mutually exclusive would present a problem for the disjunctive ordering principle if ablaut and suffixation were accounted for by distinct morphological rules; the disjunctive ordering principle would incorrectly predict that only one of these rules could apply in a given case.

One solution to this problem would be to effect ablaut and −*er* suffixation by a single rule. However, diminutives are also formed by ablaut plus suffixation, as can be seen in (2) and (14). The distinct plural and diminutive rules would then partially duplicate each other in that both would derive ablaut stems in addition to suffixation. Further, the ablaut stems are always the same in both cases. For example, while stems in *oy* can have corresponding ablaut stems either in *ay* or in *ey*, no noun in *oy* uses a stem in *ay* for plurals and one in *ey* for diminutives, or vice versa. That situation should be excluded, but with plural and diminutive rules effecting both ablaut and suffixation, nothing would exclude it.

Of course, other ways could be found to save the disjunctive ordering principle in such cases (discussed in some detail by Anderson, 1986). Under the stem suppletion analysis, however, the problem does not arise. Since there is no rule deriving the ablaut form from the nonablaut form, the problem disappears.

4. Diminutives with Ablaut

4.1 The Proposal

We now return to the split morphology hypothesis and its prediction, summarized in (1), about the interaction of plural and diminutive formation in Yiddish. The data in (2) initially seemed to falsify its predictions, since diminutives seemed to be derived from the plural form. Under the stem suppletion analysis of Section 3, however, there is no problem for the split morphology hypothesis. Both ablaut and nonablaut stems are listed in the lexicon, and diminutives are formed from ablaut stems, not from plural forms.[7] Interestingly, there is evidence internal to Yiddish for this analysis.

---

[7] The rules that derive diminutives are discussed in the appendix.

4.2 Argument One: Nonappearance of the Plural Suffix

Diminutives appear to be derived from plural forms in (2) because *cop* and *šux* form their plurals with ablaut alone, like the nouns in (10). If we examine the type illustrated in (11), which form their plurals with ablaut plus −*er*, we see clearly that the diminutive is derived from the ablaut stem alone, not from the plural form. The plural suffix −*er* does not appear in the diminutive:[8]

(14)		Sg	Pl	1st dim sg	2d dim sg	1st dim pl	2d dim pl
	face	*ponim*	*penimer*	*peniml*		*penimlex*	
	nose	*noz*	*nezer*	*nezl*	*nezele*	*nezlex*	*nezelex*
	forest	*vald*	*velder*	*veldl*	*veldele*	*veldlex*	*veldelex*
	book	*bux*	*bixer*	*bixl*	*bixele*	*bixlex*	*bixelex*
	room	*štub*	*štiber*	*štibl*	*štibele*	*štiblex*	*štibelex*
	house	*hoyz*	*hayzer*	*hayzl*	*hayzele*	*hayzlex*	*hayzelex*
	tree	*boym*	*beymer*	*beyml*	*beymele*	*beymlex*	*beymelex*
	belly	*boyx*	*bayxer*	*bayxl*	*bayxele*	*bayxlex*	*bayxelex*

Forms like **penimerlex*, **nezerlex*, **velderlex*, do not exist.[9] The diminutives are thus derived from ablaut stems, not from inflected plural forms.

4.3 Argument Two: Nouns with Distinct Stems in the Plural and Diminutive

The final argument that diminutives with ablaut (with the exception of *kinderlex* and *dernerlex*) are not derived from plurals comes from a small class of nouns that are exceptions to the generalization that the ablaut stem appears in both the plural and diminutive. These nouns have an ablaut stem used to form diminutives but undergo the regular plural rule (7):

(15)		Sg	Pl	1st dim	2d dim
	street	*gas*	*gasn*	*gesl*	*gesele*
	cheek	*bak*	*bakn*	*bekl*	*bekele*
	hare	*hoz*	*hozn*	*hezl*	*hezele*
	bundle	*bunt*	*buntn*	*bintl*	*bintele*
	broth	*yoyx*	*yoyxn*	*yayxl*	*yayxele*
	dove	*toyb*	*toybn*	*taybl*	*taybele*
	eye	*oyg*	*oygn*	*eygl*	*eygele*

These examples show clearly that the diminutive is formed not from the plural

---

[8] *Ponim* does not have a second diminutive because it fails to meet the stress requirements of the second diminutive rule, discussed in the appendix. The rules given there also account for other gaps in diminutive paradigms.

[9] The forms in (3) are discussed in Section 4.4.

form, but from a separate ablaut stem.[10] Forms like those in (2) are therefore fully consistent with the split morphology hypothesis.

4.4 Ablaut Plurals and the Split Morphology Hypothesis

(14) and (15) show that diminutives are formed on ablaut stems, not on plural forms. The grammar must treat the examples in (3) as exceptions. However, even these exceptions do not counterexemplify the split morphology hypothesis. Since only a restricted class of nouns have plurals in *−er* (see Section 2.4), affixation with *−er* must be stated by a lexical rule, which means that these plurals are in the lexicon. They are therefore available for the derivation of diminutives. The fact that they undergo diminutive formation in the lexicon is entirely consistent with the split morphology hypothesis.

These forms contrast with the few nouns with ablaut stems that do not have lexical zero or *−er* plurals. By the disjunctive ordering principle, they undergo (7). Since (7) is extralexical and derivational rules are in the lexicon, the split morphology hypothesis predicts that the diminutive suffix cannot follow the plural suffix due to (7). This is correct:

(16)   Sg   1st dim sg   Pl   1st dim pl
    maiden   *moyd*   *meydl*   *meydn*   *meydlex*   **meydnlex*

The contrast between (3) and (16) brings out what the split morphology hypothesis predicts. It allows forms listed in the lexicon to undergo derivational rules, whether they are stems like the ablaut stems that form the diminutives in (14) and (15) or inflected forms like the plurals that form the diminutives in (3). It predicts that inflected forms due to extralexical rules like (7) cannot undergo derivational rules. (16), like (8), confirms this prediction.

5. Diminutives of Hebrew/Aramaic Loan Words

Yiddish has a large number of loan words from Hebrew and Aramaic. Those ending in an unstressed vowel regularly form their plurals by rule (7a), as illustrated in (6a). The plural suffix *−s* cannot occur in their diminutives, as (8) shows. Hebrew/Aramaic nouns ending in a consonant, however, appear in the patterns of (4) and (17).

---

[10]These examples also provide evidence for the disjunctive ordering of morphological rules. For nouns with an ablaut plural, the existence of this special plural form prevents application of the regular plural rules in (7). Where there is no such plural form, as in the cases in (15), (7) applies, producing "regular" plurals.

(17)   Sg   Sg dim   Pl   Pl dim
    smart person   *xoxem*   *xoxeml*   *xaxomim*   *xaxomimlex*
    Chasid   *xosid*   *xosidl*   *xasidim*   *xasidimlex*
    delicacy   *mayxl*   *mayxele*   *mayxolim*   *mayxolimlex*

The problem for the split morphology hypothesis is the fact that in the plural, the diminutive suffix follows the plural − *im*.

Nouns in this class exhibit a high degree of irregularity in their singular–plural alternations:

(18)   Sg   Pl
    a.   thief   *ganef*   *ganovim*
         miracle   *nes*   *nisim*
         dead person   *mes*   *meysim*
         sin   *xet*   *xatoim*
         rabbi   *rov*   *rabonim*
         fool   *nar*   *naronim*
         condition   *tnay*   *tnoim*
         religious school   *xeyder*   *xadorim*
         custom   *mineg*   *minhogim*
         month   *xoydeš*   *xadošim*
         merchant   *soyxer*   *soxrim*
         murderer   *receyex*   *rocxim*
         king   *meylex*   *mloxim*
         portion, share   *xeylek*   *xalokim*
         seder   *seyder*   *sdorim*
         ignorant person   *amorec*   *ameracim*
         Gentile (pej.)   *šeygec*   *škocim*
         prophet   *novi*   *neviim*
         way, means   *oyfn*   *oyfanim*
         shy person   *bayšn*   *baysonim*
         friend, comrade   *xaver*   *xaveyrim*
    b.   house of study   *bes-medreš*   *bote-medrošim*
         hospitable person   *maxnes-oyrex*   *maxnise-orxim*
         adulterer   *mexalel-ziveg*   *mexàlele-zivugim*
         only son   *ben-yoxed*   *bney-yexidim*
    c.   villain   *roše*   *rešoim*
         rabbi of the Mishnah   *tane*   *tanoim*

The examples in (4) are unusual in showing no stem changes; they appear to be straightforward cases of suffixation of − *im*. (18) makes clear, however, how much the singular and plural forms can differ. The examples in (18b), which have internal structure in the source language, have secondary stress on the first term but otherwise behave like irregular singular–plural alternations in Yiddish. Those in (18c) end in an unstressed vowel in the singular, but do not undergo (7a).

For all these examples, I propose a full suppletion analysis: The singular and plural forms are listed separately in the lexicon, the former marked [−pl] and the latter [+pl]. There is no reason to posit a suffix −*im*.[11] Given this analysis and the disjunctive ordering principle, the fact that the plural forms in (18) are marked [+pl] will block the application of the regular plural rules in (7).

The full suppletion analysis proposed for these Hebrew/Aramaic loans contrasts with the stem suppletion analysis proposed for ablaut, where the suppletive forms in the lexicon are stems that undergo inflection and diminutive formation. The reason for the different analysis comes from diminutive formation. (2) and (14) show that both singular and plural diminutive suffixes can attach to ablaut stems, which are unmarked for number. Forms like those in (18), however, are inflected for number, and only a diminutive suffix agreeing in number can attach to them. This analysis entails a treatment of the diminutive suffixes under which −*l* and −*ele* attach to singular forms, while −*lex* and −*elex* attach to plural ones. This is necessary to prevent diminutives like those in (19) instead of the correct forms in (17).

(19) **xoxemlex*   **xaxomiml*
      *xosidlex   **xasidiml*
      *mayxlex   **mayxoliml*

Let us now return to the consequences of this analysis for the split morphology hypothesis. The forms in (4) and (17) initially appeared problematic for the split morphology hypothesis on the assumption that they arise from plural suffixation prior to diminutive suffixation. Since plural forms ending in −*im* are listed as such in the lexicon, the forms in (4) and (17) are no problem for the split morphology hypothesis. They show a diminutive suffix on a lexical plural form.[12]

Parenthetically, it should be noted that another class of Hebrew/Aramaic loans presents somewhat different issues.

(20) | | Sg | Pl |
|---|---|---|
| hostage | *maškn* | *maškones* |
| victim | *korbm* | *korbones* |
| dream | *xolem* | *xaloymes* |
| language | *lošn* | *lešoynes* |
| victory | *nicoxn* | *nicxoynes* |

---

[11]The fact that all these forms end in −*im* can be stated by a lexical rule. Nothing crucial to the concerns of this chapter hinges on whether this is done.

[12]I assume that −*lex* and −*elex* are unanalyzable plural diminutive suffixes. An alternative would be to posit a plural suffix −*(e)x* that attaches only to the diminutive suffixes −*l* and −*ele*, since no other forms (including those with other diminutive suffixes) have plurals in −*(e)x*. I do not see what would be gained under this alternative.

secret	*sod*	*soydes*
treasure	*oycer*	*oycres*
shofar	*šoyfer*	*šoyfres*
strength	*koyex*	*koyxes*
generation	*dor*	*doyres*
cup	*kos*	*koyses*
letter	*os*	*oysyes*
tablet	*luex*	*luxes*
disgrace	*bizoyen*	*bizyoynes*

Since the singular–plural correspondences are irregular, the singular and plural forms must be listed separately in the lexicon, as with the examples in (18). Because the plural forms end in unstressed *e* followed by *s*, two analyses are available. Under the full suppletion analysis, they would be listed as inflected [+pl] forms like those in (18), for example, *maškones, korbones, xaloymes*. Under the stem suppletion analysis, they would be listed as stems unmarked for number, for example, *maškone–, korbone–, xaloyme–*, in which case, ending in an unstressed vowel, they would undergo the regular plural rule in (7a). (The situation therefore differs from that with the forms ending in −*im*, since the grammar already contains an extralexical rule to derive plurals in −*s* from stems ending in an unstressed vowel.)

Under the two analyses, the split morphology hypothesis makes different predictions about diminutives. The full suppletion analysis treats the forms in (20) like those in (18) and therefore predicts well-formed diminutives of the full plural forms, for example, *maškoneslex, korboneslex, xaloymeslex*, like those in (4) and (17). The stem suppletion analysis derives the plural forms in (20) by extralexical application of (7a) and therefore predicts *maškonelex, korbonelex, xaloymelex*. Unfortunately, the situation is not clear. The speakers I consulted rejected both types of diminutives for this class. However, Bochner (1984) cites several diminutives of the first type and one of the second as grammatical, based on the judgments of one informant. Additional research is needed to determine the status of these examples. Significantly, either state of affairs is consistent with the split morphology hypothesis, depending on how the plural forms are analyzed in individual speakers' grammars. Since different speakers might enter them differently, variation on this point would also be consistent with the split morphology hypothesis. (Without some additional device(s), the split morphology hypothesis would not account for speakers' systematically rejecting both types of diminutives of these forms.)

In sum, Hebrew/Aramaic loan words like those in (4) and (17) are not problematic for the split morphology hypothesis. The singular–plural alternations are so irregular that they must be treated as suppletion. Under the full suppletion analysis, diminutive suffixation to suppletive forms is entirely consistent with the split morphology hypothesis.[13]

6. Conclusions

The results of this study bear on the analysis of Yiddish, the treatment of suppletion and ablaut in morphological theory, and the split morphology hypothesis.

Internal to Yiddish, we have seen that there is evidence to treat both ablaut and the singular–plural alternations in many Hebrew/Aramaic loan words as suppletion in the lexicon. Instead of the traditional nine classes ($-s$, $-en$, $-er$, ø, ablaut, ablaut + er, $-ex$, $-im$, plus a class with irregular plurals), we posit (7) to derive the regular plurals in $-en$ and $-s$, and lexical rules for the zero plurals and plurals in $-er$. We treat $-ex$ as part of the diminutive suffixes. Other types are analyzed as suppletion in the lexicon. Ablaut is stem suppletion, while the Hebrew/Aramaic loans whose plurals are not derived by (7) are analyzed as full suppletion.

Our results support the distinction between stem suppletion and full suppletion. Ablaut illustrates stem suppletion: Ablaut stems are unmarked for number. They can therefore undergo plural inflection and occur with both singular and plural diminutive suffixes. Irregular Hebrew/Aramaic loans illustrate full suppletion. Since each form is marked for number, they cannot undergo plural inflection and can occur only with the diminutive suffix of the appropriate number.

Our treatment of ablaut differs from most earlier generative treatments,

---

[13]After presenting this paper at the Milwaukee conference, I became acquainted with Bochner, 1984, which concludes that the Yiddish data counterexemplify the split morphology hypothesis. Bochner's argument is based primarily on Hebrew/Aramaic plurals ending in $-im$, examples like those in (4) and (17), which, as we have seen, are consistent with the split morphology hypothesis. Bochner also presents an argument against one of Lieber's (1980) predictions that could bear on the split morphology hypothesis. The argument is based on adverbs ending in $-vayz$, e.g., *bislexvayz* 'bit by bit,' in which the plural form *bislex* is combined with $-vayz$. The crucial point is the appearance of plural inflection "inside" the derivational suffix $-vayz$. The only forms that could bear on the split morphology hypothesis are those in which a plural derived by (7) undergoes a rule of derivational morphology. Of the five forms with $-vayz$ that Bochner cites, only two are relevant: *teylnvayz* 'part by part,' and *šuresvayz* 'line by line.' The speakers I consulted would accept only the first. Further attempts to construct adverbs in $-vayz$ on plurals derived by (7) met with failure. As far as I can determine, there is not a productive derivational rule suffixing $-vayz$ to plurals derived by (7). Adverbs ending in $-vayz$ seem to be sporadic and would therefore have to be listed individually in the lexicon. If this is correct, these forms present no problem for the split morphology hypothesis.

which exemplify different forms of the rule analysis. The study of German ablaut (umlaut) has revealed that it cannot be accounted for by a single rule applying uniformly in different morphological categories. For example, Robinson (1975) has argued that its generality has changed over time in different categories, and that its ordering relative to other rules (in low German dialects) varies in different categories. Janda (1982) shows that the phonological conditions on ablaut vary across categories, as does the class of vowels and diphthongs undergoing it.[14] He also shows that stems vary with respect to the categories in which they undergo or resist ablaut. Joseph and Janda (1986) cite German ablaut as an example of what they call a "rule constellation"— a "group of formally similar morphological processes sharing at least one characteristic property of form but distinguished by individual formal idiosyncrasies which prevent their being collapsed." The problem is to capture what the various cases of German ablaut have in common while accounting for the data that prevent them from being collapsed into a single rule. Analyzing ablaut as stem suppletion, as proposed here, may offer a solution. With separate stems listed in the lexicon and related by lexical rules, it then remains to state the conditions on their distribution. The question of whether a solution along these lines is appropriate for German ablaut remains to be explored.

With respect to the split morphology hypothesis, we have seen that the examples in (2–4), which initially seemed to be counterexamples, are not problematic. The diminutives in (2) are formed not on plurals but on ablaut stems, those in (3) are formed on lexical plurals, and those in (4) are formed on fully suppletive plural forms. On the contrary, the Yiddish evidence supports the split morphology hypothesis. Forms in which a diminutive suffix follows one of the productive plural suffixes ($-en$ and $-s$) due to the extralexical rule (7) are systematically impossible, as (8) and (16) show. This fact supports and is explained by the split morphology hypothesis.

Our results point to a characterization of the split morphology hypothesis based on two sets of criteria. Anderson's (1982) proposal that only syntactically relevant morphology can be extralexical is essential, for this is what assigns derivational morphology to the lexicon and makes only inflectional morphology eligible to be extralexical. At the same time, it is necessary to distinguish between two types of syntactically relevant morphology: irregular and closed-class inflection, which is in the lexicon, and regular, productive inflection, which is extralexical. This has elements in common with Lieber's (1980) proposals, from which it would follow that productive concatenative affixation will occur outside idiosyncratic and irregular affixation. However,

---

[14]There are also such differences in Yiddish. For example, in the comparatives and superlatives of adjectives, *oy* ablauts to *e* (rather than to *ay* or *ey*) and *ey* (which does not ablaut in the noun morphology) ablauts to *e*. However, *u* ablauts to *i*, as in the noun morphology. We have ignored this because our study is limited to noun morphology.

Lieber does not make the distinction between derivational and inflectional morphology that is crucial to our results here and to Anderson's characterization of the split morphology hypothesis. We are therefore led to a characterization of the split morphology hypothesis with the following properties:

(21) THE SPLIT MORPHOLOGY HYPOTHESIS
    a. Derivational morphology is in the lexicon.
    b. Stems are listed in the lexicon. Consequently, suppletive stems are listed in the lexicon.
    c. Irregular and closed-class inflected forms are listed in the lexicon. Consequently, suppletive inflected forms are listed in the lexicon.
    d. Regular, productive inflection is extralexical.

(21a) and (21d) assume a distinction between inflectional and derivational morphology in terms of Anderson's distinction between rules that refer to morphosyntactic representations and those that do not. Given (21b) and (21c), the regularities holding among separately listed stems and inflected forms must be stated by lexical rules, as in the work of Jackendoff (1975), Lieber (1980), and others. (21b) and (21c) provide the basis for a theory of suppletion that distinguishes between stem suppletion and full suppletion. The evidence from Yiddish noun morphology supports a theory with these properties.

Appendix—On the Derivation of Diminutives

Nouns ending in a vowel or syllabic *l* fail to form first diminutives. This is easily accounted for if phonetically syllabic *n* and *r* are not syllabic but are still preceded by *schwa* at the point where the First Diminutive Rule applies. Then the rule can apply to nouns ending in a [−syllabic] segment:

(22) FIRST DIMINUTIVE RULE
$$[X \ [-\text{syll}]]_{N([+\text{abl}])} \ \rightarrow \ [X \ C \ + \ l]$$
$$[+\text{syll}]$$

The specification "([+abl])" ensures that for those nouns that have ablaut stems, only the ablaut stem can serve as input to (22). The more specific environment is the one containing the specification "[+abl]." If a noun has a [+abl] stem, then, (22) will apply to it. The disjunctive ordering principle will then prevent it from applying to the nonablaut stem.

    Two epenthesis rules that apply in the environment created by the first diminutive suffix provide evidence that second diminutives are derived from first diminutives. The epenthesized consonants also appear in second diminutives. (23) accounts for the fact that stems ending in *n* epenthesize a *d* before the first diminutive suffix.

(23) D-EPENTHESIS

ø → d/n __ + l

(24)

	Sg	1st dim	2d dim
bridegroom	xosn	xosndl	
leg	beyn	beyndl	beyndele
hen	hun	hindl	hindele
son	zun	zindl	zindele
stone	šteyn	šteyndl	šteyndele

(25) accounts for the fact that a *x* is epenthesized before the diminutive suffix if the stem ends in *l*.

(25) X-EPENTHESIS

ø → x/l __ + l

(26)

	Sg	Pl	1st dim	2nd dim
mouth	moyl	mayler	maylxl	maylxele
voice	kol	keler	kelxl	kelxele
part	teyl	teyln	teylxl	teylxele

The epenthesized consonants appear in second diminutives although these forms do not satisfy the epenthesis rules' environments; compare the presence of *d* in the second diminutives in (24) with its absence in *xanele* in (34). Further, a few nouns ending in *n* drop the *n* in the first diminutive, and it is absent in the second diminutive as well:[15]

(27)

	Sg	1st dim	2d dim
bow, arch	boygn	beygl	beygele

All this indicates that second diminutives are derived from first diminutives. (28) accounts for this.[16]

(28) SECOND DIMINUTIVE RULE

$$[\text{X V C}_\text{O} \, [+\text{syll}] \,]_{\text{N}([+\text{abl}])} \rightarrow [\text{X V C}_\text{O} \, ele]$$
$$[+\text{str}] \qquad\qquad\qquad\qquad [+\text{str}]$$

The Second Diminutive Rule applies to forms ending in an unstressed syllabic segment, that is, a vowel or syllabic *l*, replacing the final syllabic segment with *−ele*. Except for the Second Diminutive Rule's stress requirement, the First and Second Diminutive Rules have complementary environments, but since the forms produced by the First Diminutive Rule end in syllabic *l*, the Second Diminutive Rule will apply to them, deriving the second diminutives. This accounts for the appearance of epenthetic *d* and *x* in the second

[15]These nouns must be marked as exceptional. The deletion of *n* will make (23) inapplicable.

[16]As with the First Diminutive Rule, this formulation assumes that *l* is syllabic, while *n* and *r* are not, at the point when this rule applies.

diminutives in (24) and (26). The Second Diminutive Rule also accounts for the fact that in second diminutives the stress is always on the syllable immediately preceding the suffix *−ele*.

The effects of the two diminutive rules can also be seen in the diminutives of proper names that end in syllabic *l*.

(29)		1st dim	2d dim	
Hershel	*heršl*	**heršlxl*	*heršele*	**heršlele*
Rachel	*roxl*	**roxlxl*	*roxele*	**roxlele*
Herzl	*hercl*	**herclxl*	*hercele*	**herclele*

Since the basic form ends in syllabic *l*, no first diminutive can be derived. The Second Diminutive Rule derives the second diminutive from the basic form, whose final syllabic *l* is replaced by *−ele*. It thus treats a final syllabic *l* in the same way, regardless of whether it is the first diminutive suffix, as in earlier examples, or part of the stem, as in (29) and (30). It does not simply add *−ele* to the stem.

Both diminutive rules have the specification "([+abl])." We have already seen that this specification is necessary in the First Diminutive Rule, but since second diminutives are parasitic on first diminutives, it might be thought unnecessary in the Second Diminutive Rule. Its necessity can be seen in the fact that nouns that fail to form first diminutives nonetheless can have second diminutives, and that these second diminutives are formed on the noun's ablaut stem if it has one.

(30)		Sg	Pl	1st dim	2d dim
blackboard		*tovl*	*tovlen*		*tevele*

Tovl is in the category in (15); the ablaut stem *tevl* is used for diminutives but not for the plural. Since it ends in syllabic *l*, however, it cannot undergo the First Diminutive Rule. It does undergo the Second Diminutive Rule, which derives *tevele*. To prevent **tovele*, the Second Diminutive Rule, like the First, must operate on the ablaut stem if there is one. The specification "([+abl])" ensures this.

Since diminutives are formed on the ablaut stems of those nouns that have them, it might be thought that ablaut is conditioned by the diminutive suffix. There is evidence against this. First, by itself it would not account for the fact that, except for the small class in (15), the ablaut stem is also used to form plurals. Second, there are many examples in which the diminutive suffix does not condition ablaut. While most phonologically eligible nouns of Germanic origin have an ablaut stem, not all do:

(31)		Sg	Dim
tower		*turem*	*tureml*
valley, dale		*tol*	*tolxl*

shawl, scarf	*šal*	*šalxl*
cloud	*volkn*	*volkndl*
warning signal	*vorn*	*vorndl*
drop	*tropn*	*tropl*

Ablaut does not occur in the Hebrew/Aramaic vocabulary:[17]

(32)

	Sg	Sg dim	
bridegroom	*xosn*	*xosndl*	**xesndl*
smart person	*xoxem*	*xoxeml*	**xexeml*
Chasid	*xosid*	*xosidl*	**xesidl*
friend, comrade	*xaver*	*xaverl*	**xeverl*
pupil	*talmid*	*talmidl*	**telmidl*
body	*guf*	*gufele*	**gifele*
gift	*matone*	*matonele*	**matenele*
family	*mišpoxe*	*mišpoxele*	**mišpexele*

(33)

	Pl	Pl dim	
smart people	*xaxomim*	*xaxomimlex*	**xaxemimlex*
delicacies	*mayxolim*	*mayxolimlex*	**mayxelimlex*
sins	*xatoim*	*xatoimlex*	**xateimlex*

Proper names form diminutives productively, but without ablaut:[18]

(34)

		1st dim	2d dim		
David	*doved*	*dovedl*		**devedl*	
Hannah	*xane*		*xanele*	**xenele*	
Menachem	*menaxem*	*menaxml*		**menexml*	
Moyshe	*moyše*		*moyšele*	**mayšele*	**meyšele*
Broche	*broxe*		*broxele*	**brexele*	
Fruma	*frume*		*frumele*	**frimele*	
Bluma	*blume*		*blumele*	**blimele*	

Not all these names are of Hebrew/Aramaic origin, and *frume* is felt to be related to *frum* 'pious,' which has an ablaut stem in the comparative (*frimer* 'more pious'). These facts argue against an analysis in which ablaut is conditioned by the diminutive suffix. They are consistent with our analysis, under which ablaut and nonablaut stems are listed in the lexicon.

[17] What is relevant is not a word's historical origin but how it is treated by the grammar. For example, *ponim* 'face,' though of Hebrew origin, is treated by the grammar as Germanic. The plural *penimer* shows this in three ways: the ablaut stem, the −*er* suffix, and the fact that stress is on the initial syllable. Similarly, *nar* 'fool,' though Germanic in origin, is treated by the grammar as a Hebrew-Aramaic loan, as can be seen in the plural *naronim*, which ends in −*im* and has penultimate stress.

[18] I know of one exception to this generalization: *avrom* 'Abraham,' dim. *avreml*. These should probably be treated as distinct items, like English pairs such as *Henry-Hank, Richard-Dick*.

For ease of exposition the diminutive rules were formulated in (22) and (28) as deriving only singular diminutives, but they also derive plural diminutives—the First Diminutive Rule with the suffix −*lex* and the Second Diminutive Rule with −*elex*. Most nouns, which get their plurals by (7), are unmarked for number in the lexicon and therefore can undergo suffixation with either singular or plural diminutive suffixes. This also holds for ablaut stems, which are unmarked for number in the lexicon. Lexical plurals like *kinder* 'children' and *derner* 'thorns' are marked as plural in the lexicon and therefore can take only plural diminutive suffixes. Hebrew-Aramaic loan words whose plurals are not derived by (7) are marked for number; they can therefore be suffixed only with the diminutive suffix of the appropriate number. We leave open the question of what formal device is appropriate to ensure this.

Acknowledgments

This chapter owes a great deal to discussions with Stephen Anderson, without whom it would probably not have seen the light of day. I also owe a great debt to Fruma Perlmutter for assistance with the research, and to her and Bella Shapiro for checking many of the examples. Harry Bochner provided useful information.

References

Anderson, S.R. (1969). *West Scandinavian vowel systems and the ordering of phonological rules.* Doctoral dissertation, MIT, Cambridge, Massachusetts.

Anderson, S.R. (1982). Where's morphology? *Linguistic Inquiry* **13**, 571–612.

Anderson, S.R. (1986). Disjunctive ordering in inflectional morphology. *Natural Language and Linguistic Theory* **4**, 1–31.

Aronoff, M. (1976). "Word Formation in Generative Grammar." MIT Press, Cambridge, MA.

Bochner, H. (1984). Inflection within derivation. *The Linguistic Review* **3**, 411–421.

Chomsky, N. (1967). Some general properties of phonological rules. *Language* **43**, 102–128.

Chomsky, N., and Halle, M. (1968). "The Sound Pattern of English." Harper, New York.

Jackendoff, R. (1975). Morphological and semantic regularities in the lexicon. *Language* **51**, 639–676.

Janda, R. (1982). On limiting the form of morphological rules: German umlaut, diacritics, and the cluster constraint. *NELS* **12**, 140–152.

Joseph, B., and Janda, R. (1986). *E pluribus unum: The rule constellation as an expression of formal unity amidst morphological fragmentation.* Paper presented at the Milwaukee Morphology Meeting.

Kiparsky, P. (1973). 'Elsewhere' in phonology. *In* "A Festschrift for Morris Halle," (S.R. Anderson and P. Kiparsky, eds.), pp. 93–106. Harper, New York.

Kiparsky, P. (1982). Lexical morphology and phonology. *In* "Linguistics in the Morning Calm," (I.S. Yang, ed.). Hanshin, Seoul.

Kiparsky, P. (1983). Word formation and the lexicon. *Proceedings of the 1982 Mid-America Linguistics Conference, University of Kansas* pp. 3–29.

Lieber, R. (1980). *On the organization of the lexicon.* Doctoral dissertation, MIT, Cambridge, Massachusetts.

Robinson, O. (1975). Abstract phonology and the history of umlaut. *Lingua* **37**, 1–29.

Sapir, E. (1915). Notes on Judeo-German phonology. *The Jewish Quarterly Review*, n.s., **6**, 231–266. Reprinted in "Selected Writings of Edward Sapir in Language, Culture, and Personality" (David G. Mandelbaum, ed.). Univ. of California Press, Berkeley.

Weinreich, U. (1965). "College Yiddish"[4] Yivo Institute for Jewish Research, New York.

Weinreich, U. (1968). "Modern English-Yiddish Yiddish-English Dictionary." Yivo Institute for Jewish Research and McGraw-Hill, New York.

Zarecki, A. (1929). "Yidiše Gramatik." Vilner Farlag fun B. Kleckin, Vilne.

Chapter 6

Are Inflected Forms
Stored in the Lexicon?

Joseph Paul Stemberger & Brian MacWhinney

Lexical items are a fundamental part of a speaker's knowledge of language. However, it is not always clear what items should be listed in the lexicon. There has been major disagreement in both linguistic theory and psycholinguistics over the status of inflected forms. Should all members of an inflectional paradigm be given separate entries in the lexicon? Or should there be only one entry for each paradigm, with the individual inflected forms being created by applying an inflectional rule to a base form? We examine this issue from a psycholinguistic perspective, bringing to bear data that we hope resolve this issue for language production. In addition to addressing the question of whether inflected forms are stored, we also address the question of how they might be stored.

Proposals about the representation of inflected forms fall into three main "generic" approaches. One approach is full suppletion: all inflected forms are stored in the lexicon as single units, as if they were monomorphemic (Leben and Robinson, 1977; Bybee, this volume). There may additionally be some form of redundancy rule that relates an inflected form to the other members of its paradigm and to other forms with the same affix. Regular and irregular forms are parallel in this approach, as in (1).

(1)   {FREEZE} → /frouz//[+past]
                          |
                    /fri:z/ elsewhere
       {WALK}   → /wa:kt//[+past]
                          |
                    /wa:k/ elsewhere

Theoretical Morphology Copyright © 1988 by Academic Press, Inc.   101

An opposite approach is possible, where no inflected forms are stored in the lexicon, but are rather produced by lexical-item-free rules that take a base form as input and give an inflected form as output. This is possible with regularly inflected forms as in (2), but not with irregular forms, where some form of lexical conditioning is required.

(2)   Regulars: $_v$] T $_v$]/[+past]

The last generic position is an intermediate one; it holds that at least some regularly inflected forms are stored in the lexicon, but that they are stored as two items. Minimally, this would involve storing the words as a sequence of two morphemes (Jackendoff, 1975), but could also involve the use of lexically conditioned rules, as in (3).

(3)   æ
           |
       [... V C_1 $_v$]/[+past],{SING, STINK, RUN, ...}

       $_v$] T $_v$]/[+past],{WALK, ASK, SNEEZE, ...}

Of course, there is no reason why one must take any one of these positions for all inflected forms. It is fairly popular to take one position for irregular forms (generally suppletion) and a different one for regular forms (generally lexical-item-free rules) (Bybee and Slobin, 1982; Kiparsky, 1982). There is very little data that allow us to choose between these options. All of them can account for the basic linguistic data, differing primarily on simplicity and what generalizations are captured. And there is little agreement on what is simple or on what generalizations should be captured. (In order to account for productivity, the full-suppletion approach requires an explicit formulation of analogy or the assumption that rules exist but are used only to relate forms in the lexicon and to create forms not stored in the lexicon (Aronoff, 1976; Butterworth, 1983)).

Psycholinguistics has only been able to partially resolve the issue (see Butterworth, 1983). It has generally been assumed that irregular forms are stored in the lexicon, but it is not clear how. Perceptual studies have often maintained that the base and inflection of regularly inflected forms are perceived independently (Stanners *et al.*, 1979; Kempley and Morton, 1982), but other researchers have suggested that the results are compatible with suppletive storage, as long as members or a paradigm are clustered in some special way (Bradley, 1980; Lukatela *et al.*, 1980). There is some evidence that young children may store inflected forms (and syntactic phrases) as unanalyzed units (MacWhinney, 1978; Peters, 1983), but no evidence that such storage continues into adulthood (or even past the age of 6). Walsh and Parker (1983) report that the /s/ of the plural morpheme is 9 msec longer than a nonmorphemic /s/ in homophonous words, suggesting that inflected forms are at least analyzed into two morphemes. Stemberger (1985b) reviews evidence from speech errors and argues that regularly inflected forms appear to be controlled as two morphemes in language production, and that inflectional rules are needed to account for errors where irregular forms are regularized (e.g., *choosed* instead of *chose*), at least within one type of language-production model. Thus, there is some evidence for inflectional rules, but none that really addresses the question of whether inflected forms are stored in the lexicon. Since lexical storage and rules are compatible (the third position outlined above), this leaves us uncertain about what is stored in the lexicon.

Psychology provides us with two clear tests of whether forms are stored as units or not. (a) Given storage, units that are of high frequency should be produced faster and more accurately than units that are of low frequency (Atkinson and Shiffrin, 1968; MacKay, 1982). Frequency effects derive from storage and cannot differentiate two items if neither is stored. (Of course, if a frequency effect is present, it only tells us that high-frequency forms are stored. It gives no information about whether low-frequency forms are stored, since storage is assumed to increase the speed and accuracy of processing relative to no storage.) (b) Given storage, items that are similar will tend to reinforce each other and lead to faster, more accurate performance (Rumelhart and McClelland, 1982; McClelland and Elman, 1986). This is a form of analogy and has sometimes been termed EXTENDED ANALOGY (e.g., Stemberger, 1985b). These "gangs" of similar items also tend to interfere with the processing of other lexical items that are similar to the members of the gang. Such "gang effects" must be present if items are stored, and cannot be present if items are not stored.

Frequency effects are present if inflected forms are stored in the lexicon, but absent if no inflected forms are stored in the lexicon. Some inflected forms are of high frequency and are used very often, for example, *ended* (Francis and Kucera, 1982). Other inflected forms are of low frequency and are used comparatively rarely but are nonetheless quite familiar, for example, *mended* (Francis and Kucera, 1982). If both are stored in the lexicon, the higher frequency of *ended* will entail that it is produced more rapidly than *mended* is, and that it will be less susceptible to error than *mended* is. This is especially true of a particular type of error that we call a NO-MARKING ERROR, where the speakers errs by accessing the base form where an inflected form was required, for example, *end* or *mend*. (We focus on no-marking errors in this chapter, since this is the most common type of error on regularly inflected forms in English.) The high frequency of *ended* guarantees more accurate access of the inflected form and fewer errors where the base form is accessed instead. If neither inflected form is stored, the difference in frequency of the inflected form is irrelevant, since this frequency is not represented anywhere in the system. The only frequencies that can matter are the frequency of the inflection and the frequency of the base. The frequency of the inflection is relevant only to access of the inflection, with more accessing failures (no-marking errors) on low-frequency inflections than on high-frequency inflections; Stemberger (1985a) demonstrates that this is at least partly the case. However, it cannot differentiate *ended* and *mended*, since the same inflection (and the same allomorph of that inflection) is involved in both forms. The frequency of the base should matter to the access of the base, with high-frequency base forms showing fewer accessing errors than low-frequency base forms (Stemberger, 1984; Stemberger and MacWhinney, 1986a). However, there is no reason to expect that success or failure with accessing the base should in any way influence the success or failure with accessing the inflection, since the two morphemes are being accessed independently. Thus, the high frequency of a base such as *end* could not lead to a more accurate access of the following *-ed* than the low frequency base *mend*. (We argue this point in more detail below.) Thus, we expect to find frequency effects if inflected forms are stored in the lexicon in some fashion, but no frequency effects if they are not stored in the lexicon.

Study 1: Naturally Occurring Error Data

Naturally occurring speech errors were taken from the first author's corpus of 7220 errors that occurred spontaneously in natural speech. All errors were made by adult native speakers of English. (For details of collection procedures, see Stemberger 1984, 1985a.) No-marking errors on the past and perfect forms of all verbs (except for the auxiliaries *was*, *were*, *did* and *had*) were identified. In all cases, the linguistic and/or extralinguistic context clearly required the verb to be in the past or perfect form, but it was produced with the simple base form of the verb instead, as in (4).

(4)　a.　*Boy, that **draw** him out—drew him out.*
　　b.　*What was it you just **sing**? (sang)*
　　c.　*So we **test** 'em on it. (tested)*
　　d.　*That's what I **need** to do. (needed)*

Frequency values per million words of printed text for each of the past and perfect forms of English were derived from Francis and Kucera (1982). The verbs were divided into regular and irregular verbs. The regular and irregular verb groups were then divided into high-frequency and low-frequency groups. The high-frequency groups contained those inflected forms with a frequency of 35 occurrences per million words or greater; the low-frequency groups contained the inflected forms with a frequency less than 35. A frequency of 35 was chosen because it is close to the midpoint of the frequency distribution of all inflected forms, such that half the tokens of inflected forms are accounted for by forms with a frequency of 35 or greater, and half by forms below 35. The frequency distribution for any given inflection differs from this, but 35 was used to ensure uniform treatment across inflections. The number of verbs in each group was summed, giving an estimate of chance for each group. The raw number of errors on verbs in each group was divided by the group frequency to yield an approximation of the error rate.

The results for the irregular verbs are given in (5).

(5)	Individual frequency	Group frequency	Number of errors	Rate
	low	1735	17	.00980
	high	15012	39	.00260

The first column tells if the past tense verb is of high or low frequency. The second column gives the number of verb tokens in these groups in Francis and Kucera (1982). The third column gives the number of observed errors in the corpus, and the fourth gives the approximation of an error rate discussed above. Most tokens of irregular past and perfect forms belong to high-frequency verbs. While there are more errors on high-frequency verbs, this is due solely to the greater level of chance. In fact, 30.4% of the errors occurred on low-frequency forms, which is significantly greater than the chance rate of 10.4% (χ^2 (1) = 23.90, $p < .0005$). This frequency effect entails that at least high-frequency irregular forms are stored in the lexicon.

The results for the regularly inflected forms are given in (6).

(6)	Individual frequency	Group frequency	Number of errors	Rate
	low	21305	24	.00113
	high	16315	11	.00072

Somewhat fewer than half of the tokens of regular past and perfect forms are associated with high-frequency forms. There is a greater error rate on low-frequency forms than on high-frequency forms, but this failed to reach significance (χ^2 (1) = 2.03, $p < .10$). The observed differences in error rate imply that at least high-frequency regularly inflected forms are stored in the lexicon, but we cannot be certain of this, since the differences were not significant. Note that the error rate on the low-frequency regular forms is nonetheless lower than the error rate on the high-frequency irregular forms (χ^2 (1) = 10.97, $p < .001$), suggesting that regular forms are easier to access than irregular forms. This might water down the effect of frequency differences through a floor effect; the production of regular forms is so easy that low-frequency forms are not at that great a disadvantage, and there were consequently too few errors in the corpus to detect a significant difference.

To more reliably test our hypothesis, we turn to an experimental task that can yield errors more quickly and under more reliable conditions (MacKay, 1976; Bybee and Slobin, 1982; Stemberger and MacWhinney, 1984, 1986a,b): having subjects produce a given member of a paradigm on presentation of a different member of the same paradigm. In Study 2, we contrast high-frequency and low-frequency verbs in this experimental task.

Study 2: Frequency and Regular Forms

A list of 40 English verbs was constructed, consisting of 10 high-frequency verbs, 10 low-frequency verbs, and 20 distractors. The high- and low-frequency verbs all ended in /t/ or /d/, since such verbs have fairly high error rates (Stemberger, 1981; Bybee and Slobin, 1982; Stemberger and MacWhinney, 1986b). All verbs were monosyllabic and were balanced for frequency and length. We chose the 10 highest-frequency regular past tense forms that fit these criteria and 10 very-low-frequency past tense forms.

The verbs were presented one at a time in the frame *was ____ing* in the center of the CRT display screen of an IBM personal computer. The subject read each verb silently, then spoke the past tense form of the verb out loud into a microphone. The instructions emphasized the need to react as quickly as possible. The subject's verbal responses were recorded on audiotape and analyzed for all errors. Subjects were 75 undergraduate students at Carnegie-Mellon University, receiving credit in an introductory psychology course for their participation in the experiment. Note that, unlike with the naturally occurring errors above, the exact error rate can be determined by dividing the number of errors by the total number of trials.

The results are shown in (7).

(7)

Verb type	Number of errors	Number of trials	Rate
low frequency	28	700	.037
high frequency	13	700	.017

There are significantly more errors on low-frequency forms than on high-frequency forms, using a Wilcoxon signed ranks test (two-tailed) over subjects ($p < .05$). This implies that at least high-frequency regularly inflected forms are stored in the lexicon in some fasion. The results are compatible with low-frequency forms being stored in the lexicon, but are also compatible with low-frequency forms being created on-line by a lexical-item-free rule.

There is only one other possible interpretation of these data that does not assume that high-frequency regularly inflected forms are stored in the lexicon, and this interpretation is clearly incorrect. In order for the access of the base form to affect the accessing of the inflection, one must make the access of the inflection a secondary action that follows the access of the base. One must also assume that there is a limited amount of attentional resources available for the access of both base and inflection, so that if all the resources are used up on the base, there will be none left for accessing the inflection. Since low-frequency bases use more resources, it is more likely that none will be left for the inflection, and a no-marking error will result. This predicts a greater error rate on inflections than on base forms, and implies that an error on the base form will invariably lead to an error on the inflection. These predictions are false for normal language production (Garrett, 1980;

Stemberger, 1984, 1985b) and for jargon aphasia (Butterworth, 1983). The data from both normal and aphasic behavior imply a certain amount of autonomy between the access of the base and the access of the proper inflected form of that base. Since this alternative makes clearly incorrect predictions about language production, we must conclude that at least high-frequency regularly inflected forms are stored in the lexicon.

There are some data that suggest that high-frequency forms are nonetheless stored as a sequence of two morphemes. Stemberger and MacWhinney (1986a) review the natural speech-error data that suggest that inflected forms have two morphemes in them, in particular the occurrence of shifts of affixes to an incorrect position in the sentence, such as *tell-us-ing* for 'telling us.' They report that such shifts are actually more common with high-frequency inflected forms than with low-frequency inflected forms, consistent with the finding that high-frequency lexical items are differentially involved in shifts (Stemberger, 1984). Insofar as shifts are a good argument for analysis into two morphemes (e.g., they are common with inflections but very rare with similar nonmorphemic sequences), it appears that high-frequency items are so analyzed. Since shifts are generally viewed as a postlexical phenomenon (Garrett, 1980; Stemberger, 1984), this entails that inflected forms are treated as two units even postlexically; we return to this implication below.

While these data allow us to draw conclusions about high-frequency regularly inflected forms, they do not allow us to draw any conclusions about low-frequency forms. To address the question of how low-frequency forms are treated in language production, we must turn to another phenomenon that is sensitive to the presence or absence of items from the lexicon: gang effects (Rumelhart and McClelland, 1982; McClelland and Elman, 1986). Gang effects arise in interactive activation models of cognitive processing. Since such models are beyond the scope of this chapter, we just describe the effects without going into detail on how they arise. The interested reader is referred to the articles cited above.

In a gang effect, several words in the lexicon that are similar in form reinforce the patterns of phonemes or letters that they have in common. The strength of the gang (i.e., the degree to which they reinforce the shared pattern) is a function of two things. First, the effect is greater when more phonemes or letters are shared. All other things being equal, a gang with three shared phonemes has more effect than a gang with two shared phonemes. Similarity of the phonemes involved in terms of position in the word and in terms of contiguity also has an effect. Homogeneous gangs that have the shared phonemes or letters in identical positions with the same items contiguous are stronger gangs. Second, the number of members in the gang has an effect. If two gangs are identical in terms of similarity of phoneme or letter patterns, the stronger gang is the one that has more words in it.

Gang effects can influence the pronunciation of nonwords such as *mave*.

The letter sequence *ave* can be pronounced /æ:v/ (as in *have*) or /eiv/ (as in *cave*). When we examine the lexicon, we find that there is only one word where *ave* is pronounced /æ:v/, while there are 14 monosyllabic words where it is pronounced /eiv/. All 14 /eiv/ words reinforce that pronunciation, while only *have* reinforces the alternative pronunciation. The greater size of the /eiv/ gang leads to greater reinforcement of the pronunciation /eiv/ and leads to the result that subjects are far more likely to pronounce *mave* as /meiv/ than as /mæ:v/. In essence, gang effects are a new form of analogy in which a word that is being processed is compared to a larger number of words than in traditional analogy (where it is compared to only a single word), and these words affect processing by each contributing a small amount of reinforcement to bias the system toward a certain outcome. By their very nature, gang effects are only possible if forms are stored in the lexicon, and must be present if forms are stored in the lexicon.

Gang effects may be able to account for some of the known phenomena in inflectional processing. Since gang effects are the result of interactions among lexical items, it is necessary to assume that inflected forms are stored in the lexicon in order to obtain any gang effects. Novel words can be made into, for example, a past tense form by interaction with known past tense forms in the form of gangs. The past tense form of *bick* will be *bicked* because a final /t/ is reinforced by a gang made up of past tense forms like *tricked*, *picked*, *kicked*. Note that there is no need to explicitly build in any connection between base and inflected forms such as *trick* and *tricked* to get this effect; it derives solely from the semantic and phonological similarities between different inflected forms. In Rumelhart and McClelland's (1986) computer model of the acquisition of past tense forms, they show that this is possible. They also argue that no-marking errors on regular verbs can arise through interference from gangs of irregular past tense forms. For example, their model produced a high rate of no-marking errors on the verb *kid* because of its resemblance to a gang of irregular verbs like *rid* that do not show an *-ed* in the past tense. The presence of gang effects with inflected forms requires lexical storage of inflected forms, while the absence of gang effects implies that inflected forms are created by lexical-item-free rules.

We first demonstrate experimentally that gangs of past tense forms can and do arise, and that these gangs can affect the processing of known regularly inflected forms. We begin by looking for the effect of irregular forms on regular forms. There are a number of regularly inflected forms with bases that resemble irregular forms. For example, the regular verb *spank* resembles the irregular past tense forms *drank*, *sank*, and *stank*. We would predict that an *-ank* gang would form and reinforce their shared phonological characteristics, including the absence of a final /t/. The word *spank* should thus have a high rate of errors without a final /t/, that is, of no-marking errors. There are other regular verbs which share fewer phonemes with the irregular forms that they resemble. For example, the regular verb *snore* shares only two phonemes with the irregular past tense forms *wore*, *bore*, *swore*, and *tore*. The regular verb *chew* shares only a single phoneme with the irregular past tense forms *knew*, *grew*, *flew*, *drew*, *blew*, *threw*, and *slew*. Gang effects predict that the gangs will be stronger and have greater effects on processing as a function of the number of phonemes shared by the members of a gang, given that the gangs are of roughly equal size (as they are in the examples given here). We thus predict that the rate of no-marking errors will be greatest for verbs like *spank* that share three phonemes with their gang, intermediate for verbs like *snore* that share two phonemes with their gang, and least for verbs like *chew* that share only one phoneme with their gang. Study 3 examined this question.

Study 3: Regular Verbs that Resemble Gangs of Irregulars

Three lists of verbs were made up, one for each of the types of regular verbs mentioned above. Each list contained 16 monosyllabic regular verbs that resemble irregular past tense forms, 16 regular verbs that do not resemble irregular past tense forms, 16 regular verbs that do not resemble any irregular past tense forms very closely, and 16 unrelated irregular verbs that acted as distractors; the two groups of regular verbs in each list were balanced for length and frequency. List 1 contained regular verbs that shared an average 3.1 phoemes with the members of their gang; half had the vowel /æ:/ and half had the vowel /ʌ/, and all ended in /ŋk/ (as in *spank* and *flunk*). List 2 contained regular verbs that shared an average 2.1 phonemes with the members of their gang; all had the vowel /ou/ and ended in /k/, /r/, or /z/ (as in *choke*, *snore*, and *doze*). List 3 contained regular verbs that shared an average 1.1 phonemes, with the members of their gang; all ended in /u:/ (as in *chew*). The procedure was the same as in Study 2. A different group of subjects were run on each list, all from the same subject pool as in Study 2.

No-marking errors were identified and analyzed. The error rate on each group of verbs is presented in Fig. 6.1. There were significantly more no-marking errors on verbs that resembled irregular past tense forms than on verbs that did not for those forms that shared approximately two or three phonemes with those irregular forms. There were also more no-marking errors on regular verbs that shared only one phoneme with irregular forms than on other regular verbs, but this did not reach significance. There was a significant effect of the number of phonemes shared with the irregular forms ($p < .05$), with more errors on forms that shared more phonemes. In fact, the error rate was almost a linear function of the number of shared phonemes.

To further reinforce the effect of shared phonemes, we can do a post hoc examination of the performance of the subjects who saw List 1 on other

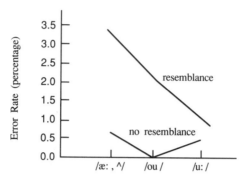

Fig. 6.1: Error rate for verbs in Study 3.

regular verbs that also had the vowels /æ:/ and /ʌ/ but shared few other phonemes with irregular forms. Each subject saw 11 such verbs, for example, *pass* and *bump*, sharing an average 1.2 phonemes with irregular forms. There were only 3 errors on these regular verbs out of 550 trials, as compared to 26 errors on the List 1 verbs out of 750 trials. This difference is significant ($\chi^2(1)$ = 12.42, p < .001). The number of shared phonemes does appear to have a great effect on error rate for regular verbs. These results are predicted by gang effects, and we have been able to devise no other explanation to account for them. (The schema hypothesis of Bybee and Slobin, 1982; and the prototype hypothesis of Bybee and Moder, 1983, cannot account for the differences in the rate of no-marking errors between the different groups of verbs, at least as currently described. See Stemberger, 1983; Stemberger and MacWhinney, 1986b, for additional arguments against these approaches.)

These data provide additional evidence that irregular inflected forms are stored in the lexicon, as the theory predicts. However, it is not particularly surprising that irregular forms are stored in the lexicon. It is of greater interest to determine whether all regularly inflected forms are stored in the lexicon. We must thus examine regular verbs that resemble regularly inflected forms. If regularly inflected forms are in general in the lexicon, then a gang effect should be present. If few regularly inflected forms are in the lexicon, then there should be no gang effect. It is relatively difficult to examine this question using past tense forms, since there are so many irregular past tense forms. We thus shift to examining third person singular present tense forms, where there are almost no irregular forms at all. Any obtained gang effects can then be due only to regularly inflected forms being stored in the lexicon. We contrast base forms that closely resemble present tense forms (as *gaze* resembles *plays*) and base forms that do not (as with *buzz* and *cross*). Gang effects predict that base forms that resemble actual inflected forms should show a greater rate of no-marking errors than forms that do not.

Study 4: Regular Verbs that Resemble Regularly Inflected Forms

A list of 90 monosyllabic English verbs was constructed. Thirty of these verbs ended in /s/ and /z/ and were designed to address the current hypothesis. The other 60 verbs ended in other segments and were designed to address other hypotheses; they are not discussed further here (but see Stemberger and MacWhinney, 1984, 1986b). Half of these closely resembled regularly inflected present tense forms and half did not. The groups were balanced for length and frequency. For the verbs that resembled actual present tense forms (e.g., *cause, coax, gaze, please*), there was an average of 3.3 present tense forms that shared at least three contiguous phonemes with them, which is comparable to the size of the gangs of irregular past tense forms in Study 3, and there was an average of 19.5 present tense forms that shared at least two contiguous phonemes. In contrast, for those verbs that did not closely resemble actual present tense forms (e.g., *buzz, force, race, toss*), there was an average of 0.3 present tense forms that shared at least three contiguous phonemes with them, and an average of 6.5 that shared at least two contiguous phonemes. These differences in gang size and the number of shared phonemes would lead us to predict a greater rate of no-marking errors on the verbs that resembled actual present tense forms.

The procedure was similar to that in Study 2, except that the frame *is ____ing* was used, and subjects produced the present tense forms of the verbs. There were 60 subjects from the same subject pool as in Study 2.

No-marking error rates on the two groups of verbs were identified and analyzed. the results are shown in (8).

(8)	Item type	Number of errors	Number of trials	Rate
	Resemblance	36	900	.040
	No resemblance	32	900	.036

The two groups of verbs show essentially identical error rates. Number of shared phonemes and gang sizes thus have no apparent effect. Gang effects are not present. Regular verbs are not penalized for physically resembling regularly inflected forms.

The lack of a gang effect here implies that regularly inflected forms are not in general stored in the lexicon. If they are stored in the lexicon, we would have obtained a gang effect. We conclude that speakers use inflectional rules instead, creating regularly inflected forms on-line during language production by adding an affix directly to the base form.

We have arrived at an apparent contradiction. In Study 2, we demonstrated, via a frequency effect, that at least high-frequency regularly inflected forms are stored in the lexicon in some fashion. In Study 4, we demonstrated, via (the lack of) a gang effect, that regularly inflected forms are not in general stored in the lexicon. This contradiction is only apparent. In point of fact, the results of the two studies are quite compatible. The results of Study 2 require only that high-frequency regularly inflected forms be stored in the lexicon and are compatible with the hypothesis that low-frequency regularly inflected forms are not stored in the lexicon. The results of Study 4, on the other hand, require that low-frequency regularly inflected forms are not stored in the lexicon but are compatible with the storage of just high-frequency regularly inflected forms. The reason for this is quite simple. There are relatively few high-frequency present tense forms that closely resemble the base forms of regular verbs. How frequent an inflected form must be before it is stored in the lexicon is unknown, but let us suppose a (probably too-low) frequency of 15 occurrences per million words. The only gang of present tense forms that could have an impact on present tense verbs that physically resemble them is made up of four verbs that end in /ouz/ (*knows, goes, shows,* and *grows*), as no other forms with a frequency over 15 are similar enough phonologically to form a strong gang. We would thus predict that resembling actual present tense forms would in general have no effect on processing, because the present tense forms that regular verbs resemble are in general too infrequent to be stored in the lexicon. We might expect a higher error rate only on verbs that end in /ouz/, since this one gang should be present in the lexicon. There is in fact a nonsignificant difference in that direction in our data, with 25.0% of the errors in the high-resemblance group occurring on such verbs, compared to 18.8% expected by chance. However, the difference is small and nonsignificant, and we did not set up our stimuli to be able to test this suggestion. This prediction should be followed up. There are too few stimuli available to test it with the present tense, but there are enough to test it with perfect forms and (marginally) with plural forms. At any rate, the results of Study 4 are problematical for the gang effect hypothesis if all regularly inflected forms are stored in the lexicon, and are compatible with it if only high-frequency regularly inflected forms are stored in the lexicon.

Discussion and Conclusion

We began by laying out three generic positions taken by researchers on the representations of inflected forms: having them stored fully suppletively, having them stored as morphologically complex lexical items or through lexically conditioned rules, and having no inflected forms stored but creating them on-line via lexical-item-free rules. Our data allow us to say that irregular forms are stored, but do not allow us to say how they are stored. However, our data require storage of high-frequency regularly inflected forms as bimorphemic or with lexically conditioned inflectional rules and require that low-frequency regularly inflected forms not be in the lexicon at all. We prefer the alternative given in (3) for high-frequency regulars, with lexically conditioned rules (see Stemberger, 1985b), but we know of no data that require it.

Given that high-frequency regularly inflected forms are stored, we can consider at what stratum they are stored in a lexical phonology framework. Irregular inflected forms are placed in Stratum 1 by Kiparsky (1982) and Halle and Mohanan (1985), while regularly inflected forms are placed on the final lexical stratum. Since high-frequency forms are explicitly listed in the lexicon, should they be at Stratum 1? Halle and Mohanan implicitly assume that this must be the case, since their analysis of engma in English requires that *longer*, *stronger*, and *younger* were placed in Stratum 1 at a historical period when they were fully regular semantically and phonologically. However, this is not possible for high-frequency past tense forms. Many of our high-frequency forms have long vowels, for example, *need*. If inflection were to take place at Stratum 1, the other rules that are posited for that stratum would give us /nɛd/, just as they give us /spɛd/ as the past tense of *speed*. Thus, regularly inflected forms are lexicalized on the final lexical stratum, not at Stratum 1. (Ramifications for Halle and Mohanan's analysis of engma are left to the reader.)

The storage of high-frequency regularly inflected forms has ramifications for compounding. Kiparsky has noted that irregular plurals can show up as the first part of a compound, but that regular plurals cannot. Sproat (1985) and Anderson (this volume) have suggested that this is because irregular forms are listed in the lexicon but regular forms are not. Our data suggest that this explanation is incorrect, since some regulars are listed. Whatever underlies this phenomenon, it cannot be the simple fact of whether something is stored or not.

We mentioned above that affix shifts (*tell-us-ing*) appear to be a postlexical phenomenon, reflecting a very late problem with the ordering of lexical items in sentences (Garrett, 1980; Stemberger, 1984). Shifts imply that high-frequency regularly inflected forms are treated as two morphemes even at this late point in processing. In lexical phonology, however, it is assumed that all inflected forms are treated as monomorphemic elements postlexically, due to the operation of Bracketing Erasure at the end of each lexical stratum. The shift data imply that there is no operation of Bracketing Erasure in language production, since the status of the affix as an independent morpheme must be preserved in order to account for the data. (Note that there are also problems for Bracketing Erasure in linguistic theory, as certain morphological phenomena such as morphological haplology require that morphological structure be maintained through all lexical strata and into the postlexical domain; see Stemberger, 1981, for relevant data.)

We note one possible problem for our approach as well. We have been assuming that the prototype effects reported by Bybee and Moder (1983) derive from gang effects, as Bybee (this volume) also assumes. Gang effects imply that the largest effects come with the greatest number of phonemes shared with the greatest number of words, but Bybee and Moder report that the greatest effect in their study was with /ʌŋ / rather than /ʌŋk/. This is counter to our predictions. Further, studies of the phonological processing of word-initial clusters in language production by Stemberger and Treiman (1986) have found that competing single consonants tend to reinforce a cluster that contains both of the consonants involved. By implication, the presence of irregular forms like *rung* and *stuck* should reinforce /ʌŋ k/ (which shares two phonemes with all the forms and contains a cluster with both /ŋ / and /k/) more than it reinforces either /ʌŋ / or /ʌk/. Bybee and Moder's morphological data thus appear to be somewhat problematical, given what we currently know about phonological processing. However, more study is needed on the phonological processing of word-final consonant clusters in language production (which could conceivably differ from word-initial clusters), as well as on these gang effects. We point out this possible difficulty, however, to emphasize the point that morphological processing cannot be studied completely separately from phonological processing. The two interact in many ways, and theories of morphological processing may fail because they are incompatible with what we know about phonological processing.

In conclusion, we have presented data that we think provide an answer to the question of whether inflected forms are stored in the lexicon. The answer is yes and no. Irregular forms appear to be stored in the lexicon, as do high-frequency regularly inflected forms. Low-frequency regularly inflected forms, which include the inflected forms of most English words, are not stored in the lexicon, however. Further study is now needed to determine whether stored inflected forms might be created in language production using lexically conditioned rules.

Acknowledgments

This research was supported by a Sloan Post-Doctoral Fellowship to Joseph Paul Stemberger while he was at CMU, and by NICHHD Grant 1-R01-HD17790 to Brian MacWhinney. The data in Studies 1 and 2 have been reported in another context in Stemberger and MacWhinney (1986a). The data in Studies 3 and 4 have been reported in other contexts in Stemberger and MacWhinney (1984, 1986b).

References

Aronoff, M. (1976). "Word Formation in Generative Grammar." MIT Press, Cambridge, MA.
Atkinson, R.C., and Shiffrin, R.M. (1968). Human memory: A proposed system and its control processes. *In* "The Psychology of Learning and Motivation" (K.W. Spence and T.J. Spence, eds.), Vol. 2. Academic Press, New York.

Bradley, D. (1980). Lexical representation of derivational relation. *In* "Juncture" (M. Aronoff and M.L. Kean, eds.). MIT Press, Cambridge, MA.

Butterworth, B. (1983). Lexical representation. *In* "Language Production: Vol. 2. Development, Writing, and Other Language Processes" (B. Butterworth, ed.), (pp. 257–294). Academic Press, London.

Bybee, J., and Moder, C. (1983). Morphological classes as natural categories. *Language* 59, 251–270.

Bybee, J., and Slobin, D.I. (1982). Rules and schemas in the development and use of the English past tense. *Language* 58, 265–289.

Francis, W.N., and Kucera, H. (1982). "Frequency Analysis of English Usage: Lexicon and Grammar." Houghton Mifflin, Boston.

Garrett, M. (1980). Levels of processing in sentence production. *In* "Language Production, Vol. 1: Speech and Talk" (B. Butterworth, ed.), (pp. 177–220). Academic Press, London.

Halle, M., and Mohanan, K.P. (1985). Segmental phonology of English. *Linguistic Inquiry* 16, 57–116.

Jackendoff, R. (1975). Morphological and semantic regularities in the lexicon. *Language* 51, 639–671.

Kempley, S.T., and Morton, J. (1982). The effect of priming with regularly and irregularly related words in auditory word recognition. *British Journal of Psychology* 73, 441–454.

Kiparsky, P. (1982). From cyclic phonology to lexical phonology. *In* "The Structure of Phonological Representations" (H. van der Hulst and N. Smith, eds.), (Part 1), pp. 130–175. Foris, Dordrecht.

Leben, W., and Robinson, O.W. (1977). Upside-down phonology. *Language* 53, 1–20.

Lukatela, G., Gligorijevic, B., Kostic, B., and Turvey, M.T. (1980). Representation of inflected nouns in the internal lexicon. *Memory and Cognition* 8, 415–423.

McClelland, J.L., and Elman, J.L. (1986). The TRACE model of speech perception. *Cognitive Psychology* 18, 1–86.

MacKay, D.G. (1976). On the retrieval and lexical structure of verbs. *Journal of Verbal Learning and Verbal Behavior* 15, 169–182.

MacKay, D.G. (1982). The problems of flexibility, fluency, and speed-accuracy trade-off in skilled behavior. *Psychological Review* 89, 483–506.

MacWhinney, B. (1978). The acquisition of morphophonology. *Monographs of the Society for Research in Child Development* 43, whole no. 1.

Peters, A.M. (1983). "The Units of Language Acquisition." Cambridge University Press, Cambridge England.

Rumelhart, D., and McClelland, J. (1982). An interactive activation model of the effect of context on perception, Part 2. *Psychological Review* 89, 60–94.

Rumelhart, D., and McClelland, J. (1986). On learning the past tenses of English verbs. *In* "Parallel Distributed Processing: Explorations in the Microstructure of Cognition (D. Rumelhart and J. McClelland, eds.), Vol. 1. Bransford, Cambridge, MA.

Sproat, R.W. (1985). *On deriving the lexicon.* Unpublished doctoral dissertation, MIT.

Stanners, R.F., Neiser, J.J., Hernon, W.P., and Hall, R. (1979). Memory representation for morphologically related words. *Journal of Verbal Learning and Verbal Behavior* 18, 399–413.

Stemberger, J.P. (1981). Morphological haplology. *Language* 57, 791–817.

Stemberger, J.P. (1983). Inflectional malapropisms: Form-based errors in English morphology. *Linguistics* 21, 573–602.

Stemberger, J.P. (1984). Structural errors in normal and agrammatic speech. *Cognitive Neuropsychology* 1, 281–313.

Stemberger, J.P. (1985a). Bound morpheme loss errors in normal and agrammatic speech: One mechanism or two? *Brain & Language* 25, 246–256.

Stemberger, J.P. (1985b). An interactive activation model of language production. *In* "Progress in the Psychology of Language" (A. Ellis, ed.), Vol. 1. Erlbaum, London.

Stemberger, J.P., and MacWhinney, B. (1984). Extrasyllabic consonants in CV phonology: An experimental test. *Journal of Phonetics* 12, 355–366.

Stemberger, J.P., and MacWhinney, B. (1986a). Frequency and the lexical storage of regularly inflected words. *Memory and Cognition* **14**, 17–26.

Stemberger, J.P., and MacWhinney, B. (1986b). Form-oriented inflectional errors in language processing. *Cognitive Psychology* **18**, 329–354.

Stemberger, J.P., and Treiman, R. (1986). The internal structure of word-initial consonant clusters. *Journal of Memory and Language* **25**, 163–180.

Walsh, T., and Parker, F. (1983). The duration of morphemic and nonmorphemic /s/ in English. *Journal of Phonetics* **11**, 201–206.

Part II

Rules and Representations

Chapter 7

Morphology As Lexical Organization

Joan L. Bybee

Most current conceptions of the apparatus behind linguistic behavior postulate separate components for rules and representations. Representations are static and fixed, the individual and idiosyncratic content of the morphology, while the rules are the "moving parts," the dynamic, the general statements that range over the representations. In the years of intensive research into the structure and domain of morphological and phonological rules since the mid-1960s, it has become apparent that many different types of rules exist and that they differ from one another in their freedom of application. Current work in modeling phonology and morphology attempts to adjust and divide the rule component in various ways in order to describe differences among rule types. Leaving aside autosegmental phenomena, representations and their properties have been the subject of interest only to the extent that they feed into the rules, which means that their form must be adjusted as rules and their mode of application are changed. This chapter takes a different perspective on representations, focusing on the lexicon directly and approaching rules as generalizations that arise from representations.

Among the descriptive frameworks for morphology utilized in the twentieth century, the one that has enjoyed the longest popularity and the widest application is the Item and Process (IP) model, currently best known as developed in generative phonology. The defining characteristic of an IP model is that it sets up one underlying form for alternating allomorphs and derives the surface forms by applying feature-changing rules to the underlying form (Hockett, 1954). Consider the stem vowel alteration in the present indicative of the following Spanish verbs, which are representative of a large lexical class of verbs:

Theoretical Morphology Copyright © 1988 by Academic Press, Inc.
All rights of reproduction in any form reserved.   119

(1)   'to begin'   'to tell, to count'
  1sg *empiézo*   1p   *empezámos*   1sg *cuénto*   1pl *contámos*
  2sg *empiézas* 2pl *empezáis*   2sg *cuentas*   2pl *contáis*
  3sg *empiéza*   3pl *empiézan*   3sg *cuénta*   3pl *cuéntan*

The stem has two forms in each case, *empiez-*, *empez-*, and *cuent-*, *cont-*; the choice is usually regarded as conditioned by the position of the stress. In an IP model, the stem is represented in the lexicon as a single form—either one of the surface alternants or a third form which does not occur on the surface but from which both alternants may be derived. Each verb has only one representation in the lexical component, and a series of rules in a separate component change the features in this underlying form to generate all the surface variants.

In contrast to the IP model, the Item and Arrangement (IA) model (which enjoyed some popularity during the 1940s and 1950s) would list all surface stem alternants, for example, *empiez-*, *empez-*, *cuent-*, *cont-*, in the lexicon and include with them a rule which states the distribution of each alternant (see Hockett, 1954). A third model, called the Word and Paradigm (WP) model, is a formalization of the intuition behind traditional grammar, which chooses the word (rather than the stem) as the unit of lexical representation and includes in the lexicon a full listing of paradigms (Matthews, 1972).

The main advantage of the IP model over the other two is that it allows the lexicon to contain a much smaller set of items, since the IA model must list all alternants and the WP model must list all words.[1] It is also sometimes argued (Kiparsky, 1968) that the IP model is superior because it allows alternations to be described in terms of very general rules that apply to many instances of the same alternation, while the IA model (in its early versions) requires a separate statement for each instance of an alternation.[2]

The IP model is the most used and the most extensively elaborated of these descriptive models, but it has also been subject to criticism. The major criticisms that have been leveled against it in its generative version are that it fails to distinguish between productive and nonproductive alternations, between morphologically and phonetically conditioned alternations, and that it allows underlying forms to differ too radically from the surface forms (Kiparsky, 1968; Vennemann, 1972, 1974; Hooper, 1976a; Hudson, 1980, etc.). Various refinements of the basic model have been proposed which introduce

---

[1] There seems to have been the feeling in the descriptive frameworks that lead to the IP model that a smaller number of lexical listings was preferable because it made for a simpler and more elegant description. This notion that the lexicon must be small and simple is disappearing as linguists realize the extent of lexical idiosyncrasy, especially in morphological and syntactic properties. Moreover, considering the enormous storage capacity of the human brain, there is no reason to insist on a small lexicon.

[2] Of course, it is not impossible to formulate a version of the IA model that allows general statements regarding the distribution of allomorphs (Hudson, 1980).

these distinctions and constrain the relation between surface and underlying forms.

Despite the extensive investigations of the relation of the IP model to natural language data, and the many proposed constraints and refinements, there are still certain basic facts about the organization of morphological systems in the languages of the world that cannot even be described in an IP model of morphology, much less predicted or explained. These facts cannot be dismissed on the grounds that they are evidence from performance, for while some of the evidence does involve the results of psycholinguistic experimentation and child language acquisition, this evidence points in the same direction as the evidence from sources accepted even by those who wish to maintain a distinction between performance and competence, that is, evidence from synchronic distribution, historical change, and language universals.[3] In response to this accumulation of evidence against the IP model, I argue that the problem lies in IP's most fundamental tenet—that item and process are two distinct and discrete components of the description. I argue instead that the best exemplar of a rule and the best exemplar of a representation are two poles of a continuum, and that some rules have properties we associate with representations while some representations bear a resemblance to rules.[4] I propose some features of a model which can account for the rule-like nature of human language without forcing unnatural dichotomies.

1. Facts about Morphology That IP Models Neglect

It has often been pointed out that IP models have no way of representing paradigms, since each word of a paradigm is derived independently from an underlying form that may not correspond to any particular form of the paradigm. This would not be a serious problem were it not for the fact that some very strong cross-linguistic generalizations, as well as some significant tendencies in historical change and child language, can only be predicted in terms of paradigmatic relations. Here are some of the facts that an IP model misses because of its inherent structure:

First, the semantically least-marked forms of a paradigm are usually the morphologically least marked and usually have the highest text frequency. These unmarked forms are basic to the paradigm in the sense that children

---

[3]Theoreticians may limit the scope of their theories in whatever way they wish and thus ignore some sources of evidence which another theory may utilize. However, I see no reason to limit linguistic theories to theories of knowledge (or competence) when theories that integrate knowledge and use are within our grasp.

[4]In an IP model, a lexical representation may be thought of as a very specific rule, a rule that rewrites a semantic representation as a phonological one. This idea gets to the same basic point that I argue below, but I approach the question from the other direction.

learn them earliest and then use them to create the more marked forms. Moreover, the "analogical leveling" of diachronic change is the remaking of a more marked form using the less marked form as a base (Vennemann, 1972; Mańczak, 1980; Hooper, 1979; Bybee, 1985).

Second, there are differing degrees of relatedness among the forms of a paradigm, depending on their semantic relations. For instance, the second and third singular forms of a present tense are more closely related to one another than each is to the same person form in a past tense. These differential relations are reflected in formal differentiation—the distribution of allomorphy as well as the propensity for one form to condition the restructuring of another in diachronic change (Hooper, 1979; Bolozky, 1980; Bybee and Pardo, 1981; Bybee, 1985).

A third set of questions for which IP morphology offers no account concerns the relative productivity of morphological and morphophonemic rules. Why are some rules more productive—better able to apply to new forms— than others? How does the extant set of forms a rule applies to determine its ability to apply to new forms? To what extent are nonce formations predictable? In an IP model these questions are not answerable, since a rule is structurally the same whether it applies to three forms, thirty, or three hundred.[5]

A fourth set of issues has to do with deviations from the one-to-one correspondence between meaning and form. An IP model takes the lack of allomorphy to be the simplest case: The combinatory rules can concatenate underlying forms and no processes need apply. The complications and the major work of the "processes" come about because of allomorphy. In such a model, unless allomorphic variation is phonologically motivated, it has no motivation whatever, and it is treated as though its occurrence were random. Such a model fails to describe a whole set of predictable phenomena: that stem allomorphy tends to follow the lines of major morphological categories and cut across minor categories (see Section 5); that irregularities tend to be greater in number in unmarked members of categories (in both stem and affix) (Greenberg, 1966); that allomorphy and suppletion are more likely in frequent lexical items than in infrequent ones. None of these generalizations can be stated in current versions of IP representation, nor can such a model explain why allomorphy persists over time rather than being eliminated rapidly.

The foregoing are a few reasons for entertaining thoughts about new and different models of representing morphology; these are important facts that

---

[5]Structural differences in rules, e.g., whether they contain a diacritic or a morphological feature, may correspond to some extent to productivity, since phonetically conditioned, transparent rules are usually productive, while morphologically conditioned rules are often not. But this correspondence is not direct enough to be predictive. For instance, the English vowel change rules for past tense would be structurally similar in an IP treatment, yet some of them (i.e., *string–strung*) are more productive than others (e.g., *bite–bit*).

can perhaps be represented more directly in a different sort of model. In addition I argue that there is motivation for rejecting the IP model specifically because of its major premise, which has gone completely unquestioned for decades: that rules and representations are discrete and distinct elements of the grammar. It is this point to which I now turn.

2. Rules and Representations

Morphological and morphophonemic rules cover the full range of types, from extremely productive and general (e.g., the suffixation of -*ing* to form participles and gerunds in English), to semiproductive (e.g., the "rule" which produces past forms such as *stung*, which sometimes applies to new forms), to minor rules (such as that governing the voicing alternation in *wives, leaves*, and so on), to "rules" dealing with admitted irregularities (such as *bring, brought*), and finally to suppletion (exemplified by *go, went*). The productive and general rules are the most independent of the representations to which they apply, but as we go down the scale, more and more information about particular representations has to be built into the rule. Thus a rule that applies to a particular lexical class (such as the class of nouns that has a final fricative that voices in the plural) must contain some particular signal—a diacritic feature or a phonological feature used as a diacritic—to match it with the particular representations to which it applies and prevent it from applying to forms which do not undergo the alternation (e.g., nouns such as *chief*). In other words, part of the representation has to be built into the rule. And of course, so-called rules governing suppletion are nothing more than representations.

A characteristic of alternations that are lexically and morphologically restricted is that they usually are not extendable to new lexical items. Consider the vowel alternations in Spanish verbs illustrated in (1). This diphthong/mid vowel alternation resulted from the diphthongization of lax mid vowels in stressed syllables, but this process is no longer phonetically conditioned in Spanish (indeed, the lax vowels that produced the diphthongs no longer exist). The alternation is usually approached as a problem in verb derivation. Although a large number of verbs undergo these alternations, there is also a large number of verbs that have nonalternating mid vowels, for example, *comer* 'to eat' with 1sg *cómo*, and *aprender* 'to learn' with 1sg *apréndo*. If in a generative treatment the mid vowel is taken as the underlying vowel, then it must be marked with a diacritic, since some mid vowels do not alternate (Harris, 1969). On the other hand, the diphthong could be taken as underlying, since there are very few verbs with a nonalternating diphthong, and these are all derived verbs, for example, *amueblar* 'to furnish' from *muebles* 'furniture' and *aviejar* 'to grow old' from *viejo* 'old.' This would suggest that a rule "a diphthong becomes a mid vowel in an unstressed syllable" could be formulated, and indeed an IP treatment along these lines could be made to work. However, additional facts indicate that these alternations are highly lexically restricted, that is, dependent upon the particular items to which they apply, and not extendable to new items.

Kernan and Blount (1966) used a nonce-probe task to test adult speakers of Mexican Spanish on the productivity of these alternations. They presented their subjects with a nonce form such as *suécha* in a context where it was clear that it was a 3sg of the present indicative, and then they asked the subjects to use it in a preterite context, where the stem is unstressed, so that the expected response is *sochó*, based on the rule stated above and the recurrent alternation pattern. However, their subjects uniformly answered *suechó*, producing a form which not only ignores the rule, but which also has an unstressed diphthong, which occurs only rarely in Spanish.

In Bybee and Pardo (1981) we tried even harder to get Spanish speakers to apply the rule. In our nonce-probe task, we presented nonce verbs in both diphthong and mid vowel alternates (e.g., *sochár* and *suécha*), but despite this very clear indication that the alternation exists for the nonce verb, in 25% of the responses the subjects produced a diphthong in an unstressed syllable. My interpretation of these results is that the rule governing these alternations is not independent of the existing lexical forms to which it applies. In some sense it is not a rule at all, but more a part of the representation of certain verbs.

Even rules that seem more independent, that is, that apply to new or nonce forms, have to emerge in acquisition from representations. In order to acquire rules, the child must extract them from the comparison of sets of related forms, which are entered in the mental lexicon. Studies by MacWhinney (1978) and Peters (1983) indicate that rule-like generalizations gradually emerge from stored rote forms, which are initially processed and stored as unanalyzed wholes.

Other evidence suggests that even though certain generalizations, especially over subregularities such as the English strong verbs, are recognized at some level by speakers, the generation of strong verb past tense forms is by lexical access rather than by feature-changing rule. We reported in Bybee and Slobin (1982) that experimentally induced errors involving vowel changes for past tense result in almost all cases not in the production of nonce forms such as the past tense of *heap* as **hept*, but rather in the replacement of one pre-existing word for another, usually within the same semantic domain. Thus in 91% of the cases the wrong vowel-change response was a real English word; in 80% of the cases it was not only a real word, but also a verb; in 75% of the cases it was a past tense form of a semantically related verb. For instance, the past tense of *raise* was given as *rose*, the past of *seat* as *sat*, of *search* as *sought* (Bybee and Slobin, 1982).[6] These errors can only be explained by postulating that the production of strong verb past tense forms is a matter of accessing the lexicon rather than applying a rule to a base form to change the vowel.

These considerations lead to the conception of a model in which morphological rules and lexical representations are not separate from one another. Rather, morphological and morphophonemic rules are patterns that emerge from the intrinsic organization of the lexicon. Patterns that range over large numbers of lexical items are highly reinforced or strengthened and apply more readily to new items, while patterns that are found in a smaller number of items are correspondingly weaker and less apt to be productive. Thus the difference between major productive rules, minor rules, and suppletion is just a matter of degree, not a matter of qualitative difference.

The model I am proposing does not have a lexicon and a morphological component as separate compartments of the grammar. Rather the model has only a lexicon. The morphological facts of natural language are described in terms of independently necessary mechanisms of lexical storage: the ability to form networks among stored elements of knowledge and the ability to register the frequency of individual items and patterns. I discuss these mechanisms and their interactions under the headings of LEXICAL CONNECTION and LEXICAL STRENGTH.

3. Lexical Connections

It is uncontroversial that stored knowledge is organized, and that the lexicon is storage governed by multiple and diverse organizational patterns. Chief among these are semantic parameters by which morphemes are associated. Morphemes are connected via the semantic field they belong in (such as verbs for cooking, *boil, fry, roast, bake*), by the scripts they participate in (such as the restaurant script), by relations such as synonymy, antonymy, hyponymy (the relation between *rose* and *flower*), and many others.

Similarly, phonological connections exist among stored forms. The evidence for this is that we have a certain amount of access to the lexicon via the phonological shape of words: We can list words with particular initial segments; we can list words that rhyme; we can list words with a particular stress or tone pattern and a certain number of syllables. Some sort of phonological mapping function is required for speech perception, and speech

---

[6] Out of 46 errors, only three were nonwords: *hept* (as the past of *heap*), *snoze* (as the past of *snooze*), and *glew* (as the past of *glow*).

errors and punning behavior show that associations based on phonological similarity are accessible.

In this model, morphologically complex items are stored in the lexicon, and I refer to them as "words" although it is conceivable that some may be larger than traditional words, and some may be smaller, and there may even be typological differences among languages regarding the size of the lexical unit. Each lexical word is a pairing of a set of semantic features with a set of phonological features. Relations among words are set up according to shared features. For instance, the close relation between *dog* and *puppy*, shown in (2), can be derived from the fact that the semantic representations of these items have many of the same features. In fact, the semantic representation of the one can partially map onto the other. We may represent this as proximity in the lexicon, or, with the notation I have adopted here, as connecting nodes from one feature to the other. In the diagrams where phonological features are connected, for simplicity I have used solid lines to indicate that all features of two segments are identical, and broken lines to indicate that only some features are identical.

(2)

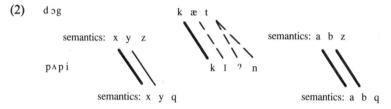

The pair *cat* and *kitten* have a similar semantic relation, since they share all features common to the species, but the latter term is restricted to the young of the species. A number of connections relate the semantic features of *cat* and *kitten*, and in addition, some connections exist between their phonological representations, since they share an initial consonant /k/, a front vowel, and an alveolar consonant. Now *kitten* and *puppy* are also semantically related, since they both designate the young of similar species, and they bear a phonological relation to one another also, since they both consist of a stressed obstruent–vowel–obstruent syllable, followed by an unstressed syllable. We could go on and show how the number of relations quickly multiplies and defies visual representation, except perhaps as something that resembles a bowl of spaghetti.

However, things are not entirely spaghetti-like. Sets of connections that parallel one another by running between the same two items may accumulate to form connections of varying strength, depending on the number of features connected, and in some cases on the content of the features.

Sets of connections such as those between *cat* and *kitten* are the basis of morphological analysis and morphological relations, for morphological relations are semantic and phonological connections that run in parallel. Consider the word *cats*. It forms both a semantic and a phonological connection with the singular form *cat* as shown in (3).

(3)

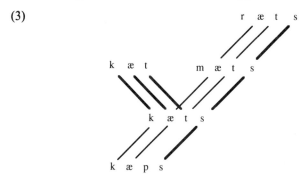

It also forms connections with other plurals, such as *mats*, *nats*, *laps*, *naps*, *tips*, *mits*, and so on, on the basis of the shared semantic feature plural and the identity of the final fricative. Thus where semantic and phonological connections coincide exactly, morphological identity can be established. This is drawn in (3), where parallel semantic and phonological connections are indicated by darkened lines, and connections that are only phonological are indicated with lighter lines.

In explicating this model, I first show how phenomena associated with the segmentation of words into morphemes are accounted for and argue that this model resolves a number of traditional problems in this area. I then introduce the notion of LEXICAL STRENGTH and the range of phenomena associated with this concept. Finally I return to the question of morphological rules and show how what appears to be rule-like behavior can be derived strictly from relations among representations.

4. Segmentation

Consider now the actual process by which we, both as speakers and linguists, discover that a word consists of more than one morpheme: We find a relation of phonological and semantic identity or similarity between some subpart of the word and a subpart of another word. This process is represented quite directly in this model: As shown in (3), *cats* forms connections with *cat*, as well as other plurals. The learning process involved here is very simple: When a new morphologically complex word is learned, it forms connections with existing lexical material on the basis of its meaning and phonological shape. The word is not physically dismembered, but its parts are nonetheless identified.

There are two major advantages to this method of representing segmentation. The first, which I have already mentioned, is that the mechanisms used, that is, the ability to form phonological and semantic associations among lexical elements, are necessary in any case, and probably differ little from the mechanisms used in storing nonlinguistic information. The second is that this model allows us to describe morphological relations in a gradient fashion, which accommodates the description of phenomena that must be ignored in an IP model.

The traditional definition of a morpheme as the smallest meaningful unit makes constancy of meaning the major criterion for identification of morphemes. In the ideal case, all the phonetic material in an utterance can be assigned to one meaningful unit or another. In such a case the semantic and phonological connections run parallel. But not all linguistic material is organized in this fashion. Deviations have been discussed for decades, for instance, the famous *cranberry* morph which results when *berry* is segmented from *cran*. Of course, this particular problem was solved by the makers of cranapple juice, but the general dilemma remains. Consider the days of the week: *Monday, Tuesday, Wednesday*, and so on all have the morpheme *day* in them, but what do *Mon, Tues, Wednes*, mean? With lexical connections we can associate the *day* sequence in these words with each other and the word *day* without requiring that the remainder of the word be meaningful. Rather the first syllable remains as a part of the whole word, but it has no connections to other items.[7]

Similarly, the formatives of generative grammar, such as the *-ceive* and *-cep-* of *receive, reception, deceive, deception* which Aronoff (1976, pp. 10–15) argues have formal behavior that identifies them as significant units, even if they are not meaningful, can be given some status in this model. *Deceive* is related to *deception* and *receive* to *reception* by both semantic and phonological connections. *Deceive* and *receive* are connected phonologically and by the fact that they are both verbs. Similarly, *deception* and *reception* are related phonologically and by the fact that they are both nominalizations. The semantic connections are weak between *deceive* and *receive* and *deception* and *reception*, but the phonological connections are strong.

Closely related to the *ceive* phenomena are phonaesthemes and other submorphemic units. In English there are sets of words with the same initial cluster that have a general semantic feature in common, such as having to do with the nose, in the case of *sneeze, snore, snort, sniff, sniffle, snivel, snoot, snout, snot*, and so on; or movement through air, as in the case of *flit, fly, flutter, fling*. These words may be connected phonologically in their initial clusters

---

[7] The sequence *Wednes* would seem to be perfect example of a uniquely occurring morph. However, I recently discovered that there is a town in England named *Wednesbury* and another called *Wednesfield*!

and semantically through one particular property. The relative weakness of such relations is due to the general nature of the semantic connection, as well as to the fact that the part of the word not involved in the connection is not meaningful, nor does it enter into any connections of its own. Phonaesthemes cannot be awarded any status in an IP model, nor can *cranberry* morphs. Formatives, such as *ceive*, can only be given status by relaxing the definition of the basic unit so that it need not be meaningful. The current model allows the description of the full range of phenomena and also allows for differential status according to whether both semantic and phonological connections are made, and how strong these connections are.

5. Degree of Relatedness

This model also allows a way of grading relations among words, so that we may say that certain pairs of words are more closely related than others. DEGREE OF RELATEDNESS is determined by the number of phonological and semantic connections. Why do we need a notion "degree of relatedness"? A series of experiments by Derwing and Baker (1977) shows that speakers can consistently rank pairs of words for semantic and phonological relatedness. In another experimental paradigm (Stanners *et al.*, 1979), the recognition of particular words can be speeded up more by priming with a closely related word than with a more distantly related one. For instance, *walked* increases the speed of recognition of *walk* more than *deception* increases the speed of recognition of *deceive*.

These experimental results point to the same conclusion as does the range of diachronic and cross-linguistic facts which I present in detail in Bybee (1985). There I argue further that it is not just the number of connections between forms that determines the degree of relatedness, but that the degree of relatedness can vary according to the semantic features involved.

If we consider first just words related through a shared stem, and in particular, inflectional paradigms, we can identify varying degrees of semantic relatedness depending on the meaning of the affix category. Some inflectional categories affect the meaning of the whole word more than others and thus produce forms that are less closely related semantically to the base form. As an example, consider the verbal category of aspect compared to person agreement with the subject. Aspect affects the meaning of the verb more, since it modifies the "internal temporal constituency" of the event or state described by the verb (Comrie, 1976). In fact, a change in aspect can produce quite a difference in the event described by the verb. Consider the example of the Spanish preterite/imperfect distinction, which is an aspectual distinction. The verb meaning 'sleep' in the preterite, *durmió* 's/he slept,' describes a completed event, which includes falling asleep and sleeping. The imperfect *dormía* translates approximately as 's/he was sleeping,' implying a state someone was in when something else occurred. For some verbs this aspectual distinction is large enough to produce distinctions that are expressed by separate verbs in another language. For instance, the preterite of the Spanish verb *saber* 'to know' translates into English as 'found out.'

Now compare aspect to person agreement. The function of agreement is to index the participants in the state or event described by the verb and has nothing to do with the inherent meaning of the verb. Two verb forms that differ only by person are much the same semantically if their tense, aspect, and mood are the same. The semantic differences produced by person markers are not the type that would be expressed by entirely different verbs. Thus such forms are more closely related than forms that differ in aspect.

Degree of relatedness is diagrammed by morphophonemic alternations: The more closely related two forms are semantically, the more likely they are to be similar morphophonemically. This means, for example, that stem changes in verbs are more likely to distinguish aspects or tenses than to distinguish person forms across aspects or tenses. Thus in Spanish there is a set of irregular verbs that have stem changes for the preterite aspect. The verb *saber* 'to know' has the 3sg preterite form *supo*, as shown in (4); similarly *tener* 'to have' has the 3sg preterite form *tuvo*; *querer* 'to want' has the 3sg preterite form *quiso*, and so on.

(4)   Imperfect 'knew'   Preterite 'found out'

1sg	*sabía*	1pl	*sabíamos*	1sg	*supe*	1pl	*supimos*
2sg	*sabías*	2pl	*sabíais*	2sg	*supiste*	2pl	*supisteis*
3sg	*sabía*	3pl	*sabían*	3sg	*supo*	3pl	*superion*

These irregular stems occur throughout the preterite person forms, and thus set off the preterite from the present and imperfect. On the other hand, there are no stem changes in Spanish that set off, for example, all first person forms in all aspects and tenses from all other person forms. Indeed, the hypothesis is that such a situation would be very rare. This hypothesis has been tested on a sample of 50 unrelated languages and was not disconfirmed. On the contrary, it was found that stem alternations of consonants or vowels are extremely frequent where aspectual distinctions are concerned and extremely rare where person distinctions are concerned (Hooper, 1979).

There are two mechanisms behind this cross-linguistic pattern, one of which concerns the order of affixes. First, since aspect (and other categories that affect the meaning of the verb more) tend to occur closer to the verb stem than agreement affixes, they are more likely to produce phonological alternations in the stem. Second, when morphophonemic alternations are eliminated in analogical leveling, this takes place preferentially among more closely related forms, often leaving alternations intact in less closely related forms. Thus a leveling is more likely to occur among person–number forms of the same aspect or tense, than among forms in different aspects or tenses.

Further evidence for a hierarchical ranking among grammatical categories is the distribution of forms in suppletive or split paradigms. When inflectional paradigms split and realign, forming suppletive paradigms, the splits occur more often among forms that are less closely related semantically, than among forms that are more closely related. Rudes (1980) studied suppletive verbal paradigms in a large number of languages and found that splits occur in general along aspect or tense lines, as with *go* and *went*, and along person agreement lines only in the present tense, the most frequent tense. (The relation between frequency and suppletion is discussed in the following two sections.)

To summarize, the degree of relatedness among words is primarily determined by the number and type of semantic features shared. The degree of phonological similarity often parallels the degree of semantic relatedness.

6. Lexical Strength

The other theoretical construct that I propose for the lexicon that distinguishes this model from an IP lexicon, or even a WP lexicon, allows for the gradient representation of lexical strength. Previously the lexicon has been conceived of as the mental counterpart of a dictionary, a list of forms set down once and for all. I propose a more dynamic representation in which not all forms have the same status, but rather in which forms are affected by use or disuse. Frequently used forms gain in lexical strength and forms that are not used lose lexical strength. Lexical strength, then, is an index of word frequency, and the main reason for proposing the introduction of this notion into a model of the lexicon is to account for the psycholinguistic, historical, and cross-linguistic effect of frequency on morphology.[8]

One of the strongest and best-known effects on lexical access is the word-frequency effect. In various sorts of tasks, words that are more frequent are more quickly accessed or recognized. This alone is enough reason to build an index of frequency into a model of the lexicon. But there is also plenty of evidence outside of experimental contexts that frequency is an important dimension in the lexicon and in morphology. Most of this evidence is well known, but it has been ignored in models that emphasized rules and paid less attention to representations.

[8]For the moment, it is sufficient to define lexical strength as based solely on token frequency, but I would like to leave open the possibility that other factors may be involved. If lexical strength is based only on frequency, then it is not equivalent to the notion of "autonomy" as used in Zager (1982), Bybee and Brewer (1980), and Bybee (1985).

First, we need a notion of lexical strength to account for the maintenance of irregularity and suppletion in high-frequency forms. Conversely, the proposal that infrequently used forms fade accounts for the tendency to regularize infrequent irregular forms, for an irregular form that is not sufficiently reinforced will be replaced by a regular formation. The correlation of irregularity with high frequency can be documented in almost any language, but the historical mechanism behind the correlation is also easily demonstrated. For instance, as I pointed out in Hooper (1976b), the average frequency of a past tense Old English strong verb that has remained strong is more than 20 times greater than the average frequency of a strong verb that has regularized.

Second, lexical strength accounts for the tendency for lexical and inflectional splits to occur more often among high-frequency words. Lexical split describes the diachronic process by which previously related words lose their morphological relatedness as the originally derived word takes on a nonpredictable semantic representation. In a study of words with the prefix *pre-* in English, Pagliuca (1976) found a strong correlation between the frequency of the prefixed word and loss of a transparent semantic and phonological relation to its nonprefixed base. This cannot be accounted for in a model in which all words with the same affix are derived in exactly the same way. It requires a model in which a particular word, despite its morphological complexity, can be autonomous and develop semantic and phonological peculiarities. The same argument applies to inflectional splits, which, as is well known, occur only among the most frequent lexical items.

7. The Interaction of Lexical Strength and Lexical Connection

Lexical strength interacts with lexical connection in some very interesting ways. The first interaction we consider concerns what I have called elsewhere the BASIC/DERIVED RELATION. There is considerable historical evidence that speakers construct unidirectional relationships (or lexical connections) between morphologically related stem forms in such a way that the semantically unmarked or basic form is also morphophonologically basic (Watkins, 1962; Vennemann, 1972; Bybee and Brewer, 1980; Bybee, 1985). To give only the simplest sort of example, consider the potential regularization of a verb such as *creep* or *weep*. In these verbs, the vowels [iy] and [ε] alternate. In order for the verb to regularize, the alternation must be eliminated, that is, the same vowel must occur in base and past tense forms. As is well known, there is no question about which vowel will prevail: it is always the [iy] of the base form, not the [ε] of the past form. The reason for this is that the regularization takes place precisely because the irregular past form is either not represented in the lexicon or is extremely weak, while the base form is stronger.

An inability to access the irregular past tense form leads to the formation of a regular past form.

Cross-linguistic evidence for an asymmetrical relation among forms can be found in the prevalence of zero-marking in semantically basic forms of a paradigm, and non-zero marking in semantically complex forms. Such marking gives evidence that one form, the stronger form, is autonomous—not analyzable in terms of other forms—while the remaining forms of a paradigm may be stored and analyzed in relation to that basic form.

I describe this asymmetrical relation in the following way: Words are acquired and stored much as other types of knowledge, by integration with knowledge already stored. A word that is morphologically simple and highly frequent is likely to be acquired more or less independently of other words and may also be acquired earlier than other related words. The more complex related words of lower frequency are learned and stored in terms of the simpler, more basic words that are already present in the lexicon. In (5) strength is indicated by a boldface representation.

(5)

The continued frequency imbalance between the two forms will maintain the dependent relation of the more complex form on the simpler one.

It is not clear whether token frequency or morphological basicness is the main factor in establishing the directionality of such relationships. Evidence exists for both positions. In word-recognition experiments on Serbo-Croatian nouns, Lukatela *et al.* (1980) found that the least-marked form, the nominative singular, has the shortest response time even in paradigms where it does not have the highest token frequency. They argue for a satellite-entry model in which the basic form of a paradigm is the nucleus entry about which other forms cluster, which resembles in some respects the proposal I am making here.

On the other hand, Tiersma's (1982) paper on local markedness shows that frequency is an important factor in determining what is conceived of as the basic form. Tiersma discusses a number of interesting examples in which the semantically marked form serves as the basis of morphophonological regularization. For example, vowel alternations between singular/plural pairs in Frisian usually regularize with the use of the vowel of the singular for both forms, but a small set of nouns shows the opposite directionality—the vowel of the plural comes to be used in the singular. However, as Tiersma argues, these are all nouns in which the plural is more frequent than the singular, nouns that refer to objects that ordinarily appear in pairs or groups, for example, *arm, goose, horn* (of an animal), *stocking, tooth, splinter, thorn, tear.* For these nouns the plural is stronger than the singular. (See also Bybee, 1985, pp. 74–77.)

Lexical strength determines the directionality of morphological relations in the sense that the weaker words are learned and stored in terms of related stronger words. The more frequent words, even if they could be analyzed and stored in terms of other words, may be strong enough to be stored separately and may thus serve as the basis for innovations. A notion of lexical strength, then, is able to account for the basic/derived relation as well as local markedness. Moreover, lexical strength allows us to explain why irregularity and suppletion are characteristic of more frequent items. It allows us to explain how suppletion develops: if a form, even a morphologically complex one like *went* when it was the past tense of *wend*, can have its own representation, it can grow in frequency independently of *wend*, and gradually undergo a generalization of meaning that allies it semantically with *go*.

8. Affixes and Morphological "Rules"

In the diagrams presented so far, it can be seen that affixes are represented lexically, attached to their hosts, and that affixes form phonological and semantic connections with other instances of the same affix. What are represented as affixation rules in other models are in this model patterns of connections, such as that shown in (6) for the present participle suffix of English.

(6)

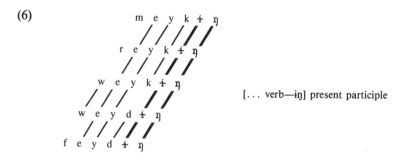

[... verb—iŋ] present participle

The same type of representation may be used for patterns that consist of internal changes in the stem rather than affixes. Diagram (7) shows a fragment of the pattern for the semiproductive strong verb class whose prototype is *strung*. In Bybee and Moder (1983) we showed that this class is fairly productive, given certain phonological features of the stem, including both the final and initial consonants.

(7)

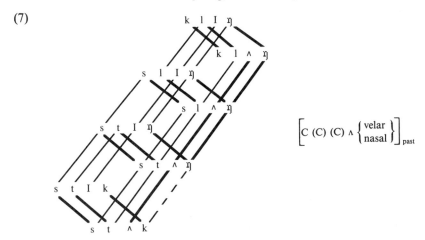

$$\left[C \ (C) \ (C) \ \wedge \left\{ \begin{array}{l} \text{velar} \\ \text{nasal} \end{array} \right\} \right]_{\text{past}}$$

I am suggesting, then, that what are usually thought of as morphological rules do not have a representation that is independent of the lexical items to which they are applicable. Rather, rules are highly reinforced representational patterns or schemas (Bybee and Slobin, 1982; Bybee and Moder, 1983). A schema may be thought of as an abstraction from existing lexical forms which share one or more semantic properties. The schema contains the features most strongly represented (i.e., represented most often) in existing forms in their positions of occurrence. Since the schema resembles a prototype, matching of form to schema works on a family resemblance basis rather than a categorical basis. Schemas may be complex, with some features being more strongly represented than others. Thus a schema may range over several allomorphs of the same morpheme, if the allomorphs have features in common. For example, the English plural suffix allomorphs may all be represented together, with the features that [s] and [z] share as the most strongly represented, the feature of voicing less strong and the features of the reduced vowel [ɨ] weaker still. While linguists today tend to think of schemas as being abstracted from lexical forms and stored in a separate component, I suggest that the evidence points toward schemas as tied ultimately to the forms from which they arise.

The tie to the lexicon is clearer for some schemas than for others. In particular, the schema that applies to fewer forms shows more evidence of being tied to the lexicon than the schema that applies to a large number of forms. The general, widely applicable morphological schemas (what are usually called "rules"), such as the regular suffixation for English past tense, appear to be free of the lexicon in the sense that they apply readily to new forms. In fact, such cases would appear to be qualitatively different from lexically restricted patterns because in acquisition they show real independence from particular lexical items. The usual sequence of acquisition for the English past tense is assumed to provide the strongest evidence that morphological rules are independent of the lexicon. This sequence of developments is as follows: In the first stage in which children produce past tense forms, they often produce the high-frequency, irregular forms, such as *went, came,* and *took,* correctly, as well as regulars, such as *looked.* In the second stage, however, they tend to regularize all past forms, producing *goed, comed,* and *taked.* This stage gives evidence for the formation of a rule, since forms are produced that are not present in the input. A third stage involves the correct relearning of the irregular form and the acquisition of the adult system.

Rumelhart and McClelland (1986) demonstrate that our assumption that this sequence of events can only be accounted for by positing the formation of explicit rules is erroneous. Rumelhart and McClelland used a parallel distributed processing model to simulate the acquisition of the English past tense. Their model and simulation did not involve the full problem of lexical storage, but only the problem with which we are concerned at the moment— the formation of rule-like patterns based on phonological features.

The main part of the model that interests us here is called the PATTERN ASSOCIATOR. The pattern associator contains two pools of units, which are phonological units of a type that I do not explain here. One pool of units is for the input and the other for the output. In this case, the input is the base form of a verb and the output is a past tense form. The pattern associator contains a modifiable connection linking each input unit to each output unit. Learning in this model involves modifying the weights of these connections. The model is given the base form of a verb and the target, which is the past form. From the base form, the model computes the past form it would generate, given the current connection strengths. It then compares its answer with the target and makes adjustments of the weights of the connections accordingly.

Rumelhart and McClelland simulated the learning of English past tense forms by supplying the model with verbs in a way that at least grossly duplicates the way verbs come into the child's system. For the learning trials they used a total of 420 English verbs, of which 20% were irregular. To begin with, they used the 10 most frequent verbs, presenting the model with these verbs for 10 trials each. This highest-frequency group had 8 irregulars and 2 regulars. These 10 learning trials were enough to produce good performance on these verbs. Then the remaining 410 verbs, mostly regular, were added to the first 10 and the trials continued. At this point, the performance on the original 8 irregular verbs reversed dramatically. For a short period, these verbs were regularized more often than produced correctly. Then gradually, correct responses for high frequency irregulars increased until they climbed over 90%. The simulation produced the same learning pattern that is observable in children, but without formulating an explicit rule. Rather the model adjusts the weights of connections, increasing or decreasing the probability of a certain output. Because the number of regular verbs so far outweighs the number of irregular verbs in English, the probability that the regular pattern will be followed is extremely high, but we need not assume that it is categorical.

Not only does the pattern associator learn the regular pattern and the irregular verbs it is given, it also learns the subregularities among the irregular verbs, so that when it is tested on verbs it has not encountered before, it behaves very much like an adult English speaker in a nonce-probe task. The majority of forms it produces have the regular suffix, including some that should not, such as *thrusted* and *sticked*. However, it also produces some correct irregulars, such as *bid* for the past tense of *bid*, *crept* for *creep*, and *clung* for *cling*. It also produces some incorrect, but highly probable vowel changes, such as the past tense of *slip* as *slept*, and some doubly marked pasts, such as *dripted* for *dripped*.

The connections made by the Rumelhart and McClelland pattern associator do not precisely parallel any connections in the model that I am proposing. The importance of their simulation is to show that, given fairly realistic input in terms of the frequency of regular versus irregular verbs, a model which only registers probabilities and never formulates an explicit rule produces behavior very similar to that of a human language learner. Let us see now briefly where these patterns show up in our model.

To begin with, recall that in our model connections are formed only between identical features, so that a pattern for the formation of the past *stung* will not be based on a connection between the [ɪ] of *sting* and the [ʌ] of *stung*. That this is correct can be seen from the fact that the members of the *stung* class of verbs do not all have the same vowel in the base. This is particularly true of the newer members, such as *strike*, *sneak*, and *drag*. Rather the basis for the formation of the pattern is an attempt to find a phonological schema with which to associate the semantics of past tense. Since there are many different shapes for past tense verbs in English, the pattern of connections is rather complex. It must be built up much as the Rumelhart and McClelland model builds up patterns: by registering probabilities for each feature paired with past tense according to how many times that feature appears in the representation of a past tense verb. As in the Rumelhart and McClelland model, the features that go into building up the pattern may be features of the stem as well as a suffix. Unlike that model, however, it is only the features of the past form that go into building the schema.

In Bybee and Slobin (1982) and Bybee and Moder (1983), we argued that the subregularities in English past forms could be accounted for by schemas, which specify the shape of a past verb form. The features of such a schema, we argued, are not categorical, but probablistic, like a Roschian natural category. The work by Rumelhart and McClelland shows that even the regular suffixation pattern should be treated in this way. The only difference between it and the subregularities is that the probabilities for suffixation are extremely high.

Thus the strongest features associated with past are alveolar and stop (in final position). The verbs that take the [ɪd] allomorph contribute the sequence "alveolar stop (the last consonant of the stem), reduced vowel, voiced alveolar stop" to the schema. Since the suffixation mode of forming the past tense involves so many verbs of such diverse phonological shapes, the rest of the schema is mostly unspecified. On the other hand, the schema for the *strung* class will have probability rankings for the initial consonants, the final consonant, and the vowel, since, as we showed in Bybee and Moder (1983), all of these features have at least some effect on the selection of this schema for new verbs.

Degree of productivity, then, is determined automatically in this system by several factors: First, how open the phonological definition of the schema is. The English past schema involving a final alveolar stop is associated with verbs of all phonological shapes, so it is open to extension to new verbs of any shape. A more strictly defined schema has correspondingly fewer chances to extend to new verbs. Second, the number of items participating in the schema. A larger number of distinct verbs participating in the same pattern will serve to strengthen it. Note that this is type frequency rather than token frequency. A verb of high token frequency will not serve to strengthen a schema; in fact, it appears that very high-frequency verbs have very little effect on productivity, since, as I mentioned in the preceding section, such forms seem to be processed without forming connections with other items. The third factor determining productivity may be termed CUE VALIDITY following Rosch. A more productive class has high cue validity, that is, most of the forms that fit the schema actually belong to the class. Thus the *strung* class has high cue validity since almost all of the verbs that could belong to the class do. On the other hand, the class that includes *tear, tore*; *bear, bore*; *wear, wore* has low cue validity, since so many regular verbs such as *snared, glared, aired, stared* exist.[9]

---

[9]Köpcke (1986), in a discussion of schemas for German plurals, suggests that the "salience" of a marker of a category may contribute to its productivity. SALIENCE refers to phonological size and shape: An affix consisting of two segments is more salient than a vowel change, such as umlaut, which affects only one or two features.

9. Conclusion

Of course, this chapter has not dealt with all the problems of lexical storage, of creating meaning–form correspondences, or of creating categories. I have proposed that lexical storage and organization involves the application of several principles, all of which appear to be well motivated and independently necessary: first, the ability to store strings of linguistic material in phonological and semantic representation; second, the ability to form, among stretches of this material, connections of a semantic and phonological nature; third, the accumulation of lexical strength due to token frequency; and fourth, the ability to organize sensory stimuli into categories. I have argued that these properties of lexical storage and organization allow us to account for a number of morphological phenomena that other models cannot account for.

First, this model allows us to conceptualize the internal structure of a word as a set of relations with other words, rather than as a string of discrete meaningful sequences, that is, morphemes. The problem of submorphemic units— *cranberry* morphs, formatives, and phonaesthemes—disappears, since the model allows the identification of a part of a word as a recurring meaningful unit without the necessity of assigning meaning to the remainder, and it allows the identification of phonological relations even in the absence of a clear semantic relation. Further, it postulates that morphological analysis proceeds directly from the discovery of relations among words, which is precisely how speakers and linguists accomplish morphological analysis.

Second, this model provides for varying degrees of relatedness among words as the consequence of both phonological and semantic features. I have proposed that some semantic connections are stronger than others because of the nature and number of shared semantic features. This proposal in turn predicts that analogical reformation is more likely among certain pairs of related forms than among others, depending upon their degree of semantic relatedness. As a result, leaving aside very high frequency forms, the degree of phonological connection reflects the degree of semantic connection.

Third, the notion of lexical strength, an index of word frequency, has been built into the model to account for the effect of word frequency on lexical access, and additionally to account for two major facts about morphological systems in the languages of the world: (a) that irregularity and suppletion are more common among high-frequency words and paradigms (because high-frequency items are less prone to analogical reformation); (b) that the more-frequent form of a pair of closely related forms is the one that serves as the basis for the analogical reformation of the other.

Finally, recurring morphological patterns emerge as accumulations of similar or identical sets of connections and are described as SCHEMAS. The notion of schema accommodates a range of pattern types from the most lexically specific and idiosyncratic to the most general and productive. The shape of a schema and the likehood that it will influence the formation of new words is directly determined by the number and types of items over which it ranges and does not have to be indicated separately.[10]

The most important difference between this theory and previous theories is that in this theory the generalizations that in other theories are called "rules" are here part of the representations. They arise out of the organization of phonetic and semantic substance of the language, and they have no existence independent of the substance that brings them to life.

Acknowledgments

I acknowledge fruitful discussions on the model I present here with Uli Frauenfelder, Klaus-Michael Köpcke, Carol Lynn Moder, William Pagliuca, Revere Perkins, Sandra Thompson, and Lolly Tyler.

References

Aronoff, M. (1976). "Word Formation in Generative Grammar." MIT Press, Cambridge, MA.

Bolozky, S. (1980). Paradigm coherence: Evidence from Modern Hebrew. *Afroasiatic Linguistics* **7**, 2–24.

Bybee, J.L. (1985). "Morphology: A Study of the Relation between Meaning and Form" Benjamins, Amsterdam.

Bybee, J.L., and Brewer, M.A. (1980). Explanation in morphophonemics: Changes in Provençal and Spanish preterite forms. *Lingua* **52**, 271–312.

Bybee, J.L., and Moder, C.L. (1983). Morphological classes as natural categories. *Language* **59**, 251–270.

Bybee, J.L., and Pardo, E. (1981). Morphological and lexical conditioning of rules: Experimental evidence from Spanish. *Linguistics* **19**, 937–968.

Bybee, J.L., and Slobin, D.I. (1982). Rules and schemas in the development and use of the English past tense. *Language* **58**, 265–289.

Comrie, B. (1976). "Aspect." Cambridge Univ. Press, Cambridge.

Derwing, B., and Baker, W.J. (1977). The psychological basis for morphological rules. *In* "Language Learning and Thought." (J. Macnamara, ed.). Academic Press, New York.

Greenberg, J. (1966). "Language Universals." Mouton, The Hague.

Harris, J. (1969). "Spanish Phonology." MIT Press, Cambridge, MA.

Hockett, C. (1954). Two models of grammatical description. *Word* **10**, 210–231.

Hooper, J.B. (1976a). "An Introduction to Natural Generative Phonology." Academic Press, New York.

Hooper, J.B. (1976b). Word frequency in lexical diffusion and the source of morphophonological

---

[10]In models that have separate rules components, productive and unproductive rules can be assigned to different components. Such assignment, however, is completely ad hoc and allows no way of associating the relevant variable—how many words a pattern occurs in—with the degree of productivity.

change. *In* "Current Progress in Historical Linguistics" (W. Christie, ed.). North Holland, Amsterdam.

Hooper, J.B. (1979). Child morphology and morphophonemic change. *Linguistics* **17**, 21–50; also in "Historical Morphology" (J. Fisiak, ed.). Mouton, The Hague.

Hudson, G. (1980). Automatic alternations in non-transformational phonology. *Language* **56**, 94–125.

Kernan, K.T., and Blount, B.G. (1966). The acquisition of Spanish grammar by Mexican children. *Anthropological linguistics* **8**, 1–14.

Kiparsky, P. (1968, 1973). How abstract is phonology? *In* "Three Dimensions of Linguistic Theory" (O. Fujimura, ed.), pp. 5–56. TEC, Tokyo.

Köpcke, K. (1988). Schemas in German plural formation. *Lingua* **68**, in press.

Lukatela, G. *et al.* (1980). Representation of inflected nouns in the internal lexicon. *Memory and Cognition* **8**, 415–423.

MacWhinney, B. (1978). "The Acquisition of Morphophonology." Child Development Publication, Univ. of Chicago Press, Chicago.

Mańczak, W. (1980). Laws of analogy. *In* "Historical Morphology" (J. Fisiak, ed.). Mouton, The Hague.

Matthews, P. (1972). "Inflectional Morphology: A Theoretical Study Based on Aspects of Latin Verb Conjugation." Cambridge Univ. Press, Cambridge.

Pagliuca, W. (1976). *PRE-fixing*. SUNY at Buffalo Master's Project.

Peters, A.M. (1983). "The Units of Language Acquisition." Cambridge Univ. Press, Cambridge.

Rudes, B.A. (1980). On the nature of verbal suppletion. *Linguistics* **18**, 655–676.

Rumelhart, D.E., and McClelland, J.L. (1986). Learning the past tenses of English verbs: Implicit rules or parallel distributed processing? *In* "Mechanisms of Language Acquisition" (B. MacWhinney, ed.). Erlbaum, Hillsdale, NJ.

Stanners, R., Neiser, J., Hernon, W., and Hall, R. (1979). Memory representation for morphologically related words. *Journal of Verbal Learning and Verbal Behavior* **18**, 399–412.

Tiersma, P.M. (1982). Local and general markedness. *Language* **58**, 832–849.

Vennemann, T. (1972). Rule inversion. *Lingua* **29**, 209–242.

Vennemann, T. (1974). Words and syllables in natural generative grammar. "Natural Phonology Parasession," pp. 346–374. Chicago Linguistic Society, Chicago.

Watkins, C. (1962). "Indo-European Origins of the Celtic Verb." Dublin Institute for Advanced Studies, Dublin.

Zager, D. (1982). *A real time process model of morphological change*. SUNY at Buffalo dissertation.

Chapter 8

Preferences vs. Strict Universals in Morphology: Word-Based Rules

Wolfgang U. Dressler

1. For decades theoretical linguistics has been plagued by the following scenario:

(1) The most frequent/(intuitively) natural state of affairs (e.g., in American structuralist phonology the principle of biuniqueness, i.e., of a biunique relation between a phoneme and an allophone) is elevated to the only state of affairs allowed by the given theory/model.

(2) This is encapsulated in a theoretical principle capturing valid generalizations about it, e.g., in the slogan "once a phoneme, always a phoneme."

(3) Counter-examples are found which cannot be explained, e.g., the merger of the two phonemes /t/ and /d/ in one and the same allophone "flap" (*writer = rider*).

(4) Therefore principle (2) and generalizations about natural states of affairs are abandoned or watered down.

(5) Thus preferences originally observed in (1) still await a theory explaining them.

This research strategy has been attacked by Zwicky (1973). Still the same strategy of proposing overly strong hypotheses in the first place and of discarding them altogether thereafter has flowered as always. In Dressler (1985a) I illustrated the advantageous alternative of replacing absolute constraints with preferences for biuniqueness (p. 130, 136, 312, 373f), MSRs (p. 229), rule order (p. 304), abstractness (p. 306), metatheses (p. 308), and abstract deletion rules (p. 309f).[1]

---

[1] I will use the following abbreviations: MR, morphological rule; NM, Natural Morphology; WBC, word base constraint; WBP, word base preference; WFR, word formation rule.

2. Here I limit my discussion to the Word Base Hypothesis or Word Base Constraint (WBC, part of which is the No Phrase Constraint) and enlarge my earlier sketchy outline (Dressler, 1981, p. 4ff).[2]

Aronoff (1976, p. 21) claimed that "all regular word-formation processes are word-based. A new word is formed by applying a regular rule to a single already existing word." The essential part of this proposed constraint, that only words can be bases of word formation rules (WFRs), but neither smaller units such as morphemes or larger units such as phrases, has been assumed under different formats by many linguists (e.g., Roeper and Siegel, 1978). It has also been watered down to allowing (1) stems as bases, (2) potential/possible (but not actually existing) words, (3) possible deep structure constituents, (4) bases of regular and productive WFRs; or it has been completely given up.[3] On the other hand, Bauer (1978), Brogyanyi (1979), Kageyama (1982), Plank (1981, p. 202ff), Toman (1983, p. 46f) have called phrase-based WFRs a marked option, but without providing a proper markedness theory. In this way the original intuition about words being the most natural bases of WFRs has been lost. However a proper theory of preferences can capture this generalization.[4] And this is possible within the framework of Natural Morphology (NM), which consists of three pertinent subtheories:

1. a subtheory of universal naturalness (markedness) which contains several parameters of naturalness and derives binary relations of more/less markedness (i.e., preferences) for morphological phenomena on each parameter from (a) very few basic functions, (b) from a restricted semiotic metatheory (based on Peirce, 1965) and (c) from extra-linguistic bases of preferences.
2. a subtheory of language typology where I elaborate on Skalička's (1979) theory of ideal language types.
3. (little used here) a subtheory of language-specific system adequacy (see particularly Wurzel, 1984).[5]

3. The first relevant parameter refers to the principle of the optimal size of a sign (or better: signans, see Dressler, 1981, p. 5ff; 1985a, p. 330ff). Too big or small a signans is difficult to perceive for the hearer and to store or speaker and hearer. Since each language type has its own typological

---

[2]In Dressler (1987), I discuss the Morphological Island Constraint or Lexical Integrity Hypothesis.

[3]See the roster in Scalise (1984, p. 72) and add Anderson (1981); Aronoff (1979, 1983, p. 26f); Bauer (1978, 1979a,b, 1980, 1983, p. 164ff); R. Botha (1980, 1981, 1984, p. 144); T. Botha (1982, 1983); Carroll (1979); Drapeau (1980); Hagen (1982); Hoekstra *et al.* (1980, p. 20); Jensen and Stong-Jensen (1984); Savini (1984); van Santen (1974, p. 27ff, 75ff).

[4]cf. also Plank (1981), Vennemann (1983).

[5]cf. Mayerthaler (1981), Wurzel (1984), Dressler (1983, 1985a–c); Dressler *et al.* (1987); cf. the special issue of *Studia Gramatyczne* **7** (1985): "Natural Approaches to Morphology."

preferences on this parameter we can derive from it for the moment only the prediction that phrase and sentence bases should be universally disfavored (when compared with word bases)—which is correct as we will see.[6]

4. But bases for what? There is no reason why a WBC (or preference) should be restricted to bases of WFRs and not to MRs in general. Thus we have to develop a preference account for (II) derivational MRs, (II) compounding WFRs, and (III) inflectional MRs. All of these MRs have the two functions of (1) producing complex words (i.e., words derived via WFRs: I, II) or inflectional word-forms (III) and of (2) motivating their base morphosemantically and morphotactically (thus reducing memory load). This second function can be served better and worse, and one factor of efficiency is the parameter of the best/more or less natural base of MRs: and here preferences can be derived from the semiotic meta-level and supported empirically.

Semiotics (see Peirce, 1965) delivers us the first premise: Words (i.e., lexically stored words) are primary signs (i.e., the most basic signs logically and in communication); morphemes, stems, roots are signs on signs, i.e., secondary signs. Phrases and sentences are supersigns (i.e., composite signs), thus secondary signs as well. Inflected word-forms are only primary signs if they are lexically stored, which is not the case for inflectional word-forms generated by regular and productive inflectional MRs (pace Bybee, 1985; cf. Stemberger and MacWhinney, Chapter 6, this volume).[7] Thus such word-forms are secondary signs as well. Complex words derived by WFRs are primary signs if they are lexically stored, which is the case for all words accepted by the respected linguistic norm (level of institutional/sociolinguistic norms as opposed to the competence level of potential/possible words). The function of morphosemantic/tactic motivation is the better served (ceteris paribus) the better/faster the base can be perceived/identified. Fast identification of the base (e.g., *read* in *re-read* or *read-s*) allows direct reference of the perceived derived word (e.g., *re-read*) or word-form (*read-s*) to the base instead of having to refer first to the stored model of the respective word-form, i.e., stored *re-read, read-s*. And in terms of semiotic primacy we can claim that primary signs, i.e., lexically stored words, should be better bases of MRs than secondary signs. For if primary signs are more basic than secondary signs, they should be easier to identify in search processes.

If we add as a second premise that human beings prefer (ceteris paribus) locally "better" operations to "worse" ones in performance, in acquisition and in diachronic change (cf. Jespersen, 1949), we can derive the following predictions:

---

[6] This is a kind of parametrization which is present in NM since its beginnings about 1977.

[7] Psycholinguistic evidence for regular inflectional word-forms being processed and not stored is abundant; see Stemberger and MacWhinney (Chapter 6, this volume).

5. Prediction I: Cross-linguistically, word-based MRs should be more frequent than root-, stem-, word-form-, phrase-, sentence-based MRs. This is a prediction over a representative set of languages (cf. Bybee, 1985), and need not hold for a single language where the specific language type may favor stem-based MRs, as in the inflecting type and in the introflecting type.[8] In order to increase falsifiability, let us sharpen Prediction I into

Prediction II: In any language the existence of root/stem/word-form/phrase/sentence-based MRs implies the existence of word-based MRs, but not vice versa. The underlying assumption is that children will learn an easier operation earlier than a more difficult one (where relative ease refers to the same parameters, whereas there is no difference on other relevant parameters). Thus they will learn non-word-based applications of MRs only after having learned word-based applications. If children do not arrive at this stage, then their language will have only word-based MRs. Since sentences are parsed into phrases and into words, the parsing of sentences into words is more complex as well. Therefore we can add:

Prediction III: In any language the existence of sentence-based MRs implies the existence of phrase-based MRs. In reference to productivity, premise II allows us to transform Predictions I–III into

Prediction IV: Productivity of secondary-sign-based MRs implies productivity of (more) primary-sign based MRs, but not vice versa.

6. In word-formation, due to the lexicalization of derived complex words (and on the semiotic metalevel due to priority of lexical over morphological biuniqueness) the set of productively derived words is a subset of all derived words, and new words can be derived by surface analogy.[9,10] Or in Aronoff's (1976) terms, a WFR may either serve only as a redundancy rule, or it may serve as a generative rule and a redundancy rule. In language acquisition, according to MacWhinney (1978), a child first processes (and parses) passively complex words (where the MR functions as a redundancy rule for motivation), then forms new words by (surface) analogy and only then learns to use a MR productively. Therefore, productive use of a MR implies the possibility of its unproductive use, but not vice versa.

Next we may assume that the child progresses to the stage of productive use of MRs earlier with better/more natural MRs rather than with less natural MRs. Put together with Predictions II, III, and IV a new prediction can be derived:

Prediction V: In a language, unproductive use of secondary-sign-based MRs implies productive use of (more) primary-sign-based MRs.

---

[8]In Dressler (1981) I followed the current belief that Semitic languages have discontinuous-consonant-root-based MRs, which is wrong; see Kilani-Schoch and Dressler (1984).

[9]See for the derivation of this principle Dressler (1977, p. 6f, 1985a, p. 322f).

[10]Motsch (1977, p. 192ff); Dressler (1977, p. 20f); Plank (1981, p. 225); cf. MacWhinney (1978).

7. Since one factor that the degree efficiency of motivation depends on is lexical storage (cf. premise I), we can derive:

Prediction VI: Existing (= lexically stored) words can be directly referred to, whereas potential but nonexisting words must first be derived before they can be referred to. Therefore existing words are better bases than potential (but nonexisting) words, so that the occurrence of potential words as bases of MRs implies occurrence of existing (actual) words as bases of MRs, but not vice versa.

8. Derivatives (i.e., complex words derived via derivational WFRs) are more tightly bonded than compounds, cf. the possibility of syntaxlike coordination reduction in composition, but not in (prototypical suffixing) derivation (e.g., Booij, 1985; Toman, 1985). Compounds are also more descriptive than derivatives (see Walter, 1976; Stachowiak, 1978, 1979). Therefore it is easier to identify the motivating base of compounds than of derivatives.[11] And as a consequence, better-motivating WFRs are needed for derivatives than for compounds, in order to compensate for this disadvantage. This allows us to formulate:

Prediction VII: If a language has derivational and compounding WFRs, the occurrence of secondary-sign-based WFRs in derivational morphology implies the existence of secondary-sign-based WFRs in compound formation, but not vice versa (and similarly the degree of productivity, etc. as in Predictions IV–VI, which can be easily formulated as Predictions VIII–X).

9. After the deductive part of deriving predictions we come to the inductive part of testing these predictions:

All the predictions hold in a language where all MRs apply to actual (existing) words only. This can be tested only with very detailed descriptions of languages, which hardly exist. For example, even in Turkish there are a few and entirely unproductive exceptions where causative and reflexive WFRs apply to stems which do not exist as actual words (cf. Schlögel, 1985; p. 55f).

10. If we turn to bases smaller than words, then stem-based morphology coexists with word-based morphology (cf. Prediction I) in inflecting (e.g., Latin) and introflecting languages (e.g., Arabic). In English, stem-based Latinate derivations such as *in-sipid, in-ert, in-trepid, lu-cid* are not formed by productive MRs, but are only extendable by surface analogy which confirms Prediction V.[12,13] However, stem-based Latinate compounding is productive, at least in scientific and technical terminology,[14] which confirms

---

[11]For language acquisition cf. Clark and Hecht (1982); Stephany (1980); for aphasia cf. Stachowiak (1979).

[12]These are acephalous derivations according to Malkiel (1970, p. 7).

[13]See Allen (1978, p. 4ff, 18ff, 53); Aronoff (1976, p. 20); Bauer (1979a, 1980, p. 77); Hoekstra *et al.* (1980, p. 20, note 52); Plank (1981, p. 204ff); Dressler (1981, p. 6).

[14]Bauer (1979a); Dressler (1981, p. 6f); Plank (1981, p. 217f); Scalise (1983, p. 186ff, 1984, p. 74ff).

Predictions IV, VII. That this occurs only in Latinate WFRs fits the typological criterion (of Prediction I): English Latinate WFRs are of the inflecting (fusional) type, "Germanic" WFRs are not.

Even worse than stem-based is root-based morphology. German (in support of Prediction V) has it just in three isolated derivations from the Germanic prefixes *ur-* 'proto-' and *miss-* 'dis-': *ur-ig* = *ur-tümlich* 'original,' *miss-lich* 'precarious' which consist just of prefix and suffix. For Russian see Hagen (1982); for Montagnais, Drapeau (1980). A semi-productive (Prediction V) and marginal status is represented by root-based onomatopoetic echo-word formation as in French (Mayerthaler, 1977) *frou-frou* 'rustle' (→ verb *frou-frou-t-er*), *glou-glou* 'coo' (→ verb *glou-glou-t-er*), *put-put* 'cry of a hoopoe' (verb *pu-pu-l-er*), *ron-ron* 'purr' (→ *ron-ronn-er*), cf. Plank (1981, p. 224).

11. If we turn to bases bigger than lexically stored words (in their basic form) we have first inflected word-forms[15] as bases (for Greenlandic cf. Sadock, 1985, p. 395ff): German and English allow plurals as bases of compounds, but not of derivations (according to Prediction VII),[16] though rarely (presumably not productively: Predictions IV, V) and particularly if the plural is morphosemantically opaque and therefore lexically stored (Predictions I, VI), e.g., (at least British) English: *customs duty, incomes tax, news man, clothes press*, less opaque: *arms race, sales clerk, sports woman*; G. *Geschicht-en-buch* 'story book' (i.e., book full of stories) vs. *Geschicht-s-buch* 'history book,' *Wört-er-buch* 'dictionary' [containing pl *Wört-er* '(unconnected) words,' pl II of *Wort* 'words'] vs. *Wort-e-macher* 'idle talker,' from *Wort-e* '(connected) words,' for Dutch cf. Booij (1977, p. 48).

Predictions VII and IV are also supported by plurals as bases of the WFR of Afrikaans reduplicated compounds (Botha, 1984), e.g., *bottel-s-bottel-s* 'bottles over bottles,' *heuwel-s-heuwel-s* 'hill upon hill,' and of the one WFR of Italian verb–noun compounds, e.g. *spremi-agrumi* 'citrus-fruit-presser' (from the plurale tantum *agrumi*), *porta-letter-e* 'mail man' (litt. *carry-letter-s*), *porta-contenitor-i* = *porta-container-s* 'container-carrier.' Occasional case-forms as bases of Icelandic compounds have been cited by Jensen and Strong-Jensen (1984, p. 475) [Prediction V, VII]. In Tzotzil (Cowan, 1969, p. 12f, 97) complex words can be derived (via WFRs) from inflectional words-forms expressing, with special suffixes, aspects (perfective), mood (subjunctive), passive; in accordance with Predictions II, IV cf. for Zoque Singh and Ford (1980, p. 328).

12. In Ancient Greek less than a dozen morphosemantically opaque perfect stems may be bases for WFRs, e.g., *apo-t^{h}néiskō* (< *apo # t^{h}nā + isk + ō*) 'I die' → perf. *té-t^{h}nē-ka* = Doric *té-t^{h}nā-ka* → compound *tet^{h}nāk-o-khalkidas* (with interfix *-o-*) 'who would die for a farthing'; *horá-ō* 'I see' _ perf. *óp-ōp-a* → *opōp-ḗ* 'sight'; *páskh-ō* 'I suffer' (< *pat^h-sk-ō* < *pn̥t^h-sk-ō*) → *pé-ponth-a*

---

[15]cf. Booij (1977, p. 48); Selkirk (1982, p. 52f).
[16]The often-cited German plural diminutive *Kind-er-chen* (sg, *Kind-chen* 'small child') is isolated.

→ new present *peponth-é-ō* 'I am affected' → action noun *pepónth-ē-sis*; *peith-ō* 'I persuade' → rather transparent perfect *pé-pei-k-a* (*/thk/ is not permitted) 'I have persuaded' vs. opaque *pé-poith-a* 'I trust' → *pepoith-ē-sis* 'trust, confidence.'

There are only two fairly transparent perfect stems which can be further derived: *kráz-ō* 'I croak, scream' (/*krág-ĭ-ō*/) → perf. *ké-krag-a* → *ké-krag-ma* = *ke-krag-mós* 'a scream, cry,' *ke-krák-tēs* 'bawler,' *ke-krak-s-i-dámas* 'he who conquers all in bawling'; *khain-ō* (/*khán-ĭ-ō*/) 'I yawn, gape' → perf. *ké-kh-ēn-a*, perf. participle *ke-khan-ódēs* → *kekh-ēn-aîoi* 'Gapenians' for *Athēnaîoi* 'Athenians.' These forms are in accordance with Predictions V, VII.

13. Now let us turn to the phrase level: Noun-phrases consisting of definite article and noun are the bases of a few, unproductive Italian compounds (verb stem ## article # noun; never of sentence-based compounds), if the noun starts with a vowel so that the article has the vowelless suppletive form /l/ (vs. *il*, *lo*, *la*): *metti-l-oro* 'gilder' (litt. 'put-the-gold') *batti-l-oro* (litt. 'hit-the-gold') *tira-l-oro* (litt. 'draw out-the-gold'), *guasta-l-arte* = *guasta-mestiere* 'crooked professional' (litt. 'waste-(the)-art'), *bevi-l'acqua* 'water drinker.' [Predictions III, V, VII].

Lexicalized (opaque) adverbial phrases and noun-phrases consisting of modifier and noun can be the basis of three Italian suffixing WFRs (cf. Scalise, 1984a, p. 156): *press'a poco* 'approximately' → *pressapoch-ismo* 'satisfaction with approximate results' and *pressapoch-ista* 'person who is satisfied with approximate results,' *doppio gioco* 'double play' → *doppiogioch-ista* 'person who indulges in double play,' *tiro a volo* 'trap shooting' → *tiravol-ista*, *la terza internazionale* 'the Third International' → *terzinternazionalista* [Predictions IV, V, VI].

Compounding is less restricted in Italian [Prediction VII], although complex compounding is very restricted cf. *sala personale viaggiante* 'traveling staff room,' *sala dirigente capo* 'chief-executive room,' *campo tiro a volo* 'trap shooting field,' *nave pesca d'altomare* 'high-sea fishing ship,' *Essa é il tipo di ragazza acqua-e-sapone* 'she is the type of a girl water-and-soap (= without make-up)'[17] or cf. the verb–prepositional phrase compound *salt-im bocca* litt. 'jump-into-mouth' (= special veal cutlet), *salt-im-banco* = *cantambanco* (< *canta-in-banco*) 'itinerant singer.'

14. Also in English only fairly lexicalized/opaque phrases can be bases of derivational WFRs (and only of a few suffixing WFRs),[18] e.g., *black and blueness, fed-up-ness, at-home-ish, short-sightedness, up-to-date-ness, with-it-ness, get-at-able, hot/cold mooner, I feel particularly sit-around-and-do-nothing-ish today* [Prediction V].

---

[17] I owe these examples to Lavinia Merlini.

[18] Allen (1978, p. 236ff); Bauer (1979b, 1980, 1983, p. 75); Th. Botha (1983); Romaine (1983, p. 180f); Selkirk (1982); Scalise (1984, p. 155f). But many word-based cases can be reanalyzed as nonlexicalized-phrase-based ones, see Meijs (1987).

Compounds based on phrases are much less restricted, e.g., *two chamber system* (Booij, 1977, p. 44; cf. van Santen, 1974, p. 75ff) [Prediction IV, VII]. For German cf. Toman (1983, p. 46f); for Afrikaans cf. R. Botha (1981), Savini (1984); for Japanese cf. Kageyama (1982). For Russian cf. *serp-i-molotov-skij* 'hammer-and-sickle-interfix-adjectivizing suffix' and acronymic compounds such as *rab-sel'-kor* 'workers-and-village-correspondent,' cf. Dutch *de van de boom vallende appels et-er* 'the from the tree falling apples eat-er.'

15. Phrase-based inflectional MRs would be phrasal affixing via clitics such as in *the Queen of England's palace*, if the identification of cliticization with phrasal affixing is correct (cf. Sadock, 1985, p. 381ff). However, it is not clear whether the existence of 'inflectional clitics' in a language implies the existence of word- or stem-based inflectional MRs in the same language [Prediction II].

16. In accordance with Prediction III, sentence-based WFRs (there are apparently no sentence-based clitic rules) and especially affixing rules are still more restricted, as in English *a what-do-you-think-move-ment, a girl-that-says: 'Mama'-doll*, where there is only compounding (not necessarily of lexicalized/opaque bases) [Prediction VII].[19] G. *Eine Friss-Vogel-oder-stirb-(artig-e) Attitüde* 'a take-it-or-leave-it-(adjectivizing suffix-fem) attitude' (Dressler, 1977, p. 15, 1981, p. 5), *Eine wer-war-das-frage* 'a who-was-it-question,' *der Jeder-kann-es-schaffen-Tarif* 'the tariff which everybody can pay' (Brogyanyi, 1979, p. 159ff; Toman, 1983, p. 46f). Compounding is easier than affixation [Prediction VII] and bases are lexicalized/opaque (Prediction VI).

Many Afrikaans examples (and mostly of compounding: Prediction VII) such as *Good-is-dood-teologie* 'God-is-dead-theology,' *laat-in-die-bed-kom + ery* 'late-in-bed-get + ing,' *ons-word-mishandel-klag + te* 'we-are-ill-treated-complain + t' can be found in R. Botha (1980, 1981), Th. Botha (1982, 1983), Savini (1984). Swedish and Danish examples in Bauer (1983, p. 164), Dutch ones in Booij (1987).

For Italian cf. *un non-so-ché X* 'an I-don't-know-what/which X,' *il sistema'fai-da-te'* 'the do-it-yourself (litt. 'doest-from-you') system.' A Russian example is *čert-mne-ne-brat-stvo* 'devil-(is)-me-not-brother-hood' = 'foolhardiness' (Kalnijazov, 1978).[20]

A complex Hungarian sentence as base is given by Brogyanyi (1979, p. 160): *a ha-érdekli-úgyis-elolvassa-vers + ek* 'the if-interest + him-anyway-will-read-verse + s = the verses which will be read anyway, if they interest one.' The base-sentence is clearly nonidiomatic, but of course idiomatic sentences may serve as bases as well. Particularly the poet and writer Ferenc Juhász is said to be famous in producing sentence-based ad hoc compounds.

---

[19]Carroll (1979); Bauer (1979a, 1980, 1984, p. 164, 175).

[20]Michael Noonan draws my attention to clause-based WFRs in the Western Nilotic language Lango.

17. Especially the longer ones among the English, etc. phrase/sentence-based complex words are most often occasionalisms and do not succeed in being accepted as neologisms. But this has nothing to do with the shape of their bases, but rather their own size, i.e., they go against the preference for the optimal sizes of a signans. It would have been easy to find far more examples of stem-based MRs, but otherwise the literature does not abound in illustrations of non-word-based morphology, which seems to fully confirm Predictions I and II.

18. The material given and cited here fits the predictions deduced from the first (and particularly second) subtheory of Natural Morphology, and falls neatly into the parametrizing approach of NM. Any more detailed description and explanation of language-specific parameter fixation would have necessitated going deeply into the third subtheory of language-specific system adequacy, impossible here for lack of space. Moreover, the concentration on the explanation of universal preferences may have shown that this approach of NM might be useful for adherents of other morphological models as well.

From a methodological point of view I wanted to present an alternative to the strategy of first proposing, then watering down and finally discarding strong constraints. And in this spirit I mention finally that the often-proposed generalizations[21] (a) derivational affixes are placed inside inflectional affixes, (b) inflectional MRs follow derivational WFRs in rule application can be deduced from the WBP as follows:

1. Since the outputs of WFRs are words, but the outputs of inflectional MRs not (in the sense of the WBP), the WBP favors (b) over its inverse.
2. On the parameter of affixing, the suffixing and prefixing operations are universally preferred over infixing and interfixing (a preference which can be deduced from more general principles), which permits the following deduction:

1st premise: preference for inflectional following derivational MRs (b).
2nd premise: preference for suffixing and prefixing.

Conclusion: preference for inflectional MRs being suffixed/prefixed to words derived via derivational MRs = proposal (a).

References

Allen, M.R. (1978). Morphological Investigations. Ph.D. Thesis, University of Connecticut.

[21]cf. Bybee (1985, p. 96f); Sadock (1985, p. 398); Scalise (1984, p. 103f); Wurzel (1984, p. 41, 47, 49).

152 *Wolfgang U. Dressler*

Anderson, S. (1981). Where's Morphology. *Linguistic Inquiry* **13**, 571–612.

Aronoff, M. (1976). "Word Formation in Generative Grammar." MIT Press, Cambridge, MA.

Aronoff, M. (1979). A reply to Moody. *Glossa* **13**, 115–118.

Aronoff, M. (1983). A decade of morphology and word formation. *Annual Review of Anthropology* **12**.

Bauer, L. (1978). "The Grammar of Nominal Compounding with special reference to Danish, English and French." University Press, Odense.

Bauer, L. (1979a). Against word-based morphology. *Linguistic Inquiry* **10**, 508–509.

Bauer, L. (1979b). Patterns of productivity in new formations denoting persons using the suffix -er in modern English. *Cahiers de Lexicologie* **35**(II), 26–31.

Bauer, L. (1980). In the beginning was the word. *Te Reo* **23**, 73–80.

Bauer, L. (1983). "English Word-Formation." Cambridge Univ. Press, Cambridge.

Booij, G. (1977). "Dutch Morphology." de Ridder, Lisse.

Booij, G. (1985). Coordination reduction in complex words: A case for prosodic phonology. *In* "Advances in Nonlinear Phonology" (H. van der Hulst and N. Smith, eds.), pp. 143–60. Foris, Dordrecht.

Booij, G. (1987). The external syntax of complex words. *AL Hung*, in press.

Botha, R. (1980). Word-based morphology and synthetic compounding. *SPIL* **5**.

Botha, R. (1981). A base rule theory of Afrikaans synthetic compounding. *In* "The Scope of Lexical Rules" (M. Moortgat and T. Hoekstra, eds.), pp. 1–77. Foris, Dordrecht.

Botha, R. (1984). A Galilean analysis of Afrikaans reduplication. *SPIL* **13**.

Botha, T. (1982). *Primary compounds as bases of affixation rules*. MA thesis, University of Stellenbosch.

Botha, T. (1983). Allen's defense of the extended ordering hypothesis: A critical appraisal. *SPIL* **11**, 49–113.

Brogyanyi, B. (1979). Bemerkungen zu den Phrasenkomposita. *In* "Fs. Szemerényi" pp. 159–65. Benjamins, Amsterdam.

Bybee, J.L. (1985). "Morphology." Benjamins, Amsterdam.

Carroll, J.M. (1979). Complex compounds: Phrasal embedding in lexical structures. *Linguistics* **17**, 863–77.

Clark, E.V., and Hecht, B.F. (1982). Learning to coin agent and instrument nouns. *Cognition* **12**, 1–24.

Cowan, M. (1969). "Tzotzil Grammar." SIL, Norman.

Drapeau, L. (1980). Le rôle des racines en morphologie dérivationelle. *Recherches Linguistiques à Montréal* **14**, 299–312.

Dressler, W.U. (1977). Elements of a polycentristic theory of word formation. *Wiener ling. Gazette* **15**, 13–22.

Dressler, W.U. (1981). Word formation in natural morphology. *Wlg* **26**, 3–13 (= *PICL* **13**(1983), 172–82.

Dressler, W.U. (1985a). "Morphonology." Karoma Press, Ann Arbor, Michigan.

Dressler, W.U. (1985b). On the predictiveness of natural morphology. *Journal of Linguistics* **21**, 321–37.

Dressler, W.U. (1985c). Typological aspects of natural morphology. *Wlg* **35–36**, 3–26.

Dressler, W.U. (1987). Morphological islands: Constraint or preference? *In* "Language Topics" (R. Steele, Fs. M. Halliday, eds.)

Dressler, W.U., and Merlini, L. (1987). "Interradical Interfixes." Fs. R. Filipović, in press.

Dressler, W.U., Mayerthaler, G.W., Panagl, O., and Wurzel, W.U. (1987). "Leitmotifs in Natural Morphology." Benjamins, Amsterdam.

Dressler, W.U., Schaner-Wolles, Ch., and Grossmann, G.W. (1985). On the acquisition of morphology in normal children and children with Down's syndrome. *Studia Gramatyczne* **7**, 13–26.

Hagen, St. (1982). A root morph hypothesis in Russian word formation. *FoL* **16**, 136–180.

Hoekstra, T., van der Hulst, G.H., and Moortgat, G.M., eds. (1980). "Lexical Grammar." Foris, Dordrecht.

Jensen, J.T., and Stong-Jensen, M. (1984). Morphology is in the lexicon! *Linguistic Inquiry* **15**, 474–98.

Jespersen, O. (1949). Efficiency in linguistic change. *Historik-Filologiske Meddelelser* **27**, 4; (here cited after: "Selected Writings," pp. 381–466). Senyo, Tokyo.

Kageyama, J. (1982). Word formation in Japanese. *Lingua* **57**, 215–58.

Kalnijazov, M. (1978). "Okkazional'nye i potencial'nye slova v jazyke sovremennoj periodiki." Moscow University, Moscow.

Kalini-Schoch, M., and Dressler, W.U. (1984). Natural morphology and classical vs. Tunisian Arabic. *Wlg* **33–34**, 51–68 (= *Studia Gramatyczne* **7**(1985), 27–47).

MacWhinney, B. (1978). "The Acquisition of Morphophonology." Univ. of Chicago Press, Chicago.

Malkiel, Y. (1970). Patterns of derivational affixation in the Cabraniego dialect of East-Central Asturian. *Univ. of California Publications in Linguistics* **64**.

Mayerthaler, W. (1977). "Studien zur theoretischen und französischen Morphologie." Niemeyer, Tübingen.

Mayerthaler, W. (1981). "Morphologische Natürlichkeit." Athenaion, Wiesbaden.

Meijs, W. (1987). Over the borderline: Words or phrases? *ALHung*, in press.

Motsch, W. (1977). Ein Plädoyer für die Beschreibung von Wortbildungen auf der Grundlage des Lexikons. *In* "Perspektiven der Wortbildungsforschung" (H. Brekle and D. Kastovsky, eds.), pp. 180–202. Bouvier, Bonn.

Peirce, Ch. S. (1965). "Collected Papers" (Ch. Hartshorne and P. Weiss, eds.). Harvard Univ. Press, Cambridge, MA.

Plank, F. (1981). "Morphologische (Ir-)Regularitäten." Narr, Tübingen.

Roeper, Th., and Siegel, E.A.M. (1978). A lexical transformation for verbal compounds. *LInq* **9**, 199–260.

Romaine, S. (1983). On the productivity of word formation. *Australian Journal of Linguistics* **3**, 177–200.

Sadock, J.M. (1985). Autolexical syntax. *Natural Language and Linguistic Theory* **3**, 379–439.

Savini, M. (1984). Phrasal compounds in Afrikaans: A generative analysis. *SPIL* **12**, 37–114.

Scalise, S. (1983). "Morfologia Lessicale." CLESP, Padua.

Scalise, S. (1984). "Generative Morphology." Foris, Dordrecht.

Schlögel, S. (1985). Zur Kausativierung im Türkischen. *Arbeitspapier, Institut für Sprachwissenschaft der Universität Köln* **48**.

Selkirk, L. (1982). "The Syntax of Words." MIT Press, Cambridge, MA.

Singh, R., and Ford, A. (1980). Flexion, dérivation et Panini. "Progress in Linguistic Historiography" (K. Koerner, ed.), pp. 323–332. Benjamins, Amsterdam.

Skalička, V. (1979). "Typologische Studien." Vieweg, Braunschweig.

SPIL = *Stellenbosch Papers in Linguistics.*

Stachowiak, F.-J. (1978). Some universal aspects of naming as a language activity. *In* "Language Universals" (H. Seiler, ed.), pp. 207–228. Narr, Tubingen.

Stachowiak, F.-J. (1979). "Zur semantischen Struktur des subjektiven Lexikons." Fink, Munich.

Stephany, U. (1980). Zur psychischen Realität der Dimension der Deskriptivität. "Wege zur Universalienforschung" (G. Brettschneider and Ch. Lehmann, eds.), pp. 549–55. Narr, Tübingen.

Toman, J. (1983). "Wortsyntax." Niemeyer, Tübingen.

Toman, J. (1985). A discussion of coordination and word-syntax. *In* "Studies in German Grammar" (J. Toman, ed.), pp. 407–432. Foris, Dordrecht.

van Santen, A. (1974). "De Morfologie van het Nederlands." Foris, Dordrecht.

Vennemann, T. (1983). Theories of linguistic preferences as a basis for linguistic explanations. *FLH* **4**, 5-26.

Walter, H. (1976). Zum Problem der Deskriptivität am Beispiel deutscher Verbalderivation. *Arbeitsberichte Kölner Universalienprojekt* 26.

Wlg = *Wiener Linguistische Gazette*

Wurzel, W.U. (1984). Flexionsmorphologie und Natürlichkeit. *Studia Grammatica (Berlin)* **21**.

Zwicky, A.M. (1973). The analytic leap: From 'some Xs are Ys' to 'all Xs, are Ys'. *PCLS* **9**, 700-709.

Chapter 9

Zero Derivation and the Overt Analogue Criterion

Gerald Sanders

1. Introduction

A lexical form sometimes has two distinct syntactic and semantic functions in a language. For example, in English, forms like *walk, answer, hammer,* and *milk* can function both as nouns and as verbs, and forms like *dry* and *calm* can function both as verbs and as adjectives. Traditionally, for situations like this, linguists have generally tended to view one of the functions as more basic than the other, and to assume, moreover, that a word serving the less basic function is in fact morphologically or lexically derived from a word serving the more basic function, in spite of the fact that there are no formal differences between the words and no overt mark of any derivational relation between them.

This particular type of asymmetric word-formation process is known as CONVERSION, or ZERO DERIVATION, and it plays a major conceptual and analytical role in nearly all systematic studies of grammatical structure.[1] Rarely, though, has any explicit evidence or argumentation been presented in support of the particular zero derivation relations that linguists have assumed, in spite of the great abundance of such assumptions and the crucial role that they sometimes play in the application and evaluation of proposed generalizations about natural language grammar.

[1]Most linguists seem to use these two terms as synonyms. Lyons (1977) referring to Quirk *et al.* (1972, p. 1009), on the other hand, seeks to differentiate the two terms, saying "arguably, the term 'conversion'—"the derivational process whereby an item is adapted to a new word-class without the addition of an affix"—carries different implications from the term 'zero-affixation,' which can be understood as implying the addition to the stem of the identity-element function-ing as an affix" (1977, p. 523).

It is implicitly quite clear, nevertheless, that the primary traditional basis for the recognition of zero derivation relations has been the existence of appropriate analogues involving overt morphological marking of the same derivational function. Thus, for example, given sentences like those in (1), we recognize the analogy schematized in (2).

(1) a. *I'll **answer** that again : This is my final **answer***
     b. *I'll **announce** that again : This is my final **announcement***

(2) $answer_V$: $[answer_V \; ø]_N = announce_V$: $[announce_V \; ment]_N$

And on the basis of this analogy we argue that just as *announcement* is derived from *announce* by the addition of the overt noun-forming suffix alternant *-ment*, so too the noun *answer* is derived from the verb *answer* by the addition of an alternant consisting of no overt form, or zero, in the position of the derivational suffix.

The same type of analogical reasoning also underlies the common postulation of zero alternants of inflectional affixes, for example, as illustrated in (3) and (4), the noun plural affix in English.

(3) a. *This **sheep** is nice : These **sheep** are nice*
     b. *This **cat** is nice : These **cats** are nice*

(4) $[sheep]_{sg}$: $[sheep \; ø]_{pl} = [cat]_{sg}$: $[cat \; s]_{pl}$

Although we are concerned at present chiefly with zero derivation, it is clear that for zero inflection and zero derivation alike it is the existence of an analogous pattern involving overt morphological marking of a given lexical relation that constitutes the primary rationale and justification for the recognition of zero elements or zero-marked relations of any type.

To explicitly recognize the kind of analogical argumentation that is involved here, we can construe the existence of overt analogues of zero derivation relations to be an explicit condition for the recognition of such relations. We refer to this condition as the OVERT ANALOGUE CRITERION; it is with the investigation of this criterion that the present chapter is primarily concerned.

Our inquiries in particular seek to determine the actual empirical and methodological status of this constraint as a basis for the recognition of zero derivation relations in languages. On the basis of these inquiries it is shown that there are several crucial problems that arise if the existence of overt analogues is taken as a general criterion for zero derivations in all cases. Through consideration of these problems it will be seen that while the overt analogue criterion can be appropriately construed as a useful heuristic principle and even as a sufficient condition for the recognition of zero derivation relations, it cannot be construed as a necessary condition for the recognition of such relations in all cases. Its incompleteness as an absolute criterion, moreover, will follow from the incompleteness of the overridingly formal assumptions about lexical derivation that underlie it. An appropriate absolute criterion for zero derivations will thus evidently require the incorporation of appropriate nonformal principles as well as a supplement or alternative to the primarily form-centered principle embodied in the overt analogue criterion alone.

2. Lexical Relatedness

Given a form with two distinct syntactic functions and a basic invariance of core meaning across these functions, there are four alternative analyses that are possible, representing three significantly distinct types of analysis. These are schematized in (5), where A and B are distinct functions of form F.

(5) a. A is derived from B. }
    b. B is derived from A. }   ZERO DERIVATION

    c. There is a single basic form con-
        stituting a polysemous archiform of
        A and B, with A and B as its   POLYSEMY
        context-sensitive alternants.

    d. A and B are separate and independent
        words or morphemes, i.e., homophones.   HOMOPHONY

The homophony alternative (5d) is clearly the weakest of the four analyses and in fact constitutes the null hypothesis for this type of situation. Thus, to claim that there are two separate and independent lexical items, equally basic or equally primitive in status, is to claim that any formal and/or semantic similarities between the two items are, in terms of language structure, purely accidental and nonsystematic. For example, to say that *wrinkle* the noun and *wrinkle* the verb are simply homophonous lexical items in English would be to claim that the striking phonological and semantic resemblances of the two *wrinkle*s are merely accidental and exactly on a par with the resemblance between *buy* the verb and *by* the preposition, for example, or between *bare* the adjective and *bear* the noun. Because it claims no systematic basis for the observed similarities at all, then, the null hypothesis of homophony is acceptable in a given situation only if none of the other possible claims about relatedness can be supported.

The strongest of the four alternatives, on the other hand, are those that claim a directed relation of zero derivation between the two functions of a form. This is because a derivational analysis claims not only that the two functions are nonaccidental variants of the same fundamental linguistic unit, which would also be claimed by a polysemy analysis of the form, but also that one of the variants is significantly subordinate and dependent in some way upon the other. Thus a homophony analysis is acceptable only if there are no grounds for recognizing either polysemy or derivation, and a polysemy analysis is acceptable only if there are no grounds for recognizing a relation of directed derivation. It is important, then, for purposes of adequate linguistic description and analysis, to determine some reasonably objective basis for establishing or disestablishing such grounds, and, more specifically, to determine the extent to which principles like the overt analogue criterion can effectively serve to differentiate relations of polysemy proper from relations where one of the polysemous terms is a dependent or subordinate derivative of the other.

The present endeavor thus addresses one aspect of the general problem of justification and evaluation of empirical claims about the morphological structures of words and about the relationships that hold between one word and another. The importance of such an endeavor is indicated by the nearly total absence of evidence or argumentation concerning the numerous actual claims about zero derivation that have been made in the linguistic literature. Clark and Clark (1979), for example, cite hundreds of instances of purported zero derivations of verbs from nouns in English without once stating for any of these instances why they believe that the verb is derived from the corresponding noun rather than the noun from the verb or in fact neither from either. The same is largely true for Kiparsky (1982) and Marchand (1969), who both give many examples of both zero-derived denominal verbs and zero-derived deverbal nouns without any significant comment on the basis or rationale for the categorizations they assert. For such categorizations to have empirical import, though, there obviously must be some objective basis for justifying and evaluating them. It is thus important to determine whether something like the overt analogue criterion is capable of providing such grounds.

On the basis of native-speaker intuition alone, I would tend to agree with most of the specific categorizations that linguists like Clark and Clark, Kiparsky, and Marchand have made concerning the existence and directionality of zero-derivation relations in English. In a number of instances, however, I find the claims made to be counterintuitive or at least decidedly unclear. For some words, moreover, different scholars have in fact made mutually incompatible claims about their derivational analysis. For example, Quirk and Greenbaum (1973, p. 441) claim that the English noun *cover* is derived by zero derivation from the verb *cover* while Clark and Clark (1979, p. 770) claim that the verb is derived by zero derivation from the noun. Similarly, where Clark and Clark (1979, p. 776) consider the verb *shampoo* to be derived from the homophonous noun, Marchand (1969, p. 303) considers the noun to be derived from the verb.

But quite apart from the need to evaluate unclear or competing analyses of this sort, we have the more general obligation to explicate our intuitions about the clear cases of zero derivation and to determine what general or possibly universal principles underlie these intuitions about lexical structure.

It is thus necessary to try to find out what makes one word simple and another complex and in what ways and for what reasons one word can be derivationally dependent upon another.

Finding out these things is important simply for the sake of accuracy and conceptual clarity of linguistic description. Of equal, or perhaps even greater, importance, though, is the fact that there are a number of proposed theoretical claims and lawlike generalizations about natural language that make crucial reference to the relations of lexical complexity and morphological derivation and which can thus be empirically evaluated only if it is possible to determine independently and with reasonable certainty whether these relations hold for actual linguistic situations in particular languages. Among the most prominent of such proposals are those found in the works of Kiparsky (for example, Kiparsky 1976, and, especially, 1982), who in fact has suggested some principles, cited here in (6), that are defined on the class of zero derivations itself.

(6)   a. A restricted set of verbs allow nouns to be made at level 1 by such suffixes as *-ant* or zero derivation (which I take to be a phonologically empty suffix).... The interesting generalization is that verbs subject to one of these level 1 rules tend not to get the otherwise productive *-er* suffix added by the corresponding rule...at level 2. (Kiparsky 1982, p. 135)

   b. As a broad generalization it can be said that verbs are freely zero-derived from nouns whenever not blocked by a synonymous formation at Level 1, such as *systematize* (**to system*), while nouns are zero-derived from verbs in special cases which themselves block the productive agent and action suffixes at level 2 such as *-er*...and *-ing*. (1982, p. 140)

   c. If we stipulate that zero suffixes cannot be added to suffixed forms... (1982, p. 141)

   d. Nouns zero-derived from verbs should be capable of receiving level 1 suffixes, while verbs zero-derived from nouns should not be so capable. (1982, p. 142)

To evaluate proposed generalizations such as these, it is necessary to determine in at least most individual instances whether or not a relation of zero derivation holds between two words and, if so, which word is derived from the other. And to avoid vicious circularity, this must be determinable independently of the proposed generalizations themselves. It is thus necessary to seek objective grounds for the identification of zero derivations and therefore to investigate the extent to which principles like the overt analogue criterion can provide such grounds.

3. Traditional Versions and Uses of the Overt Analogue Criterion

3.1

As an implicit basis for the postulation of nonovert, or zero, elements in linguistic analysis, the overt analogue principle undoubtedly goes back as far as the concept of zero elements itself. An almost explicit appeal to something like the overt analogue criterion in justification of a particular zero analysis can be found in Bloomfield's *Language* (1933, p. 223):

> The occurrence of one form [in an inflectional paradigm] usually guarantees the occurrence of all the others. It is this parallelism of the inflections which forces us to treat a single phonetic form like *sheep* as a set of homonyms, a singular noun *sheep* (corresponding to *lamb*) and a plural noun *sheep* (corresponding to *lambs*).

A more general, and perhaps somewhat even more explicit, appeal to an overt analogue principle is evident in Lyons's (1977, p. 523) discussion of zero derivation:

> The reason why these nouns [*release, attempt,* etc.] are said to be derived from the corresponding verbs, and by means of suffixation, is that they belong to the same subclass of nouns as 'extension,' 'justification,' 'arrangement,' etc., which are clearly deverbal and derived by suffixation.... Conversion, or zero-derivation, is very productive in English; and it is usually, though not always, clear which of the pair of lexemes related by conversion is simple and which is complex in terms of the general patterns of derivation manifest in the language.

Occasional attempts have been made, moreover, to codify the type of analogical reasoning involved here in the form of explicit constraints on the recognition of zero elements and relations. The most well known and most widely discussed constraint of this sort is that proposed by Bloch (1947): "One of the alternants of a given morpheme may be zero; but no morpheme has zero as its only alternant" (in Joos, 1957, p. 245). This constraint, which Haas (1957, p. 39) refers to as "the alternation rule," has the effect of excluding the postulation of any zero element that is not in an alternation relation with at least one analogous overt, or nonzero, element in the language. With specific reference to zero derivation, then, we can express the effect of Bloch's alternation rule by the general principle stated in (7), which we refer to as the "restricted version" of the overt analogue criterion.

(7)   THE OVERT ANALOGUE CRITERION (RESTRICTED)
        One word can be derived from another word of the same form in a
        language (only) if there is a precise analogue in the language where

the same derivational function is marked in the derived word by an overt (nonzero) form.

3.2

Among structural linguists, both American and European, there was quite widespread agreement with at least the spirit of Bloch's constraint. Two major criticisms, however, have been leveled against it: the first suggesting the constraint is insufficient, or too weak; the second suggesting it is nonnecessary, or too strong. The first criticism, however, voiced, for example, by Haas (1957), Matthews (1947), and Nida (1948), is really not particularly significant, since it merely points out that Bloch's constraint, not surprisingly, fails in itself to assure that all analyses involving zero alternants will be reasonably natural ones.

Moreover, what was primarily being objected to in connection with the sufficiency of Bloch's constraint was not the constraint itself but merely Bloch's own analyses of certain strong verbs of English—analyses that were considered intolerably counterintuitive by most linguists, but which were not precluded by the overt analogue criterion or any of the other then generally accepted constraints on morphological analysis. Thus, for example, Bloch's (1947) analysis of the word *took* is as follows: *took* consists of two morphemes, the first being the verbal root morpheme that also occurs in *take, taken, taking*, and the second being the preterite or past tense morpheme that also occurs in *walked, waited, bought, sang*; the preterite morpheme is expressed by the morphologically conditioned allomorph zero, which occurs after the morphemes *take, sing, cut*, etc., and the root morpheme is expressed by the morphologically conditioned allomorph *took*, which occurs only before the preterite morpheme, with *take* occurring as the allomorph of {*take*} in all other environments.

The primary, and quite reasonable, objection that was raised to this kind of analysis, by linguists such as Haas (1957), Hockett (1947), and, perhaps most clearly, Nida (1948), was that it located the semantic contrast between *take* and *took* at a position where there is no formal difference between the words—that is, in the completely imperceptible contrast between the zero allomorph of the preterite suffix in *took* and the absence of any suffix morpheme at all in *take*—while treating the formal difference between the two words, namely, their different root vowels, as being contextually predictable, and hence semantically nondistinctive. "By this procedure," as Nida says (1948; Joos, 1957, p. 256), "an overt distinction...is treated as meaningless, while the covert distinction becomes the meaning-carrier."

The overt analogue criterion alone is also clearly insufficient to exclude postulations of zero that would violate the fundamental biuniqueness condition assumed by metatheories of grammar such as that presented in Zellig Harris's *Structural Linguistics* (1951). According to Harris's metatheory, the rules of a grammar must determine a unique sequence of phones for any given sequence of morphemes and a unique sequence of morphemes for any given sequence of phones. A zero element can be said to occur in a given environment, then, only if it is possible to determine that the zero in that environment is an alternant of one and only one specific morpheme. Thus, for example, Harris (1951; pp. 214–215) allows for the postulation of a zero allomorph of the past participle suffix on *cut* in the sentence *I've cut it*, since the overt auxiliary consistently co-occurs with overt forms of the past participle morpheme in analogous expressions like *I've walked* or *I've broken it*. On the other hand, he prohibits postulation of a zero alternant of the preterite suffix on *cut* in the sentence *I cut it*, since "we cannot say uniquely what elements it contains, i.e., whether or not it contains the morpheme {*ed*}" (1951, p. 215).

The existence of morphemic and lexical homonymy in languages demonstrates that the biuniqueness condition is an empirically incorrect constraint on natural-language grammar since it dictates factually incorrect analyses of all sentences containing homophonous expressions. Thus it would dictate the claim that a sentence, for example, like *I'll meet you near the bank* has only one sequence of morphemes associated with it and hence only one meaning, when in fact, of course, it has at least two. Similarly, Harris's analysis of *I cut it*, which is dictated by the biuniqueness condition, falsely claims that the sentence has only one interpretation, where it actually has two, and where these are related to each other, moreover, in exactly the same way as *I push it* and *I pushed it, I buy it* and *I bought it*, and so on. The most natural thing to say about *I cut it*, in fact, is that *cut* does indeed have two alternative morphemic interpretations in this situation, one of which includes a zero alternant of the preterite morpheme and one of which includes no variant of this morpheme. This analysis is sanctioned by the overt analogue criterion by virtue of the occurrence of overtly differentiated analogues like *walk–walked, wait–waited, sing–sang*.

3.3

Bloch's version of the overt analogue criterion, while allowing zero allomorphs, excludes the postulation of ZERO MORPHEMES, that is, any morpheme that has no overt alternants at all. This has sometimes been considered too strong a constraint on linguistic analysis. For example, Bazell (1949; Hamp *et al.* 1949, p. 225) says that "one cannot go so far as to deny, with some American scholars, that a morpheme can consistently be expressed by a zero suffix; if there is reason to attribute a positive meaning to zero a morpheme must be assumed." Haas (1957, p. 38), even more critical of Bloch's constraint, says

"It might even be claimed that some zero-elements introduced in defiance of the rule would be more acceptable than many of those that are sanctioned by it."

The idea of zero morphemes, indeed, goes back at least as far as de Saussure, who said that "a material sign is not necessary for the expression of an idea; language is satisfied with the opposition between something and nothing" (de Saussure, 1931; 1959, p. 86). The postulation of a zero morpheme has been most often favored in situations where several different forms occur in a given position, each associated with a distinct meaning, and where when none of these contrasting forms occurs in that position, there is also a distinct meaning expressed which is not included in the meanings of the other forms that occur in that position.

For example, given Dakota verb paradigms like that in (8), it is reasonable to provide an analysis like that in (9), where a zero prefix meaning 'neither first person nor second person subject' contrasts in both form and with the overt prefix morphemes *wa*, *ya*, and *un*.

(8) *wadowan* 'I sing'
     yadowan 'you (sg) sing'   *yadowanpi* 'you all sing'
     undowan 'you and I sing'   *undowanpi* 'we all (+/−) you) sing'
      dowan 'he/she sings'   *dowanpi* 'they sing'

(9) Verb: Prefix-Stem-(Suffix)
     Stem: *dowan*,...
     Prefix: *wa* '1st person subject'
            ya '2nd person subject'
            un '1st person plus other(s) subject'
             ø 'neither 1st person nor 2nd person subject'
     Suffix: *pi* '3rd person plus other(s) subject'

Another quite similar example is provided by the schematic verb paradigm for Totenac in (10), taken essentially from Nida (1949, p. 46).

(10) *k*-stem '1 sg'   stem-*wi* '1 pl'
      stem-*ti* '2 sg'   stem-*tit* '2 pl'
       stem '3 sg'   stem-*qú·* '3 pl'

About this example Nida says,

> The absence of some other form is what actually indicates the third singular. Structurally, this is a type of significant absence; it is not, however, an allomorphic zero, but, rather, a morphemic zero. That is to say, this significant absence does not occur in a series of allomorphs, but in a series of morphemes (1949, p. 46).

Thus there would seem to be good reasons in cases like these to consider zero to be the expression of a particular morpheme in spite of the fact that this morpheme has no overt expression anywhere. This in turn would imply that Bloch's restricted version of the overt analogue criterion cannot be a strictly necessary condition for the appropriate recognition of zero elements in all cases.

However, though the postulation of any zero morpheme would violate Bloch's version of the overt analogue criterion, it is clear that the postulation of zero morphemes in paradigmatic set situations of the sort illustrated from Dakota and Totenac are always crucially dependent on an overt analogue too—only in this case the analogy of zero is with other morphemes of the same structural set rather than, as previously, with other allomorphs of the same morpheme. This suggests that it should be possible to generalize the overt analogue criterion to embrace the appropriate postulation of zero morphemes as well as zero allomorphs of morphemes.

Consider, first, the nature of the analogical relation that holds between the members of any set of overtly contrasting morphemes, for example, the inflectional endings of the Latin verbs, *amō, amas, amat*. The distinctive characteristic that is shared by all of these is simply that of being distinctively different, in form and meaning, from each and every one of the other members of the set. Their relatedness can thus be represented in the form of an analogical proportion of the type given in (11).

(11) $-\bar{o}$: $\{-as, -at\}$ :: $-as$: $\{-\bar{o}, -at\}$ :: $-at$: $\{-\bar{o}, -as\}$

Exactly the same analogy schema is applicable when one of the contrastive forms has no overt marking other than the absence of any of the other forms, as represented in (12) for the Dakota verb prefixes exemplified in (8).

(12) $\emptyset$: $\{wa, ya, un\}$ :: wa : $\{\emptyset, ya, un\}$ :: ya : $\{\emptyset, wa, un\}$
          :: un : $\{\emptyset, wa, ya\}$

The analogy schema for allomorphs of a morpheme are of this same form, too, of course, except that each element of the set is not just a form but a conjunction of a form and a specification of the context in which the form occurs. For example, the analogical proportion for the allormorphs of the English noun plural morpheme are based on a set with members like "/s/ after voiceless nonsibilants," "/z/ after voiced nonsibilants," "/ən/ after the morpheme *ox*," etc.

An appropriate generalization of the overt analogue criterion can thus be quite readily arrived at and can be explicitly expressed, for example, as in (13).

(13)   THE OVERT ANALOGUE CRITERION (GENERALIZED)
          Zero, or the absence of form, is a member of a set of (meaningful) linguistic elements (only) if
          a.   there are other elements in the set;
          b.   at least one of the other elements is not a zero element; and

c. zero is related to each of the other elements in the set in the same way that each of the other elements is related to each of the other elements in the set.

This generalized version of the overt analogue criterion would now apply to the determination of zero morphemes and zero allomorphs alike, and indeed to the determination of other linguistic zero elements as well.[2] It imposes the overt analogue requirement as a condition—hypothetically sufficient and, for the moment at least, possibly necessary as well—for the recognition of linguistically significant zeros of any sort. As such, it appears to be both conceptually and methodologically coherent, and seems to properly express the type of analogical reasoning that underlies, at least implicitly, most of the reasonable postulations of zero elements that have traditionally been made in the linguistic literature. The question that remains then is whether this constraint is empirically adequate for the particular purpose that is of concern here, namely, the determination of the existence and directionality of specific zero-derivation relations in languages. The remainder of our investigations is devoted to this question.

4. Problems with the Overt Analogue Criterion

A number of crucial problems arise if the existence of overt analogues is taken as a general criterion for the recognition of zero derivations in all cases. For example, since the overt analogue principle makes zero derivation dependent upon nonzero derivation, it would imply that zero derivation is universally marked relative to nonzero derivation. Such a conclusion would appear to be seriously questionable, however, particularly in view of the fact that zero derivation patterns in a language—such as the zero derivation of verbs from nouns in English—are often at least as general and productive as any of the language's nonzero patterns, as well as the fact that there are some languages, such as Chinese, that have essentially no nonzero derivational morphology at all.

It appears, however, that most of the problems that arise when we attempt

---

[2]Although we are concerned at present only with morphemic zeros, it is clear that the recognition of lexical or phrasal zeros (i.e., ellipsis sites, empty categories, etc.) is also consistently based on the existence of overt analogues. For example, the basis and justification for the postulated zero constituents in the second conjuncts of the following coordinations are the analogous nonzero constituents occurring in the corresponding structures of the associated first conjuncts:

(i) [*tall*]$_A$ *men and* [ø]$_A$ *women*
(ii) [*John*]$_{NP}$ *opened the door and* [ø] *came in*
(iii) *Pat has* [*eaten lunch already*]$_{VP}$ *and Tom has* [ø]$_{VP}$ *too*
(iv) *Ruth* [*likes*]$_V$ *the white* [*meat*]$_N$ *and Bill* [ø]$_V$ *the dark* [ø]$_N$

to make general use of the overt analogue criterion in linguistic analysis are to a large extent simply the problems that are associated with any investigation or reasoning based on analogy. These are indeed simply the basic problems of inductive inference in general: the problem of quality and quantity of instances of a pattern, and the problem of alternative or competing patterns instantiated by the same phonomena.

4.1

The quantity problem is the question of how many examples of an overtly marked derivational relation are needed in order for us to feel confident that there is really a significant pattern involved. Given only the pairs *man–manly* 'having characteristics of men' and *woman–womanly* 'having characteristics of women,' it would hardly be reasonable to seek to generalize from these two instances to a purported zero-derivational analogue like, for example, the noun *cold* and the adjective *cold*, meaning 'having characteristics of cold things.' But what about the set of pairs {*prince–princess, author–authoress,...*} Is this set large enough to warrant the analysis *professor* ('any/male professor')-*professor-ø* ('female professor')?

Essentially the same issues of evaluation apply to the problem of quality of instances, that is, the question of how clear our cases have to be, or, more specifically, how strong the parallelism between two relations must be for them to be considered instances of the same general relation. For example, are the similarities and differences clear enough for us to decide whether or not *trail* is to *trailer* as *work* is to *worker*, or *winter* is to *winterize* as *lion* is to *lionize*, or whether the verb *love* is to the noun *love* as the verb *govern* is to the noun *government*?

But, of course, with respect to quantity and quality of instances alike, there is no possible way to establish a minimum value needed to justify a given proportion or any given analogical extension of it. As with all inductive generalizing, in fact, the only principle here is necessarily just the more cases, and the more clear cases, the better.

4.2

One of the most serious problems with analogical reasoning, however, and the one that is most troublesome of all in reasoning about zero derivations in particular, stems from the fact that for any natural domain there are a multiplicity of distinct analogies, in fact, one analogy for every relation that holds for any two or more pairs of elements within the given domain. Typically, then, every element of a domain belongs to more than one analogical series. Thus, for example, the English phoneme /t/ belongs, on the basis of its laryngeal relation, to the series /t/ : /d/ :: /k/ : /g/ :: /s/ : /z/, and so on, and simultaneously, on the basis of its continuance relation, to the series which includes /t/ : /s/ :: /d/ : /z/ :: /p/ : /f/. Similarly, on the basis of different semantic relations, the English *boy* is analogous both to *man, father, uncle, king*, and to *girl, kitten, puppy, cub*.

The existence of multiple and intersecting analogies should not be disturbing in itself, of course, since it is just a natural reflection of the multipropertied and multirelationed nature of the natural contents of our universe. A problem arises only when different analogies intersect upon a particular pair of elements in such a way as to suggest that there are CONTRARY or CONTRADICTORY relations between the elements of the pair. Since the relation of derivational dependence is asymmetric, this is precisely the situation that could arise in the case of potential zero derivations.

It would be possible, therefore, that one analogy might suggest that function A is derived from function B and another analogy that function B is derived from function A. The question then is whether use of the overt analogue criterion does in fact lead to contradictory ascriptions of this sort about the nature and directionality of derivational relations in languages.

Apparent cases of alternative, mutually incompatible analogues for zero derivations can indeed be found. Consider, for example, the noun and verb *cover* in English. According to Clark and Clark (1979, p. 770), the verb *cover*, as in *cover the cushion*, is derived by zero derivation from the noun *cover*. According to Quirk and Greenbaum (1973, p. 441), on the other hand, the noun *cover* is derived by zero derivation from the verb. There are overt analogues, as shown in (14), for each of these opposite directions of derivation.

(14) a. *cover*$_N$: [ø *cover*$_N$]$_V$ 'put cover(s) on'
          :: *chain*$_N$: [en *chain*$_N$]$_V$ 'put chains on'
      b. *cover*$_V$: [*cover*$_V$ ø]$_N$ 'instrument for covering'
          :: *cleave*$_V$: [*cleav*$_V$ er]$_N$ 'instrument for cleaving'

A similar situation of competing analogues is evidenced by the noun and verb *knight* in English. Thus, as indicated in (15), the overt analogue criterion would suggest both that the verb *knight* is derived from the noun (on the basis of the overt analogue *victim–victimize*) and that the noun is derived from the verb (on the basis of the analogue *create–creation*).

(15) a. *knight*$_N$: [*knight*$_N$ ø]$_V$ 'make a knight of'
          :: *victim*$_N$: [*victim*$_N$ ize]$_V$ 'make a victim of'
      b. *knight*$_V$: [*knight*$_V$ ø]$_N$ 'product of knighting'
          :: *create*$_V$: [*create*$_V$ ion]$_N$ 'product of creating'

For cases like these, then, the overt analogue criterion is incapable of determining a unique analysis of the words involved and provides no basis in itself for reconciling the mutually incompatible claims about zero derivations that it generates. But the criterion suffers from a more fundamental and perhaps even more serious inadequacy as well, since there are some situations involving multiple function that intuitively constitute exceptionally clear cases of zero derivation but that seem to present no sufficiently clear evidence of overt analogues at all.

4.3

The absence of overt analogues of possible zero derivation relations is most striking, of course, in languages, like Chinese, that have essentially no overt derivational morphology at all (on derivation and multiple function in Chinese, see Tai, 1983, 1985). For such languages, it follows from the overt analogue criterion that since there are no nonzero derivational relations between words there can be no zero derivational relations either, and hence that all forms with multiple functions must have either a polysemy or a homophony analysis, as in (5c,d), rather than a derivational one, as in (5a,b). It might perhaps be argued that this is in fact the correct conclusion for languages of this type. But there appear to be crucial absences of overt analogues even in languages, like English, that have an abundance of explicit morphological marking of lexical relationships.

One of the most critical examples of this type of situation involves the exceptionally clear and productive zero derivation of denominal verbs in English. As indicated by the examples in (16), taken from Clark and Clark (1979), this pattern is essentially open-ended, there being a possible verb for every possible noun or nominal expression of the language.[3]

(16)   a.   *They **oil-painted** the house.*
       b.   *You'd better **zip-code** the letter.*
       c.   *They **rotten-egged** the speaker.*
       d.   *The paperboy **porched** the paper.*
       e.   *She **salt-and-peppered** the food.*

On syntactic grounds alone it is clear that the stems of the verbs in sentences like these are basically nominal rather than verbal, and that their function as verbs is dependent or parasitic upon their more direct or more fundamental use as nominals. Thus, for example, the constituents and constituent orderings of expressions like *oil paint* and *rotten egg* are standard and unexceptional for expansions, or projections, of the lexical category noun but not for the

---

[3]The proper set of inputs to denominal verbalization could be specified more precisely, perhaps, as the set of nonmaximal projections of N, that is, any nominal not initiated by a specifier or determiner. Thus, for example, sentences like *She **big-girled** them* or *She **girl-on-the-cornered** them* seem perfectly grammatical, while those like **She **a-big-girled** them* or **She **the-girl-on-the-cornered** them* appear to be decidedly less English-like.

category verb. The existence and directionality of a derivational relationship here is also quite clear on the basis of semantic considerations. Thus the meaning of a verb like *to porch* or *to rotten-egg* cannot be specified independently of the meaning of the noun, and perhaps in general must be so specified.

The semantic-pragmatic asymmetry that is involved here underlies Hopper and Thompson's (1984, p. 745) generalization that "a nominalization names an event taken as an entity; however, a 'verbalization' does not name an 'entity taken as an event,' but simply names an event associated with some entity." The naturalness of the nominal-to-verbal direction of derivation and the empirical appropriateness of defining the verbals on the basis of their corresponding nominals, rather than the reverse, are also clearly evidenced by the generality and simplicity of the general interpretation principle for all zero-derived denominal verbs in English proposed by Clark and Clark (1979, p. 767).

[The use of zero-derived denominal verbs in English] is regulated by a convention: in using such a verb, the speaker means to denote the kind of state, event, or process that, he has good reason to believe, the listener can readily and uniquely compute on this occasion, on the basis of their mutual knowledge, in such a way that the parent noun (e.g., *porch* or *Houdini*) denotes one role in the state, event, or process, and the remaining surface arguments of the denominal verb denote other of its roles.

But the strongest evidence of all for the zero derivation of denominal verbs in English is provided by examples of the sort illustrated in (17), where the stem of the verb is a proper name or definite description.

(17) a. *She **Lincoln Tunneled** her way to New York.* (from *Vogue*, cited by Clark and Clark, 1979, p. 777)
      b. *It's wrong to try to **uncertainty-principle** everything.*
      c. *She **relational-grammared** the syntax chapter of her book.*
      d. *They **Jessica Wirthed** their guests.*

Names and definite descriptions are prototypically nominal, if anything is, and have the prototypical nominal function of referring. Moreover, it is not possible to arrive at any appropriate understanding of the verbal uses of such forms except through knowledge of the characteristic attributes and behavior of the individual entities that are referred to by means of the nominal uses of the forms in question. It is thus exceptionally clear that the verbal use of forms like *Jessica Wirth* and *relational grammar* are crucially dependent upon, and subordinate to, their nominal uses, and therefore that if there is any zero derivation at all there should be zero derivation of verbs in English.[4] The question then is whether there are any overt analogues to such derivation in the language.

As noted by Marchand (1969, p. 296), "The only overt derivative morphemes that P[resent-day] E[nglish] has for denominal verbs are *-ate*, *-ize*, and *-ify*." These are thus the only possible candidates for overt analogy with the zero derived denominal verbs of English. And as can be seen from the data in (18), (19), and (20), none of the three suffixes really qualifies as an appropriate analogue here.

(18) $[X_N \; \emptyset]_V$ vs. $[X_N \; ize]_V$

    a. *They've **lioned** this zoo too much.*
        ≠ *They've **lionized** this zoo too much.*
    b. *He **patroned** many fine artists.*
        ≠ *He **patronized** many fine artists.*
    c. *She **charactered** the novel very well.*
        ≠ *She **characterized** the novel very well.*
    d. *They **vitamined** the milk at the dairy.*
        (?)= *They **vitaminized** the milk at the dairy.*
    e. *I **sectioned** the article.*
        = *I **sectionized** the article.*

(19) $[X_N \; \emptyset]_V$ vs. $[X_N \; ify]_V$

    a. *They **gassed** the enemy.*
        ≠ *They **gasified** the enemy.*
    b. *They **fished** at the north end of the lake.*
        ≠ *They **fishified** at the north end of the lake.*
    c. *She **classed** the inscriptions as Etruscan.*
        (?)= *She **classified** the inscriptions as Etruscan.*
    d. *He **Chomskied** the whole analysis.*
        (?)= *He **Chomskified** the whole analysis.*

---

[4]Extensive zero derivation of denominal verbs occurs in other languages as well. The following small samples, for example, indicate the generality of the pattern in Latin and French:

	nouns		verbs	
Latin	*corōna*	a crown	*corōnare*	to crown
	cumulus	a heap	*cumulare*	to heap
	locus	a place	*locare*	to place
	lacrima	a tear	*lacrimare*	to shed tears
French	*épice*	spice	*épicer*	to spice
	guide	guide	*guider*	to guide
	groupe	group	*grouper*	to group
	clou	nail	*clouer*	to nail
	piste	track, trail	*pister*	to track

(20) $[X_N \; \emptyset]_V$ vs. $[X_N \; ate]_V$
   a.   *I circled the answer.*
        ≠ I circulated the answer.
   b.   *He aliened the workforce at his factory.*
        ≠ He alienated the workforce at his factory.
   c.   *They oriented themselves quickly.*
        = They orientated themselves quickly.
   d.   *She filtered the solution.*
        = She filtrated the solution.

From these data we must conclude (a) that zero is not in complementary distribution with any of the overt denominal verb-forming suffixes of English, (b) that zero is sometimes, but not always, in contrast with each of the overt suffixes, and, therefore, (c) that zero derivation of verbs from nouns in English does not satisfy the overt analogue criterion in either its restricted or its generralized version. Since the existence and directionality of a zero derivation relation is exceptionally clear in this case, these data demonstrate that the overt analogue criterion is clearly not a necessary condition for the appropriate recognition of zero derivation relations in all cases.

5. Other Possible Criteria for Zero Derivations

Where there is no formal evidence of a derivational dependency relation— either direct, or indirect through analogy with other overtly marked dependencies—there still might be some other grounds for considering one function of a form to be dependent upon another.

5.1

One logically possible supplementary criterion of this type might be some sort of developmental precedence criterion, according to which the function of a form that appears later—either in the course of language history or in the process of language acquisition by individual speakers—would be taken to be derived from the function that appears earlier. But, in addition to all of the usual problems associated with the use of diachronic or developmental data as a basis for justifying synchronic analyses, there seems to be no clear evidence in the present case of any systematic general correspondence between the temporal precedence of functions and the evident derivational relationships between them. Thus, for example, as suggested by the sample of earliest OED attestations from Marchand (1969, p. 297) given in (21), there appears to be no systematic differences between the dates of first use of a multiple-function English word as a noun and as a verb.

(21)   Date of earliest attested use   Precedence

	as noun	as verb	
annoy	1230	1250	N by 20 years
accord	1297	1123	V by 174 years
array	1300	1297	V by 3 years
change	1225	1230	N by 5 years
charm	1300	1300	none
count	1325	1325	none
cry	1275	1225	V by 50 years
dance	1300	1300	none
rule	1225	1225	none
touch	1297	1297	none
trouble	1230	1225	V by 5 years
vow	1290	1300	N by 10 years

5.2

Another type of principle that might be considered as a supplement to the overt analogue criterion is a principle of relative markedness, according to which a typologically marked function of a word would always be taken to be derived from the corresponding unmarked function of that word.[5] Thus, for example, there are languages that have a word with the meaning and function of the English noun *bottle* but no word with the meaning and function of the English verb *bottle*. (Chinese is such a language; see Tai, 1985.) On the other hand, it is very likely that every language that has a verb meaning 'to bottle' also has a noun meaning 'bottle.' If this is the case, then the verbal function of 'bottle' words is typologically marked relative to their nominal function and would thus be taken to be derived from the latter, according to the relative markedness principle, even when, as in Chinese, the overt analogue criterion is incapable of determining any derivational relation between these functions.

Markedness relations of this sort, however, could be used as a basis for determining the existence and directionality of derivational relations in a language only if it can be established on independent general grounds that there is in fact some systematic and invariant relationship between typological markedness relations and derivational dependency relations—for example, such that if a language has both terms of a lexical markedness relation, the marked term is always derived from the unmarked term. To determine whether or not something like this can be established and, more generally, whether markedness relations do in fact hold between the functions of multiple-

---

[5]A is TYPOLOGICALLY MARKED relative to B (and B is TYPOLOGICALLY UNMARKED relative to A) if and only if every language that has A also has B, but not every language that has B has A.

function words, it is clear that a great deal of typologically oriented study of morphology and lexis remains to be carried out.

5.3

The incompleteness of the overt analogue criterion as an absolute condition for the recognition of zero derivation relations really follows, however, from the incompleteness of the fundamental assumption about lexical derivation that underlies it, namely, that the prototype of lexical dependency is a relation such that the form and occurrence of one word in a language depends on the form and occurrence of another word, regardless of the particular semantic and pragmatic relations involved. Actually, though, the prototype of lexical dependency involves both a dependency between the forms of two words and a dependency between their appropriate interpretations and uses, where the two species of dependency, moreover, have the same directionality. This would suggest then that any appropriate absolute criterion for zero derivations must incorporate an appropriately restricted principle of semantic-pragmatic dependency as an addition or alternative to the primarily form-centered principle expressed by the overt analogue criterion alone.

It would thus seem to be appropriate, for example, to assume that if the interpretation of function A of a form is necessarily presupposed or entailed by the interpretation of function B, but not the reverse, then a direction of derivation from A to B can thereby be argued, even if formal indications of such dependence are totally lacking. This is precisely the type of argumentation that is employed by Marchand (1969) in support of his claim that the French verb *scier* 'to saw' is derived by zero derivation from the noun *scie* 'saw,' rather than the noun being zero derived from the verb, as Godel (1953) suggested on the basis of the analogy *scier* : *scie* :: *hâcher* 'to chop' : *hâchoir* 'chopper' :: *passer* 'pass, sift, strain' : *passoire* 'strainer, colander.'

In arguing for the zero derivation of the verb from the noun in this case, Marchand (1969, p. 3) says,

> The equation...does not hold from the point of view of the significate: the action of 'passer' does not presuppose the existence of a 'passoire' (any more than a tamis ['sieve'] or filtre ['filter, strainer']), nor is the action of 'hâcher' subject to the existence of a 'hâchoir' (one could chop with any kind of knife). Yet one cannot 'saw' without a 'saw,' i.e. the concept 'saw' is implied in the verbal concept 'saw.' Though the problem is more complex than this isolated case suggests, the general principle will be to assume that the concept which for its definition is dependent on the concept of the other pair member must be considered that of the derived word. Applied to *scier* : *scie* it means that *scier* is the marked form, derived by a zero morpheme from the substantive *scie*.

Although this appeal to definitional dependency is basically reasonable, the problem of applying this principle is indeed, as Marchand acknowledges, quite complex. It is not literally true that "one cannot 'saw' without a 'saw,' " since it is perfectly possible to saw off a branch with a pocket knife, to saw the air with one's hand, to saw through a rope with a piece of broken glass, and so on. But it is true, nevertheless, that the normal and prototypical instrument that is used for sawing is indeed a saw, and unless there are good reasons for believing otherwise this is the instrument that will be assumed. Thus it would be communicatively inappropriate to answer the question *Where's Bob?* simply with *He's out back sawing wood* unless it is a saw that Bob is using to cut the wood.

A more serious problem with this type of semantic–pragmatic dependency criterion, though, is the difficulty of determining in all cases a unique direction of dependence. The typical situation, in fact, at least for instrumental cases like *saw* seems to involve mutual dependence. Thus while it is true that to saw is to cut as with a saw, it is equally true that a saw is that kind of instrument that is prototypically used for sawing things. Nevertheless, in this as in all other things linguistic, unclear cases are to be expected and do not in themselves cast doubt on the appropriateness of general principles.

The fundamental appropriateness and utility of the concept of definitional or semantic–pragmatic dependence is, in any event, quite readily apparent from the consideration of clear cases of zero derivation like that of the denominal verbs of English discussed above. For example, to define or make effective communicative use of the verb *to John Wayne*, as in *He John Wayned the part*, depends on shared knowledge of the characteristic attributes of the jointly understood referent of the expression *John Wayne* when it is used in the prototypically nominal function of referring. In this type of case, then, where the overt analogue criterion would fail to generate any claims about derivational relatedness, a general criterion of semantic–pragmatic dependence would make what is surely the empirically correct claim that the verb is zero derived from the nominal, and not the reverse. It remains to be determined, of course, to what extent this criterion of semantic–pragmatic dependency can be generalized to less clear and less prototypical cases of multiple function and thus to what extent it can serve, either alone or in conjunction with the overt analogue criterion, as an appropriate basis for the recognition of zero derivation relations in all languages.

Acknowledgments

I am grateful to Linda Schwartz for valuable comments on the preliminary manuscript. I have also benefited from discussion of various points with Gregory Iverson and James Tai.

References

Bazell, C.E. (1949). On the problem of the morpheme. *Archivum Linguisticum* 1, 5–15. (Reprinted in E. Hamp, F.W. Householder, and R. Austerlitz, eds. "Readings in Linguistics," Vol. 2, pp. 216–26. Univ. of Chicago Press, Chicago, 1966.)

Bloch, B. (1947). English verb inflection. *Language* 23, 399–418. (Reprinted in Joos (ed.), pp. 386–99.)

Bloomfield, L. (1933). "Language." Holt, New York.

Clark, E.V., and Clark, H.H. (1979). When nouns surface as verbs. *Language* 55, 767–811.

deSaussure, F. (1931). "Course in General Linguistics." English translation by W. Baskin. Philosophical Library, New York, 1959.

Haas, W. (1957). Zero in linguistic description. "Studies in Linguistic Analysis," pp. 33–53. Blackwell, Oxford.

Harris, Z.S. (1951). "Structural Linguistics." Univ. of Chicago Press, Chicago.

Hockett, C.F. (1947). Problems of morphemic analysis. *Language* 23, 321–43. (Reprinted in Joos (ed.), pp. 229–42.)

Hockett, C.F. (1954). Two models of grammatical description. *Word* 10, 210–31. (Reprinted in Joos (ed.), pp. 386–99.)

Hopper, P.J., and Thompson, S.A. (1984). The discourse basis for lexical categories in universal grammar. *Language* 60, 703–52.

Joos, M. (ed.) (1957). "Readings in Linguistics." American Council of Learned Societies, Washington, D.C.

Kiparsky, P. (1976). Abstractness, opacity, and global rules. *In* "The Application and Ordering of Phonological Rules" (A. Koutsoudas, ed.), pp. 160–86. Mouton, The Hague.

Kiparsky, P. (1982). From cyclic phonology to lexical phonology. *In* "The Structure of Phonological Representations" (H. van der Hulst and N. Smith, eds.), Part 1, pp. 131–76. Foris, Dordrecht.

Lyons, J. (1977). "Semantics." Cambridge Univ. Press, Cambridge.

Marchand, H. (1969). "The Categories and Types of Present-Day English." Beck, Munich.

Matthews, P.H. (1947). "Morphology." Cambridge Univ. Press, Cambridge.

Nida, E.A. (1940). The identification of morphemes. *Language* 24, 414–41. (Reprinted in Joos (ed.), pp. 255–71.)

Nida, E.A. (1949). "Morphology," 2nd Ed. Univ. of Michigan Press, Ann Arbor.

Quirk, R., and Greenbaum, S. (1973). "A Concise Grammar of Contemporary English." Harcourt, New York.

Quirk, R. *et al.* (1972). "A Grammar of Contemporary English." Longman, London.

Tai, J.H.-Y. (1983). *On the absence of denominal verbs in Chinese.* Presented at the Annual Meeting of the Linguistic Society of America, December 28, 1983, Minneapolis, Minnesota.

Tai, J.H.-Y. (1985). Category shifts in Chinese. In preparation.

Part III

Historical/Areal Studies

Chapter 10

Prefixation in Kannada

Mark Aronoff & S.N. Sridhar

We have isolated a phenomenon in modern literary Kannada which, to our knowledge, has escaped notice. In this chapter, we analyze the phenomenon and demonstrate that it can be described as prefixation. This claim, if true, is interesting to Dravidianists, because no prefixes have previously been found in any Dravidian language. Moving to a more general theoretical plane, we also defend the more delicate claim that there is a structural distinction between compounding and prefixation. This distinction is so well known in the general literature on morphology that our exercise might seem over-nice, but in fact the boundaries are not so clear as they have been presumed to be, even to the point where the distinction has been called into question (Wolff, 1984).

Let us begin with this theoretical and, indeed, general descriptive problem: How do we demonstrate that those entities that we are calling prefixes are just that and not first members of compounds? After all, in both cases, we have a word of the form AB. Why are some As first members of compounds and other As prefixes?

There are two general types of reasons for making the distinction. One concerns the sets of elements and the other concerns the manner of their combination. The two sets, first members of compounds and prefixes, are always defined differently. In any given type of compound, the set of first elements is defined categorically: it consists of one or more of the major lexical categories of the language (noun, verb, adjective). A set of prefixes, by contrast, is always defined extensionally. Because of its categorial definition, the set

Theoretical Morphology   Copyright © 1988 by Academic Press, Inc.

of first elements of compounds is open, while, by contrast, the set of prefixes is closed.[1]

The difference in the manner of combination between first members of compounds and prefixes lies in the bound nature of prefixes. Prefixes are what Bloomfield calls BOUND FORMS; they cannot appear anywhere else than as prefixes. First elements of compounds, by contrast, may occur freely wherever other members of the same lexical category may occur. Prefixes are also more closely bound in another sense of the word: They are always more closely tied to their surroundings by morphological and/or phonological means than are first elements of compounds.

Prefixes, then, should be a small set of bound forms which are tightly tied phonologically and morphologically to their heads. First members of compounds, by contrast, are members of an open major lexical category and have looser phonological and morphological ties to their heads. These are the general criteria that we use in our investigation.

There is, as always, an intermediate case. Here it is the COMBINING FORM, wherein a member of a major lexical category has a special idiosyncratic form that is found only in compounds. The classic examples come from Germanic (Bloomfield, 1933; Botha, 1969). The problem with combining forms is to determine whether a particular combining form is an allomorph of a member of a major lexical category or whether it is a prefix. This problem does not have a solution that extends to all instances, but must rather be answered on a case-by-case basis. The simplest way to show that a combining form is not a prefix is to show that it contrasts with a prefix, and luckily, this is what we find in Kannada. Also, if it can be shown that a combining form has the characteristics of a first member of a compound rather than of a prefix, then we may conclude that the combining form is indeed a first member of a compound. This is also the case in Kannada.

There are other types of intermediate cases. These include morphologically and syntactically bound stems. Because, however, these other types do not occur in Kannada we do not discuss them further. Readers interested in morphologically bound stems should consult the relevant pages in Bloomfield, while those interested in syntactically bound stems should look at the literature on Neo-Latin compounds in English (Hatcher, 1951; Wolff, 1984).

In short, although there are entities that fall midway between prefixes and normal members of major lexical categories, it is still possible to distinguish these entities from prefixes. Furthermore, although intermediate cases may meet some of the criteria that are associated with prefixes, only prefixes meet all of these criteria. This is the crucial difference between prefixes and combining forms or bound stems.

---

[1]It is often difficult to determine what category, if any, a given prefix belongs to. This is in large part because it does not occur elsewhere.

More than Tamil or Telugu, Kannada, like Malayalam, has borrowed extensive vocabulary from Sanskrit. Because of the large number of productive prefixes in Sanskrit, one might be tempted to turn to that sector of the vocabulary of the language to find productive prefixes. However, we do not do so. Instead, we show that prefixes may be found in the Dravidian portion of the vocabulary of Kannada.

The first clues that there might be prefixes in Kannada come from examples of the sort found in (1). In Column A are regular compounds, words whose first and second elements both may appear elsewhere as free forms. In Column B are words whose first element is a combining form, or bound stem, related to a free form but not found elsewhere. The first elements in the words in Column C are what we consider prefixes.

(1)

A	B	C	
mundevari	*munduvari*	*munnari*	go forward
	mundugade	*mungade*	front side
hinde munde			back and front
	hindumundu		back and forth
hinde ga:lu		*hinga:lu*	back leg
hindesari		*hinjari*	back slide
	hindugaDe	*hingaDe*	back side

If it were not for examples like those in Column B, one might conclude that the first elements in Column C were combining forms. However, the simple existence of forms like those in Column B militates against this solution and suggests the possibility that the forms in Column C are indeed prefixes. Our task is to provide additional evidence for this claim.

We have said that the set of prefixes in any language should be closed and small, and this is indeed true of those elements which we are calling prefixes in Kannada. They number no more than a dozen; (2) lists all those elements for which we have evidence of prefixhood.

(2)

mun-	fore	*kaD-*	intense
hin-	back	*teL-*	clear
ili-	down	*ken-*	red
ir-	two	*in-*	sweet
her-	big		

What sorts of features do these elements share? Semantically, they are somewhat diverse. Most seem to be adjectives or modifiers; the meanings of some are more or less what one would expect of prefixes, but the meanings of others are more specific. Because they do not appear elsewhere as free forms, it is generally impossible to assign any lexical category to prefixes; nonetheless, by looking at their semantics, we can see that these elements are heterogeneous in their categories. Some are adjectival, and some adverbial. This heterogeneity, though it may seem peculiar, is in fact exactly what we normally find in classes of bound forms. We return to syntax and semantics in our discussion of the combinatorial behavior of this set. For the moment, we turn to phonology in order to demonstrate that, despite their semantic heterogeneity, these elements that we are calling prefixes are remarkably uniform in their phonological properties.

As the examples in (3) show, prefixed words are characterized by assimilation of both the final consonant of the prefix and the initial consonant of the stem. Except for *I*, the final oral consonant of a prefix assimilates in both place and manner or oral articulation to the initial consonant of the stem.

(3)　　*kengaNNu*　　red eye　　　　　*kaNNu*　　eye
　　　kendaLir　　red sprout　　　*taLir*　　sprout
　　　kembal　　red tooth　　　*hallu*　　tooth
　　　kengiraNa　　red rays　　　*kiraNa*　　rays
　　　kenjiguru　　red sprout　　　*ciguru*　　sprout
　　　kendale　　red head　　　*tale*　　 ˙head
　　　kenna=lige　　red tongue　　　*na=lige*　　tongue
　　　kemmugilu　　red sky　　　*mugilu*　　sky
　　　heddere　　big screen　　　*tere*　　screen
　　　hebbandi　　big pig　　　*handi*　　pig
　　　heggumbaLa　　big pumpkin　　　*kumbaLa*　　pumpkin
　　　hejje=nu　　big bee　　　*je=nu*　　bee
　　　hemmara　　big tree　　　*mara*　　tree

Nasal consonants assimilate in place of articulation but remain nasal. This assimilation is summarized in the rule given in (4).

(4)　　$[+\text{nasal}] \rightarrow [\alpha\text{place}]/\underline{\quad\quad}[\alpha\text{place}]$
　　　$C \rightarrow C_i/\underline{\quad\quad}C_i$

In the correct phonological theory, it should be possible (perhaps even necessary) to state these rules as a single rule without baroque abbreviations. We do not concern ourselves with such a theory here (though see Sagey, 1986). As for the initial consonant of the stem, it becomes voiced after the prefix. For the most part, this is a simple matter. However, a few peculiarities, which are characteristic of voiced/voiceless pairs throughout the language, should be noted. The voiced counterpart of *s* is *j*, there being no *z* phoneme in the language, while the voiced counterpart of *h* is *b*, a peculiarity due to the fact that *h* is derived historically from initial *p*.

Except after one prefix, which we return to below, voicing is categorical in prefixed forms in Kannada. There is an interesting contrast here between prefixed forms and compounds, which lends some further support to our analysis. Voicing does occur in compounds, but it is highly limited. Certain individual compound words undergo voicing, others never undergo voicing, while in a few cases voicing seems to be variable. Whether voicing occurs in any given compound cannot be attributed to either the first or the second member of that compound. That is to say, there is no word which, when it occurs as a first member of a compound, triggers voicing; similarly there is no word which, when it occurs as the second element of a compound, always undergoes voicing. There are certain types of compounds, such as *dvandva*, where voicing never occurs, but there is no type of compound in which voicing is obligatory. Voicing in compounds also seems to correlate with semantic lexicalization: Semantically lexicalized and more frequent forms are more likely to undergo voicing, while novel forms do not. Voicing is thus a mark of a closer binding between the two elements of a compound. This is exactly what is expected on universal grounds; lexicalized compounds should be closer in their phonology to affixed forms, and rules which are categorical for affixes should apply in individual compounds. For example, in English, it is well known that vowel reduction is found in the more-frequent compounds.

One way to formalize this difference between compounds and prefixed forms is to distinguish them in terms of boundaries or lexical levels. We have argued elsewhere (Aronoff and Sridhar, 1983) that Kannada, like English, has two morphological levels, stem level and word level. We may thus say that assimilation occurs at the stem level but not at the word level, that prefixation is stem level and compounding is word level. Lexicalization, which is normally interpreted as boundary decay, results in stem-level compounds in certain individual cases. This is exactly parallel to the standard interpretation for similar phenomena in English and is probably universal.

There is further evidence for the claim that compounding is a word-level phenomenon. This evidence lies in the rule of enunciative *u* (Bright, 1958). In Kannada, the vowel *u* is inserted after a word-final consonant. *u* also appears before the word-level plural suffix *galu* (Aronoff and Sridhar, 1983). The same *u* shows up in compounds, which is exactly what we expect if compounding is a word-level phenomenon. This *u* never appears after a prefix, reinforcing the argument that prefixation is stem level. The patterning of combining forms is instructive with regard to this phenomenon. The major difference between combining forms and related free forms is that the combining forms show *u* postconsonantally, while the free forms have another vowel. We do not know why the vowel is different, however the fact that *u* shows up in the combining form shows that combining forms are also concatenated at word level.

We have argued elsewhere that the number of morphological levels found within words is limited to just the two that are permitted by *The Sound Pattern of English* (Chomsky and Halle, 1968) (SPE) and Selkirk (1982), which we call STEM LEVEL and WORD LEVEL. There is evidence from many languages that, while affixational phenomena may be found at both word level and stem level across a wide variety of languages, compounding is a strictly word-level phenomenon. What we consider prefixation in Kannada must be analyzed as a stem-level phenomenon, both because of the lack of word-level characteristics and because the assimilation found in prefixation is a stem-internal characteristic of the language. We take this stem levelhood as further support for our analysis, for otherwise we would be forced to admit stem-level compounds.

Before we leave phonology, we point out one subtle but major phonological difference between what we are calling prefixed forms and compounds: The nature of exceptionality in each domain. We have already seen what exceptional compounds are like: Individual compounds may exceptionally undergo initial voicing. This is determined by neither the first nor the second member of the compound; it is rather a lexical property of the individual compound word. With prefixes, the situation is different. We noted above that initial voicing is categorical for prefixes—all prefixed forms undergo the rule—with one exception. The prefix *ir* (unlike the other *r*-final prefix, *her*) does not trigger voicing, as we see in (5).

(5)   *ikkay*   both hands   *kay*   hand
      ikka=valu   double guard   *ka=valu*   guard
      igga=li   two wheels   *ga=li*   pair
      ibbadi   two sides   *badi*   side
      itterige   double taxation   *terige*   tax
      innu=ru   two hundred   *nu=ru*   100
      ippattu   twenty   *hattu*   ten
      immana   two minds   *mana*   mind
      ikkoTi   two crores   *koTi*   10 million

Assimilation, the rule that is particular to the prefix level, does apply in all *ir* forms.[2] Note what is happening here: The rule to which these forms are exceptional would apply to the stem, not to *ir-. ir-* is thus a negative trigger. It idiosyncratically blocks the application of a rule in the stem to which it is attached. With this prefix, all prefixed forms are exceptional. With compounds, by contrast, individual compound words are exceptional.

This difference in the patterning of exceptions is traceable to a fundamental distinction between affixes and roots. The distinction can best be understood through the theory of phonological levels as first elaborated in SPE. According to this theory, each phonological level or juncture type can be identified with the operation of a specific set of rules on a specific set of affixes. A priori, as Strauss (1982) first observed, any given affix can undergo any rule—there is no logical necessity for a set of affixes all to undergo the same set of rules. But what we find instead in language is a sort

---

[2]In fact, these forms show that the last consonant of the prefix assimilates in voicing as well as in place and manner.

of clustering, each cluster constituting a level or boundary type. One unclarity in SPE is what types of entities must be stipulated for the boundaries or levels. Are all arbitrary segmental strings—roots, stems, words—stipulated for boundaries, or are only some? This question has not been addressed directly in the literature, but the answer may be found in Siegel (1979): Only affixes are stipulated for a particular level. Roots and members of major lexical categories carry no labels and are associated with no level. Thus, in English, a monomorphemic word like *telegraph* carries no boundaries. It is not a Level I word nor a stem-level word. However, suffixes like +*y* and #*er* do carry such information. *Telegraph*, if left alone, will go through all the levels, stem and word, + and #, I and II, as will any unaffixed word. Affixes differ. Attach +*y* and stem-level rules apply twice, once to *telegraph* and once to *telegraphy*, before word-level rules are invoked. Attach #*er* and there is no second application.

The reason that all and only affixes must be specified for a given level or boundary is that they are dependent, while lexical roots are not.

Phonological rules are associated, through the levels, with individual affixes. The affixes trigger the rules, not only because of their segmental properties, but often simply because they belong to a certain level. Thus, two affixes may be segmentally identical, yet each triggers the rules associated with the level it belongs to. This is clear from such pairs as +*er*/#*er* (Sapir, 1925), +*able*/#*able* (Aronoff, 1976), and many others in the literature. Kiparsky (1982) even claims that there are two levels of zero affixation in English.

Affixes are thus connected arbitrarily through levels to phonological rules. Roots do not have the same arbitrary connection to phonological rules, because they belong to no level.

Because of the arbitrary nature of the connection between affix and rule, this connection may sometimes be broken, in which case a given affix will not trigger a given rule. Conversely, a given affix may arbitrarily become a trigger for a rule which other affixes of the same level do not trigger. Because of the dependent nature of the affix, if the connection is lost, the rule will fail to apply not just in one case or in one word, but across the board, in all words to which the affix is productively attached. This is exactly what we see in the case of *ir-*. All words beginning with *ir* fail to undergo voicing. English *-ic* is an example of an affix which arbitrarily triggers an idiosyncratic rule of its own: It attracts stress to the preceding syllable, and this rule too operates in nearly all cases (Prince, 1972).

Lexical roots may be exceptional, but in different ways. They may be exceptional positive triggers of minor morphological rules. This has been amply demonstrated in various works on lexical phonology, especially Kiparsky (1982). Thus, certain English words have irregular plurals. They are marked positively to take the irregular plural marker. The elsewhere condition blocks the application of the regular plural rule to these forms, so that the blocking of the regular rule is not stipulated. To our knowledge, there are no cases of lexical roots acting as negative triggers for morphological rules. In fact, this possibility is explicitly ruled out in Aronoff (1976) as well as in most cyclical theories of phonology.

Also, as we know from the large literature on exceptions (Leben and Robinson, 1977; Zonneveld, 1978), individual complex words may be exceptional with respect to individual phonological rules (e.g., *obesity* is an exception to Tri-Syllabic Laxing in English). In these cases, though, it is the individual word that is exceptional and not a particular morpheme. By contrast, when affixes are exceptional, their exceptionality extends to all cases.

To sum up this long excursus, we have argued that the dependent nature of affixes leads to a particular pattern of exceptions that is not found with free roots. The existence of this type of pattern in Kannada thus supports our argument for prefixes in that language.

We now move from phonology to more morphological matters. So far, we have shown that Kannada prefixes are very few in number, that they are more closely tied phonologically to their heads than are first members of compounds, even combining forms, and that their morphophonological peculiarities are typical of dependent elements. We now show that prefixes may be distinguished from their parallel free forms in their privilege of occurrence as well.

Affixes are always very closely constrained in their distribution. They are not simply dependent forms. Rather, each affix must be labeled as to exactly where in a word it may appear. Even in the most liberal cases, such as in most of English morphology, every affix must be either a prefix or a suffix or an infix, in which case the manner of infixation is invariably completely determined. Frequently, however, affixes are more highly restricted, so that we find complex and very rigid templates, where each affix may appear in only one particular position with respect not only to the stem but also to other affixes, for example, the sorts of templates that we see in Iroquoian and Athapaskan languages such as Mohawk and Navajo.

In Kannada, if we compare a prefix to its corresponding free form, this difference in distribution becomes clear. Prefixes are always prefixes; they cannot appear in any other position in a word. Elements that serve as first members of compounds, on the other hand, because compounding is categorial, are members of major lexical categories and may occur as second members as well. This is shown clearly in the examples in (6).

(6) *kenje=nu* ⎫
     *je=nuken ⎰   red bee
     je=nu tuppa   honey (lit. bee oil)
     kenni=li   reddish blue
     kempuni=li   reddish blue or red blue

$$\left.\begin{array}{l} *ni=liken/m \\ ni=lik(g)empu \end{array}\right\}$$ bluish red (?)

kenduTi   red lip

$$\left.\begin{array}{l} *tuTigen/m \\ tuTigempu \end{array}\right\}$$ redness of the lip (?) (e.g., lipstick)

This fixedness of prefixes emerges even more clearly when we look at compound verbs, which are very common in Kannada, but which we have not discussed up to this point. While Kannada noun compounds have their head as the second element, just as English compounds do, in compound verbs the head comes first; the second member is either an auxiliary verb or a member of a relatively small class called VECTORS. If prefixed forms were just another type of compound, we might expect to find suffixed rather than prefixed verbs, on the analogy of compounds. However, this is not the case. Prefixes are always prefixes, regardless of whether they attach to nouns or verbs:

(7)   a.   V(head) + V(auxiliary/vector) structure in compound verbs
         ha=L-agu   'ruin become' (i.e., 'come to ruin')
         hogi-biDu   'go-leave' (i.e., 'go away')
   b.   Prefixes, though vectorlike in meaning, occur to the left of the verb (semantic head).
         munnuggu   'push forward' (*nuggu* 'push')
         hinjari   'hesitate' (*sari* 'move/slide')

Prefixes are not only fixed, they are also closely bound to their stems. Nothing may intervene between a prefix and its stem. For example, neither the inclusive conjunctive clitic *u* nor the exclusive conjunctive clitic *o* may attach to a prefix. This is demonstrated in (8).

(8)   a.   *kempu= niliyu= a=da   a=ka=sha*
         red-u   blue-u "being" sky
         'red and blue sky'
   b.   *kempo= niliyo= a=da   a=ka=sha*
         red-alt. blue-alt. "being" sky
         'either red or blue sky'
*c.   *kenno= ni=liyo= a=da a=kasha*, compare with
   d.   *kenni=liyo=   kembiLupo=   a=da   a=ka=sha*
         reddish blue-alt. reddish white-alt. "being" sky
         'The sky which is (either) reddish-blue or reddish-white.'

This close binding of prefixes extends finally to semantic scope. A prefix may have scope only over the stem to which it is attached, while the scope of the first element of a compound may be broader, sometimes leading to ambiguities, as shown in (9).

(9) a. *kempu maNNu go=De*
          red   earth   wall
          'red earthen wall' or 'wall (made) of red earth'
     b. *kemmaNNu go=De*
          'wall made of kemmannu (i.e., a special type of red soil)'
          'wall painted with kemmannu'

Any one of the distinctions that we have drawn, taken separately, might be construed as little more than a curiosity. However, falling together as they do, they make it difficult to conclude anything but that there is a distinct prefixal construction in Kannada. It remains to be shown, however, that those forms that we have termed prefixed are not merely relics, that prefixation in Kannada is productive. Otherwise, one might argue that prefixed forms in Kannada are like compound Latinate verbs in English of the type *revert.* Any real demonstration of productivity would entail an experimental task that is beyond the scope of this chapter [see Anshen and Aronoff (1981) for an example]. Nonetheless, it is clear from anecdotal evidence that at least some of these prefixes are productive and that a fair number of prefixed words are recent coinages.

We now turn to history. What, we may naturally ask, is the origin of these Kannada prefixes? The answer to this question, though somewhat speculative, is very simple. The major difference between prefixes and corresponding first members of compounds is, as we have noted above, the lack of the enunciative *u* in the prefixes. We know from comparative evidence that this enunciative *u* is fairly recent. The prefixes are therefore relic forms. We also know that the rules of initial voicing and final assimilation are relatively new. At an earlier stage of the language, therefore, the normal compound consisted of two words concatenated without an intervening *u.* When the enunciative *u* appeared inside compounds, at least some of the old compounds without *u* were retained. This led to pairs similar to the ones we noted in our first set of examples. The rules of stem-initial voicing and sonorant assimilation served to further distinguish the two sets. Eventually, and this last step may have been quite recent, the morphologized relic forms, the ancient compounds, became a productive type, brought back to life in a different guise.

Why? One possible answer may lie in the productivity of Sanskrit and other Indo-Aryan prefixes in modern Kannada. As the examples in (10) demonstrate, certain Sanskrit and other borrowed prefixes are highly productive in modern Kannnada.

(10) *upa-jilla=dhikari*   deputy district commissioner
      upa-ra=shtrapati   vice president
      upa-kulapati   vice chancellor
      upa-ji=vi   parasite

nir-udyo=ga	unemployment
nir-a=s'rita	refugee
nir-aksharate	illiteracy
antar-ra=shtriya	international
antar-ja=ti=ya	intercaste
antar-ra=jya	interstate
antar-vibha=ga	interdepartmental
antar-jilla= sa:rige vyavasthe	interdistrict transport system (*jilla* Urdu)
bahu-mukha pratibhe	multifaceted talent
bahu-mata	plurality/majority
bahu-ra=shtriya	multinational

None of the examples in (10) may be found in Sanskrit and most of them are very recent. In fact, the status of Sanskrit morphology is similar to that of Latinate morphology in modern English. It is possible, therefore, that the native Dravidian prefixes that are the subject of this chapter became productive under the influence of the Sanskrit prefixes. There is some similarity between the two types of prefixes. Most notably, both types may be found only in derivation. All of modern Kannada inflectional morphology, which is quite extensive, is entirely suffixing, in accordance with the Dravidian pattern. Although we would like to go beyond structural similarity, there is unfortunately no empirical or theoretical way to demonstrate conclusively that the Sanskritic model was an impetus for the development of prefixes in the Dravidian sector of the Kannada lexicon. We therefore leave this tantalizing question and bring matters to a close. Assuming that we are correct, that there are indeed productive derivational prefixes in modern literary Kannada, what is the value of this finding?

That depends on the reader's particular interests. For the Kannada grammarian, and Dravidianists in general, it tempers the traditional exclusivist view. We suspect that closer scrutiny of other Dravidian languages, especially Malayalam, which is even more heavily influenced by Sanskrit, may have similar results, but we leave that task to specialists in those languages.

From a typological perspective, it shows that even the most perfect of holds may, under the proper circumstances, be broken. This is a comfort, for otherwise, given enough time, we would expect all the world's languages to converge on a small number of fixed types, rather than moving about in Sapirian fashion in a multidimensional space. Sapir's abstract view of typology is also more convenient to data of this sort than is a less-abstract parametric system.

For morphologists, we believe that there are two important points. First, our findings cast some doubt on the generality of the trash compactor theory of morphology. This theory, in its simplest form (Givón, 1979), views all morphology as the result of the morphologization of more productive syntactic phenomena. Certain recent formal phonological theories, such as lexical phonology (Kiparsky, 1982), are also easily reduced to the trash compactor model. If this model is correct, then morphology is intrinsically uninteresting from a theoretical point of view. Happily, there is some evidence that morphology does have its own properties. Bybee (1985) has shown that reanalysis plays an important role in morphological change. What we have shown is that a productive morphophonological system may arise at the stem level, Kiparsky's Level I. Such a development is impossible within the trash compactor model.

Our second morphological point is more formal. There has been an unfortunate tendency (Lieber, 1980; Marantz, 1984) to lump together affixes and members of major lexical categories and to call them all lexical items. To our mind, this is equivalent to calling a horse a cow, because both are mammals. There may be many similarities between affixes and members of major lexical categories, but there are also clear differences (Hoeksema, 1985). In this particular work, we have used phonological, morphological, and semantic evidence to distinguish compounding from prefixation. All of our evidence makes perfect sense within a traditional framework that distinguishes affixes from members of major lexical categories. All of the properties that we have found for Kannada prefixes are properties that are characteristic of affixes. We believe that it would be difficult for these other recent theories to account for these differences without at least implicitly making the distinction that we have made between affixes and members of major lexical categories. We hope that it is impossible.

Acknowledgments

An earlier version of this work was presented at the annual meeting of the LSA in Seattle, December 1985. Thanks to Sandy Steever, Bh. Krishnamurti, and Bill Bright for comments and discussion. The research that led to this chapter was supported in part by a grant from the National Science Foundation, #8418914. S.N. Sridhar's research was also supported by a Senior Faculty Research Fellowship of the American Institute of Indian Studies during 1983–84.

References

Anshen, F., and Aronoff, M. (1981). Morphological productivity and phonological transparency. *Canadian Journal of Linguistics* **26**, 63–72.
Aronoff, M. (1976). "Word Formation in Generative Grammar." MIT Press, Cambridge, MA.
Aronoff, M., and Sridhar, S.N. (1983). Morphological levels in English and Kannada. "The Interplay of Phonology, Morphology and Syntax," pp. 3–16. CLS, Chicago.
Bloomfield, L. (1933). "Language." Holt, New York.
Botha, R.P. (1969). "The Function of the Lexicon in Transformational Generative Grammar." Mouton, The Hague.
Bright, W. (1958). "An Outline of Colloquial Kannada." Deccan College, Poona.

Bybee, J. (1985). "Morphology." Benjamins, Amsterdam.

Chomsky, N., and Halle, M. (1968). "The Sound Pattern of English." Harper, New York.

Givón, T. (1979). "On Understanding Grammar." Academic Press, New York.

Hatcher, A.G. (1951). "Modern English Word-Formation and Neo-Latin." Johns Hopkins Press, Baltimore.

Hoeksema, J. (1985). *Categorial Morphology.* PhD dissertation, Groningen.

Kiparsky, P. (1982). "From Cyclic Phonology to Lexical Phonology. The Structure of Phonological Representations (Part 1)" (H. van der Hulst and N. Smith, eds.), pp. 131–176. Foris, Dordrecht.

Leben, W., and Robinson, O.W. (1977). Upside-down phonology. *Language* **53**, 1–20.

Lieber, R. (1980). *The Organization of the Lexicon.* PhD dissertation, MIT University (distributed by IULC).

Marantz, A. (1984). "On the Nature of Grammatical Relations." MIT Press, Cambridge.

Prince, A. (1972). -ic. Ms. MIT.

Sagey, E. (1986). *The Representation of Features and Relations in Non-Linear Phonology.* PhD dissertation. MIT.

Sapir, E. (1925). Sound patterns in language. *Language* **1**, 37–51.

Selkirk, E.O. (1982). "The Syntax of Words." MIT Press, Cambridge, MA.

Siegel, D. (1979). "Topics in English Morphology." Garland, New York.

Strauss, S. (1982). "Lexicalist Phonology of English and German." Foris, Dordrecht.

Wolff, S. (1984). *Lexical Entries and Word Formation.* NYU dissertation (distributed by IULC).

Zonneveld, W. (1978). "A Formal Theory of Exceptions in Generative Phonology." de Ridder, Lisse.

Chapter 11

The How and Why of Diachronic Morphologization and Demorphologization

Brian D. Joseph & Richard D. Janda

1. Introduction

Morphology and diachrony have exhibited a puzzling complementary distribution within generative linguistics. When, some years ago, diachrony was in vogue, morphology was not in fashion. Of late, however, morphology has become all the rage, yet diachrony is now in a state of relative neglect by generativists.[1] As a result, there currently is comparatively little work being done on morphological change within the generative framework. Thus, with notable exceptions such as Bybee (1985) and Dressler (1985), most recent investigations in morphology (as represented, for example, by the work of Anderson, Kiparsky, Lieber, Marantz, McCarthy, Williams, and Zwicky) have focused almost entirely on the testing of theoretical claims and constructs in purely synchronic terms and with purely synchronic data.

There is, however, clearly another important side to morphology—and to the study of language structure in general—namely, the diachronic aspect:

[1] Thus, e.g., while Kiparsky (1968, 174) could confidently state that linguistic change "is a window on the form of linguistic competence that is not obscured by factors like performance," Kiparsky (1982, viii) expresses the more pessimistic view that "language change is not as direct a 'window' on linguistic structure as one might have hoped." Given that the earlier concentration on historical linguistics by Kiparsky and certain other generativists involved an unquestionably formalistic bent, the present complementarity between morphology and diachrony does not reduce to a formalist/functionalist opposition, nor is it an accidental result of the fact that there just happen to be relatively few functionalists working on morphology at the moment. As we emphasize in this chapter, historical morphology has much to gain from and contribute to both formal and functional approaches to linguistic analysis.

Theoretical Morphology Copyright © 1988 by Academic Press, Inc.

193

the manner in which earlier synchronic states give way, across time, to new and somewhat-altered later synchronic states. Diachrony is best viewed as the set of transitions between successive synchronic states, so that language change is necessarily something that always takes place in the present and is therefore governed in every instance by constraints on synchronic grammars. As a result, synchronic morphological theory not only should consider the results of diachronic morphological investigations but must be responsive to—and should ultimately explain—morphological changes.

This notion of the interconnection of synchrony and diachrony is not idiosyncratic to us; it originates with Halle (1962) and continues through such works as Kiparsky (1965), Chomsky and Halle (1968), and King (1969). More recently, it has been advocated by Lightfoot in several of his works, most notably Lightfoot (1979), and Culicover (1984, p. 118) has labeled such a view "reasonable." If diachrony were not linked to properties of the grammars of a language to be found at individual synchronic points in time, then that language would have to be viewed as a disembodied entity that somehow exists apart from its use by speakers at such particular points in time. Indeed, one of the underlying tenets of diachronic linguistic investigation is the assumption that, as the surface forms of a language—the stuff from which grammars are constructed by speakers—are transmitted through time (i.e., across generations and/or peer groups consisting of members relatively close in age), aspects of such transmitted forms and their underlying grammars can be uncovered and can lead to meaningful comparisons between stages of a particular language.

We recognize that some linguists (especially variationists such as Bailey, 1973) deny the distinction between synchrony and diachrony, instead advocating for the study of language a single perspective which is claimed to be "dynamic." With all due respect, we do not believe that this view is supported by either logical or empirical considerations. On the one hand, we take it as beyond question that, at any one moment, a given speaker has some particular linguistic system in his or her head—a synchronic grammar. The existence of such a system is not belied by the mere presence in it of variation; after all, a major thrust of modern sociolinguistics has been to show that variation is systematic. Hence synchrony indeed exists as a distinguishable phenomenon. On the other hand, it is indisputable that, as already stated, some language change arises via the transmission of linguistic phenomena between speakers of different generations or between lects spoken by speakers of the same generation. Hence diachrony also exists as a distinguishable phenomenon. In denying synchrony and diachrony, the view that there is only a panchronic or achronic dynamism in language suggests that there exist grammatical principles or mechanisms which direct speakers to change their languages in certain ways other than through cross-generational and cross-lectal transmission. To the best of our knowledge, however, there is absolutely no evidence suggesting that this kind of asocial individual causation of linguistic change really exists. But such questionable devices can be dispensed with on the usual view, taken here, that language change occurs solely via two independently motivated entities: the present (synchrony) and time (a succession of presents, i.e., diachrony).

The interplay of synchrony and diachrony can be illustrated by a schematic example representative of numerous real cases. Consider a situation of the following sort: A linguistic stage in which a particular phenomenon can be analyzed as only phonologically conditioned is succeeded first by a stage where the same phenomenon is amenable to analysis with either phonological or morphological conditioning and finally by a stage in which morphological conditioning is an analytic necessity. In the second stage, *ex hypothesi*, neither analysis is favored over the other by any data. Consequently, it would seem that some synchronic grammatical mechanism, made available through universal grammar either as part of the language-acquisition device or as a general constraint on the form of individual grammars, must be posited in order to explain why a morphological analysis—actually a reanalysis of the earlier situation—is preferred and ultimately chosen at the third stage. Only if linguistic theory (via universal grammar) is suitably enriched so as to include the relevant grammatical mechanism can such a diachronic development be accounted for. In cases of this type, therefore, not only are diachronic examples directly relevant to the form of synchronic linguistic theory, but also synchronic linguistic theory becomes indispensable to the explanation of language change.

Given this conclusion, diachronic morphology obviously has no shortage of issues to explore, questions to address, and problems to solve. At the top of the agenda for research in this regard is the challenge presented by the common diachronic phenomenon of morphologization, alluded to in our schematic example. This phenomenon is frequently alleged to be widespread and thus certainly deserves a focused investigation that not only identifies real examples but also carefully defines the nature of the elements involved (e.g., what is meant by "morphological" and "phonological").

By PHONOLOGICAL as applied to a rule, constraint, and so on, we mean a generalization which makes exclusive reference to phonological features (such as coronal, nasal, labial, strident, voiced, continuant, and/or phonological boundaries/domains (of syllable, word, phonological phrase, etc.). By MORPHOLOGICAL we mean a generalization with any morphological and hence nonphonological feature(s); these include features which are morphosyntactic (e.g., [+dative] or [+3sg]), morphosemantic (e.g., [+agentive], for nouns), or morpholexical (e.g., [+ō-stem]), as well as other, difficult-to-classify morphological features (see also Zwicky, 1986, on classifying feature types). MORPHOLOGIZATION, then, describes any transition (via dephonologization or desyntacticization) from a state in which a generalization is nonmorphological in nature to a state in which the corresponding generalization is morphological in nature. DEMORPHOLOGIZATION [which could potentially occur via either (re)phonologization or (re)syntacticization] describes the opposite process. Our use of this latter term should be distinguished from that of Klausenburger (1976), who employed it to label a historical development whereby an already-morphological generalization becomes (more) lexicalized. For us, demorphologization in Klausenburger's sense constitutes nothing more than a subtype of morphologization, namely, greater (morpho)lexicalization. It is no accident that we group together morphology and the lexicon. It is universally recognized that there are intimate ties between these domains, and, in most current theories of grammar, the lexicon contains at least some morphological rules (see especially lexical morphology and phonology).

Two things make morphologization especially interesting. First, the diachronic phenomenon of morphologization is exemplified by the movement of syntactic phenomena into morphology as well as by the movement of phonological phenomena into that domain. Second, it is widely presupposed that these processes are virtually unidirectional, so that probably most linguists would agree that transitions into morphology are in fact the norm. On the other hand, movement out of morphology into phonology or syntax, demorphologization, is generally held to be rare or even nonexistent. In keeping with these views, most investigations of morphologization deal only with the how of that diachronic change and do not even mention the possibility of the existence of the opposite type of development, diachronic demorphologization.

In this chapter, we point out that, while instances of diachronic demorphologization are admittedly rare, they are nevertheless known to exist. In view of this fact, we submit that the more important question to be addressed in this regard is why diachronic morphologization occurs, and furthermore, why so often, whereas the converse direction of reanalysis is so (relatively) infrequent.

Our answer is that both the how and the why of diachronic morphologization (and, for that matter, demorphologization) can be understood only by assigning to morphology a more central position and role in grammar than has heretofore been done, even in approaches like the lexical morphology and phonology of Kiparsky, Mohanan, and others. That is, nothing short of a conception of language in which grammar, even syntax, is morphocentric can explain the facts and trends of diachronic morphology, and of much of diachronic phonology and diachronic syntax as well.

2. Diachronic Morphologization

The phenomenon and the frequency of historical shifts from both syntax and phonology into morphology are familiar enough that they do not need much in the way of detailed explanation. Here, in fact, we merely present a brief listing of some representative cases. The classic example illustrating morphologization of an originally phonologically conditioned process is provided by Germanic umlaut. This phenomenon represents numerous different morphologizations in a variety of Germanic languages at a variety of different times in the course of their development, but for our present purposes these can all be brought together under a single rubric.[2]

Other such cases include the subpart of Grassmann's Law in Sanskrit which survives as part of the morphological processes of reduplication (see Sag, 1976; Schindler, 1976; Janda and Joseph, 1986), many of the consonant mutations in Celtic, and accent shifts in Modern Greek compared with their Ancient Greek counterparts (see Warburton (1970), where a pseudophonological account with a phonetically/phonologically unmotivated feature [+long] is used, as well as Bubenik (1979) and Joseph and Philippaki-Warburton (1986, Chap. 3)).[3,4] The most solidly established examples of morphologization of phonology have been provided from within the tradition of Indo-European studies. Nevertheless, further cases from other language families can be found, although they are not as widely known and thus require more extensive discussion than can be presented here.[5]

As regards the morphologization of syntax, a familiar case concerns the development of person-agreement affixes from free pronouns in many Bantu languages as analyzed by Givón (1971), who formulated the now well-known slogan, "Today's morphology is yesterday's syntax." Similar instances of this kind of desyntactization include noun incorporation in Iroquoian (see Mithun, 1984, 1985) and the evolution of a synthetic future in Romance from a Late Latin analytic future with *habēre* (see Benveniste, 1968; Fleischmann, 1982). Finally, the standard handbooks have made familiar yet other morphologizations of syntax, such as the Romance development of an adverbial suffix *-mente* out of a free word in Late Latin, as well as numerous parallel transitions from free words to derivational affixes in various Germanic languages (as for English/German *-hood/-heit, -less/-los,* etc.).

[2]The morphologization of umlaut in Germanic has been most extensively treated for High German (see Wurzel 1970, 1980; Robinson 1972, 1975; Janda 1982a,b, 1983a, and references there).

[3]This is most massively the case under the traditional analysis, e.g., that implicit in Lewis and Pedersen (1937). We are aware, by the way, that some of the Celtic facts can be given a phonological treatment. Still, this is possible only at the expense of assuming fairly abstract triggers, and there are other mutations in various Celtic dialects for which even such an abstract analysis cannot work and has therefore never been suggested. See, for example, Thomas-Flinders (1981) on lenition in the Scots Gaelic of Leurbost, Isle of Lewis.

[4]We take it as beyond argument that the mere manipulation of sound by some linguistic rule does not *ipso facto* render that rule phonological.

[5]For example, Holman (1985) presents consonant gradation in Finnish as a morphologized originally phonological process (though he argues that the process has further been "semasiologized"). An instance of desyntacticizing morphologization from the history of Japanese is discussed by Vance (1982) (following traditional Japanese scholarship, although this analysis is disputed by Miller, 1985, pp. 140–141, 158n.2, 159n.9), and a similar example from Cantonese is provided by Wong (1982).

3. Diachronic Demorphologization

As we noted earlier, though, the opposite developments—both the syntacticization of a former morphological element or process and the phonologization of a once morphologically determined alternation—have also been argued to exist. All of the cases known to us, however, are controversial, a property which is not at all surprising, given that demorphologization is generally held to be a rare phenomenon. Accordingly, in this section, we present and discuss the facts of four such possible cases of demorphologization, limiting ourselves to those in which the facts are known to us in sufficient detail to allow a judicious consideration and evaluation of their merits. While it is clearly not possible to examine all reported instances of such a development, we nonetheless strongly believe that these examples are representative of the general situation to be found with instances of demorphologization. The cases in question—taken up in turn below and then reevaluated in Section 4—are the following: the conditions under which a prefix marking past tense appears in Ancient and Modern Greek, allomorphy in the Hittite quotative particle, the development of the English possessive ending, and the deaffixation of the Saame (Lappish) abessive morpheme.

In Ancient Greek, a prefix traditionally known as the "syllabic augment" served as one of the elements marking a verbal form for the past tense, the other possible elements being stem change, different endings, and a different stress pattern. The prefix in question was usually *e-*, though the prefixation process was occasionally realized differently under conditions irrelevant here. (1) lists some examples of regular augment-prefixation in Ancient Greek.

(1)   *paidéu-o:* 'teach, 1sg present'   ~ *e-paídeu-on* 'taught, 1sg imperfect'
       lambán-ete 'take, 2pl present'   ~ *e-láb-ete* 'took, 2pl aorist'
       lambán-ei 'take, 3sg present'   ~ *é-lab-e* 'took, 3sg aorist'

In some forms, though, the augment was the sole marker of past as opposed to present tense. That is, in such cases, none of the other possible marking devices happened to be present, as in (2), for example.

(2)   *paidéu-omen* 'teach, 1pl present' ~ *e-paidéu-omen* 'taught, 1pl impf'
       lambán-ete 'take, 2pl present'   ~ *e-lambán-ete* 'took, 2pl impf'

The augment, therefore, must be considered to be present in the underlying morphological structure of Ancient Greek past tense forms; furthermore, its occurrence there is not linked to any phonological feature(s).

Under one analysis of the occurrence of the same prefix in Modern Greek (see Kaisse, 1982, pp. 77–79), however, the augment is assumed to be a completely phonologically determined element, one which is present only on the surface and occurs only when it can be stressed. Because of the predictable antepenultimate placement of stress in certain types of past tense formations, the augment apparently serves as a mere phonological placeholder for that stress. Thus, under this analysis, the augment occurs only when there is no syllable in a verb stem which can bear the necessarily antepenultimate stress— necessarily antepenultimate because the form at issue is by definition an appropriate past tense:

(3) Underlying morphological form: $/lav\text{-}a/_{[+past]}$ 'took, 1sg'
     Antepenultimate past tense stress: $[' + lav\text{-}a]$
     Phonological augment epenthesis: $[é + lav\text{-}a]$ 'I took'

The form *élava* can be contrasted with the 1pl form *lávame*, where no augment is needed because the combination of a bisyllabic stem (*lava-*) with a mono-syllabic ending (*-me*) provides an antepenultimate syllable that can carry stress. Under such an analysis, then, the once purely morphologically conditioned rule of augment prefixation has become phonologized in Modern Greek.[6]

Similarly, the Hittite quotative particle, which introduces direct speech, has two forms: *-wa* before consonants and *-war* before vowels. According to one proposed etymology for this particle, Joseph (1981; see also Joseph and Schourup, 1982), this phonologically based alternation between *-wa* and *-war* derives from an originally morphological distinction. To wit, a Proto-Indo-European particle *-wo (which would directly yield Hittite *-wa*) was contrasted with a variant form of the same particle which differed in its morphological makeup by having an additional adverbial (actually locatival) suffix *-r, their combination giving *-wor (which would in turn directly yield Hittite *-war*). Here, too, a once-morphological difference appears to have been transformed into a matter of phonological conditioning.

An example of demorphologization via syntacticization has been discussed for the history of English by Janda (1980, 1981), who argues at length that, during the late Middle English period, the possessive inflectional affix (i.e., the genitive singular suffix *-(e)s*) was reinterpreted by at least some speakers as the reduced version of an independent form, the possessive pronominal deter-miner *his*. In this way there arose syntactic expresssions like *John his book* (= [*John* [*his book*]]), where possession is indicated by a presumably clitic form of an underlyingly free word rather than a bound affix (as in *John's book* = [[*John-'s*] *book*]). The construction with *his* in fact persisted well into the Early Modern English period, its gradual demise apparently being principally attributable to the concerted attacks of Latinizing prescriptive grammarians.

---

[6] Kaisse's analysis could be translated into more current terms by positing an empty prefix for the past consisting of a V-slot which can be stressed and which, if stressed, is spelled out as *e* (a default specification—other values are found) but which, if not stressed, is either deleted or simply not realized. Describing these facts in such terms does not change the basic thrust of an analysis of this phenomenon as apparent demorphologization, for there would still have been a change in the type of conditions under which the augment appeared: from purely mor-phological to more phonological (though see Section 4 for a reevaluation of this view).

A parallel case is provided by Nevis (1985b), who discusses the course of events by which the Saame (Lappish) abessive morpheme *taga* was demorphologized via its syntacticization from an affix to a clitic to a free word by speakers of the Northern Saame Enontekiö dialect. The form *taga* derives from an affixal sequence **pta-k-ek/n* consisting of caritive **pta* + lative **-k* + an extra lative suffix **-k* or **-n* (with epenthetic *-e-*); other Finno-Permic languages show reflexes of **pta-k* (without the extra lative suffix). One might think that Enontekiö Saame is archaic in having a reflex of **pta-k(-ek/n)* as a free word and that the other dialects and languages were the innovators here in developing a clitic or affix from an original free word or sequence of free words. Compelling evidence, however, supports the reconstruction of the entire protosequence in question as affixal. For one thing, in the vast majority of Saame dialects and in fact throughout Finno-Permic in general, the reflexes of **pta-k* are suffixal. Moreover, the sequence is clearly composed of two (or three, in the case of Northern Saame) morphemes, each reconstructible on its own, and the single-segment elements **-k* and **-n* simply could not have been independent words in the protolanguage. Finally, in most of the Finno-Permic languages, **-pta* shows idiosyncrasies of combination—in particular, attachment as a case suffix to verbal stems—which are unpredictable and unexpected and thus unlikely to have occurred independently in each language. Thus it seems safest also to reconstruct affixal status for **-pta* in the protolanguage.[7]

The most relevant fact for the matter at hand, though, is that, in all dialects of Saame, *(-)taga* has undergone deaffixation and has been reanalyzed as a true clitic (on this term, see Nevis, 1985a). In Enontekiö, however, *(-)taga* has further undergone decliticization, thereby gaining status as an independent word. In particular, it seems now to be a stressless postposition. (A similar case from Old Estonian is discussed in Nevis, 1987.)

4. A Reconsideration of Demorphologization Cases

The importance of these putative cases of demorphologization cannot be denied. However, they are only as strong as the data and interpretations upon which they rest. As it happens, though, at least some of these putative cases of demorphologization are not without problematic aspects and thus are subject to challenge concerning whether they truly constitute examples of demorphologization. It is significant that such is the case far more often with demorphologization examples than with morphologization examples (e.g., those in Section 2 above). In particular, this fact points up the difficulty of finding real examples of demorphologization and thereby attests to the rarity of the phenomenon. In what follows, we briefly indicate some of the problems faced by the proposed examples.

[7]It may well be that the origin of these protolanguage affixes is to be sought in free words in some preprotolanguage stage, but we know of no evidence requiring such a conclusion. For the directly reconstructible protolanguage stage, the affixal status of the morphemes in question seems assured.

In the case of the Modern Greek augment, the analysis given is based on an idealized version of the standard language. Due to decades of a diglossic situation within Greek, however, there are now—and have always been, to a greater or lesser extent—several verbs with unstressed augments that are borrowings from the "high"-style language but which are nonetheless in relatively common use. For example, the past tense of *prókite* 'it is a question of, it is about to' is commonly *e-prókito*, with an unstressed augment. Furthermore, many verbs occur with an augment (the so-called internal augment) even though they have a lexical prefix which provides enough syllables to allow the form to satisfy the antepenultimate-stress requirements of the past tense without epenthesis of the augment. For example, the past tense of *meta-frázo* 'I translate' (prefix *meta-* with bound verbal root *-fra(z)-* '(having to do with) speech or language'; see also *ek-frázo* 'express,' *frásis* 'phrase,' etc.) is commonly *met-é-frasa* 'I translated,' with an internal augment, and not, for many speakers, *metá-frasa*.[8]

Such facts make it clear that a strictly phonological solution for the Modern Greek augment cannot work, and consequently one cannot say that past tense augmentation in Greek has truly become phonologized. Moreover—and this bears directly on the issue of defining such terms as "phonologization" and "morphologization" in the first place (see Section 1)—even if the facts concerning the augment were such as to allow the phonological solution outlined in Section 2 to stand, the change in question would be a matter of a morphological process becoming not completely phonologically determined but instead only somewhat more phonological in nature. That is, the epenthesis rule would still apply solely in past tense forms and not generally, since antepenultimate stress is not called for everywhere in Modern Greek (as, for instance, with neuter nouns in *-ma*, e.g., *ónoma* 'name, nom' ~ *onómatos* 'name, gen' but *ríma* 'verb, nom' ~ *rímatos* 'verb, gen' instead of **érima* ~ *rímatos*).[9]

---

[8]Forms such as *metá-frasa* do occur, but many speakers reject them as "unnatural" and favor the *met-é-frasa* type. See Mackridge (1985, pp. 182–187) for general discussion of the augment in Modern Greek and a consideration of the complex sociolinguistic factors involved in any individual's choice of augmented versus unaugmented forms.

[9]Matters are similar with the case of the German perfect-participal prefix *ge-* (see e.g., Paul, 1917, pp. 276–279; Kiparsky, 1966, pp. 70–75). The Germanic perfective marker **ga-* (as in Gothic *ga-*), which essentially could appear on any verb form in any tense, was in Old High German restricted to marking perfect participles, as *gi-* (which became Middle High German *ge-*). Such participles lacked *gi-* only if they belonged to an inherently perfective verb or already contained certain other prefixes. By the Modern High German period, these conditions had been reanalyzed (and altered) so that *ge-* now always occurs prefixed to perfect participles except when the initial syllable of a verb stem to which it would otherwise be added is unstressed. This development clearly represents a phonologization of the rule(s) for the occurrence of a morphological element. But, as with (one account of) the Greek augment, the case of German *ge-* does not represent an instance of demorphologization in the sense developed here, since the relevant process—of *ge-* omission or deletion—remains a fact about a particular morpheme (or set of morphemes). That is, the rule for *ge-* has not been so phonologized as to become a morphemically/lexically free process of German sound structure. Rather, it has remained a morphological rule, albeit one with greater phonological conditioning.

The Hittite example is similar, but it has an added problem. Just as in the case of the Greek augment, the phonologization of the *-wa/-war* alternation is really just increased phonologicity of conditioning. It represents a shift in the direction of greater phonological determination for two allomorphs of a single lexical item and is not the result of a general phonological rule of intervocalic *r*-insertion at word boundary. Moreover, the case for demorphologization depends crucially on the etymology proposed above, which, it should be recalled, derives *-wa/-war* from **-wo/*-wo-r (*wo* being the etymon of the particle found in Sanskrit *i-va* 'like, as if' and **-r* being the locatival adverbial suffix also found in English *there, where,* and the like). As is well known, though, etymology is the most brittle of the linguistic sciences, and, as it turns out, there is another possible etymology for *-war.* Many scholars (e.g., Friedrich, 1952, s.v.) connect it with the Hittite verb *wer-iya-* 'say' (cognate with Latin *ver-(bum),* etc.) and take the *-wa* form to be a generalization of a sporadic *r*-loss process found elsewhere in the language. Under that proposal, there is no demorphologization, because the original difference between the two Hittite quotative morphs did not reside in their morphological makeup.

Finally, it must be noted that, when the common Middle English expression of possession by the *John his book* construction later fell out of use in Early Modern English, it gave way to a situation where the only way to express possession prenominally was use of the phrasal affix *-'s* (on this term and concept, see especially Nevis, 1985a, and earlier references there). This change, then, represents a kind of desyntacticizing remorphologization of the periphrastic possessive with full-word *his,* since the full sequence of changes was *-'s > his > -'s.*

These difficulties notwithstanding, we believe that demorphologization must be recognized as a possible type of linguistic change. In particular, there seems to be nothing standing in the way of accepting the Saame example, and it appears indisputable that some Middle English speakers did reanalyze their language's affixal-possessive construction in such a way as to express possession syntactically where speakers at earlier stages had done so morphologically. Thus, demorphologization does exist, after all.

5. Explaining the Preponderance of Morphologization Cases

Unobjectionable examples of this phenomenon are so few and far between, especially compared with the easily found examples of morphologization (see Section 2), that we must recognize a lopsided asymmetry between historical morphologization and historical demorphologization in grammatical change.

Perhaps more importantly, though, this lopsidedness is totally unexpected in any linguistic theory where there is no separate morphological (sub)component, even in the lexicon—as in most generative theories until recently—or where phonology, morphology, and syntax are all accorded equal status in the overall organization of grammar.

As we noted at the outset of this chapter, we feel that this relative asymmetry can be accounted for by embedding a diachronic view of morphology in a synchronic theory of language where the various aspects of word formation and word structure, along with the lexicon, constitute the central component of grammar.

Synchronically, the best evidence for such morphocentricity comes from the fact that there is no aspect of grammar which interacts with all the others to the extent that morphology does. The connection of morphology with phonology via morphophonology is obvious, and the connection of semantics with morphology both in lexical entries and in morphological rules goes almost without saying. Much of syntax can actually be seen as concerning either the ordering and grouping of morphologically defined categories or the co-occurrence properties of various morphemes, especially affixes. Relevant here are such inflectional phenomena as case marking and agreement, as well as the correlation of different derivational affixes with different argument structures. Finally, even phonetics interfaces with word formation via such phenomena as sound symbolism and onomatopoeia.[10]

Rather than diagramming our conception of morphocentric grammar, we simply point out that the centrality of morphology in language is reflected in the fact that, of the various subparts of grammar, morphology alone may refer to all the other subparts in its rules and principles. Thus, analysts rarely comment when morphological rules refer to or manipulate all of semantics, syntax (categories, subcategories, configurations, etc.), phonology, and even pragmatics. But much recent work attempts to show that syntax is autonomous, that is, phonology-, semantics-, and even morphology-free. Furthermore, we maintain that a proper conception of phonology takes that realm to be morphology-free and syntax-free. This is because, on the one hand, sound-structure rules referring to morphological features are really morphological rules, while on the other hand, syntactic considerations are only indirectly relevant to phonology (insofar as they define phonological phrases and other related domains).

Against the claim that grammar is morphocentric, it might be objected that some languages (like Chinese) are said to lack morphology and that all languages participate in a great cycle of downgrading whereby analyticity and

---

[10]Recent work on sound symbolism and onomatopoeia, e.g., Ohala (1983), suggests that universal semantic associations must be posited for certain phonetic phenomena such as particular tonal/intonational pitches, vowel quantities, and consonantal places of articulation. This is so because the association of such meanings and sounds with one another is so cross-linguistically widespread as to be clearly nonaccidental and hence presumably part of universal grammar, at least as an unmarked tendency or default setting of some parameter.

syntactic expression give way to syntheticity and morphological expression, which themselves give way to analyticity and syntactic expression again, ad infinitum. Clearly, morphocentricity cannot be a linguistic universal if some languages now lack morphology or if all languages pass through stages where they lack and then regain morphology.

However, neither of these situations is actually the case. On the one hand, we know of no language that lacks both affixation and compounding; Chinese for example, certainly has compound morphology. Furthermore, clitics and free morphemes (or words) which structure sentences also seem to be present in all languages (like the Chinese enclitics discussed by Huang, 1985). On the other hand, the fact that downgrading seems to be constantly at work wearing away morphology—and provoking its replacement with syntactic means—at the same time that it converts syntax into morphology does not disprove the grammatical centrality of morphology. It is not as if syntax first decays into morphology, and morphology then eventually decays into nothing and thereby dies. Morphology is not a graveyard. Instead, it is more as if syntax feeds morphology, while morphology itself undergoes (greater) lexicalization which, for speakers of the world's languages, does not apparently resemble death so much as nirvana. And, since syntax continues to pass into morphology even as the latter undergoes lexicalization, morphology indeed remains as a central constant of grammar.

Of further relevance to our notion of a centrality for morphology in synchronic grammar is an evaluation of the opposite claim made by Roeper and Siegel (1978). These authors maintain that, in cases where morphological rules might come into competition with syntactic rules, as in their analysis of English compounding, the generativity and general freeness of syntactic rules lead them to prevail over even productive morphological or morpholexical rules. For Roeper and Siegel, this principle accounts for the absence of [adverb + noun] deverbal compounds of the type *beautifully dancing* (which would otherwise be predicted by their general morpholexical rules for English verbal compounds), since syntactic [adjective + noun] sequences are independently generated by the phrase structure rules for noun phrases and thus would block the morphological formation of the relevant compounds.

For us, such a principle would be directly at odds with the view of the role of morphology in synchronic grammars that we are espousing here. However, even if Roeper and Siegel's principle might work for the English case at hand—and note that other analyses have been proposed for English verbal compounds which do not need such a blocking of morphology by syntax[11]—it

---

[11]For example, for Selkirk (1982, p. 46 et passim), the absence of adverbs in compounds with final deverbal noun heads follows from a broader restriction excluding adverbs from noun compounds and certain other compound types as well. Furthermore, Allen (1978, 182n. 23) points out that Roeper and Siegel's use of syntax to block morphology effectively constitutes a transderivational constraint. To these considerations, we add two further criticisms. First, Roeper and Siegel's

cannot be universally valid. Joseph (1980) has shown that their principle is contradicted by developments in Medieval and Modern Greek involving adjectival compounds with *tough*-Movement semantics, for example, *efkoló-spastos* 'easy to break, easily broken' (cf. *éfkolos* 'easy' and *spázo* 'I break'). These compounds have become widespread in Greek despite the availability of syntactically generated *tough*-Movement patterns and in fact seem to be spreading at the expense of the syntactic construction, to judge from the general avoidance by speakers of the syntactic patterns and their extremely low text frequency.

An even more powerful argument for assigning to morphology the central place which we believe it requires in synchronic grammars comes from certain recurrent types of diachronic developments. The diachronic evidence for morphocentricity comes not only from the numerous cases of morphologization already alluded to (Section 2), but also from such developments as the morpholexical particularization and fragmentation over time of umlaut in German (sketched briefly above but treated in more detail in Janda (1982a,b, 1983a; Joseph and Janda, 1986) and of Sanskrit reduplication. In what follows, we summarize our fuller treatment of the Sanskrit facts presented in Janda and Joseph (1986).

Both proto-Indo-European (in the standard reconstruction) and Sanskrit have reduplication in five verbal categories (present, perfect, and aorist tenses; desiderative and intensive secondary conjugations). Proto-Indo-European is usually reconstructed as having had relative unity within each reduplicated category (e.g., the vocalism in perfect reduplication was generally **e*, in present reduplication generally **i*, and few if any irregularities in its reduplicative formations. By contrast, Sanskrit has a variety of vocalisms within all reduplicated categories (although there is usually one default value for each category), as well as numerous highly particularlized forms not even obviously reduplicative such as the perfect stems *u-va:c-* (for √*vac-* 'speak), *a:n-ṛdh-* (for √*ṛdh-* 'thrive'), *ja-bhar-* (for √*bhṛ-* 'bear'). Within Sanskrit, forms such as these latter can be explained only as particularized replacements for more regular forms (*u-va:c-* by lexicalization of a former sound change grown opaque, *a:n-ṛdh-* by analogy, *ja-bhar-* probably by contamination, etc.).

Such changes reveal a strong and constant tendency on the part of speakers to particularize formerly more general morphological processes as markers of more specific lexical and grammatical categories, and, in so doing, to make

---

principle would incorrectly predict that [adjective + noun] compounds like *blackbird* and *highchair* should be blocked by the existence of their (syntactically derived) phrasal equivalents (see also Joseph, 1980). Second, their use of syntax to block morphology runs directly counter to current assumptions about the "blocking" of syntax by morphology and the lexicon; e.g., Kiparsky (1983) argues that the nonexistence of the phrase **the day after today* is due to the lexical existence of *tomorrow*. This kind of blocking moreover provides further evidence for morphocentricity.

local generalizations over (unified) subsets of the totality of the relevant data.[12]

Under the usual generative assumption that language change is governed primarily by constraints of synchronic grammar, the above evidence regarding speakers' preference for particularized (i.e., morpholexical) analyses of reduplication and morphological processes in general requires that grammars be constructed so as to place a premium on morpholexical solutions to linguistic problems involving sounds as well as sentence structure.[13]

Clearly, much work is needed in order to transform our programmatic statements here into an elaborated representation of the notion MORPHOLEX-ICAL PREFERENCE within the valuation metric of a generative grammar. Still, the outlines of the mechanism and its consequences are clear. For example, the famous Maori case discussed by Kiparsky (1971) and Hale (1973) shows speakers disregarding an apparently obvious and simple purely phonological solution in favor of a fragmented morphological analysis involving considerable allomorphy. As a syntactic example, we cite the following: Like Modern German, Old English had case marking and a presumably base-generated double-object construction where indirect objects preceded direct objects. When the Old English case system was lost and, concomitantly, the use of prepositions was generalized, the continuing occurrence of nonpreposi-tional indirect object + direct object sequences was apparently evaluated as much more marked and thus, on many synchronic analyses of Modern English, is now taken to be the result of (something analogous to) a Dative Movement transformation. However, this reanalysis clearly involved a morpholexical restriction, since it was basically not generalized beyond the then-existing stock of appropriate verbs in Old English (e.g., Latinate verbs are still resistant to Dative Movement alternations, so that *explain me the text* is unacceptable).

Unmistakable historical trends involving increased splintering of already-morphologized processes bespeak a tendency on the part of speakers to opt, in their internalized grammars, for analyses which focus on individual morphological and lexical elements, rather than alternative analyses which are

---

[12]As discussed by Janda and Joseph (1986) and Joseph and Janda (1986), fragmentation over time of affixation, and, in fact, of morphological processes in general, is also common. Regarding fragmented affixes, consider, e.g., English *-al/-ar* (as in *linear/lineal*) and the various *-able*s (as in *movable/survivable/comfortable/potable*), as well as German *-(e)n/-ern* and *er/-ler/-ner*. As for fragmented replacement processes, consider umlaut in German (Janda 1982a,b, 1983a) and in Rotuman (see Janda, 1983b, 1984; Hoeksema and Janda, 1985). Concerning fragmentation of both subtractions and permutations in morphology, consider the "incomplete-phase" apocope and metathesis also found in Rotuman (treated in the references just given).

[13]See Section 1. Note also that, on this assumption, language change occurs by innovations either in underlying/base forms or in rules, e.g., by addition, reordering, alteration, and/or loss. All of these phenomena obviously are subject to the constraints of synchronic grammars. However, our own view is that analyses couched in such terms must be strongly tempered by a sharper focus on the role of surface forms in triggering the reshaping of grammars.

generalized over broader, less idiosyncratic classes of grammatical elements (whether phonological or syntactic).

The explanation for this morpholexical preference may well have to do with the apparent fact that, in their dealings with language, speakers are severely constrained in scope by a highly limited window determining how much grammatical and lexical structure they can consider at one time. If speakers do not have available to them pencils, papers, and notebooks full of charts and tables for performing morphological and general grammatical analysis, we suggest that linguists should at least think twice about proposing descriptions and theories arrived at through a heavy reliance on the aforementioned tools.[14] Instead, imposing a more lexically based limitation on morphological analysis and reanalysis seems to yield exactly the right predictions regarding both morpholexical fragmentation and—to return the focus to our more central concern—morphologization.[15]

We believe that finding one or more answers regarding the asymmetry which exists between historical morphologization and historical demorphologization depends largely on asking the right question. In the morphological literature, most attention has been focused on the important issue of how morphologization occurs diachronically, for example, by such mechanisms as the obscuring of phonological conditioning (for such processes as umlaut) or else just simple reanalysis (as in the case of agreement markers). Nevertheless, an even more important question would seem to concern why it is that both "lower-level" phonological processes and "upper-level" syntactic constructions (and/or processes) so often have morphology as the ultimate target of their diachronic development.[16] We know of no current conception

---

[14] Appearances to the contrary, we deny that this suggestion concerns only the methodology and practice of linguists and so is irrelevant to linguistic theory and analysis. After all, linguistic analyses and theories are usually based on the full range of available relevant data in a language. But if speakers do not or cannot consider more than a limited window of data, then linguists' deviation from speakers in this regard is not only methodologically ill-conceived but also analytically and theoretically so. If children are indeed "little linguists" but differ from adult, professional linguists in not always considering the totality of available and relevant linguistic data, then surely it is the members of the latter group who should change their theory and practice.

[15] This centrality of morphology (with its concomitant of frequent morphologization) can thus be overcome, via demorphologization, only by massive accidental convergences of linguistic circumstances. We in fact know of no valid cases where a morphological process was completely (re)phonologized (i.e., so as to become a morphemically/lexically free process of some language's sound structure) and thereby completely demorphologized. Furthermore, the cases of (re)syntacticizing demorphologization in Middle English and in Enontekiö-Saame discussed earlier seem to have resulted, respectively, from accidental homophony of an affix (ME -(e)s) with a preexisting free word (ME *his*) and from a rather convoluted intersection of the results of certain sound changes (including loss of vowel harmony) with particular phonotactic restrictions. Given the number of unsystematic coincidences required to set the stage for such demorphologizing reanalyses, it is not surprising that demorphologization is so rare.

[16] Our suggestion that the frequency of morphologization is due to morphology's status as the nexus of all grammar represents both a convergence with and an expansion on the semiotically based proposals of Dressler (1985).

of word formation and grammar overall from which this situation could be predicted. But in a morphocentric theory, one in which morphology occupies a central place in the grammars of particular languages and hence in the underlying architecture of universal grammar, it is only to be expected that the morphological component should come to be, via dephonologization and desyntacticization, the final resting place of so many different kinds of originally nonmorphological linguistic phenomena.

Acknowledgments

The two authors' respective contributions to this chapter have been equal in every respect; the nonalphabetical order of the names here is dictated by our practice of following an onomastic "alternation condition" in the various results of our collaboration as they appear.

We would like to thank Wolfgang Dressler, Paul Kiparsky, and Jürgen Klausenburger for their helpful comments at the oral presentation of this chapter. Keith Johnson and Brad Getz also deserve thanks for their technical assistance in making that presentation possible.

References

Allen, M. (1978). *Morphological Investigations*, Ph.D. dissertation, University of Connecticut.
Bailey, C.-J. (1973). "Variation and Linguistic Theory," Center for Applied Linguistics, Arlington, VA.
Benveniste, E. (1968). Mutations of linguistic categories. *In* "Directions for Historical Linguistics. A Symposium." (W. Lehmann and Y. Makiel, eds.), pp. 83–94. University of Texas Press, Austin, TX.
Bubenik, V. (1979). Historical development of the Ancient Greek accent system, *Indogermanische Forschungen* **84**, 90–106.
Bybee, J. (1985). "Morphology. A Study of the Relation Between Meaning and Form." Benjamins, Amsterdam. (*Typological Studies in Language,* **1**.)
Chomsky, N., and Halle, M. (1968). "The Sound Pattern of English." Harper, New York.
Culicover, P. (1984). Review article [on] "The Logical Problem of Language Acquisition," L. Baker and J. McCarthy, eds. *Language* **60**, 115–122.
Dressler, W. (1985). "Morphology: The Dynamics of Derivation." Karoma, Ann Arbor, Michigan. (*Linguistica Extranea Studia* **12**.)
Fleischmann, S. (1982). "The Future in Thought and Language: Diachronic Evidence from Romance." Cambridge Univ. Press, Cambridge. (*Cambridge Studies in Linguistics* **36**.)
Friedrich, J. (1952). "Hethitisches Wörterbuch. Kurzgefasste kritische Sammlung der Deutungen hethitischer Wörter." Winter, Heidelberg.
Givón, T. (1971). Historical syntax and synchronic morphology: An archaeologist's field trip. *CLS* **7**, 394–415.
Hale, K. (1973). Deep-surface canonical disparities in relation to analysis and change: An Australian example. *Current Trends in Linguistics* **11**, 401–458.
Halle, M. (1962). Phonology in generative grammar. *Word* **18**, 54–72.
Hoeksema, J., and Janda, R. (1985). *Implications of Process-Morphology for Categorial Grammar.* Paper presented at the Conference on Categorial Grammars and Natural Language Structures; Tucson, AZ, May 31–June 2.
Holman, E. (1985). On the semasiologization of phonological rules: The semiotic evolution of Finnish consonant gradation. *ICHL* **6**, 281–290.

Huang, C.-R. (1985). *Chinese Sentential Particles: A Study of Cliticization*. Paper presented at the Annual Meeting of the Linguistic Society of America; Seattle, WA, December 27-30 (abstract published in *Meeting Handbook* 18).

Janda, R. (1980). On the decline of declensional systems: The overall loss of OE nominal case-inflections and the ME reanalysis of *-es* as *his*. *ICHL* 4, 243-252.

Janda, R. (1981). A case of liberation from morphology into syntax: The fate of the English genitive marker *-(es)*. "Syntactic Change (Natural Language Studies 25)" (B. Johns and D. Strong, eds.), pp. 59-114. Department of Linguistics, University of Michigan.

Janda, R. (1982a). Of formal identity and rule-(Un)collapsbility: On lost and found generalizations in morphology. *WCCFL* 1, 179-197.

Janda, R. (1982b). *Umlaut and Morphologization*. Unpublished paper, University of Arizona.

Janda, R. (1983a). Two *Umlaut*-heresies and their claim to orthodoxy. *Coyote Papers (Working Papers in Linguistics, University of Arizona)* 4, 59-71.

Janda, R. (1983b). Morphemes aren't something that grows on trees: Morphology as more the phonology than the syntax of words. *CLS* 19 Parasession (Interplay), 79-95.

Janda, R. (1984). Why morphological metathesis rules are rare: On the possibility of historical explanation in linguistics. *BLS* 10, 87-103.

Janda, R., and Joseph, B. (1986). One rule or many? Sanskrit reduplication as fragmented affixation. *Proceedings of the Second Eastern States Conference on Linguistics [ESCOL '85]*, OSU, Department of Linguistics. Columbus. pp. 103-119. [Revised version published in *Ohio State University Working Papers in Linguistics* 34(1987).]

Joseph, B. (1980). Lexical productivity versus syntactic generativity, *Linguistic Inquiry* 11, 420-426.

Joseph, B. (1981). Hittite *iwar, wa(r)* and Sanskrit *iva. Zeitschrift für vergleichende Sprachforschung* 95, 93-98.

Joseph, B., and Janda, R. (1986). *E Pluribus Unum: The Rule Constellation as an Expression of Formal Unity Amidst Morphological Fragmentation*. Paper presented at the Milwaukee Morphology Meeting (Fifteenth Annual UWM Linguistics Symposium), April 4-6.

Joseph, B., and Philippaki-Warburton, I. (1986). "Modern Greek." Croom Helm, London.

Joseph, B., and Schourup, L. (1982). More on *(i)-wa(r). Zeitschrift für vergleichende Sprachforschung* 96, 56-59.

Kaisse, E. (1982). On the preservation of stress in Modern Greek. *Linguistics* 20, 59-82.

King, R. (1969). "Historical Linguistics and Generative Grammar." Prentice-Hall, Englewood Cliffs, NJ.

Kiparsky, P. (1965). *Phonological Change*. Ph.D. dissertation, MIT.

Kiparsky, P. (1966). Über den deutschen Akzent. *In* "Studia Grammatica VII. Untersuchungen über Akzent und Intonation im Deutschen," pp. 69-98. [East] Berlin: Akademie-Verlag (Deutsche Akademie der Wissenschaften zu Berlin, Arbeitsstelle Strukturelle Grammatik).

Kiparsky, P. (1968). Linguistic universals and linguistic change. *In* "Universals in Linguistic Theory" (E. Bach and R. Harms, eds.), pp. 170-202. Holt, New York.

Kiparsky, P. (1971). Historical linguistics. *In* "A Survey of Linguistic Science" (W. Dingwall, ed.), pp. 577-649. Univ. of Maryland Linguistics Program, College Park, MD.

Kiparsky, P. (1982). "Explanation in Phonology." Foris, Dordrecht.

Kiparsky, P. (1983). Word formation and the lexicon. *Proceedings of the 1982 Mid-America Linguistics Conference. Lawrence, KA: University of Kansas Department of Linguistics* pp. 3-29.

Klausenburger, J. (1976). (De)morphologization in Latin. *Lingua* 40, 305-320.

Lewis, H., and Pedersen, H. (1937). "A Concise Comparative Celtic Grammar." Vandenhoeck & Ruprecht, Göttingen.

Lightfoot, D. (1979). "Principles of Diachronic Syntax." Cambridge Univ. Press, Cambridge.

Mackridge, P. (1985). "The Modern Greek Language." Oxford Univ. Press, Oxford.

Miller, R. (1985). Externalizing internal rules: Lyman's Law in Japanese and Altaic. *Diachronica* 2, 137-165.

Mithun, M. (1984). The evolution of noun incorporation. *Language* 60, 847-894.

Mithun, M. (1985). Diachronic morphologization: The circumstances surrounding the birth, growth, and decline of noun incorporation. *ICHL* **6**, 365–394.

Nevis, J. (1985a). *Finnish Particle Clitics and General Clitic Theory.* Ph.D. dissertation, Ohio State University. [Published as *Ohio State University Working Papers in Linguistics* **33**(1986).]

Nevis, J. (1985b). *Decliticization and deaffixation in Saame: Abessive taga.* Paper presented at the Annual Meeting of the Linguistic Society of America; Seattle, WA, December 27–30. [Published in *Ohio State University Working Papers in Linguistics* **34**(1987), 1–9.]

Nevis, J. (1987). Declitization in Old Estonian. *Ohio State University Working Papers in Linguistics* **34**, 10–28.

Ohala, J. (1983). Cross-language use of pitch: An ethological view. *Phonetica* **40**, 1–18.

Paul, H. (1917). "Deutsche Grammatik. Band II. Teil III: Flexionslehre." Niemeyer, Halle an der Saale.

Robinson, O. (1972). *Synchronic Reflexes of Diachronic Phonological Rules.* Ph.D. dissertation, Cornell University.

Robinson, O. (1975). Abstract phonology and the history of umlaut. *Lingua* **37**, 1–29.

Roeper, T., and Siegel, M. (1978). A lexical transformation for verbal compounds. *Linguistic Inquiry* **9**, 199–260.

Sag, I. (1976). Pseudosolutions to the pseudoparadox: Sanskrit diaspirates revisited. *Linguistic Inquiry* **7**, 609–622.

Schindler, J. (1976). Synchronic and diachronic remarks on Bartholomae's and Grassmann's Laws. *Linguistic Inquiry* **7**, 622–637.

Selkirk, E. (1982). "The Syntax of Words." MIT Press, Cambridge, MA. (*Linguistic Inquiry Monographs* **7**.)

Thomas-Flinders, T. (1981). Initial Lenition in Celtic: Evidence for Inflection as a Phonological Process. Inflectional Morphology: Introduction to the Extended Word-and-Paradigm Theory (UCLA Occasional Papers #4: Working Papers in Morphology), pp. 72–83.

Vance, T. (1982). On the origin of voicing alternation in Japanese consonants. *Journal of the American Oriental Society* **102**, 333–341.

Warburton, I. (1970). Rules of accentuation in classical and modern Greek. *Glotta* **48**, 107–121.

Wong, M. (1982). *Tone Change in Cantonese.* Ph.D. dissertation, University of Illinois.

Wurzel, W. (1970). Studia Grammatica VIII. Studien zur deutschen Lautstruktur. [East] Berlin: Akademie-Verlag (Deutsche Akademie der Wissenschaften zu Berlin, Arbeitsgruppe Strukturelle Grammatik).

Wurzel, W. (1980). Ways of morphologizing phonological rules. *In* "Historical Morphology." (J. Fisiak, ed.), pp. 443–462. Mouton, The Hague [*Trends* in Linguistics, Studies and Monographs **17**].

Zwicky, A. (1986). *Phonologically Conditioned Agreement and Purely Morphological Features.* Paper presented at the Milwaukee Morphology Meeting (Fifteenth Annual UWM Linguistics Symposium), April 4–6, University of Wisconsin-Milwaukee, Milwaukee, WI.

Chapter 12

Lexical Categories and the Evolution of Number Marking

Marianne Mithun

Number has traditionally been considered a property of entities, a characteristic of objects and people. Accordingly, it has usually been assumed to be an inflectional category of nouns. When number distinctions appear on other words, such as verbs or adjectives, they are often automatically classified as agreement markers, indicators of the syntactic relationship between those words and associated nouns, rather than inherent features of the words themselves. They are thus frequently described in terms of rules that copy features of nouns onto associated lexical items. For some languages, such an analysis seems adequate. For many others, however, copying rules fail to capture the essence of number marking. In these languages, the number markers that appear on different kinds of lexical items operate independently of each other and perform subtly different functions. The functional differences result in formal differences in morphological number-marking systems. In what follows, the nature of these functional and formal differences is examined and the diachronic processes behind them explored.

Frajzyngier (1985) and Durie (1986) have shown that nominal and verbal number markers operate independently in many languages. This is the case with most of the several hundred languages indigenous to North America. The problems introduced by an agreement analysis for these languages become apparent as soon as spontaneous speech is examined. In the majority of North American languages, verbs can constitute grammatical predications in themselves. Separate nominal constituents are not only unnecessary for grammaticality, they are frequently absent. Still, even when no nouns appear, verbs can bear number markers. Note the plural prefix in the verb below from Ineseño Chumash, a California language of the Chumash family.

(1)　Ineseño Chumash
　　　s-iy-axi-　　kum
　　　3pl iterative dance
　　　'They are dancing.' (Applegate, 1972, p. 458)

There is no nominal source for the number specification, nothing for a copying rule to copy.

In order to maintain a strict agreement analysis, one might posit underlying nominal constituents as part of every sentence, allow copying rules to duplicate their number features on associated verbs, then permit optional nominal deletion. This analysis would run into a second set of problems, however. When separate nominals are actually present, they do not necessarily agree in number with associated verbs.

(2)　Ineseño Chumash
　　　s-iy-axi-　　kum　　ha-ku
　　　3pl iterative dance　　the person
　　　'The people are dancing.' (Applegate, 1972, p. 458)

In many of these situations, plural forms of the nouns simply do not exist. In fact, in the majority of North American languages, nouns referring to nonhumans are not marked for number at all. Yet even when plurals do exist, they are not necessarily used. The Ineseño Chumash noun *ku* 'person' has a counterpart *kuhkuʔ* 'people,' but it was not chosen for the above context. Such mismatches are usually not the result of sloppiness on the part of speakers, although this possibility has sometimes been suggested by frustrated grammarians.

1. Number Marking with Different Lexical Categories

1.1 Nouns

In some languages in North America, among them Taos, Kiowa, Zuni, and the Algonquian languages, all nouns are inflected for number, just as in Indo-European. In the vast majority of North American languages, however, only certain nouns have plural forms. In most of these, only nouns referring to human beings have plurals, or only some nouns referring to humans, often kin terms. (Multiple animals that are considered 'sentient beings,' such as pets or characters in legends, are also often referred to by plural nouns.) The plurals that do exist are used only on some occasions, not every time multiple participants are discussed.

1.2 Adjectives

Many North American languages lack a special lexical class of adjectives. Modification is accomplished by stative verbs. Where adjectives do constitute a separate category, they often have plural forms, but use of these forms is usually not obligatory, independently of whether human beings, animals, or objects are described.

1.3 Verbs

Verbs typically include a variety of number markers. Number is most frequently marked on verbs by bound pronouns, stem alternations, and various derivational processes.

1.3.1 Bound pronouns   In the majority of North American languages, pronouns referring to the core arguments of a predication are bound to verbs or auxiliaries as affixes or clitics. They are usually obligatory whether separate nominal constituents are present or not, as in (1) and (2). Languages vary in their repertoires of bound pronouns. Bound pronouns may represent all persons, or only first and second. They may distinguish number systematically throughout, or only for certain human referents, or, surprisingly often, not at all.

1.3.2 Stem alternation   In many North American languages, verb stems alternate according to the number of participants involved. The set of alternating stems consists of a limited number of common verbs, in some languages only two or three, in others up to several dozen. They usually include intransitives such as 'sit,' 'lie,' 'stand,' 'go,' 'walk,' 'run,' 'fly,' 'die,' and transitive such as 'take,' 'pick up,' 'carry,' 'throw,' 'kill.' Note the complete lack of phonological resemblance between the singular and plural verbs for 'sit' and 'kill' in the languages (3) and (4), for example.

(3)	'sit/dwell'		'(one to) sit'	'(group to) sit'
	Shuswap	(Gibson, 1973, p. 52)	ʔém	łéq
	Southern Paiute	(Sapir, 1930, p. 242)	qari̇̀-	yuʀwi̇̀-
	Haida	(Swanton, 1911, p. 276)	q!ao	L!ū
	Zuni	(Newman, 1965, p. 55)	ʔimo	tina
	Upper Chehalis	(Kinkaid, 1975, p. 48)	tawíłš	lákʷł
(4)	'kill'		'kill (one)'	'kill (several)'
	Shuswap	(Gibson, 1973, p. 52)	púl	ʾíkʷ
	Southern Paiute	(Sapir, 1930, p. 242)	paq·a	qɔʾi̇̀-
	Haida	(Swanton, 1911, p. 276)	tia	L!da
	Zuni	(Newman, 1965, p. 55)	ʔayna	łata
	Upper Chehalis	(Kinkaid, 1975, p. 263)	x̣ə́lq̇	-ə́x̣ʷ

For intransitive verbs, the selection of a stem reflects the number of subjects involved, whether they are agents (walkers, runners, flyers) or patients (fallers, sitters, corpses). For transitive verbs, it reflects the number of objects involved: how many people are killed, how many objects are picked up, thrown, given, dropped, and so on. The pattern remains the same regardless of whether other parts of the grammar operate on an active, accusative, or ergative basis. This is no accident. The subjects of intransitives and patients of transitives share an important role: They are the participants most directly affected by an action. The primary function of stem alternation is not to enumerate entities, but to quantify the effect of actions, states, and events.

This stem alternation has sometimes been referred to as suppletion. In the strictest sense, suppletion refers to allormorphic alternation conditioned by a systematic inflectional distinction. A prototypical example of stem suppletion in English, where every verb is obligatorily inflected for tense, is the alternation between *go* and *wen-*. The relationship between verbs like *kick* and *slap*, by contrast, is not considered suppletive, since we do not systematically specify the instrument involved in every action. *Kick* and *slap* simply happen to include different instruments as parts of their basic meanings. The North American verbs that alternate according to the number of entities affected are related in a similar way. The implied plurality of effect is a feature of their basic meaning. Walking alone is classified lexically as a different activity from walking in a group; speaking is different from conversing; murdering an individual is different from massacring a village. The pairs of verbs are related semantically but not inflectionally.

Reactions of speakers confirm the lexical independence of these alternating stems. An excellent speaker of Central Pomo, a California Pomoan language, was asked for the plural of the verb *yow* '(one) goes.' She supplied *hlaan* '(several are) walking.' On another occasion, when asked for the singular form of *hlaan*, she provided *waan* '(one is) walking.' Such chains are not unusual, even from the best speakers.

Not all verbs implying multiple effects even have specific singular counterparts, or vice versa. Note the asymmetry in the sets of verbs used with singular, dual, and plural subjects for 'sit' and 'dwell' in Koasati, a Muskogean language of Lousiana:

(5) Koasati

Singular	Dual	Plural	
cokkó:lin	*cikkí:kan*	*í:san*	'sit'
á:tan	*áswan*	*í:san*	'dwell' (Kimball, 1985, p. 273)

The transitive verbs in (6) from Klamath, an Oregon language, constitute another common type of set. Different handling verbs are used depending upon the nature of the substance handled: round, flat, alive, or multiple, but not 'multiple round' or 'multiple flat.'

(6)   Klamath
       ˡoy   'to give a round object'
       nᵉoy   'to give a flat object'
       ksᵛoy   'to give a live object'
       sʔewanʔ   'to give plural objects (round, flat, live, etc.)' (Barker, 1964,
                      p. 176)

The lexically plural verbs are not unlike English *congregate, disperse, gather,*
and *scatter.* These English verbs also imply multiple subjects when intransitive and multiple patients when transitive, but it is not immediately obvious
what their singular counterparts should be. Here, too, the number distinction is semantic rather than grammatical. Pants (grammatically plural, semantically singular) could not scatter, but a crowd (grammatically singular,
semantically plural) could gather and disperse. (See Durie, 1986, for a detailed
discussion of similar issues.)

Although verb stems implying multiple effects may appear to agree with
plural nouns or pronouns, a match is not obligatory. Lexically plural verbs
may denote events involving groups, not simply multiple participants. In
English, if each solitary hiker who passes a bench rests there for a moment,
they have not necessarily congregated; if a murderer kills three victims during
his lifetime, they have not necessarily been massacred. Verbs with plural subjects or objects may contrast with lexically plural verbs. In Yurok, a California Algic language, the verb *nep* 'eat' has a counterpart *ʔeʔgah* 'have a meal
together.' It also has a plural form *nepoh*, which could be used if several people
ate individually. The verb *cwinkep* 'speak' has a semantic counterpart *tohkow*
'talk together, converse,' but it also has a plural *cwinkepoh* '(several) speak'
(Robins, 1958, p. 42). In his grammar of Sarcee, an Athabaskan language
of Alberta, Cook remarks that "like the unmarked stems, the plural stems
may occur with either a singular or a plural subject. With a plural subject,
-dáɬ means 'three or more move,' and with a singular subject it means 'one
moves in company with two or more' (1984, p. 59). Kinkaid (1975, p. 49) reports
similar systems in Salish languages.

1.3.3 Derivational Processes   Most North American languages show derivational processes in their verbal morphology that appear to reflect number.
Compare the verbs below from Karok, a language of Northern California.

(7)   Karok
       θivrú·htih   '(one object) to be floating'
       θivru'hti·h·va   '(several objects) to be floating'

       ikyí·m-kurih   '(one) to fall in'
       ikyimku'rih·va   '(several) to fall in'

       ʔákunv-ař̃   '(one) to go hunting'
       ʔákunvan·va   '(several) to go hunting' (Bright, 1957, p. 92, 93)

The suffix -*va* appears to indicate a plural subject, at least with intransitive verbs. When it appears with transitive verbs, it can indicate a plural patient.

(8)   Karok
    pasnáp-iš(rih)   'to glue down (one)'
    pasnapi' šri·h-va   'to glue down (several)'

    itráa·mnihtih   'to be looking into (one object)'
    itramni' hti·h-va   'to be looking into (several objects)'
                           (Bright, 1957, p. 92, 93)

Actually, the suffix need not pluralize any particular entities at all.

(9)   Karok
    taknah   'to hop'
    takná·h-va   'to play hopscotch'

    mah   'to see'
    má·h-va   'to see'

    ví·k-paθ   'to weave around (once)'
    vikpá·θ-va   'to weave around and around' (Bright, 1957, p. 92)

The primary function of -*va* is to multiply actions. It may imply that the actions are distributed over multiple agents or multiple patients, but this is a secondary effect. The actions can just as well be distributed over time or space:

(10)   Karok
    ikre·myáhiš(rih)   'to start to blow'
    ikre·myahi' šri·h-va 'to blow off and on'

    ʔápakunih   '(earth) to slide down'
    ʔapaku' ni·h-va   'to be a landslide' (Bright, 1957, p. 92)

Multiple event or distributive suffixes do not appear every time multiple agents or patients are involved. The first verb in (11) involves a single cook, as shown by the singular pronominal prefix *ʔu-* 'he/she.' The second involves several cooks, as shown by the plural pronominal prefix *kun-* 'they.' In both cases, however, the cooking is considered a single activity, so no multiple-event suffix appears.

(11)   Karok
    ʔú-mniš   'he cooks'
    kun-imnis 'they cook'

The Karok multiple event suffix -*va*, like those in other languages, is derivational, not inflectional. It creates lexical items with specific meanings. Etymologically, *takná·hva* 'to play hopscotch' ('jump'-*va*) could just as well mean 'to hop up and down repeatedly,' or 'to hop around in different directions,' but it has been lexicalized with the specific meaning it was derived to express.

Although multiple-event or distributive markers are by far the most common verbal quantifiers in North American languages, other kinds of number markers also appear on verbs in many languages. They typically specify such features as distributive causation, collective causation, collective agency, multiple displacement, and iteration of various sorts. Coos contains special suffixes for multiple causative passives and multiple reflexives, phonologically unrelated to their singular counterparts (Frachtenberg, 1922, p. 358). The various verbal number markers do not necessarily co-occur, although they can. They quantify different aspects of the event predicated. Central Pomo, for example, exhibits extensive verb stem alternation according to the number of participants affected, and it also contains a multiple-event suffix, a multiple-displacement suffix, and a collective-agent suffix, a multiple-displacement suffix, and a colletive-agent suffix, among others. The number markers are in boldface in the commands in (12).

(12)   Central Pomo
       ʔnée-   *la-*   *m*
       throw one object down sg imp
       'Throw it down!'

       mčá-   *la-*   *m*
       throw multiple objects down sg imp
       'Throw them down!'

       mča-   *la-* *ta-*   ***m-***
       throw multiple objects down multiple event collective agency
            me?
            pl imp
       'Throw them down!' (Frances Jack, Personal Communication)

In the last command, every morpheme except the directional suffix 'down' quantifies some aspect of the action, but none requires the presence of any other grammatically.

A similar exuberance of verbal number markers can be seen in Southern Paiute, a Uto-Aztecan language of Utah described by Sapir (1930). Some distribute actions over time, functioning essentially as aspect markers. They indicate such things as continuous repetitive action ('patter') or durative iteration ('gnaw'). Southern Paiute also exhibits verb stem alternation according to number, as well as various distributive and multiple-agency markers. They can occur singly or in combination, as in (13).

(13)   Southern Paiute
       tA˟qɾ'u-   *ɣi-*   *nŋqï-*   *qa-*   *p·íɣa*
       reduce to small pieces durative iterative transitive pl agent remote past
       'They chipped it into small pieces.' (Sapir, 1930, p. 670)

Verbal number marking is pervasive in North America, but it does not represent simple agreement with nouns. It operates independently, modifying the verbs themselves.

2. The Grammaticization of Number

The number marking typical of Indo-European nouns enumerates entities, while that of North American verbs usually quantifies aspects of events. But exactly how does this come about? Do number markers bind morphologically with noun or verb stems only when their semantic contributions are appropriate? Or do their meanings shift after they have become bound?

The synchronic morphological systems of some North American languages provide glimpses of the path of development of number marking. In several languages, phonologically similar number markers appear with words from different lexical classes. Their resemblances suggest a common diachronic source and presumably a single ancestral function.

2.1 Reduplication

The most common form of number marking over multiple lexical categories is reduplication. In some North American languages, such as those in the Algonquian and Pomoan families, only verbs are reduplicated. In many languages, however, the same reduplicative processes that mark number on verbs also appear on nouns and even adjectives.

2.1.1 The functions of reduplication in different lexical categories   The Tsimshian texts recorded by Boas on the Nass River in Northern British Columbia provide excellent documentation of the function of reduplication in that language. Verbs, nouns, and adjectives can all be reduplicated according to the same patterns. (Most of the patterns are somewhat complex, but they apply to all lexical classes.) In his grammatical sketch, Boas (1911b) simply listed the reduplicated forms as the plurals of the plain forms. An examination of the texts, however, indicates that reduplication does not produce simple plurals. Reduplication appears only a fraction of the time that multiple entities are discussed.

Verbs can bear reduplicative prefixes when multiple intransitive subjects are involved as in (14), or multiple transitive objects, as in (15).

(14)   Nass Tsimshian
         *NLk·'ē **ad'ā'd'ĭk·sk^uL** wī-hē'ldEm qē'wun.*
         then   redup came   many   gull
         'Now many gulls came.' (Boas, 1902, p. 103.13)

(15) Nass Tsimshian
NLk·'ē q'ax·q'ayā'ant.
Then redup he clubbed them
'Then he clubbed them.' (Boas, 1902, p. 70.9)

Yet verbs are not reduplicated every time multiple subjects or objects are identified. The verb *hwant* 'sit' is not reduplicated in (16).

(16) Nass Tsimshian
Ga·a'aL g·at hwant aL g·ilē'lîx·g·ê.
they saw man sitting at inland
'The men who were sitting under the trees saw what he was doing.'
(Boas, 1902, p. 111.12)

The fact that several men were present is clear from the choice of the verb *hwant* '(several) sit'; a different verb *d'a* is used if one person sits alone. The verb 'several sit' does have a reduplicated form. It follows the same pattern as *hwîlp/huwî'p* 'house/houses,' and *hwā/huwā'* 'name/names.' The reduplicated form appears in contexts like that in (17).

(17) Nass Tsimshian
NLk·'ē huwa'nL *txanētkᵘL k'ōpE-ts'ō'ôts.*
then redup they sat down all the little birds
'And all the birds sat down.' (Boas, 1902, p. 124.15)

Nass Tsimshian reduplicated verbs distribute an event over multiple times or locations, including multiple participants.

The function of reduplication on nouns is interesting. The simple noun *gan* 'stick' refers to single stick in (18).

(18) Nass Tsimshian
NLk·'ēt gōL **gan.**
then he took a stick
'Then he took a stick.' (Boas, 1902, p. 68.3)

The reduplicated form *ganga'n* refers to multiple sticks in (19).

(19) Nass Tsimshian
K·'ē hwîl sagait-hā'p'aaL t'an kᵘLē-hîsya'tst aL **ganga'n,**
then all together they who all over hit him with redup stick
'Then he was attacked and beaten with sticks,

aL nî'g·ît g·a'alL g·at. *Q'am-ba'gait-bEbEsba'tskᵘL* **ganga'n**
and not he saw a person by themselves they were lifted redup stick
although he did not see a single person. The sticks moved of themselves

t'an *ĥisya'tsL lEpLa'nt, t'Em-qē'st, qa-an'ô'nt, asEsa'et.*
which hit   his body, his head, his hands, his feet.
hitting his body, his head, his hands, and his feet.'
(Boas, 1902, p. 62.12–13)

Reduplicated nouns are not simple plurals, however. The noun for *stick* is unreduplicated in (20), even though we know that multiple sticks were involved from the choice of the verb *dôq* 'to take (several).' (The verb *gō* means 'to take (one).')

(20)   Nass Tsimshian
        HuX dô'qdēL gan.
        again they took stick
        'Again they took sticks.' (Boas, 1902, p. 97.12)

Like reduplicated verbs, reduplicated nouns function as distributives, emphasizing temporal, locative, or conceptual distribution: the separateness of the entities they identify.

Reduplicated verbs and nouns often appear to 'agree.' In (16), neither the verb 'sit' nor the noun 'person' is reduplicated. In (21), both the verb 'load' and its object 'canoes' are reduplicated.

(21)   Nass Tsimshian
        huX mîx·māx·L mmāl.
        again redup they loaded redup canoe
        'Again they loaded the canoes.' (Boas, 1902, p. 108.12)

These matches reflect semantic co-occurrences rather than grammatical agreement. Distributed entities are often involved in distributed actions. The multiple canoes of (21) required multiple loading. In (16), by contrast, a single group of people was seated together at one time in one place, so neither the verb nor the noun was reduplicated.

Although reduplication is highly productive in Nass Tsimshian, Boas's texts indicate that it is not applied uniformly to all verbs and nouns. It is a derivational process, used only when needed to create new lexical items. Distribution is a more important aspect of some actions and entities than of others, and it is these that can be described with reduplication. Many verbs and nouns lack reduplicated forms, so distribution is simply not distinguished for them in any context. In (14), for example, the reduplicated verb *ad'-ā'd'ĭk·sk^uL* 'came' indicates distributed activity, but the noun for 'gull' remains unspecified for distribution.

Nass Tsimshian adjectives can also be reduplicated. The qualities they specify are distributed individually over each item described, rather than ascribed to the set as a unit. Reduplication on adjectives operates independently of the distributed status of the nouns modified. The noun for 'salmon,' for example, has no distributive form, so it is always unmarked for this feature. Nevertheless, the quality of fatness is distributed by a reduplicated adjective over the individual fish in (22).

(22) Nass Tsimshian
      DEm max-t'Elt'ē'lx· hân   aL K·san.
      fut   all redup fat   the salmon at Skeena
      'The salmon of Skeena river shall always be fat.'
      (Boas, 1902, p. 20.15)

A similar pattern can be seen in Southern Paiute. Here, as in other Uto-Aztecan languages, both verbs and nouns can show partial reduplication for number. The rich textual material collected by Sapir, along with his grammatical sketch, show that reduplicative prefixes on verbs function as prototypical verbal number markers: They characterize events, not things. They distribute actions over time, indicating iterative or continuous action, or over space, indicating multiple locations or participants.

(23) Southern Paiute verbs
      ivi-   'to drink'
      i'ï'p·i'   'drinks repeatedly, sips'
      na'a'ip·ïɣa'   'fire was burning'
      nan·a'aip·ïɣa'   'there were fires burning'
      ⲡan·aɣa-   'several go home'
      ⲡampa'n'A'qai'   '(they) go home in parties'
      tɔ'qwa'ai'   'patches one'
      tɔ'tɔ'q·wa:ai'   'patches several' (Sapir, 1930, pp. 258–261)

As in Nass Tsimshian, Southern Paiute nominal reduplication is not a simple inflectional plural marker. Sapir points out that reduplicated nouns are distributive, "not plurals, though sometimes, particularly in the case of animate nouns, practically equivalent to such" (1930, p. 257).

(24) Southern Paiute nouns
      qa'nI   'house'
      qaŋqa'nI   'houses'
      pɔ·'   'trail'
      pɔvɔ'ɔ   'trails'
      piŋwa-   'wife'
      pivi'ŋwa·mï   'their (visible) wives' (Sapir, 1930, pp. 257–258)

Distributive nouns are usually plural, but not all plural nouns are distributive. Both nouns for 'horse' in (25) can be used to refer to multiple horses, for example, but only the second is distributive.

(25)   Southern Paiute
     puŋqu' ŋwïraŋ WA   'our (inclusive) horses (owned
                                   collectively)'
     pumpu' ŋquŋwïraŋ WA   'our horses (one or more owned
                                     individually by each one of us)'
                                     (Sapir, 1930, p. 258)

Similar examples come from Maidu, a California Penutian language. Dixon (1911) remarks in his grammatical sketch that reduplication is quite frequent in verbs, where it serves a distributive function.

(26)   Maidu
     witöswitösönoitsoia   'he went about picking here and there'
                                     (Dixon, 1911, p. 689)

The same reduplicative processes can be applied to nouns, adding a distributive sense. Dixon lists four reduplicated nouns.

(27)   Maidu
     sēu' sēuto   'each, every river' (*se' wi* 'river')
     höbo' boto   'every house, or camp' (*höbo'* 'house')
     ya' manmanto   'every mountain'
     tsa' tsato   'every tree' (*tsa* 'tree')

He notes, however, that few nouns seem to have reduplicated forms, and those that do are rarely used. These distributives "appear not to be used in ordinary conversation to any extent, and are rare in the texts. The above are practically all the forms that have been noted" (1911, p. 689, 708).

The same situation was reported by Hoijer for Tonkawa, a language isolate formerly spoken in central Texas.

> Reduplication affects verb themes for the most part. . . . It symbolizes repeated action, plural [intransitive] subject, or rarely, vigorous or intense action. Examples: *totop-* 'to cut repeatedly' (*top-* 'to cut'), *wawana-* 'several fall forward' (*wa·na-* 'to fall forward'). . . . In noun themes, reduplicated forms occur rarely: *nanto?on* 'a range of mountain' (*na:ton* 'mountain'), *kʷa·kʷan* 'women' (*kʷa·n* 'woman'), *?o·?on* 'blood veins' (*?o·n* 'blood') (1946, p. 297).

Beeler described a similar system in Barbareño Chumash. Reduplication "ordinarily expresses repeated, continuing action" (ms: 31). "Nouns may show initial reduplication accompanied by glottalization and falling tone on the final syllable; this formation, though it has been called a plural, appears rather to have distributive meaning" (ms: 17).

Takelma, a language isolate of Oregon, exhibits the same characteristics. Sapir (1922) reported that

Reduplication is used in Takelma as a grammatical process with surprising frequency (p. 57).

Frequentatives, continuatives, and usitatives are formed from simpler verb forms in great part by various methods of repetition of all or part of the phonetic material of the stem. . . . The frequentative idea may have reference to the repetition of the act itself (iterative or usitative) or to the plurality of the transitive object or intransitive subject affected (distributive); any sharp characterization of the manner of the frequentative action in each case is, however, doubtless artificial apart from the context (p. 127).

Reduplicated nouns are not frequent in Takelma, particularly when one considers the great importance of reduplication as a grammatical device in the verb (p. 220).

A few adjectives form their plural or frequentative by reduplication. . . . That these plurals are really frequentative or distributive in force is illustrated by such forms as *da' k!oloi-ts·!ilit' it'* 'red-cheeked,' which has reference not necessarily to a plurality of persons affected, but to the frequency of occurrence of the quality predicated (p. 264).

This pattern is common across North America. Reduplication of verbs usually serves a prototypical verbal function of distribution. In the same language, reduplication of nouns, when present, usually shares the distributive function, rather than simply pluralizing entities. Nominal reduplication is typically rarer than verbal reduplication, appearing only when the entities it quantifies are scattered (trails, rivers, veins, houses, objects individually possessed by different owners) or especially distinctive (people). Reduplication can also be extended to adjectives, still with the same basic function, distributing the quality expressed over time, space, or individuals, rather than over a static group as a whole.

2.1.2 The functional shift of reduplication over time   There is evidence that, under certain circumstances, the function of reduplication can change over time, according to nature of the host lexical category. Kwakiutl, a Wakashan language of British Columbia, exhibits typical distributive reduplication in verbs and nouns. Boas notes in his grammar that the reduplicated verbal stem

conveys purely the idea of distribution, of an action done now and then. . . . The idea of plurality is not clearly developed. Reduplication of a noun expresses rather the occurrence of an object here and there, or of different kinds of a particular object, than plurality. It is therefore rather a distributive than a true plural (1947, p. 206).

Compare the use of the simple noun for 'wolf' in the first sentence in (28) with that of the reduplicated distributive noun in the second, for example.

(28)   Kwakiutl
   a. *lā'ᵉlae q̓ē̄⁻nEma la ᵉnEmā'dzaqwa gEmō't̓aleda ᵉaLaᵉnE'ma.*
      'Then, it is said, many wolves howled all at the same time.'
   b. *le sE'nbEndxa ᵉnā'la lEᵉwa' gā'nuLe gEmō'teda q̓ē'nEme*
      ᵉeᵉaLaaᵉnE'ma.
      'Then the whole day and night wolves were howling (singly).

At the same time, Boas detected an incipient shift in the function of nominal reduplication:

> It seems that this form is gradually assuming a purely plural significance. In many cases in which it is thus applied in my texts, the older generation criticizes its use as inaccurate. Only in the case of human beings is reduplication applied both as a plural and a distributive (1947, p. 206).

He suggests that the shift may be due to the influence of English:

> There are a great many examples of the use of reduplicated plural forms for inanimate objects. The present usage is certain, but we are under the impression that the frequent use of plural forms is due to the influence of English. There are so many cases in which the absolute form is used and we have heard the reduplicated forms so often criticized as unidiomatic that we believe the old grammar would require the absolute form for all plurals in which the single objects are not individualized (1947, p. 293).

2.2 Phonologically Constant Derivational Affixes

There are also many languages in which verbs, nouns, and sometimes adjectives bear similar, phonologically constant number affixes.

2.2.1 The functions of constant derivational affixes in different lexical categories

As noted earlier, Central Pomo exhibits an elaborate array of verbal devices reflecting number. Among them is a suffix *-ṭa-* that might at first appear to indicate multiple subjects. [All of the Central Pomo examples are from Frances Jack (personal communication).]

(29)   Central Pomo
   ʔaa madúmač'   'I woke up'
   ya madúmač'ṭam   'we woke up'

On transitive verbs, *-ṭa-* appears to correlate with the number of patients.

(30)   Central
   ts'iič'kam   'fold it'
   ts'iičṭáakam   'fold lots of things'

The suffix -*ṭa*- is actually a multiple event marker. Not all verbs involving multiple participants contain the suffix. In the second sentence in (31), the pronoun *múuṭuyal* 'them' refers to a plural patient, but there is no multiple event suffix, since a single event is predicated.

(31)   Central Pomo
    a. *ʔaa múuṭu manáač'*
        I   him   pay semelfactive
        'I paid him.'
    b. *ʔaa múuṭuyal manáač'*
        I   them   pay semelfactive
        'I paid them.' (The work crew received a single check jointly.)

The suffix appears only when several separate actions are predicated.

(32)   Central Pomo
    ʔaa múuṭuyal manáataayṭaw
    I   them   pay multiple event multiple displacement aspect
    'I paid them.' (Each worker was paid individually.)

Both verbs in (33) could describe the actions of several workers. Only the second, which predicates multiple activities, contains the suffix -*ṭa*-.

(33)   Central Pomo
    béenmaw   '(group) carrying something together'
    béṭač'   '(several) each carrying something individually'

Another Central Pomo suffix, -*y*-, indicates multiple displacement. It frequently co-occurs with the multiple event suffix.

(34)   Central Pomo
    sapáaṭu ṭíqan   '(one) putting on a shoe'
    sapáaṭu ṭíyqan   '(one) putting on a pair of shoes'
    sapáaṭu ṭíyq'ṭama   '(several) putting on their shoes'

The multiple event suffix and the multiple displacement suffix both function as prototypical verbal modifiers. They quantify aspects of events.

Most Central Pomo nouns have no plural forms. 'Plurals' can be elicited for certain nouns referring to people, as in many languages, and for the noun *lóq'* 'thing.' The basic form of the plural suffix on nouns is -*ṭay*. (The dental stop disappears following another consonant.)

(35)   Central Pomo
    máaṭa   'woman'   *qanémač'*   'relative'
    máaṭaṭay   'women'   *qanémač'ay*   'relatives'
    ṭoo č'áalʔkʰe   'my sibling'   *lóq'*   'thing'
    ṭoo č'áalʔkʰeṭay   'my siblings'   *lóq'ay*   'things'

The nominal suffix *-ṭay* bears a striking resemblance to the multiple event suffix *-ṭa-*, possibly in combination with the multiple displacement suffix *-y-*.

As in other North American languages, 'plural' nouns are not used every time multiple human beings are discussed. In fact, they are more often absent than present. When people act jointly, the suffixes normally do not appear. Note that the nouns are the same in the singular and collective plural sentences in (36).

(36)   Central Pomo
     a.   *yóohṭow   čaač'   waáda.*
        south from person go sg continuative sg
        'There's a person coming from the south.'
     b.   *yóohṭow   čaač'   hlaáda.*
        south from person go pl continuative pl
        'There's a group of people coming from the south.'

The 'plural' nouns tend to appear when people act individually, at different times, in different directions, at different locations, and so on.

(37)   Central Pomo
     a.   *Cáač'ayya   qʰadée'maw.*
        person pl topic fight reciprocal multiple agent aspect
        'There's a bunch of people fighting.'
     b.   *Méen 'e čáač'ayya   máa yhéṭač'.*
        so   it is person pl topic stuff do multiple event imperfective pl
        'That's how people do things.'

-ṭay- has retained a distributive function in the relatively rare contexts in which it appears on nouns. The fact that it appears with the noun for 'thing' as well as nouns referring to persons is consistent with this role. A term for 'all sorts of things' is useful in a language without inflectional number marking on nouns.

-ṭay- appears with adjectives as well, where it also serves as a distributive. Like the Tsimshian reduplicative prefixes, it appears somewhat more frequently with adjectives than with nouns, because the qualities specified by adjectives are usually distributed individually over members of a set, rather than attributed to the set as a whole.

Maidu contains a similar number suffix that appears with both verbs and nouns. Dixon notes, "this suffix, of general and very frequent use. . .is used in some cases to indicate iteration; in others, reciprocal action; at times it seems to point to a plural object" (1911, p. 705).

(38)   Maidu
     mo'-tōn   'to drink repeatedly' (*mon* 'to drink')
     yo'k-ō-tōn   'to strike repeatedly with fist'

(*yo'k-ōn* 'to strike')

yapai'-to-to-dom   'talking to each other' (Dixon, 1911, p. 705)

He found that *-to* was "also used as a nominal suffix in connection with the reduplicated distributives." Recall that although reduplicated verbs are pervasive in Maidu, reduplicated nouns are rare.

(39)   Maidu
        tsā'-tsa-to   'trees' (Dixon, 1911, p. 705)

In Maidu, as in Central Pomo, the suffix retains its distributive function even when applied to nouns.

Coos exhibits a similar pattern. Frachtenberg (1922, p. 327) described several verbal distributive suffixes: "All the suffixes expressing distribution have the element *n-* in common, which consequently may be regarded as the original suffix conveying the idea of distributive plurality; the more so, as in the following instances *n-* actually denotes distribution."

(40)   Coos
        a.   *djï*   'it came'
              lE djí'nīt   'they came (singly)'
        b.   *cîne$^{\varepsilon}$tî'k·E*   'you stand!'
              tsEL'nē^i ûx tîkîne   'side by side they two were standing.'
                                             (Frachtenberg, 1922, p. 327)

A similar suffix, also labeled a distributive by Frachtenberg, appears with nouns, although much more rarely. *'-înī* is suffixed to nouns of relationship only and expresses a degree of mutual kinship. It is etymologically related to the verbal distributives *-ne^i*, *-änī* (1922, p. 371).

(41)   Coos
        a.   *sla'atc*   'cousin'
              ûx sla'tcîni   'they two were mutual cousins'
        b.   *hä'Lätc*   'elder brother'
              î-n häLtcî'ni   'we are brothers mutually'
                                             (Frachtenberg, 1922, p. 371)

In the limited cases where the distributive suffix appears with nouns, it retains its primary function.

Karok also shows cross-category number marking. Recall the verbal multiple event suffix *-va* illustrated in examples (7) through (10). The suffix appears with other kinds of lexical items as well, still with the multiple event or distributive sense.

(42)   Karok
    a.   *axyara*   'full'
       axyará·vah   'all full (of various vessels)'
    b.   *iθé·kxaram*   'one night'
       iθe·kxarám-vah 'night after night' (Bright, 1957, p. 82)

Distribution is more often pertinent to events than to entities, and correspondingly more likely to be marked on verbs than on nouns and adjectives. As the Central Pomo, Maidu, Coos, and Karok data show, however, distributive markers can fuse with adjectives and nouns as well, while still retaining their original function.

2.2.2   The functional shift of derivational affixes over time   There is evidence that the functions of distributive affixes can change after they have become morphologically bound, under certain conditions. The Iroquoian languages contain several distributive verbal suffixes. As in other languages, the suffixes function to distribute actions over time, space, or participants. This effect can be seen in the verbs in (43) from Cayuga, a Northern Iroquoian language of Ontario. [All of the Cayuga examples are from Reginald Henry (personal communication).]

(43)   Cayuga
    ehsyé:tho?   'you will plant'
    ehsyéthwahsọ:?   'you will plant a lot of different things'

Most Iroquoian nouns referring to human beings contain pronominal prefixes indicating the gender and number of their referents, but number is not normally specified otherwise in nouns. Several suffixes, however, clearly cognate with the verbal distributives, do appear on nominals.

(44)   Cayuga
    a.   *kanyo:?*   'wild animal'
       kanyo?shọ́:?ọh   'game'
    b.   *enọhsọnyá?tha?*   'one builds houses with it, tool'
       enọhsọnya?tha?shọ́:?ọh 'house building tools'
    c.   *akétkw?wẹta?*   'my suitcase, my handbag'
       aketkw?ẹtá?shọ?   'my baggage'

The suffixes do not appear every time multiple entities are referred to; they specify a variety of assortment of kind. The term translated 'tools' would not be used for several identical hammers. (The words for 'game' and 'tools' are morphologically verbs, but the suffix modifies them as lexicalized nominals rather than etymological verbs. The term for 'tools' does not mean 'one builds various houses with it.')

Distributive suffixes do appear systematically with certain terms referring to more than two people. They always appear with plural terms for 'children' or 'old people,' for example, although not with duals.

(45)   Cayuga
eksá:?ah	'child, girl'	*hakẹhtsih*	'old man'
kaeks?ashǫ́:?ǫh	'children'	*kaekẹhtsíhshǫ?*	'old people'

The suffix also appears with certain kin terms whenever they are plural.

(46)   Cayuga
kakhehtsi?áhshǫ?	'they are my older siblings, older siblings'
akwatẹnóhkshǫ?	'my cousins, we all are related'
kakhéhsotshǫ?	'my grandparents'
kakheyatre?shǫ́:?ǫh	'my grandchildren'
kaǫtatháwạkshǫ?	'their children (offspring)'

With these nominals, the force of the suffix has moved from distribution to plurality. This is not surprising; human beings are often considered inherently individualistic and differentiated. Still, the suffix has not become a full-fledged inflectional plural marker. It does not appear systematically with all nouns referring to humans or even to kinsmen. It is lexically governed. The basic nouns for 'men' and 'women,' for example, do not contain it.

(47)   Cayuga
akǫ́:kweh	'woman'	*hǫkweh*	'man'
ká:kǫkweh	'women'	*honǫ́:kweh*	'men'

Although these patterns are normally maintained by all Iroquoian speakers in spontaneous speech, the influence of English can be seen on occasion, as teachers work at normalizing grammatical patterns for language curricula. As they search for paradigms on English models, younger, more English-dominant speakers sometimes take advantage of the distributive as an equivalent of the English inflectional plural. They still do not use distributives as general plurals in spontaneous discourse, however.

Another example of a shift in the function of a derivational affix comes from Chinook, a Chinookan language formerly spoken in southern coastal Washington. When Boas recorded the language in 1890–1891, there were only two remaining speakers. In his grammatical sketch, he described a verbal suffix *-Em*: "distribution at distinct times. . . followed usually by *-x* (customary)" (1911a, p. 596). The texts he recorded amply show that the suffix functioned as a verbal distributive.

(48)   Chinook
*a-tc-L-kx̄ōtE'qo-**im**-x*	'he always stood on them severally'
*a-Lg-i-o-pcō'tet-**Em**-x*	'he hides it everywhere'
*a-L-x-ā'-x-**um**-x*	'they always did here and there'
	(Boas, 1894, 1911a, p. 596)

Both verbs and nouns in Chinook contain pronominal prefixes distinguishing person, gender, and number. In the verbs in (48), the prefixes following the aorist *a-* refer to ergative and absolutive arguments. Pronominal prefixes similar in form to the absolutives distinguish masculine, feminine, neuter (indefinite), dual, or plural nouns. Gender is no longer biological, although Boas detected enough of a pattern to conclude that it once was. Compare the prefixes below: *i-* masculine singular, *o-* feminine singular, and *t-* plural.

(49)   Chinook

ī'kala	'man'	*ō-hō't!au*	'virgin'
t-kālauks	'men'	*t-hat!aunā'na*	'virgins'
i-qoa-inē'nē	'beaver'	*ō-kci*	'finger'
t-qoa-inē'nē	'beavers'	*t-kci*	'fingers'
i-q!eyō'qxut	'old man'		
o-q!eyo'qxut	'old woman'		
t-q!eyō'qtîkc	'old people'		

In addition to their pronominal prefixes, some plural nouns contain suffixes. Nouns for human beings bear a suffix, *-ikc* or *-ukc*, as in the words for 'men' and 'old people' above. A particularly interesting suffix on many plural nouns is *-ma*. Boas considered this nominal suffix to be cognate with the verbal distributive *-Em-x*: "the frequent plural-suffix *-ma* (Kathlamet - *max*) seems to have been originally a distributive element. This appears particularly clearly in the words *ē·xtEmaē* 'sometimes' (*ēx·t* 'one'; *-ma* distributive; *-ē* adverbial); *kana'mtEma* 'both' (*kana'm* 'both, together'; *-ma* distributive)" (Boas, 1911a, p. 608).

The textual material from Chinook shows that the distributive force of the suffix had been generalized toward pluralization by the time Boas recorded it. Nouns that have *-ma* forms usually appear in the texts with the *-ma* whenever multiple entities are mentioned. These are only a subset of the nouns in the language, however, and they tend to refer to entities especially likely to occur distributively, such as islands, towns, houses, things, warriors, rocks, days, or elk.

The functions of number markers can thus shift after they have become bound to nouns, toward a distinction that is more generally pertinent to nouns: pluralization. It is easy to see how the shift might come about. Distributive markers on nouns tend to recur with certain semantic classes: those that are highly differentiated. Since human beings are often considered inherently individuated, highly distinct by their very nature, nouns referring to them might easily bear distributive markers nearly every time multiple human beings are involved. The reinterpretation of the distributive marker as a plural under such conditions is a short step. It also serves a useful function: Speakers and hearers are usually more interested in the number of people involved in events than in the number of objects. Data from Kwakiutl, Cayuga, and Chinook indicate that the shift may continue one step further under special conditions. Under heavy influence from a language like English, where plural is an inflectional category of nouns, number marking may be reinterpreted as a more general category and extended to more contexts.

3. The Predominance of Verbal Number Markers in North America

North American number-marking systems still remain strikingly different from those found in many other parts of the world. Throughout North America, verbal number markers are generally more pervasive, productive, and elaborate than nominal number markers. The nominal number markers that do exist are usually verbal in origin and in character, signaling distribution rather than simple plurality. These tendencies are probably not unrelated to other characteristics of the languages themselves. A surprising proportion of North American languages share certain structural traits, although they are not demonstrably related genetically. As a whole, they are predominantly verb centered. Verbs are typically elaborate morphologically, containing bound pronouns referring to core arguments, as well as numerous locative, temporal, and other adverbial distinctions, and often even incorporated noun stems. Verbs can usually function as self-contained sentences in themselves. When they contain third person referential pronouns, separate nominal constituents are not syntactically bound to verbs as they are in English. They function more as appositives to the bound pronouns, supplying identification where necessary. It is not surprising that these appositional nominal adjuncts should fail to be inflected systematically for number.

4. Inflection, Derivation, and the Lexicon

Number distinctions in North America are typically not only verbal, they are usually lexical and derivational rather than inflectional. This is no accident. As Bybee (1985) points out, inflectional distinctions are obligatorily specified on all members of a lexical class or subclass. In English, number is marked inflectionally on all count nouns, and tense on all finite verbs. We know that every singular count noun has a plural counterpart, and every present tense verb has a past tense, although we may not know exactly what the forms are. Inflectional categories must therefore be sufficiently general in meaning to be applicable to all members of a lexical class or subclass.

The distinction between singular and plural number may be equally applicable to all nouns, but it is not equally pertinent to all verbs. For some events, number can be central: One bird flitting by can be conceived of as a different event from a flock flying by in formation; picking up one object can be classified as a different motion from gathering up a lot of objects. Such distinctions can be sufficiently important to be encoded lexically, and in North America, events of this type are frequently expressed by means of different verb stems. Such classifications can of course be culture specific, but the similarities across North America are striking. Languages differ more in the number of verb roots that encode number than in the types of verbs that do. Most common are verbs of position ('sit,' 'stand,' 'lie'), of handling ('put,' 'take,' 'pick up,' 'drop,' 'throw'), of basic motion ('go,' 'walk,' 'run,' 'fly,' 'swim'), and killing and dying. Also typical are certain social activities, such as conversing, eating, and crying (mourning).

In many cases, number may not be a sufficiently central aspect of an event to be encoded in a distinct verb root, but it may be pertinent enough to motivate the creation of a special lexical item. Hitting a man once and giving him a beating might be classified as subtypes of the same basic activity, so they might be expressed with verbs based on the same root. If the repeated hitting corresponds to a recognizable, conceptually unitary event, speakers might exploit their derivational morphology to create a word for this concept. Similarly, doing laundry may be simply categorized as washing, or a special term may be created, perhaps with multiple event suffix, for this special activity. Like all derivational processes, these devices vary in productivity from language to language.

Verbal number distinctions rarely become inflectional, because the pertinence of number varies so greatly from one type of event to another. As Bybee points out, once the most important number distinctions are expressed lexically, and other significant number distinctions expressed derivationally, there is little motivation to extend number specification to the remaining verbs in a language.

Basically verbal number distinctions are sometimes extended to nouns, but they seldom spread to all nouns, because of their specialized function. Distributive markers retain a distributive meaning, serving to emphasize the distribution or separateness of the entities referred to by nouns. In some cases, they eventually appear with all nouns referring to multiple human beings, since people can be considered inherently individualistic and differentiated. At this point, they can function essentially as plural markers, but still, only within the range of nouns referring to people. This is not an unstable state; the number of human beings involved in an event is generally more interesting to speakers than the number of inanimate objects. Even languages with no inflectional or derivational number marking at all on nouns often contain separate noun stems for 'person' and 'people,' 'man' and 'men,' 'woman' and 'women,' 'child' and 'children.'

5. Conclusion

Number is thus not necessarily a nominal category or even an inflectional one. In many North American languages, it is primarily a verbal category:

Number markers appear predominantly on verbs and quantify aspects of events. On occasion, basically verbal number markers are extended to nouns and adjectives where appropriate, but they retain their basic functions, usually marking distribution.

Once distributives are extended to nouns, their functions can shift. Because people can be viewed as inherently differentiated, distributives often come to appear with all nouns referring to multiple human beings. At this point, the markers may be reinterpreted as plurals, but only in this restricted domain. The next step, the extension of the plural function to all nouns, apparently occurs only under the heavy influence of another language with a general inflectional plural, such as English.

The functional difference between nominal and verbal number markers results in a formal difference. Plurality is a sufficiently general feature of entities to be applicable to all count nouns. It is thus often inflectional. Verbal number distinctions, by contrast, vary widely in their importance and applicability to events. They rarely become inflectional. Instead, they are encoded lexically, derivationally, or not at all.

Acknowlegments

I am grateful to Mrs. Frances Jack, of Hopland, California, for sharing her expertise on her language, Central Pomo, and to Mr. Reginald Henry, of Six Nations, Ontario, for sharing his expertise on his language, Cayuga.

References

Applegate, R.B. (1972). *Ineseño Chumash grammar*. Ph.D dissertation, University of California, Berkeley.

Barker, M.A.R. (1964). Klamath grammar. *University of California Publications in Linguistics* **32**.

Beeler, M.S. (1987). "Topics in Barbareño Chumash Grammar." University of California, Berkeley.

Boas, F. (1894). Chinook texts. *Bureau of American Ethnology Bulletin* **20**. Government Printing Office, Washington D.C.

Boas, F. (1902). Tsimshian texts. *Bureau of American Ethnology Bulletin* **27**. Government Printing Office, Washington D.C.

Boas, F. (1911a). Chinook. Handbook of North American Languages, Part 1. *Bureau of American Ethnology Bulletin* **40**, 559–678. Government Printing Office, Washington D.C.

Boas, F. (1911b). Tsimshian. Handbook of North American Languages, Part 1. *Bureau of American Ethnology Bulletin* **40**, 283–422. Government Printing Office, Washington D.C.

Boas, F. (1947). Kwakiutl Grammar. *Transactions of the American Philosophical Society, New Series*, 37, Part 3.

Bright, W. (1957). The Karok language. *University of California Publications in Linguistics* **13**.

Bybee, J. (1985). "Morphology. A Study of the Relation between Meaning and Form." Benjamins, Amsterdam.

Cooks, E.-D. (1984). "A Sarcee Grammar." Univ. of British Columbia Press, Vancouver.

Dixon, R.B. (1911). Maidu. Handbook of North American Languages, Part 1. *Bureau of American Ethnology Bulletin* **40**, 679–734. Government Printing Office, Washington D.C.

Durie, M. (1986). The grammaticization of number as a verbal category. *Proceedings of the Twelfth Annual Meeting of the Berkeley Linguistics Society* 355-370.

Frachtenberg, L.J. (1922). Coos. Handbook of North American Languages, Part 2. *Bureau of American Ethnology Bulletin* **40**, 297-430. Government Printing Office, Washington D.C.

Frajzyngier, Z. (1985). Ergativity, number, and agreement. *Proceedings of the Eleventh Annual Meeting of the Berkeley Linguistics Society* 96-106.

Gibson, J.A. (1973). *Shuswap grammatical structure*. Ph.D. dissertation, University of Hawaii.

Hoijer, H. (1946). Tonkawa. "Linguistic Structures of Native America," pp. 289-311. Wenner-Gren Foundation for Anthropological Research, New York.

Kimball, G.D. (1985). *A descriptive grammar of Koasati*. Ph.D. dissertation, Tulane University.

Kinkaid, M.D. (1975). *Pluralization in Upper Chehalis*. Paper read at the 1975 Salish Conference.

Newman, S. (1965). Zuni Grammar. *University of New Mexico Publications in Anthropology* (14).

Robins, R.H. (1958). The Yurok language. *University of California Publications in Linguistics* **15**.

Sapir, E. (1922). The Takelma language of southwestern Oregon. Handbook of American Indian Languages, Part 2. *Bureau of American Ethnology Bulletin* **40**, 1-296. Government Printing Office, Washington D.C.

Sapir, E. (1930). Southern Paiute, a Shoshonean language. Texts of the Kaibab Paiutes and Uintah Utes. Southern Paiute Dictionary. *Proceedings of the American Academy of Arts and Sciences* **65**, 1, 2, and 3.

Swanton, J.R. (1911). Haida. Handbook of American Indian Languages, Part 1. *Bureau of American Ethnology Bulletin* **40**, 205-282. Government Printing Office, Washington D.C.

Watkins, L.J. (1984). "A Grammar of Kiowa." University of Nebraska Press, Lincoln.

Chapter 13

On the Mechanisms
of Morphological Change

Dieter Stein

1.

The purpose of this chapter is not, as with most chapters in this volume, to discuss how a body of facts about morphology fits into various theories about morphology. It is rather to contribute to the equally necessary task of adding to this body of facts by an in-depth case study of one notorious case of morphological change in English which must still be considered unresolved in essential motivations and mechanisms: the transition from *th* to *s* (from *he singeth* to *he sings*) in the third person singular present indicative in Late Middle and Early Modern English. This process is embedded in a context of broader, but not unrelated changes on the way from Old English to Modern English (see Holmqvist, 1922), including the odyssey of the *s* form through nearly all of the person categories, from Late Old English up to Modern English dialects. The *s* ending appears first in Late Old English Northumbrian texts of the tenth century, and there predominantly in person categories other than the third singular present. In Middle English texts there is dialectal variation in the third singular present between *s* in the North and Northeast of England and *th* in the rest of the Midlands and the South. The question of where the *s* form in the verb-inflectional paradigm comes from and how to account for the migration through the person categories with the final place, in Standard English, in the third singular is one of the classsical problems of English historical linguistics.

   The material presented here is part of larger research with the aim of obtaining an overall view of verb-inflectional processes in English historical and modern dialects and their evolution (Stein 1985b, 1987). Here I focus on the change from *th* to *s* in the third singular indicative as manifested in written texts of the sixteenth century. There is plenty of evidence that, at this time and probably already in the fifteeth century, *s* was the normal form of the spoken language. The point of departure for the evolutional segment which this chapter treats is therefore a split state of the language: In the first half of the sixteenth century written texts of a more literary or artistic character have *th* and more colloquial texts, to the extent that such texts exist, have *s*. As an example of the latter one might cite *The Diary of Henry Machyn* (1550–1563), a "supplier of funeral trappings." This chapter, then, is a case study of a morphological replacement process in written texts which takes place in the latter part of the sixteenth century and in the first half of the seventeeth century in English written literary texts. In the light of the data to be presented it is important to point out that the observed mechanism is not a change in the language, but a change in the newly emerging written register.

1.1

This replacement process has several distinct features which are treated in turn. The chapter concentrates on those features which are of a more general linguistic interest while abstracting from more philological issues and also from those which are of more specific interest from the perspective of English historical linguistics. Section 2 looks at the internal structure of the process, establishing an isolectal structure. Section 3 discusses the relative abruptness of the process, which is also manifested in corpus-internal diachronic developments. Section 4 shows the involvement of syntax in the morphological replacement process. Section 5 demonstrates semiotic values of the isolectally obsolete form and discusses their status and place in the diachronic structure of the process. Section 6 places the features discussed in wider linguistic and historical contexts, and Section 7 summarizes the main features of the process.

2.

A first characteristic feature of the replacement process is in compliance with an implicational succession of linguistic contexts in which the new form appears. This pattern is obscured by giving mere percentages of *s* and *th* such as the often-cited list by Bambas (1947, p. 186) in Table I.

    The list indicates that there is in fact a transition from *th* to *s* in the period under consideration but it does not give an indication of an internal transition pattern. Rather, the replacement of *th* by *s* proceeds in three quite distinct

Table I   *s* and *th* According to Bambas (1947)

Author	Work	Date	Percentage
Ascham	*Toxophilus*	1545	6
Robynson	*More's Utopia*	1551	0
Knox	*The First Blast of the Trumpet*	1558	0
Ascham	*The Schoolmaster*	1570	0.7
Underdowne	*Heliodorus' An Aethiopian History*	1587	2
Greene	*Groats-Worth of Wit; Repentance of Robert Greene; Blacke Bookes Messenger*	1592	50
Nashe	*Pierce Pennilesse*	1592	50
Spenser	*A View of the Present State of Ireland*	1596	18
Meres	*Poetrie*	1598	13
Dekker	*The Wonderful Years;*	1603	84
	The Seven Deadlie Sinns of London	1606	78
Drummond of Hawthornden	*A Cypresse Grove*	1623	7
Donne	*Devotions;*	1624	74
	Juvenilia	1633	64
Fuller	*Historie of the Holy Warre*	1638	0.4
Jonson	*English Grammar*	1640	20
Milton	*Areopagitica*	1644	85
Daniel	*A Defence of Rhyme;*	1607	62
	The Collection of the History of England	1612–1618	94

isolectal stages A, B, and C, defined as a successive extension of contexts in which *s* appears, as shown in Table II.

A first stage, A, is defined by *th* as the 99% ending; there are only very sporadic occurrences of *s* in maximally 1% of the eligible cases. It is possible to identify conditions favoring the appearance of *s* forms, such the nature of the stem-final consonant and negation, which favor the new ending. Stage

Table II   Isolectal Stages in the Replacement of *th* by *s*

	Isolectal stage		
	A	B	C
Main verbs except sibilant-ending verbs[a]	*th*	*s*	*s*
Sibilant verbs and auxiliaries	*th*	*th*	*s*

[a] "Sibilant-ending verbs" indicates those verb stems ending in a sibilant, such as *purchases* or *purchaseth*. The property relevant for the present discussion is that with these verbs the ending is automatically syllabic, i.e., the ending appears with a vowel for phonetic or phonotactic reasons specific to English. For convenience we refer to these main verbs as "sibilant verbs."

B is defined by *s* being the dominant form in main verbs whose stems end in a nonsibilant. In other words, *th* is only retained in *have* and *do*, and in such main verbs which give automatically syllabic suffixes, such as *purchaseth.*[1] So in texts of this isolectal stage the grammar is split along the main verb/auxiliary line as well as along a phonological parameter. The Bambas list (Table I) does not segregate the occurrences along these lines and therefore obscures an important aspect of the change mechanism. Stage C is more or less what we have in present-day English: *s* in all contexts, with *th* available for special stylistic effect in the written registers.

It is a surprising fact that of a large number of whole texts investigated from all genres (from dramatic to prose) (see Stein, 1987), only around 5% cannot be clearly assigned to one of the three stages. Without going into details, these latter texts are cases of deliberate exploitation of the contrast for purposes of prose rhythm by writers who follow special stylistic ideals and lay claim to artistic perfection in prose writings, such as Sir Thomas Browne (second half of the seventeenth century). The remarkable fact is that by far the majority of written texts are either A, B, or C. For instance, in *The Conny-Catching Pamphlets* by Robert Greene (ca. 1590), there is only one occurrence which breaks the rule. These texts are isolectally B, so verbs ending in a stem-final sibilant have syllabic *eth*.

In the whole of these texts, there is only one case of such a verb with *es*, such is the level of regularity with these isolectal markers. It seems also remarkable that the seemingly independent parameters of syllabic suffix as a basically phonological criterion, and auxiliary/main verb as a syntactic criterion, go together in demarcating isolectal stages in a change process.

3.

Such discreteness in the isolectal status of the texts of that period implies that there is an element of abruptness in the replacement process. The Bambas list does give an indication of this relative abruptness, with jumps from single-figure percentages to 50% with few texts in between. An analysis of the Shakespeare corpus gives some interesting results here, as it contains a clear internal diachronic dimension. Within the chronological extension of the Shakespeare plays, from 1590 to 1611, there is a transition from Stage B to Stage C. Shakespeare starts out by being predominantly the B type: Table III shows a clear increase of *s* forms with syllabic suffixes, with a rather clear boundary line in the middle of the corpus. The second case of corpus-internal

---

[1] At Stage B, the different syntactic functions of *have* and *do* show no difference in their morphological behavior with respect to *s* or *th*. There is, however, such a differential effect at the transition to Stage C as briefly indicated in Section 3. The modal auxiliaries never took *th* or *s*.

Table III Third Singular Ending of Verbs with a Stem-Final Sibilant.

	Plays	eth	es
1	The second part of *King Henry the Sixth*	2	2
2	The third part of *King Henry the Sixth*	6	2
3	The first part of *King Henry the Sixth*	8	1
4	*Richard the Third*	8	4
5	*The Comedy of Errors*	3	2
6	*Titus Andronicus*	2	1
7	*The Taming of the Shrew*	3	5
8	*The Two Gentlemen of Verona*	3	2
9	*Love's Labor's Lost*	2	2
10	*Romeo and Juliet*	–	9
11	*King Richard the Second*	3	–
12	*A Midsummer Night's Dream*	1	1
13	*King John*	2	7
14	*The Merchant of Venice*	14	3
15	The first part of *King Henry the Fourth*	7	2
16	The second part of *King Henry the Fourth*	3	6
17	*Much Ado about Nothing*	1	7
18	*King Henry the Fifth*	1	8
19	*Julius Caesar*	2	3
20	*As You Like It*	4	6
21	*Twelfth Night*	–	6
22	*Hamlet*	–	13
23	*The Merry Wives of Windsor*	1	9
24	*Troilus and Cressida*	2	13
25	*All's Well That Ends Well*	–	19
26	*Measure for Measure*	1	14
27	*Othello*	2	11
28	*King Lear*	1	12
29	*Macbeth*	–	8
30	*Antony and Cleopatra*	4	11
31	*Coriolanus*	–	7
32	*Timon of Athens*	–	11
33	*Pericles*	3	6
34	*Cymbeline*	–	7
35	*The Winter's Tale*	–	15
36	*The Tempest*	1	6

development can be observed with the auxiliaries *have* and *do*: Table IV shows that *s* forms occur in greater numbers only from the middle of the corpus onwards (from *As You Like It*). Seen from the development of the auxiliaries, the first half of the corpus is clearly Stage B, the second more like Stage C.

It is interesting to look at the determining factors for *have* in the second part of the corpus (Table V). There is a first four-play period in which the verse/prose distinction is the main parameter for *have* (*Twelfth Night, Hamlet,*

Table IV Third Singular Ending of *have* and *do* in Shakespeare.

Play[a]	doth	does	hath	has
1	21	1	62	3
2	32	–	60	1
3	35	–	52	–
4	36	–	65	1
5	16	–	34	–
6	30	–	59	2
7	16	6	35	8
8	14	1	53	2
9	43	–	37	–
10	48	–	64	–
11	32	1	70	–
12	31	–	38	–
13	41	1	64	–
14	39	–	52	2
15	30	3	52	2
16	58	3	64	7
17	24	1	74	3
18	33	2	58	6
19	30	4	35	3
20	25	1	52	3
21	13	24	35	20
22	27	27	65	10
23	7	18	61	22
24	37	9	60	16
25	6	24	52	28
26	24	9	71	7
27	17	16	67	9
28	15	18	55	14
29	6	24	52	19
30	5	29	44	23
31	9	19	51	35
32	9	24	29	33
33	19	11	38	16
34	20	8	79	7
35	7	23	42	31
36	13	15	26	7

[a]Names of plays are listed in Table III.

Merry Wives and *Troilus and Cressida*), which is later given up. The other auxiliary, *do*, shows syntactic conditioning. From *Hamlet* (Play 22) onwards, the distribution of *th* and *s* is governed by syntactic criteria for the next seven plays, until *King Lear*. *Does*, the *s* form, appears in all cases except in declarative sentences. Without going into details, similar factors can be found in other texts as well. What we observe here is a further and finer internal

Table V Prose *have* in Relation to Total
have in the Later Shakespeare Plays

Play	Total *have*	*Have* in prose
21	20	19
22	10	8
23	22	21
24	16	14
25	28	18
26	7	4
27	9	2
28	14	6
29	19	3
30	23	1
31	35	16
32	33	12
33	16	6
34	7	1
35	31	13
36	7	1
37	48	0

patterning beyond the gross patterning on the auxiliary main verb level, with the parameters different for *have* and *do*. So what on a gross level of un-subcategorized frequencies must appear as mere, if comparatively sudden, increases in frequency of the new form has to be reduced to a kind of filtering through discrete types of linguistic environment factors where the comparative rapidity of this filtering-through process is manifested in corpus-internal developments.

4.

Another interesting feature of the replacement process is that it seems to involve a syntactic "bypassing" strategy of avoiding unwanted morphology. Table III showed that the sibilant verbs increasingly replace *th* by *s*. Table VI shows a distinct increase of simple forms in the second half of the corpus, which has to be interpreted as a tendency to syntactically bypass simple forms as long as the new form is not yet fully acceptable.

The same effect can be observed in *yes–no* questions in texts ranging over two centuries from Caxton to Restoration comedy, from 1480 to 1670, as shown in Table VII, charting third singular verb morphology and verb syntax in order to demonstrate a dependence between the two levels. It can be shown that the correlation between verb morphology and verb syntax defines

Table VI Number of Stem-Final Sibilant Verbs in the Shakespeare Corpus: Simple and Periphrastic Forms

Play	Sibilant ending main verb	
	es or *th*	*does* or *doth* + verb
1	4	2
2	8	3
3	9	5
4	12	3
5	5	–
6	3	6
7	8	3
8	5	1
9	4	6
10	9	6
11	3	3
12	2	2
13	9	2
14	6	8
15	9	1
16	9	2
17	8	1
18	9	3
19	5	2
20	10	1
21	6	–
22	13	3
23	10	1
24	15	5
25	19	4
26	15	2
27	13	3
28	13	1
29	8	3
30	15	3
31	7	1
32	11	1
33	9	–
34	7	–
35	15	3
36	7	1

diachronic stages which, with some overlap, correspond to the chronological position of the texts. The point of departure is at isolectal Stage A, with *th* the normal ending and no involvement of syntax. The next stages are defined by changes in syntax and morphology. Looking at *yes–no* questions first, we notice that in a period designated II, the majority of the tokens are

Table VII Simple and Periphrastic Forms, Subcategorized by Syntactic Context and Inflectional Ending, in Texts 1480–1670

Period	Author	Declarative Sentences	*Wh*-questions		*Yes–No* questions	
			Simple vs. periphrastic forms	Simple form	Simple vs. periphrastic forms	Simple form
I	Caxton (1480)	*th*	1: 0	*th*	0	
	Medwall (1497)	*th*	2: 1	*th*	1: 0	*th,*
	Atkynson (1502)	*th*	5: 0	*th*	0	
	Valentine (+)	*th*	2:10	*th*	0	
	Orson (1505)					
	Bourchier (1527)	*th*	6: 0	*th*	1: 0	*th*
	Fisher (1530)	*th*	7: 4	*th*	1: 0	*th*
II	Lud. Conventri. (1500)	*th*	1: 0	*th*	0: 1	
	Tyndale (1525–1536)	*th*	30: 7	(*th*)	0: 7	
	Palsgrave (1540)	*th*	21: 3	(*th*)	0: 2	
	Toxophilus (1545)	*th*	1: 3	(*th*)	0: 2	
	Bale (1530–1560)	*th*	7: 0	*th*	1: 2	
	C2 (1540–1560)	*th*	8: 2	*th*	0: 4	*th*
	Foxe (1555)	*th*	30: 9	*th*	4: 9	
	Painter (1566)	*th*	6: 2	4 *th*, 2 *s*	0: 1	*th*
	Gascoigne (1566)	*th*	10: 0	8 *th*, 2 *s*	2: 4	
	C1 (1565–1581)	*th*	17: 1	*th*	1: 4	*th*
	Dahl-korp.	*th*	9: 1	7 *th*, 2 *s*	0: 3	*th*
	Stubbes (1588)	*th*	9: 1	*th*	0: 3	
	Lyly (1580–1599)	*s/th*	34: 4	*th*	1:16	*s*
	Deloney (1596–1600)	*s/th*	22: 3	*th*	1: 8	*s*
III	Peele (1581–1595)	*s*	58: 6		8: 5	*s*
	Marlowe (1586–1592)	*s*	88: 6		6: 2	*s*
	Nashe (1592–1599)	*s*	14: 1	(8 *s*, 6 *th*)	1: 0	*s*
	Heywood (1603–1638)	*s*	44:10	*s*	4: 1	*s*
IV	Greene (1587–1599)	*s*	72: 9	64 *s*, 8 *th*	8:10	2 *s*, 2 *th*
	B. Jonson (1599–1641)	*s*	141:24	*s*	34:39	*s*
	Shakespeare (1590–1611)	*s*	433:50	*s*	49:62	*s*
	Chapman (1598–1639)	*s*	145:18	*s*	22:44	*s*
	Dekker (1600–1657)	*s*	114:14	*s*	11:16	*s*
	Massinger (1623–1655)	*s*	73: 8	*s*	11:29	*s*
	Congreve (1693–1700)	*s*	14:24	*s*	1:17	*s*
	Wycherley (1671–1676)	*s*	24: 8	*s*	0:12	*s*

periphrastic, at Period III, the majority of tokens are finite, but the ending is *s*. Again, *yes–no* questions are periphrastically bypassed as long as the new ending is not yet presentable. This phenomenon seems confined to *yes–no* questions; declarative sentences go with *wh*-questions in not involving syntax, but simply changing the ending. Relevant here are the John Lyly plays in the 1590s. Table VIII shows that he changes his endings corpus-internally. *Wh*-questions change verb morphology in line with declarative sentences. In declarative sentences, *th* is the predominant ending until *Endimion*, while *s* predominates from *Midas* onwards. Although the figures are much smaller with *wh*-questions, there is a distinct change of morphology in the midst of the corpus. Again, declarative sentences and *wh*-questions are in tandem, and *yes–no* questions stay aloof in syntax with only one finite form.

In summary, if the morphological process of the changeover from *th* to *s* is syntactically and phonologically conditioned, it also involves syntactic bypassing as a stage immediately prior to the appearance of the new form. This process is observed independently on two levels, with sibilant verbs within the Shakespeare corpus and on a wider diachronic level. This involvement of syntax triggered by a tendency to avoid verbal endings has also been observed in the second singular personal ending *st* as in *thou sing'st* in the form of a syntactically differentiated tendency to bypass unwanted consonantal clusters which in the latter case eventually led to the grammaticization of the bypassing strategy in questions, the origin of *do* in questions (Stein, 1985a). Apart from the two independent cases of syntactic conditioning of morphological processes and phonotactic preference discussed here, there are other cases from other compartments of the grammar where such processes do not happen across the board and which can be cited as parallel cases in this respect. For instance it is a well-known feature of the loss of case inflections in both German (ongoing) and English (largely completed) that there is differential progressiveness both along the individual cases themselves and by word class

Table VIII   Morphology and Syntax in Different Sentence Types in the Lyly Plays

Play	Declarative sentences	Finite periphrastic	
		wh-questions	*yes–no* questions
Campaspe (1580)	84:24[a]	1:0 (*th*)	0:1
Sappho and Pharo (1581)	82:14	1:0 (*th*)	0:2
Gallathea (1584)	87:21	1:0 (*th*)	0:3
Endimion (1585)	119:33	5:2 (3 *s*, 2 *th*)	1:2 (*s*)
Midas (1589)	64:59	4:0 (*s*)	0:6
Mother Bombie (1590)	20:87	5:0 (*s*)	0
Woman in the Moore (1591–1593)	24:126	10:1 (9 *s*, 1 *th*)	0:1

[a]*th:s*.

(pronouns latest). So this type of differential progressiveness in change processes along syntactic parameters is quite a general phenomenon; it is a task for future research to identify the factors behind this phenomenon.

5.

Stage B was characterized by nonsibilant-ending main verbs appearing with *s*. There are always some residual occurrences with *eth*, which are as a rule syllabic. To give an idea of the order of size of these forms: In the Shakespeare corpus they average less than 10 per play, compared to about 300 third singular main verb occurrences in *s*. So the frequency relations make it quite clear that in these texts these occurrences are extremely exceptional with nonsibilant-ending verbs. With verb stems ending in a sibilant, syllabic *eth* is normal at Stage B. This exceptional nonautomatically syllabic -*eth* (*he putteth*) is therefore an artificial form, and must have been felt as such. It provides an extra syllable and is therefore a very expedient means to get the meter right in verse. Obviously, the early Shakespeare makes use of this additional syllable, but the number decreases gradually to zero in the late plays (Stein, 1987), which gives the above-mentioned statistical average per play.

Apart from this obvious metrical use in Shakespeare's early verse, a comparison of a wide range of texts from different genres, including Shakespeare and nonmetrical genres, reveals that the artificiality of this syllabic form is the vehicle for distinct semiotic functions. One characteristic, not only of the Shakespeare corpus, is comic use. Typical cases are Holofernes and Don Armado in *Love's Labor's Lost*.

Another typical use is the *eth* of villains and rogues, where of course Richard III comes first to mind as an exemplar. It is he who produces 7 of the 18 occurrences, but he only produces *eth* in situations where he is feigning or trying to trick somebody. It is part of his rhetoric, for instance in the scene where he woos Anne. It is part not of the "keen encounter of wits," but of the "slower method" employed to win her. Not surprisingly then, two of the four occurrences in *Othello* are produced by Iago in his cynical rhetoric. In *King Lear* there are only two occurrences, one in a song, the other produced by Edmund when he is telling lies to Edgar. There is, for completeness' sake, a third use which may be called the *eth* of special poetic effect in moments of high dramatic intensity.

The same type of semiotization of what must be considered the marked form can be observed in a number of other nondramatic texts, such as Nashe's *Unfortunate Traveller*, where it appears in a number of distinct contexts, such as sayings, standing phrases, and appeals to general truths. Some texts show what can be termed a kind of discourse marking function, such as Greene's Pamphlets, where the older form occurs in the passages where the practices and tricks of conny catchers are reported generally and generically, but *s* appears where an instance is given of what happened at a specific time and place. This type of discourse use appears to be a more general phenomenon (Stein, 1985b). Generally speaking, it can be said that the kind of meaning the marked form *eth* has depends on the type of text. The form typically has quite a range of loose meanings. What are called "meanings" here is more in the nature of implicatures with a high degree of contextual determination: They involve a breaking of an isolectal rule which triggers an inferencing process under the assumption of the intentionality of the foregrounding effect. But it is an important methodological point to be able to claim that such uses should be observed in a range of heterogeneous texts. Also, with prose texts, there is a double marking of these uses by an "unnatural" additional syllable and by the use of the old form with exception status. From the more general linguistic point of view, the uses observed semiotically exploit a potentiality which is opened up by the internal structure of the diachronic process, more precisely, by the specifics of the isolectal stage. By virtue of their being a function of diachronic processes they are necessarily ephemeral, that is, tied to a specific state of the language structure at a certain point in an evolutional process. They are nevertheless systematic and observable, if only the possibility of their existence is kept in mind when reading these texts. Conversely, these uses are an indicator of the marked status of the older form in these texts.

6.

Some of the features of the change process under discussion can be compared with similar processes of other synchronic and diachronic varieties (see the discussion at the end of Section 4). The fact that the auxiliaries behave differently from main verbs in morphological processes can be related to well-known findings from American dialects and black vernacular English where the auxiliaries behave differently with respect to verbal inflectional morphology (e.g., Wolfram and Fasold, 1974, p. 155; Feagin, 1979, p. 169; Cheshire, 1978, p. 55ff). But while the cases testify to the special status of auxiliary verbs (and also negation, cf. *he don't*), the latter examples are from cases of nonagreement with *s* or nonstandard *s*, while the case under discussion here is a morphological replacement process, and a very special one at that. So while the structural conditions and tendencies are different in each individual case, there must be a common denominator that works toward the special behavior of auxiliaries in morphological processes. One clue is certainly their status as high-frequency forms which creates their relatively autonomous (Bybee, 1985, p. 57f, and passim) character. These forms are presumably not synthesized in speech production, as are other, less autonomous forms.

This touches on the general role of frequency in linguistic change. While frequency in phonology goes with an advanced state in phonological change processes, the evidence for inflectional morphology seems to point in the other direction in that the auxiliaries, possibly because of their autonomous status, are the last ones to change. This has also been shown for the second person singular ending *st*, which was easily tolerated with the auxiliaries but was syntactically bypassed with main verbs.

Another factor that an explanation of the conservativeness of auxiliaries, and also the syntactic differentiation of morphological processes and phonotactics discussed in Section 4, might make reference to is similar to the one mentioned by Naro and Lemle (1977), who invoke a notion of perceptual saliency to explain the succession of linguistic contexts in which case loss appears. The process is most frequent where it is least foregrounded.

A similar notion of informational saliency may be invoked to explain both the morphological conservativeness of auxiliaries and the higher sensitivity of *yes–no* questions to phonotactics. In the former case the unwanted form can stay on longer because auxiliaries are rarely focused, and in the latter case the lexical verb tends to be more frequently at the center of the focus in *yes–no* questions (*sing'st thou, singeth he,* in early Elizabethan English).

A functional explanation might be along these lines, but, as mentioned in Section 4, a much broader range of processes must be compared and well-described change processes reanalyzed in terms of intralinguistic, that is, syntactic, differentiation, in order to envisage a broadly based explanatory hypothesis.

One of the facts about the replacement process described here that deserves special attention is the persistence in isolect B of *th* forms with sibilant verbs and auxiliaries long (over a century) after these forms disappeared from the spoken language. The only answer can be that these were "natural" constraints in the spoken language that were carried over into the emergent written register.

While the conservativeness of the auxiliaries can be accounted for by their special status as adumbrated above, the conservativeness of the sibilant-ending verbs can be interpreted as pointing to the ultimate factor in deciding for *s* rather than *th*: The phonotactics of a verb-final segment plus ending after the vowel of the ending had first been weakened and then altogether dropped. This made for nonpreferred word-final consonant clusters. There is plenty of evidence for this hypothesis (Stein, 1987). Briefly, *th* lingered on longest in (sibilant-ending) verbs where the ending is automatically syllabic (he *hisseth*) and the phonotactic problem cannot arise. There is also a greater conservativeness in *saith*, which fulfills both conditions: no consonantal cluster and high frequency. It appears that the change process was caught in the process by the emerging written register, which in the isolectal subdifferentiation reflects the advanced stage of the replacement process at the point of its coming into being. In other words, it would be difficult to explain the existence of a clearly orally derived constraint by conditions in the written register itself, rather than as a habitualized "hang-over" from orality; the hypothesis is that it fossilizes an advanced stage of the replacement process in the written register.

More precisely, the effect of Caxton and printing established and institutionalized a new variety of written and printed literature in the narrower sense not comprising letters, diaries, and the like, and this variety came into being when the replacement process was very advanced in the London area in the latter part of the fifteenth century. The new printed variety—more precisely, Caxton—settled for the more conservative form, thus in a way arresting or at least retarding morphological change in one variety; *th* became a marker of the formal written register. This hypothesis would also go some way toward explaining a phenomenon that would otherwise be quite an embarrassment for what we know about the essential gradual nature of linguistic change processes: the abruptness of the replacement process, which is also manifestd in the corpus-internal diachronies. It is utterly improbably that there should have been an equally sharp break of the grammar in any spoken variety of the time: *Natura non facit saltum*, in the Darwinian vein. From the abruptness of the transition in the printed material, it is unlikely that it could reflect a development in the spoken language. Rather, we must assume that there was an abrupt catching up with the state of the spoken language. So this feature, too, must be considered evidence for the artificial status of the old *th* form. It is only natural that writers and poets should have availed themselves of the foregrounding potentialities of this form.

7.

Summing up, the replacement process under discussion displays a number of salient features. The linguistically interesting features of the process become transparent only if changes in respective overall frequencies of the two alternative forms *s* and *th* are reduced to successive and rather discrete extensions of contexts in which the new form appears. These changes from one isolectal stage to the next work together with corpus-internal diachronic developments to create a general impression of abruptness of the process. It may well be the case that this abruptness is due to the medium in which the change is observed, that is, in written language, after the change has long been completed in the spoken language. The mixture of syntactic and phonological factors that are the defining parameters of the isolectal stages are further characteristics of the process. Further cutting across linguistic levels is manifested in the involvement of syntax: There are correlations between verb morphology and verb syntax that suggest an effect of syntactic avoidance of structures that would yield nonpreferred endings. Finally, isolectal structure opens up potentialities for semiotic exploitation of the form with exceptional status.

Acknowledgments

This chapter has profited generally from extended discussions with Edith Moravcsik. I have also benefited from comments by Mike Noonan and Mike Hammond. The chapter would not have seen the light of day in a presentable form had it not been for the services of Christine Swoboda-Körner, Rita Hennemann, Susanne Dressler, and Traute Ewers.

References

Bambas, R.C. (1947). Verb Forms in -*s* and -*th* in Early Modern English. *Journal of English and Germanic Philology* **46**, 183–87.

Bybee, J.L. (1985). "Morphology. A study of the relation between meaning and form." Benjamins, Amsterdam.

Cheshire, J. (1978). Present tense verbs in reading English. "Sociolinguistic Patterns in British English" (P. Trudgill, ed.). Arnold, London.

Feagin, C. (1979). "Variation and change in Alabama English. A Sociolinguistic Study of the White Community." Georgetown Univ. Press, Washington, D.C.

Holmqvist, E. (1922). "On the history of the English present inflections, particularly '-th' and '-s'." Winter, Heidelberg.

Naro, A., and Lemle, M. (1977). Syntactic diffusion. *Ciencia e Cultura* **29**, 259–68.

Stein, D. (1985a). "Natürlicher Syntaktischer Sprachwandel: Untersuchungen zur Entstehung der englischen 'do'-Periphrase in Fragen." TUDUV, Munich.

Stein, D. (1985b). Discourse markers in Early Modern English. *4th International Conference on English Historical Linguistics* 283–302.

Stein, D. (1987). "At the crossroads of Philology, Linguistics, and Semiotics: Notes on the replacement of *th* by *s* in the third person singular in English." *English Studies* **68**, 406–432.

Wolfram, W., and Fasold, R.W. (1974). "The Study of social dialects in American English." Prentice-Hall, Englewood Cliffs, N.J.

Part IV

Mapping to
Other Components

Chapter 14

Clitics, Morphological Merger, and the Mapping to Phonological Structure

Alec Marantz

Clitic constructions like those in (1) share essential features with two other types of structures familiar from the literature: classic morphological bracketing paradoxes of the sort discussed in Pesetsky (1985) and cases of what I call MORPHOLOGICAL MERGER, in which an independent syntactic constituent shows up phonologically as part of a derived word. The principles independently motivated to handle these other constructions jointly provide an explanatory theory of the major distributional properties of clitics, as described most carefully in Klavans (1985). This chapter demonstrates the explanatory power of basic principles governing the affixation of morphemes within the syntax and the mapping from syntactic to phonological structures. In particular, I show that the principles rule out logically possible but actually unattested clitic positions, positions predicted to be possible by other theories.

(1) Semantic/Syntactic structure   Phonological structure
    a. [[*I*] [*will* [*go to Milwaukee*]]]   [[*I'll*] [*go to Milwaukee*]]
    b. [[*the porcupine over there*]'*s*] *cage*   [*the porcupine over* [*there's*]]*cage*
    c. *le porcupine* [$_{PP}$ *de* [$_{NP}$ *le garçon*]]*le porcupine* [$_?$[$_?$ *du*] [$_?$ *garçon*]]
              of   the boy
    d. [*ó*[$_S$[$_V$' *pi*   *iam-hu cikpan*] *g*   *Huan*]][[[*pi* + *ó*] *iam-hu cikpan*] *g Huan*]
      AUX   NEG there   work   ART John   NEG + AUX
      'John is not working there.'

To begin the investigation of clitic constructions, note that clitics involve a mismatch between the bracketing or structure motivated on semantic and syntactic grounds and the bracketing or structure motivated on phonological grounds. On the left in (1) are the semantic/syntactic bracketings, on the right the phonological bracketings. For example, the English auxiliary clitic *'ll* is syntactically and semantically related to a following VP; however, it affixes phonologically as part of the last word of the subject NP as in (1a). Similarly, the English possessive *'s* is semantically and syntactically associated with the whole possessor NP but shows up phonologically affixed to the last constituent in the NP, as in (1b). In (1c) we find a French preposition *de* 'of,' which semantically and syntactically takes a full NP as its object, surfacing in a suppletive form *du*, which phonologically represents a combination of *de* and the article *le* 'the' from the object NP. Finally, (1d) shows a Papago example from Pranka (1983) in which an AUX element with sentential scope syntactically shows up affixed to the right of a particle within the first phrase of the sentence.

The bracketing mismatches implicated by clitic constructions resemble morphological bracketing paradoxes, examples of which are found in (2).

(2)   Semantic/syntactic Structure   Phonological Structure
    a.   [[*un happy*] *er*]   [*un* [*happy er*]]
    b.   [$_N$ [$_{ADJ}$ *un* [$_{ADJ}$ *grammatical*] *ity*]]   [*un* [*grammaticality*]]

Here again semantic, syntactic, and morphological considerations motivated one bracketing while phonological considerations motivate another. In (2a) *unhappier* has the semantic and grammtical bracketing on the left—It means *more* [*not happy*], not *not* [*more happy*]. If Elmer is unhappier than Hortense he must be more unhappy than she is; he cannot be as unhappy, thus not more happy. However, phonologically, *un-* atttaches outside *-er*. The phonological bracketing cannot be that in (2a) because *-er* does not attach to trisyllabic adjectives: *redundanter*, from *redundant*, is bad.

Similarly, in (2b) *ungrammaticality* is semantically the state of being ungrammatical; thus the semantic structure on the left is motivated. Moreover, *un-* generally attaches to adjectives like *grammatical* and not to nouns like *grammaticality*, supporting the left structure as a syntactic analysis. However, since *-ity* is a stress-shifting stem-level affix, and *un-* is a stress-neutral word-level affix, the phonological bracketing on the right is called for.

In addition to bracketing paradoxes like (2), clitic constructions like (1) also resemble structures such as derived causative constructions in which a syntactically independent constituent ends up phonologically as part of a derived word. In (1a), for example, the syntactically independent *will* is phonologically part of *I'll*. A derived causative construction is illustrated in (3a). Here, in a Chi-Mwi:ni example, a semantically and grammatically independent morpheme, the causative affix *-ish-* , becomes part of a derived causative verb (Chi-Mwi:ni data from Abasheikh, 1979).

(3) a.   *Mi ni-m-big-ish-ize   mwa:na ru:hu-y-e.*
      I   sp-op-hit-cause-t/a child   self
      'I made the child hit himself.'
      (sp, subject prefix; op, object prefix; t/a, tense/aspect)

    b.   Semantic/syntactic structure   c.   Phonological structure

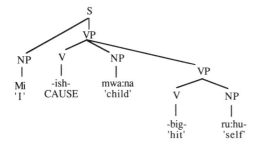
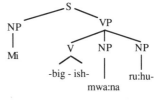

    d. *Mi ni-m-big-ish-iz-e   Ali ru:hu-y-a.*
       I   sp-op-hit-cause-t/a Ali self
      *'I made Ali hit myself.'

The Chi-Mwi:ni sentence in (3a) has the same biclausal semantic structure as its English gloss: *I made [the child hit himself]*. (Technically, the causative verb *-ish-* within the VP that it heads acts like an INFL within an S with respect to its VP complement. Like INFL, it takes a VP argument, which in turn takes a subject NP and thus establishes a second clause within the matrix VP; therefore, the governing category for any constituent governed within the embedded VP will be the matrix VP since this VP contains the subject of the embedded VP). In particular, an adverb may have scope over either the embedded or matrix semantic clause. The Chi-Mwi:ni equivalent of 'I made the child hit himself slowly' containing the same derived causative verb *-big-ish-* as (3a) would mean either 'I made him do it and I was slow about it' or 'I made him do it and be slow in doing it.' In addition, the reflexive data in (3a,d) show that the causative has a biclausal syntactic structure, again just like its English gloss (recall that since the subject of the lower VP in (3b) is within the matrix VP, the matrix VP acts as a sentence with respect to binding theory). Note in (3d) that, as in English, one cannot say 'I made Ali hit myself' in Chi-Mwi:ni because the connection between reflexive and antecedent is clause bound in Chi-Mwi:ni, as in English, and 'I' and 'myself' are in different syntactic clauses in (3d)—see (3b)—even though there is only one phonological sentence (3c). Also, the Chi-Mwi:ni reflexive must find a syntactic subject as its antecedent. In (3a), the antecedent, 'the child,' is a subject only in the biclausal syntactic structure (3b), not the monoclausal phonological structure (3c).

The clitics in (1) show properties of both the structures in (2) and (3), displaying both bracketing paradoxes and syntactic affixation. In (1a) the English auxiliary *will* syntactically associates with the verb phrase on its right but phonologically affixes to the last word of the phrase, regardless of this word's syntactic category. The French example in (1c) is a mirror image of (1b): The preposition *de* is syntactically and semantically related to the whole NP to its right, its object, yet it phonologically affixes to the initial determiner of this NP. The combination of *de* + *le* has the special suppletive form *du*. The French example highlights a general problem with clitics: The bracketings they force in the phonological structure make it impossible to assign regular syntactic category labels to some phonological constituents. What is the category of *du* in (1c)? What is the category of the NP lacking a determiner?

The Papago auxiliary clitic in (1d) is a typical second-position sentential clitic. It has syntactic and semantic scope over the whole sentence, but it (generally) appears after the first word in the sentence. Word order in Papago is fairly free with two notable exceptions. First, the order of constituents within the phrase labeled V' in (1d) is fixed. For example, the NEG morpheme, the word meaning 'there,' and the verb must appear in that order. Second, the AUX element must appear in second position, after some phrase or word. When the V' appears in initial position, as in (1d), then the AUX suffixes to the first morpheme within the V' phrase.

This chapter shows that the principles that allow for the mismatch between syntactic/semantic structures and phonological structures in (2) and (3) are jointly necessary and sufficient to explain the behavior of clitics. The principle at work in (2) is simply the principle that constrains the mapping between hierarchical syntactic structures and linearly ordered phonological structures. The principle implicated by (3) defines the situation in which an independent syntactic constituent may become part of a derived word. These two very general principles automatically describe correctly the semantic, syntactic, and phonological properties of clitics and explain their restricted distribution.

To present the two principles, I assume the terminology of the government and binding theory, although some of my assumptions are not consistent with this theory. The general structure of the grammar is diagrammed in (4).

The level of D-structure encodes semantic argument-taking relations and θ-role assignment. These relations are represented in tree structures by sisterhood—regular sisterhood for the θ-role assignment relation and asymmetric sisterhood for the argument relation. For asymmetric sisterhood, if B is an argument of A, then A and B will be sisters in a phrase headed by A. Note, then, that the order of constituents in a D-structure tree is uninterpreted; any left–right order with the correct sister relations will do.

The S-structure represents grammatical relations including what are generally called "abstract case assignment" and "government." Move α is usually assumed to map between D- and S-structures, although I argue for a different sort of mapping principle in Marantz (1984). Again, the two sorts

(4)   Model of the grammer

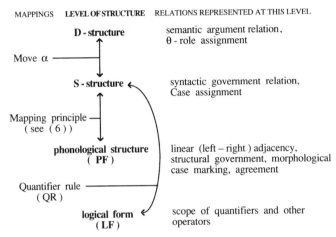

MAPPINGS   LEVEL OF STRUCTURE   RELATIONS REPRESENTED AT THIS LEVEL

D - structure   semantic argument relation,
                     θ - role assignment

Move α

S - structure   syntactic government relation,
                     Case assignment

Mapping principle
(see (6))

phonological structure   linear (left – right) adjacency,
(PF)   structural government, morphological
                          case marking, agreement

Quantifier rule
(QR)

logical form   scope of quantifiers and other
(LF)   operators

of relations at S-structure are represented in the S-structure tree by sisterhood—case assignment by straight sisterhood and grammatical government by asymmetric sisterhood. As with D-structure, the constituents of S-structure are essentially unordered.

First–last phonological order, graphically left–right linear order, is a property of phonological structures. The principle mapping between S-structure and phonological structure constrains the left–right ordering of constituents according to their grammatical relations. Before discussing this mapping principle, I emphasize that the mapping involved does not relate the S-structure tree and the phonological structure tree but rather maps between the relations represented by the S-structure tree and the relations represented by the phonological structure tree. This point is illustrated in (5). Each level of representation consists,

(5)

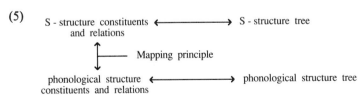

S - structure constituents   ⟵⟶   S - structure tree
and relations

        Mapping principle

phonological structure   ⟵⟶   phonological structure tree
constituents and relations

Other Constraints

General ordering constraints: head first / last, case assigner first / last

Requirements of individual lexical items

General prosodic structure constraints

essentially, of a list of constituents and relations, with a corresponding tree-structure representation of the constituents and relations (for further discussion of the nature of syntactic representations, see Marantz 1984).

The relations at each level are represented in the trees; we do not determine the relations from the trees. The mapping principle in (6) maps between S-structure and phonological structure relations.

(6)   THE MAPPING PRINCIPLE. An S-structure relation borne by B with respect to A corresponds to one or more of the following phonological relations: A structurally governs B (asymmetric sisterhood in the phonological structure tree), A is linearly adjacent to B (left/right adjacency), A morphologically casemarks B (morphology determined by A appears on B or the head of B), A agrees with B (morphology determined by B appears on A or the head of A).

One may see (6) as taking an S-structure and yielding a set of constraints on the construction of phonological structure. The language will impose other constraints on phonological structure as indicated in (5). For example, the language might require that heads of phrases appear either first or last in the phrase, or that Case assigners appear to the left or to the right of the constituents to which they assign Case. Second, individual lexical items might demand particular locations, as encoded in subcategorization features. Third, universal or language-particular principles determining the unmarked branching direction in prosodic trees may impose structure on the phonological structure of words and sentences.

Thus the mapping from S-structure and the other constraints listed in (5) determine a set of conditions that the phonological structure must meet—a set of simultaneous equations that must be solved by the phonological structure. To the extent that relations at S-structure are mapped onto case marking and agreement relations, not adjacency relations, and to the extent that individual lexical items make few demands on their ordering, a number of different phonological structures showing different orders of constitutents will meet all the constraints on phonological structures, giving the appearance of freedom of word order observed in some languages. English generally imposes sufficient constraints on phonological structure to fix the order of constituents.

The internal structure of a word as well as the internal structure of a sentence is represented at every level of syntactic analysis. Morphemes determine their relative ordering within a word by morphological subcategorization features; affixes stipulate that they appear to the left or to the right of a stem of a certain type. Thus relations between morphemes are mapped onto left/right adjacency relations at phonological structure, and the order of morphemes within a word is generally fixed.

The crucial property of the left/right adjacency relation that allows for the bracketing paradoxes in (2) is that the relation is associative (Marantz,

1984; Sproat, 1985). The meaning for the grammar of the associativity of the adjacency relation is illustrated in (7). Say the S-structure relation between X and Y is mapped onto an adjacency relation with X to the left of Y. Furthermore, the constitutents within Y are ordered by mapping such that Z ends up leftmost in the phrase. With the adjacency relation written as an asterisk, (7a) represents those constraints that the mapping to phonological structure places on the phonological structure. (Note that X * Y should be read, "X is left adjacent to Y" not simply, "X and Y are adjacent.") However, because adjacency is associative, the phonological structure in (7b) meets the constraints of (7a).

(7) a. X * [Y Z * W * ...
     b. [[X Z] W ...

Thus the associativity of the adjacency relation allows for a sort of rebracketing in the mapping from S-structure to phonological structure—a discrepancy in the bracketing between S-structure and phonological structure is allowed to the extent that the rebracketing does not cause the phonological structure to violate any of the constraints imposed on it by the mapping principle (6) or the other constraints in (5).

With the mapping principle, the associativity of adjacency, and the assumption that the internal structure of words is represented at every level of structure, we are ready to explain the bracketing paradoxes in (2). The semantic and syntactic structures of the words in (2) are displayed in (8a). Recall that the order of constituents in these structures is uninterpreted.

(8) a. Semantic/S-structure
         [er [un [happy]]]
         [NP ity [ADJ un [grammatical]]]
     b. Constraints on phonological structure
         un * happy, [un, happy] * er
         un * grammatical, [grammatical,un] * ity
     c. Phonological structure trees
         [un [happy [er]]]
         [un [grammatical [ity]]]

The relations between the constituents in the words at the S-structures in (8a) are mapped onto the adjacency relations shown in (8b), where the left/right order is determined by the lexical properties that *un-* is a prefix while *er* and *-ity* are suffixes. Given the associativity of adjacency, the constraints in (8b) are compatible with the actual phonological structure trees in (8c), where the bracketing in (8c) is determined by the lexical properties of the affixes that *un-* is a word-level affix, *-ity* is a stem-level affix, and *-er* may attach to a stem of at most two syllables.

The analysis provided for the cases in (2) would seem to extend automatically to the clitics in (1a–c), as shown in (9).

(9)   Constraints on phonological structure   Phonological structure trees

    a. [I * [*will* * [*go to Milwaukee*]]]   [[*I'll*] [*go to Milwaukee*]]

    b. [[*the* * *porcupine* * [*over* * *there*]] * *'s*] * *brother*   [[*the porcupine* [*over* [*there's*]]] *brother*]

    c. *le porcupine* * [*de* * [*le* * *garçon*]]   *le porcupine* [[*du*] *garçon*]]

On the left in (9) I have summarized the adjacency requirements imposed on phonological structure by the mapping from S-structure in each case. Given the associativity of adjacency, the bracketings in the phonological structures on the right are consistent with these requirements. Note that the clitics are meeting both their left and right adjacency requirements. For example, in (9a), *will* must appear not only to the right of *I* but also to the left of the phrase *go to Milwaukee*. Note also in (9c) that the combination of clitic *de* affixed to *le* has a special suppletive form, *du*. Suppletion is not uncommon with clitics. Note finally that there is no problem in assigning syntactic category labels to the constituents produced in the phonological structures, for example, to the constituents labeled *?* in (1c). Syntactic categories are just that, syntactic, that is, relevant to the distribution and behavior of constituents in the syntax. Such categories are irrelevant to the geometry of phonological structure trees per se, coming into play only in the mapping between S-structure and phonological structure. To the extent that syntactic category labels play a role in the operation of phonological rules, we may suppose the combination of a clitic and its phonological host takes on the category label of the host (acknowledging the adjunction nature of the affixation). Since the category labels of words do not determine the tree structures at phonological structure, this assumption causes no structural anomalies.

A major difference between the bracketing paradoxes in (2) and the clitic constructions in (1) concerns the determination of the linear position of the clitics. While the leftness or rightness of adjacency relations involving affixes like *un-* is determined by their status as prefixes or suffixes, the linear position of the clitics follows from their syntactic role in a sentence. For example, the leftness of the *un-* is fixed by its prefix status. On the other hand, the positioning of *will* in (9a) derives from *will*'s function as an auxiliary verb of a certain sort. Crucially, the position of *will* in front of the verb phrase serving as its argument is independent of *will*'s status as a suffixal clitic. On the other hand, *un-*'s position in front of the stem over which it has semantic scope is totally fixed by *un-*'s prefixal status. This positioning of clitics according to their syntax allows a clitic like *will* to have scope to the right while leaning phonologically to the left.

Given this account of the clitics in (1a–c), it should be clear that the Papago

AUX clitic in (1d) will not yield to the same solution. Rather than appearing on the periphery of the phrase to which it is semantically and syntactically related, that is, on the periphery of the whole sentence, the AUX appears inside the sentence—in fact, inside a phrase that itself is inside the sentence. The principle that accounts for the placement of the Papago AUX also licenses the causative construction in (3a) and allows the Chi-Mwi:ni causative morpheme to pass from its status as an independent argument-taking verb to its suffixal status. This is the principle of morphological merger, given in (10) and heavily discussed and motivated in Marantz (1984).

(10)   MORPHOLOGICAL MERGER. At any level of syntactic analysis (D-structure, S-structure, phonological structure), a relation between X and Y may be replaced by (expressed by) the affixation of the lexical head of X to the lexical head of Y.

The causative construction in (3) shows how morphological merger works. In the S-structure to the left in (3), the causative morpheme *-ish-* takes as its argument a VP headed by the verb *-big-* 'to hit.' According to the merger principle, this relation between *-ish-* and the lower VP may be replaced at S-structure by the affixation of *-ish-* to *-big*; the head of the VP. This merger yields an S-structure isomorphic to the phonological structure shown to the right in (3), except that order holds no significance at S-structure, of course. The S-structure on the right in (3) is entirely determined by the theory, as I show in Marantz (1984), where I discuss the full range of causative constructions and other constructions involving merger.

For the purpose of the analysis of merger at phonological structure involving clitics, the interpretation and consequences of (10) are entirely straightforward. In all cases under consideration, two morphemes X and Y will merge at phonological structure only if, by the associativity of adjacency, they may be bracketed alone together in a phrase and bear the adjacency relation with respect to one another. Merger allows clitics to cross the word boundary to take on affixal status. Since crossing the word boundary has consequences in the grammar—in particular it makes the clitics subject to certain word-internal phonological rules—we should say the merger is always involved in clitic constructions, even when the positioning and bracketing of the clitics are completely determined by principle (6) as they were for the clitics in (1a–c). Since the principle of morphological merger describes the only way in which a syntactically independent morpheme (or X⁰) may cease to project its syntactic relations and become part of another word morphologically, clitic constructions necessarily implicate merger.

Returning to the Papago AUX clitic, we may propose the merger analysis illustrated in (11).

(11)   S-structure for (1d):
         [s *ò* [s [v' *pi*   *iam-hu cikpan*] [g *Huan*]]]
              AUX   NEG there   work   ART John
         'John is not working there.'
         Adjacency constraints:
         [*ò* * [[*pi* * *iam-hu* * *cikpan*], [g * *Huan*]]]
         Phonological structure relations consistent with the constraints:
         [[[*ò* * *pi*] * *iam-hu* * *cikpan*] * [g * *Huan*]]
         Phonological structure after merger:
         [[[*pi* + *o*] * *iam-hu* * *cikpan*] * [g * *Huan*]]

   The S-structure in (11) maps onto the set of adjacency requirements shown. Recall that the order of major constituents within the S is rather free in Papago, but that the order of constituents within the phrase labeled V' is fixed. Thus, as shown in (11), the mapping to phonological structure does not put any constraints on the relative order of the V' constituent and the subject NP. Next in (11) is a premerger phonological structure consistent with the adjacency requirements. We have chosen to place the V' first in the sentence, allowing the bracketing of the AUX with the first constituent within the V'. Now merger will replace the adjacency relation between the AUX and the negative particle *pi* with an affixation relation between AUX and *pi*. The AUX clitic is a suffix and thus appears to the right of *pi*. Note that the positioning of the AUX clitic at the beginning of the sentence was determined by its syntactic status as an AUX, while its positioning after the negative particle once merger occurred was determined by its suffixal status. The key to understanding the distribution of clitics is acknowledging these dual constraints on their location.

   It might be suggested that the Papago AUX clitic derives its second-position status through the movement of some other constituent to the front of the sentence: Perhaps AUX moves to COMP and another constituent moves to SPEC of COMP position. This analysis would be appropriate when the AUX appears after a topicalized XP or fronted *wh-* phrase. However, when the AUX appears within the initial phrase, as in the example cited above, the fronting analysis of the first position constituent will not work. The initial subconstituent of the V' cannot move away from the V' and thus may not be analyzed as moving into initial position to the left of AUX. It is for these and other similar reasons that Pranka (1983) suggests both a leftward movement rule to front XPs to the left of AUX and a rightward rule to move the AUX into the initial phrase if no constituent has been fronted.

   About the analysis in (11) one might ask why the suffixation of the AUX to the NEG particle does not disturb the adjacency relation between the NEG particle and the adverbial morpheme 'there' to its right within the V'. To understand why this change of linear order is allowed, consider the internal structure of the word derived by affixing AUX to the NEG particle, as shown in (12).

(12)

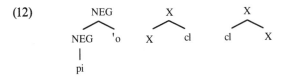

The clitic is (Chomsky-)adjoined to the word to which it attaches, creating a word with the root, rather than the affix, as head; the derived word is taking on the position of the root. (Although I have indicated the headedness of the derived word by giving it the same category label as the head, as I explained above, the syntactic category labels may not be relevant at phonological structure. What counts here is which constituent is head and thus which constituent has its relations taken on by the entire word; the category label is not relevant.) Thus any adjacency relations borne by the root word will be satisfied by adjacency relations of the whole derived word. In the case under discussion, the adjacency relation between the NEG particle and the following 'there' adverbial is satisfied by the adjacency of the combined NEG plus AUX and the adverbial. On the other hand, if the AUX element bore an adjacency relation with respect to some constituent on its left, adjacency of the derived NEG plus AUX word with this constituent would not satisfy this relation. So it is a good thing, and no accident, that the Papago AUX element has nothing to its left in the premerger phonological structure. We now can explain why, if an XP is fronted to the left of the Papago AUX, the AUX will not cliticize within a V' to its right: Such a cliticization would disrupt the adjacency relation between the AUX and the fronted constituent.

At this point we are ready to examine the full range of the distribution of clitics allowed by merger and the mapping principle. The theory allows all and only the clitic positions listed in (13).

(13)   HEAD CLITICS. By merging with the head of their syntactic dependents at D- or S-structure, a clitic may appear suffixed or prefixed to the head of the phrase to which it is semantically or syntactically related.

PERIPHERAL CLITICS

	Suffixes		Prefixes
Adjacency requirements	/Phonological structure	Adjacency requirements	/Phonological structure
a. ...[...Y * X] * cl...	/ ...[...Y X + cl]...	...cl * [X * Y...]...	/ ...[cl + X Y...]...
b. ...Y * X] * [cl * [Z...	/ ...Y X + cl] [Z...	...Z] * cl] * [X * Y...	/ ...Z] [cl + X Y...
c. cl * [X * Y...	/ [X + cl Y...	...Y * X] * cl	/ ...Y cl + X]

I have broken down the full set of clitics into head clitics and peripheral clitics. Although we have not discussed head clitics here, merger of a clitic at D- or S-structure permits a clitic to appear on the head of the phrase to which it is semantically or syntactically related. For example, the English sentential negation clitic *not/n't* as in *clitics shouldn't do that* seems to appear on the head of the sentence that it negates. The analysis of head clitics parallels the account given to the Chi-Mwi:ni causative suffix in (3), which might well be called a head clitic. Using commonly accepted terminology, we call the Chi-Mwi:ni causative a derivational suffix because the term "clitic" has been reserved for morphemes on the periphery of words. On the present theory of the distribution of clitics, any syntactically independent constituent that merges with another morpheme at some level of analysis qualifies as a clitic and should conform to (13).

In (13) I have separated the peripheral clitics into prefixes and suffixes and the pairs in (13a–c) are mirror image cases. The English possessive *'s* is a (13a) suffix; the French prepositional clitic *de* a (13a) prefix. (13b) suffixes include the English auxiliary *'ll*. Finally, the Papago AUX suffix exemplifies (13c). I have recently looked briefly at two cases that might be analyzed as (13c) prefixes. In the Hebrew "construct state," noun–noun compounds, with the head noun on the left, show the definite article prefix *ha-* on the second noun of the compound to express the definiteness of the compound as a whole. Given the head-first character of Hebrew NPs, one might analyze the definite article as a clitic syntactically positioned after the N (possibly consisting of a construct state) that it modifies. It merges with the last root of the N and prefixes to it (I thank Joel Hoffman for bringing this possibility to my attention). In Rama, a Central American SOV language, subject pronouns apparently show up prefixed to the V when they express the running topic of conversation (Ken Hale, personal communication). One might suppose that these pronouns have been topicalized to the right in the syntax, then merged with and prefixed to the adjacent V at phonological structure.

I have not encountered any good examples of (13b) prefixes. I would speculate that the general cross-linguistic preference for (productive) suffixes over prefixes might account for this gap. Bracketing paradoxes like those in (13a,c) may need the motivation, within a language, of a strong preference for suffixing phonologically reduced material.

Within the range of clitic positions allowed by the present theory, the reader may be most disturbed by the cases schematized in (13b). In (13a and c) the clitic attaches within a phrase to which it bears some syntactic relation, while in (13b) it attaches away from such a phrase. Although the English example of (13b), auxiliary *I'll*, may yield to alternate analyses, much stronger examples of this situation are found in Kwakwatal (discussed in Klavans, 1985) and Yagua (see Payne, 1986).

Among the interesting potential clitic positions ruled out by the present theory we find (14), (15), and (18). (14) shows a case related to both the English auxiliary *'ll* and the Papago AUX examples. Like the English *'ll*, this clitic is trying to attach phonologically in a different direction from that in which it leans syntactically. Like the Papago AUX, the clitic has moved inside another constituent. This case is ruled out because the clitic must remain adjacent to the constituent containing X. By appearing to the right of Y in (14), the clitic may not meet this adjacency requirement; it is no longer right-adjacent to X. Recall that in a configuration like (14), the word consisting of cl affixed to Y will take on the adjacency requirements of Y and thus Y will still count as being adjacent to Z after merger. Since a word may only have one relational head, this word may not also take on the adjacency requirements of the clitic.

(14)   Adjacency requirements: ...X] * cl] [Y * Z...]

         Phonological structure not meeting the requirements:
         ...X] [Y + cl Z...]

Similarly, even cases almost identical to the Papago example are ruled out if the clitic must meet more than one adjacency requirement, as shown in (15).

(15)   Adjacency requirements: ...X] * [cl * [Y * Z...

         Phonological structure not meeting the requirements:
         ...X] [Y + cl Z...

In (15) a clitic may not appear suffixed to Y, the first word in its syntactic dependent, because it must satisfy an adjacency relation with respect to the phrase ending in X. The theory thus predicts that second-position clitics like the Papago AUX should generally be limited to sentence-initial positions. It is in general only in sentence-initial position that a clitic is not required to meet any left-adjacency requirements because there is nothing on the left to be adjacent to. (15) represents the ungrammatical situation described above in which the Papago AUX clitic tries to cliticize into second position of the V' after some constituent XP has been syntactically moved into initial position to AUX's left. Again, in such situations, the AUX cliticizes to the left onto the initial XP; it may not cliticize within the V'.

An often-cited example of a second-position clitic that seems to exemplify (15) turns out to support rather than contradict the claims of the present theory. Sadock (1985) describes the case of the Latin conjunctive *-que* 'and' clitic that appears after the first word of the second conjunct. The behavior of *-que* is summarized in (16), with the example in (16b) from Sadock (1985, p. 423).

(16) a.

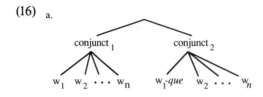

b.

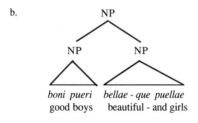

boni pueri   *bellae - que puellae*
good boys   beautiful - and girls

' good boys and beautiful girls '

Latin *-que* does not create an example of (15) precisely because conjunction is a relation among the conjuncts, not between the conjuncts and the conjunction. Thus the conjunction might best be seen as a morpheme that appears only in phonological structure, adjoined to the last conjunct as a marker of the relation among the conjuncts, as shown in (17a) (which matches the structure assumed by Sadock for conjunction; it is also possible that the conjunction should be analyzed semantically and syntactically as an *n*-place operator on *n* conjuncts). Note in (17a) that the relation between the conjuncts maps onto an adjacency relation between their phonological structure counterparts, while the conjunction itself must be adjacent to the last conjunct if, as we assume, it marks the last conjunct at phonological structure.

(17) a. [[*boni pueri*] * [*bellae puellae*]], [*-que* * [*bellae puellae*]]

      b. [[*boni pueri*] [*bellae puellae*]], [[*-que* * *bellae*] * [*puellae*]]

      c. [[*boni pueri*] [[*bellae* + *que*] *puellae*]]

(17b) shows the premerger phonological structure consistent with (17a) while (17c) shows the final phonological structure tree after the suffix *-que* has merged with the first word of the second conjunct. When the *-que* appears to the right of the first word of the second conjunct, as in (17c), the adjacency relation between the first and second conjuncts is preserved. In short, it is the special nature of the relations involved in conjunction that allows for a second-position clitic that seemingly instantiates (15); in fact, (17a) does not conform to the disallowed (15) since *-que* is not constrained to fall to the right of any constituent.

Last among the interesting clitic positions ruled out by the theory, situations like (18) are prohibited.

(18)   Adjacency requirements: ...Y * X] * cl...
        Phonological structure not meeting the requirements:
        ...[Y + cl] X]...

The suffixal clitic in (18) presents a case whose left–right ordering of morphemes is identical to that of the prefixal clitic case in (13c). The difference between them is that the clitic in (18) suffixes to the second word from the end of the phrase while the prefixal clitic in (13c) prefixes to the last word in the phrase. (18) is ruled out because the suffixation of the clitic to Y requires the bracketing of the clitic together with Y. However, such a bracketing would not satisfy the adjacency requirements of (18). Adjacency is only associative, not commutative. A clitic can move inside a phrase to which it is syntactically related only by affixing to the first or last element in the phrase.

Recent work by Klavans helps confirm the predictions of the present theory (Klavans, 1985, reports on work originally described by Klavans, 1982). After surveying the literature on clitics, Klavans concludes that the distribution of clitics may be exhaustively covered by providing each clitic with a value for each of the three parameters listed in (19).

(19)   a. Initial vs. final: Is the clitic initial or final with respect to a reference
            phrase?
        b. Before vs. after: Does the clitic appear before or after the first (if
            initial) or last (if final) constituent of this phrase?
        c. Proclitic vs. enclitic: Is the clitic a prefix or a suffix?

To translate Klavans's terminology into the language we have been using in this chapter: Initial vs. final indicates whether the clitic occurs at the beginning or at the end of the phrase with respect to which it bears a syntactic relation. Before vs. after indicates whether the clitic appears before or after the leftmost, if initial, or the rightmost, if final, word in this phrase. Proclitic vs. enclitic indicates whether the clitic is a prefix on the constituent found to its right after meeting the requirements of the first two parameters or is a suffix on the constituent found to its left after meeting these parameters. Klavans's parameters classify the clitics we examined in (1) as shown in (20).

(20)   English *'ll*: initial, before, enclitic
        English *'s*: final, after, enclitic
        French *de*: initial, before, proclitic
        Papago *'o*: initial, after, enclitic

Although it severely restricts the distribution of clitics, Klavans's typology still allows several locations for clitics ruled out by the analysis of this chapter. In particular, Klavans allows the cases in (15) and (18), as well as their mirror images. For Klavans, the case in (15) is indistinguishable from the Papago AUX clitic—simply another initial, after, enclitic. (18) is a straightforward final, before, enclitic. In her entire survey of clitics, Klavans suggests only one example of a clitic of a sort that is allowed by her typology but ruled out under the present analysis. This is the Nganhcara dative clitic, which Klavans considers a final, either after or before, enclitic. Representative Nganhcara sentences from Klavans (1985) are (21). All of the sentences mean 'The man gave the dog to the child.'

(21) a. *Nhila   pama-ng nhingu pukpe-wu ku?a wa:+ngu.*
          he.nom man-erg him.dat child-dat dog give+dat.3sg

      b. *Nhila pama-ng nhingu pukpe-wu ku?a+ngu wa:.*

      c. *Nhila pama-ng ku?a nhingu pukpe-wu+ngu wa:.*

The data represented in (21) may be summarized as follows: The dative clitic, agreeing with the indirect object, must appear either before or after the verb, which, ignoring this clitic, always appears in sentence-final position. The clitic always suffixes to the constituent on its left. Because, except for the verb, the major constituents of a Nganhcara clause may appear in any order, the dative clitic may end up attached to almost any sort of word, depending on what word finds itself in penultimate position. For example, (21a) has the clitic last, suffixed to the verb. (21b,c) show the clitic before the verb, suffixed to the penultimate word. When the clitic appears before the verb, as in (21b), the geometry of the situation looks like the case schematized in (18), which the present theory prohibits.

However, (21b) would only be correctly schematized by (18) if the dative clitic were a sentential clitic, and there is no reason to believe that this clitic takes the whole sentence as its syntactic dependent. Rather, the dative is either an indirect object agreement marker, with the verb as its domain, or a pronominal argument of the verb, which may "double" a full dative NP argument in the sentence in the familiar situation of clitic doubling. In either case, assuming that the clitic is a constituent of the verb phrase, any account of the data in (21) will implicate a structure distinct from (18). For example, suppose the clitic is an indirect object agreement marker contained in a V' phrase with the verb. The V' phrase is constrained to appear last in the sentence and the agreement clitic must appear adjacent to the verb, but the relative order of V and agreement clitic within the V' is not fixed. If the clitic shows up after the V, it merges with and cliticizes to the V at phonological structure. If it shows up adjacent to but in front of the V, it will bracket and merge with the last word in the sentence before the V'.

Since they allow for just the clitic positions observed in the world's languages, the mapping principle and morphological merger correctly predict the possible distribution of clitics cross-linguistically and seem jointly necessary and sufficient as a theory of clitics. One might ask whether any other current theory would do as well. We have seen that Klavans's account of clitics is inadequate. Even though she constructs an ad hoc, clitic-specific set of parameters to deal with clitics, her system still predicts several types of clitics that are not found in the world's languages. What about other accounts of the sort of bracketing paradoxes that clitics exemplify?

Pesetsky (1985) also proposes to handle bracketing paradoxes like those in (2) by mapping between two levels of structure. However, he takes the right-hand structures in (2), which I have labeled the phonological structures, as the S-structures for these cases and suggests using Move α to create the left-hand structures, which he equates with logical forms. For example, Move α would move *un-* out of the word in the right-hand structure, creating the structure on the left as a logical form. That is, Pesetsky claims that the bracketing paradoxes involve a mapping between S-structures and logical forms in the diagram (4), not between S-structures and phonological structures.

Many objections have been raised to Pesetsky's proposal as a solution to bracketing paradoxes; see, for example, Sproat (1985). However, for present purposes we should just note that his idea does not extend to the clitic sort of bracketing paradoxes in (1). For Pesetsky, what we have been considering the phonological structures of sentences and words must be S-structures that serve as input to the mapping to logical forms. But, as we have seen, the phonological structures for sentences containing clitics cannot be generated as syntactic structures since they involve words and phrases of no determinable syntactic category or function. Consider again the French example in (1c). How could the phonological structure on the right be generated in the syntax? To describe the syntactic properties of the word *du* would be impossible on any reasonable assumptions about the creation of S-structures. Since Pesetsky would need something like morphological merger and the mapping principle to handle clitics anyway, and since these principles automatically cover the other cases of bracketing paradoxes, Pesetsky's theory is superfluous.

Sadock (1985) introduces the notion of autolexical syntax, which involves a mapping between syntactic structure and morphological structure similar in spirit and intent to the proposed mapping between S-structure and phonological structure. Since Sadock is concerned with the appearance of syntactically independent morphemes as bound affixes inside derived words, we might think of his autolexical syntax as a theory of merger.

Sadock works inductively, examining cases that he is familiar with and trying to generalize from them to principles that would allow just those sorts of cases and no others. Sadock lists a number of ad hoc principles governing the mapping between his two structures (his Principles IV–VIII), principles that he adjusts at will to deal with further data beyond that used initially to formulate the principles. Because it is not entirely clear what governs the construction of Sadock's two levels of analysis and because the principles are not completely transparent in interpretation (consider Principle VI, p. 409, "Elements of morphological structure must be associated one-for-one with *corresponding* elements of syntactic structure *to the maximum extent possible"* (emphasis mine)), I do not know exactly what distribution of clitics Sadock would predict, nor does he explicitly make such a prediction. However, the descriptive success or failure of Sadock's inductive account is of no general interest; if counterexamples to his principles are discovered, he can again add a new principle or again modify an existing one.

In conclusion, let me emphasize that the present theory of clitics employs no clitic-specific constraints or principles, nor does it treat cliticization in any of its observed forms as a marked or special phenomenon. Rather, two general principles essential to the operation of the grammar as a whole—the mapping principle and morphological merger—account immediately for the observed behavior of clitics without allowing for logically possible but actually unobserved cases.

References

Abasheikh, M.I. (1979). *The Grammar of Chimwi:ni Causatives*. PhD dissertation, University of Illinois, 1978. Distributed by University Microfilms.

Klavans, J. (1982). "Some Problems in a Theory of Clitics." IULC, Bloomington.

Klavans, J. (1985). The independence of syntax and phonology in cliticization. *Language* **61**, 95–120.

Marantz, A. (1984). "On the Nature of Grammatical Relations." MIT Press, Cambridge, MA.

Payne, D.L. (1986). *Derivation, Internal Syntax, and External Syntax in Yagua*. Paper given at the 15th UWM Linguistic Symposium, April, Milwaukee, Wisconsin.

Pesetsky, D. (1985). Morphology and lexical form. *Linguistic Inquiry* **16**.

Pranka, P. (1983). *Syntax and Word Formation*. Unpublished MIT PhD dissertation.

Sadock, J.M. (1985). Autolexical syntax: A proposal for the treatment of noun incorporation and similar phenomena. *Natural Language and Linguistic Theory*, **3**(4).

Sproat, R. (1985). *On Deriving the Lexicon*. Unpublished MIT PhD dissertation.

Chapter 15

The Autolexical
Classification of Lexemes

Jerrold M. Sadock

1. A Sketch of Autolexical Syntax

1.1 Autonomous Components

Suppose we take a grammar to be a set of subgrammars called MODULES.
Suppose further that each of these modules is a grammar of an independent
level of linguistic representation (i.e., the "tactics" of that level in the terminology of stratificational grammar). I assume that for natural languages
at least three such modules are required, namely syntax, semantics, and morphology. The syntax specifies the surface constituent structures that the
language allows, the semantics gives us the set of well-formed meaning structures in the language, and the morphology the set of well-formed words.
Finally let us suppose that, unlike what is assumed in stratificational theory,
transformational grammar, and so on, these modules are not hierarchically
related to one another. A module need not wait for the output of another
to do its work, but has the power to generate an infinite set of representations quite independently of what is going on in any of the other components.

On this conception of grammar, an expression must satisfy the independent requirements of each of the modules in order to count as a sentence.
Each module, in other words, acts as a filter on all of the others. An expression that is syntactically well formed may fail to qualify as a sentence because
it does not have a well-formed semantic parsing, or because there is no morphologically correct clustering of morphemes corresponding to it, or for both
reasons. Similarly, an expression which is generable vis-à-vis the semantics may

not be parsed by the syntax or may not be expressible in terms of words allowed by the morphology, or both.

Even if an expression is well formed with respect to its projection on each of the levels, it may still not qualify as grammatical, for there clearly are principles relating representations in two or more modules. There is, in other words, an interface grammar that checks to see whether allowable parsings vis-à-vis the individual components fit one another. Several examples of these are mentioned below.

To lend some concreteness to this discussion, let me provide some rough approximations of what might be found in the three modules for English. I emphasize that I do not vouch for the analyses that the rules below imply. Though in some cases the rule systems presented give excellent results despite their simplicity, they are provided mainly to illustrate how a grammar of autonomous modules functions.

1.2 Syntax

I assume that a context-free phrase structure grammar is a sufficient formalism for each of the modules, including the syntactic components.[1] Such a syntax might contain the equivalent of the following rules for English (among others, of course). For the sake of clarity, these rules are written out in a fairly redundant form, though they could, of course, be reduced to virtual rules in the manner of Gazdar *et al.* (1985). Note that I have adopted the scheme from generalized phrase structure grammar (GPSG) whereby the rule that introduces a lexical head is encoded on that item as a lexical subcategorization feature. The numeral features in the rules refer to bar level. The morphosyntactic feature BSE is found on uninflected verb phrases, FIN on finite verb phrases, IND on indicative complement clauses, and [to] on verb phrases headed by the infinitive marker *to*.

SF1. $S \rightarrow N[2]\ V[1]$
SF2. $N[2] \rightarrow DET\ N[1]$
SF3. $V[1] \rightarrow V[0,\ SF3]$
SF4. $V[1] \rightarrow V[0,\ SF4]\ N[2]$
SF5. $V[1] \rightarrow V[0,\ SF5]\ V[1,[to]]$
SF6. $V[1] \rightarrow V[0,\ SF6]\ V[1,\ BSE]$
SF7. $V[1] \rightarrow V[0,\ SF7]\ S[1,\ IND]$
SF8. $S[1,\ IND] \rightarrow COMP[SF8]\ S[FIN]$

[1]The language generated by such a grammar is in the intersection of two (or more) languages each generated by a phrase structure grammar. Since the class of context-free languages is not closed under intersection, the power of such a grammar goes considerably beyond that of an individual phrase structure grammar, as Borgida (1983) has shown. Given the sort of interface conditions that I have been investigating here, the cross-serial dependencies of Dutch and Swiss German, as well as the facts of reduplication pointed out by Manster-Ramer (1983), are well within the power of this grammar to specify (see Sadock, 1987b).

1.3 Semantics

The semantic module might contain rules like the following, which closely follow McCawley (1981) in assuming that only restricted quantification is appropriate for natural language semantics. This scheme is similar in other ways to the system found in Cresswell (1973). It is meant to be a categorial syntax for an interpreted intensional language, but once again I have adopted a more perspicuous notation for purposes of exposition.[2] The category names I employ are meant to be mnemonic: "FORM," formula; "PROP," property; "REL," relation; "IOP," intransitive operator; "TOP," transitive operator. Lower case letters represent basic entity expressions of which there is an infinite supply in the logical language. They do not correspond directly to any expressions in the object language, but are variables which must be bound by the meanings of real expressions in the language. A description of the interpretation for a language similar to this can be found in Cresswell (1973).

LF1. FORM: PROP (i)
LF2. FORM: REL (i, j)
LF3. FORM: BINDER (FORM)
LF4. FORM: IOP (FORM)
LF5. FORM: TOP (i, FORM)
LF6. PROP: PROP (PROP)
LF7. BINDER: Q (FORM)

FORM is the category of both well-formed formulas and open formulas. Rule LF1, for example, combines a one-place predicate such as *bark* with a variable to form an open formula, e.g., *bark*(x). To constitute a well-formed formula (WFF), this open FORM must be combined with a BINDER whose constituent FORM contains an instance of the variable to be bound. Thus the expression *every*(*dog*(x)) can be combined with *bark*(x) to form a WFF.

The syntactic rules of this logical language do not require proper binding of variables. Unbound variables, doubly bound variables, and vacuous binding expressions are all allowed by the syntax itself. The rules of interpretation, however, cannot handle deviations of any of these sorts.

Rule LF6 produces derived property expressions by combining two property expressions. It functions in composing the semantics of adjective–noun

---

[2]Beginning with two basic categories, "0" for propositions and "1" for entity expressions, as Cresswell (1973) does, the following would be the categorial representations of the various mnemonics used in the text where these correspond to lexical items:

PROP = <0,1>	Rule LF1
REL = <0, 1, 1>	Rule LF2
IOP = < <0,1>, 0>	Rule LF4
TOP = < <0,1>, 1, 0>	Rule LF5
Q = <0, 0, 0>	Rule LF7

combinations, noun–relative clause combinations, and stacked relative clauses.

1.4 Morphology

Let us assume that a morphology for English would contain rules M1–M4.

M1. $X[-0] = AF, Y[-0]$
M2. $X[-1] = X[-0], AF$
M3. $X[-2] = Y[-1], AF$
M4. $X[-0] = Y[-0, CF], X[-0]$

This is essentially the system of morphology presented in Sadock (1985), but since it is probably unfamiliar to most readers, a little explanation is called for. The bar levels in these rules distinguish stems $[-0]$, from words $[-1]$, from "superwords" $[-2]$. Stems comprise a morphological class of items that require more morphology to become independently pronounceable words. The morphology that is required is supplied by Rule M2 and is usually termed inflectional, but more about this later. Rule M1 gives us stems from stems and includes most ordinary derivational morphology. M3 gives a class of morphological forms that can neither be inflected nor derived. The affixes involved in the production of such entities are typically labeled clitics. Finally, M4 takes two stems and returns a single compound stem. One of the two stems involved bears a special morphological feature CF, indicating that it is of the class of items that form compounds. In some languages, like Greek, all compound-forming elements are derived by a derivational rule that adds overt morphology. In other languages, English, for instance, any stem is allowed to bear this feature and to function as an element of a compound. English does, however, contain a number of lexical items like *hydro-* and *Franco-* that are marked as CF in the lexicon and can therefore only function as compounding elements.

In all of these rules except M3 there is a head in the technical sense that the head feature convention (HFC) (Gazdar *et al.*, 1985) governs the feature specification of one of the daughter categories. In M1 the head is the affix, in M2 it is the stem, and in M4 it is that stem that is labeled X (i.e., the same label the mother category bears). According to the HFC, the features that make up these morphological heads are partially redundant with the feature composition of the mother node.

1.5 Lexicon

In this theory, as in lexical functional grammar (LFG) (see for example Bresnan, 1982) and head driven phrase structure grammar (see Pollard and Sag, 1984), the lexicon plays a central role. Here it forms the axis around which the several autonomous modules pivot. It contains the basic vocabulary for each of the modules and information as to the structural properties of each item with respect to the several autonomous components. Much of this vocabulary is shared, in that the typical lexeme has semantic, morphological, and syntactic value.

For example, an English stem like *dog* is listed in the lexicon as a noun in the syntax, a noun stem in the morphology, and a property expression in the semantics:

L1. *dog:*
     syntax: N[0]
     semantics: PROP
     morphology: N[−0]

The syntactic statement in the lexical entry *dog* indicates that the lexeme may be found in structures like (1) because of the existence of a rule of English syntax SF2.

(1)

The semantic statement sanctions semantic structures like (2) on the basis of the semantic Rules LF1 and LF7, and the morphological part of the entry allows the lexeme to be found in morphological trees such as (3) because the morphological module of English contains Rule M2.

(2)

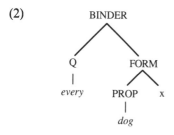

(3)

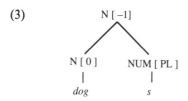

A proper noun such as *Fido* would have a different representation from *dog* in each of the three components. It would count as an NP for syntax, as a full word for the morphology, and as a binder expression (including a definite quantifier) in the semantics:

L2. *Fido:*
 syntax: N[2]
 semantics: BINDER[Q[DEF] FORM[PROP[____] *i*]]
 morphology: N[−1]

This lexical entry permits *Fido* to be found in semantic structures like (4), syntactic structures like (5), and morphological structures like (6).

(4)

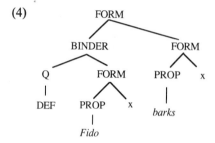

(5)

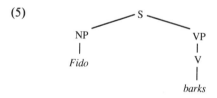

(6)   N [−1]
         |
        Fido

The following is a sampling of possible lexical entries for some other words of English. The symbols in the syntactic and semantic parts of each of these entries refer to the syntactic and semantic combinatoric rules given above. Since none of these entries behaves morphologically as an affix, what we find under morphology in these particular cases never mentions a morphological rule. As members of distinct morphological categories (verbs, particles, prepositions, and so on), the following items can only occur as whole words or as level [−0] morphological elements, that is, stems.

L3. *bark:*
    syntax: [SF3]
    semantics: PROP
    morphology: V[−0]
L4. *every:*
    syntax: DET
    semantics: Q
    morphology: PRT[−1]
L5. *bite:*
    syntax: [SF4]
    semantics: REL
    morphology: V[−0]
L6. *seem:*
    syntax: [SF5] or [SF7]
    semantics: IOP
    morphology: V[−0]
L7. *want:*
    syntax: [SF5]
    semantics: TOP
    morphology: V[−0]
L8. *it:* (expletive)
    syntax: N[2]
    semantics: nil
    morphology: N[−1]
L9. *to:* (infinitive marker)
    syntax: [SF6]
    semantics: nil
    morphology: P[−1][3]
L10. *that:* (complementizer)
    syntax: [SF8]
    semantics: nil
    morphology: COMP[−1]

To illustrate the filtering effect attained when lexemes are taken to have independent reality in more than one autonomous module, consider the fact that **Fido dog* is not a sentence of English. From the semantic point of view, this expression is flawless, having a semantic representation like (7).

---

[3]By saying that *to* has the syntax of a complement-taking verb we capture all of the syntactic generalizations listed in Pullum (1982). But by saying that it has the morphology of a preposition, we automatically predict that it will have none of the inflectional forms of a typical complement-taking verb, a fact that needs to be stipulated by Pullum.

Though *to* is homophonous with, and historically derived from, a preposition, it might better be treated as acategorical in the morphology (though not the syntax) of Modern English. I do not pursue this issue here.

(7)

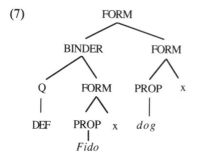

The ill-formed expression *Fido dog* predicates dogginess of Fido, at least as far as the semantic value of its lexemes goes, and for that reason is quite comprehensible, though ungrammatical. What's wrong with it is that English (as opposed to numerous other languages) has no sentences of the form NP + PRED. Russian, for example, does have such a rule, and in that language one can say the equivalent of *Fido sick, Fido in Moscow,* and of course also *Fido dog,* with exactly the meaning given by (7).

As an illustration of the mutual filtering effect that the independent representation of lexemes in separate components achieves, consider the following much-discussed paradigm:

(8) *Fido seems to bark.*
(9) *It seems that Fido barks.*
(10) **Every dog seems that Fido barks.*
(11) **That Fido barks seems.*

Examples (8) and (9) are grammatical and semantically well formed, having appropriate structures at both levels of representation. Both have exactly the same semantic representation, namely (12), a fact that turns on the semantic emptiness of the words *to, it,* and *that,* as shown in lexical entries (L8)–(L10) above.[4]

---

[4]Actually, given the semantic representations implied by LF1–LF7, both are ambiguous. In addition to the well-formed formula in (12), both can also be assigned structure (i) by these rules.

(i)

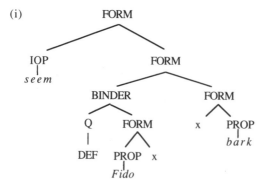

(12)

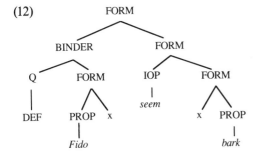

The two sentences do differ in syntax, of course, (8) having a structure like (13), and (9) corresponding to (14).

(13)

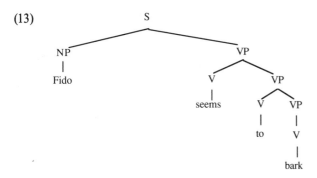

(14)

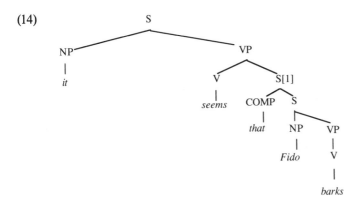

Differing syntactic structures are permitted because *seem* can be inserted into two different subcategorization frames, as indicated in L6.[5]

Now example (10) comes out as fully well formed in the syntax, having essentially the same structure as is represented in (14), except for the fact that the first NP is *every dog* rather than *it*. Its problem is in the semantics. The word *seem* is an IOP in the semantics and it may combine with a proposition *barks* (*Fido*) or *barks* (*x*). If it combines with the former, there is no variable left for the BINDER *every dog* to bind. If it combines with the latter, it may bind the variable *x*, but now there is no variable for the BINDER *Fido* to bind. In either case, we have an ill-formed semantic representation.[6]

Example (11) is bad for exactly the opposite reason. It is semantically faultless, but has no well-formed syntactic structure. The syntactic part of the lexical entry for *seem* demands that it take an S[1] or VP complement, but in (11) it has neither. Thus the syntax acts as a filter on the semantics in some cases, and in others the semantics acts as a filter on the syntax.

2. Initial Classification of Lexemes

The separation of the grammatical value of a lexeme into three quite distinct categories of information suggests a straightforward initial system of classification based on which of the several modules a lexeme is represented in. Eight classes are possible in principle. These are displayed in Table I, where a + indicates that a lexeme has a representation in the component indicated on the left, and a − indicates that its representation is nil in that component.

The lexemes we have considered so far fall into two classes with respect to Table I. The majority of them have a value which must be satisfied in all three components (i.e., they belong to Class I), but the lexemes *it*, *to*, and *that* were presumed to have no semantic value at all and thus to belong to

---

[5] While this is treated as a brute fact at the moment, regularities between lexical entries can be captured by redundancy rules over lexical entries of the sort that have frequently been proposed. In the present case, for example, we might say that the clausal object is basic and that the existence of the infinitival complement can be predicted from it. The rule might look something like the following:

LR1.   If there is a lexeme with syntax = [SF7] and semantics = IOP, then there is another lexeme otherwise identical but with syntax = [SF5].

[6] Note how this recapitulates some of the work and spirit of the theta criterion of government and binding, or the combination of the principles of functional uniqueness, completeness, and coherence in LFG. There is no need to stipulate any such principle in the present framework because the semantic theory has an explicit syntax. It is no more necessary to impose external well-formedness conditions to the effect that predicates must take the appropriate number of arguments and that arguments must be arguments of predicates in any well-formed semantic structure than it is to impose external constraints on the syntax itself to the effect that NPs must go in syntactic trees only where they go, and that everywhere there is a required NP we find one. The rules of the relevant component imply these results.

Table I Classification System for Lexemes

	I	II	III	IV	V	VI	VII	VIII
Syntax	+	+	+	+	−	−	−	−
Semantics	+	+	−	−	+	+	−	−
Morphology	+	−	+	−	+	−	+	−

Class III. I assume that there are also lexemes that are represented at only one level (see the discussion of German -*s* below), but there could apparently not be any lexemes with no representation in any component, for these would have committed intermodular suicide.

As an example of a Class V lexeme, one which has a representation in the morphology and the semantics but not in the syntax, consider the German derivational suffix -*chen*. While this affix has a meaning similar to that of the adjective *klein*, it is irrelevant to the syntax. The stem to which it is added is not independently represented in the syntax, as can be seen from the fact that it cannot be coordinated.

(15)   **Hünd- und Kätzchen*
(16)   *kleine Hunde und Katzen*

I therefore assume that the lexical entry for the morpheme -*chen* is as in (L11):

L11.   -*chen*
       syntax: nil
       morphology: N[M1, NTR]/N
       semantics: PROP

Since this suffix has no independent representation in the syntax, a word like *Hündchen* will appear no different to the syntactic component than any basic common noun in the language. Its pieces are invisible to the syntax and thus cannot be coordinated since coordination, I assume, is a rule of the syntax. (While this is the expected behavior of affixes, it is not the only behavior that is attested. There are proper pieces of morphology that coordinate and take coordinate complements in German, as example (18) shows.)

The morphological specification in this entry indicates that -*chen* functions as the head (i.e., the affix) in M1 and that it bears the feature [NTR] (neuter). Because of the HFC, the new stem that it forms will also be neuter. The notation "/N" in the morphological specification indicates that the complement to the affix (the Y[−0] in M1) must be a noun. Since no gender is mentioned here, the affix may apply to noun stems of any gender.

Though -*chen* has no representation in the syntax, it does have independent semantics. The semantics of the word *Hündchen* are complex, indeed roughly the same as the semantics of the N′ expression *Hund der klein ist*. It means, if you will, *Hund der -chen ist*, but nothing like that is grammatical in German because *-chen* is obligatorily an affix to nouns and because it has no syntactic representation.

The same two facts make it the case that *-chen* can only be combined with other semantically contentful expressions by LF6. By compositionality (Frege's principle), the meaning of an expression is a function of the meaning of its parts. Since *-chen* has no syntax, the expression of which *-chen* is a part can only be N + *chen*, and since N will (in general) be a property expression, LF6 is the only semantic combinatoric rule that can operate. Thus *Hündchen* has the semantic representation in (17), though it has only the syntax of an N[0].

(17)

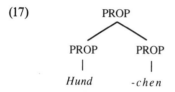

Let me also turn to German for an example of a lexeme with representation in only one component. Consider the suffix *-s* that is found on the first member of compounds such as *Lebensversicherung* or *Freiheitskämpfer*. This suffix might be confused with the genitive in the first example, but the second shows that it is really quite separate from it, for the genitive of *Freiheit* is *Freiheit*. The only function of this *-s* is to derive compounding stems of certain nouns, stems which only occur as the first member of compound forms. The suffix *-s* itself interacts in no discernible way with the syntax and appears to be free of any semantic properties as well. This *-s* of German is therefore an example of a Class VII lexeme and should have the lexical entry in L12. Its only function is to create nouns bearing the feature [CF] from noun stems of a particular class (indicated arbitrarily here by F). The resulting stem will be allowed as the nonhead member of compounds produced by M4. The derived form *Freiheits* is an N[−1], so it cannot be further derived or inflected. Assuming that no syntactic rule specifically subcategorizes this inflectional form, it can only occur in compounds.

L12.   *-s:*
        syntax: nil
        semantics: nil
        morphology: N[M2, CF]/N[F]

Finally, note that while the constituents of *Freiheit* + *s* are invisible to the syntax, the form itself need not be. Assuming, as we have, that no syntactic rule calls for a phrase bearing the feature [CF], only a syntactic rule that is completely neutral with regard to inflectional features can affect *Freiheits*. Such a rule, of course, is conjunction, and indeed it does apply to the first member of German compounds:

(18) *Heizungs- und Kühlungsanlagen*
      'heating and cooling apparatus'

3. Finer Classification

The classification of lexemes given in Table I is quite coarse, but it can easily be made more fine-grained by attending not only to whether a lexeme is represented in a certain component, but also to how it is represented there. We may ask, for example, whether a lexeme is a stem or an affix in the morphology, whether it is a member of a major class in the syntax, whether it is an argument-taking predicate in the semantics, and so on.

3.1 Intermodular Defaults

Posing such questions immediately reveals that there are strong correlations between the form of the representation of a lexeme in one component and the form of its representation in others. Such observations in fact form the basis of one tradition for the classification of lexemes. Sapir (1921, p. 101) sets up four classes of lexemes with respect not only to the type of meaning they express but also with respect to their typical manner of expression.

The first class is that of BASIC (CONCRETE) CONCEPTS which Sapir says are "normally expressed by independent words or radical elements." We may recast this in the present framework as a statement to the effect that semantic property or relation expressions are represented as morphological stems. Furthermore, the default case for morphological stems is for them to count as lexical categories in the syntax. In the symbolism of the present chapter we have:

A. CONCRETENESS OF STEMS (Sapir, p. 101: I)
    1. PROP or REL $\rightarrow$ X[−0]
    2. X[−0] $\rightarrow$ X[0]

Sapir's second class is that of "derivational concepts" which he says are "normally expressed by affixing non-radical elements to radical elements or by inner modification of these." Sapir insightfully observes that the increment of meaning that derivational affixes add applies only to the meaning of the stem to which they are affixed. Combining this observation with Bloomfield's (1933) observation (incorporated in the morphology I have presented above) that derivational morphology ("word-formation," as Bloomfield calls it) forms an inner layer of morphology with respect to inflectional morphology (p. 222), we may formulate the following further intermodular default:

B.   SEMI-CONCRETENESS OF DERIVATION (Sapir, p. 101: II)
      1. $X[M1] \rightarrow$ semantics $= F(Y[-0]')$

Sapir's remaining two classes have in common (a) the tendency to be expressed as affixes, and (b) the expression of what Sapir calls RELATIONAL CONCEPTS. Though this might be stretching things, I believe that what was intended by this term is something close to the lack of predicative content. Notions of coreference and the distinction between subject and object—two of the cases Sapir used as examples of relational concepts—would not be encoded in a model-theoretic analysis as semantic categories at all. The following principle, then, comes close to capturing some of the rest of what Sapir's classificatory scheme implied:

C.   ABSTRACTNESS OF INFLECTION (Sapir, p. 101: IV)
      1. $X[M2] \rightarrow$ semantics $=$ nil

Now Sapir did not carefully distinguish between syntactic structure and meaning, often speaking of the two in the same breath. In discussing the meaning contribution that derivational affix *-er* makes, for example, he writes that it indicates "that particular substantive concept...that serves as the habitual subject of the verb to which it is affixed" (p. 100). Furthermore, "This relation of 'subject'...does not exist for the sentence as a whole" (fn 13). As for inflections, they "serve to relate the concrete elements of the proposition, thus giving it definite syntactic form" (p. 101). From these remarks (as well as from other writings), I think it would be fair to assume that Sapir would have said that affixes are usually not elements of the syntax. Those that express pure relational concepts are surely relevant to the syntax (see Anderson, 1982), but are not parts of it. As I have claimed elsewhere, Sapir is the author of lexicalism, a strong version of which is embodied in the following principle.

D.   LEXICALIST HYPOTHESIS
      1. $X[Mn] \rightarrow$ syntax $=$ nil

Principles A, B, and C, and D give us exactly three classes of lexemes based on correlations between the subparts of lexical entries. Quite roughly, these three classes approximate the three broad classes of roots, derivational morphemes, and inflectional morphemes. The first of these have predicative content, act as stems in the morphology, and as lexical heads in the syntax. The second class forms the inner layer of morphology, have meanings that are functions of the meanings of their morphological hosts, and lack syntax. The last class, that of inflections, forms the outer layer of morphology (except for clitics—see below), are not represented as categories in the semantics, but may or may not have a syntactic vitality.

But we have already seen that other classes do exist. Consider the class exemplified by English *to*, *it*, and *that* in the tiny lexicon above. Like inflections, these are not to be represented as expressions in an independent semantic representation, but unlike inflections, they do not form an outer layer of morphology, but rather count as free words. This is, of course, the traditional class of function words, a class which is consistent with the defaults above.

3.2 Association Principles

3.2.1 Incorporation There is an extremely frequently encountered class of morphemes that departs from the defaults above. It consists of morphemes that apply to stems (like derivational or inflectional morphemes) but clearly have independent status in the syntax, and which are semantic functions of the meanings of their syntactic, rather than their morphological, hosts. There is a huge range of these with representatives from nearly every syntactic class, but I do not have space to document that claim here. Two examples will suffice.

The first is the class of noun-incorporating deverbal affixes in Greenlandic, described by Rischel (1971, 1972), and discussed in several places by me (see Sadock 1980, 1986). I do not repeat the many surprising features of the behavior of these affixes that point unequivocally to the conclusion that they have the syntax of object-taking verbs, but simply refer the reader to the works mentioned above. Such affixes depart from Principle D in having syntax. The lexical entry for the Greenlandic affix *-qar* 'to have ____' should be as follows:

L13.   (Greenlandic) *-qar:*
        syntax: V[SF3]
        semantics: REL (= 'have')
        morphology: V[M1]/N

While this is a possible lexical item on a theory that radically separates syntactic, semantic, and morphological properties of lexical items, note that it is a more complicated entry than any that conform to Principles A–D. A normal derivational affix that lacked syntax would need no separate syntactic specification at all; Principle D, the lexicalist hypothesis, would supply it. A verb root, on the other hand, would need no independent morphological specification, as Principle A would make it a stem on the basis of its semantics.

As a somewhat different example, consider Hungarian, a language with both postpositions and suffixes with relational meanings.[7] The suffixes are

---

[7] I am indebted to Donka Farkas and George Fowler for helpful discussions of the facts of Hungarian.

phonologically integrated with the noun to which they are attached and undergo vowel harmony determined by the vocalism of the stem (as well as participating in other obligatory phonological alternations):

(19)   *Magyarország-ról* 'from Hungary

(20)   *Budapest-ről* 'from Budapest'

The postpositions, however, remain separate words and do not harmonize with the noun that precedes them or undergo rules of internal sandhi.

(21)   *Magyarország mellett* 'beside Hungary'

(22)   *Budapest mellett* 'beside Budapest'

Despite the fact that some of these relational items are suffixes and some separate words, they share so many syntactic and morphological properties (not to mention semantic properties) as to demand treatment as representatives of the same class at some level. Though the suffixes are frequently called case endings in descriptions of Hungarian, they are unlike typical case endings in other languages in not demanding concord on determiners and adjectives (as do the similar Finnish cases), and in this they are just like the postpositions.

(23)   *egy/a fehér ház* 'a/the white house'

(24)   *egy/a fehér házról* 'from a/the white house'

(25)   *egy/a fehér ház mellett* 'beside a/the white house'

I conclude that the postpositions and locational suffixes represent the same syntactic and semantic classes and differ only in that the former have default (stem) morphology, while the latter happen to be suffixes, participating in Rule M2:

L14.   *mellett:*
        syntax: [$_{PP}$ N″, ____]
        semantics: REL
        morphology: P[−0]

L15.   *rÓl:*
        syntax: [$_{PP}$ N″, ____]
        semantics: REL
        morphology: N[M2]

I emphasize that nearly every lexeme that is both an affix to a stem and a syntactic head is governed by a powerful principle relating its syntactic and morphology occurrence. This principle, which loomed large in my (1985) paper, can be stated as follows:

E.   INCORPORATION PRINCIPLE

$$\left.\begin{array}{l} W[\text{-}n] = Y[-0], \underline{\qquad} \\ \qquad\qquad \text{and} \\ Z[n] = X[\text{max}], \underline{\qquad} \end{array}\right\} \rightarrow Y[-0] = H \text{ of } X[\text{max}]$$

What this says is that if a lexeme attaches to a stem Y[−0] to form any sort of morphological entity W[−n], and at the same time takes a complement phrase X[max] in the syntax to form a phrase Z[n], then Y[−0], the stem it attaches to in the morphology, must be the lexical head of X[max], the phrase it combines with in the syntax. Example (26) illustrates this for the Greenlandic suffix (compare the independent nominal in (27)):

(26)   *kunngip paneqarpoq   kusanartumik*
       king-erg daughter-have-indic/3sg pretty-inst[8]
       'There was a pretty daughter of a king.'

(27)   *kunngip pania   kusanartoq*
       king-erg daughter-3sg pretty
       'a beautiful daughter of a king'

Despite the fact that the Hungarian locational suffixes are inflection-like in that they form an outer layer of morphology, they too attach to the head noun of the object phrase, regardless of where in the phrase this head appears. This can be seen in (28), which I owe to Donka Farkas.

(28)   *a szép   kép-ről   amit tegnap   láttunk*
       the beautiful painting-rŐl which yesterday saw-we
       'from the beautiful painting that we saw yesterday'

3.2.2 Cliticization   Another extremely widespread class of lexemes that does not fit the traditional mold is the class of clitics, a sampling of which is given in (29)–(32).

(29)   *Illumut angisuumukarpoq.*
       illu-mut   angisuu-mut-kar-poq
       house-allat big-allat-go-indic/3sg
       'He went to the big house.'

(30)   *the Queen of England's crown*

(31)   *boni pueri pulchraeque   puellae*
       good boys beautiful-que girls
       'good boys and beautiful girls'

(32)   *l'ancienne ville*
       'the old city'

In these examples, the affix is attached not to the head of its presumable syntactic complement, but to a word that is on one periphery of its phrase. In (29) and (30) the host is a phrase-final word, and in (31) and (32) it is a phrase-initial word.

There is another notable difference between the grammatical behavior of clitics and incorporators besides the syntactic status of the element they attach

---

[8]For an account of the instrumental case of the modifier in this example, see Sadock (1980).

to: In contrast to the earlier examples that follow the incorporation principle, (29)–(32) all involve the affixation of a morpheme to a fully-formed word,
not to a stem; or to put it somewhat more technically, they involve affixation
to $X[-1]$ as opposed to $X[-0]$. I take it to be the normal state of affairs
that affixation to more fully complemented morphological entities than stems
does not conform to the incorporation principle and it is for that reason that
the incorporation principle was formulated narrowly, so as to demand
syntactic-head incorporation only when a stem is involved in the morphological operation.

Cliticization, that is, the addition of morphology to an inflected word, is
governed by a different principle. As observed above, the clitic can be expected
to attach to a phrase-peripheral word. In cases where we can tell, the position
of the host is adjacent to the position that the clitic would occupy if it were
a separate word. Thus the central behavior of clitics can be captured in an
autolexical model by assuming the existence of a principle associating syntactic and morphological representations which we can state as follows:

F.   CLITICIZATION PRINCIPLE

$$W[\text{-}n] = Y[-1], \underline{\hspace{1cm}} \Big\} \;\rightarrow\; Y[-1] \text{ is syntactically}$$
$$Z[n] \rightarrow X[\text{max}], \underline{\hspace{1cm}} \Big\} \qquad \text{adjacent to} \underline{\hspace{1cm}}$$

Note that in the formulation of the cliticization principle there is no implied
connection between the category of the word to which the affix is attached
and the syntactic category of its complement. Clitics, in other words, are also
typically "promiscuous" affixes, as opposed to derivational or inflectional
morphemes which we expect to impose tight constraints on their morphological hosts.

4. Summary

Instead of the traditional three classes, we now have five, whose properties
in the three components are summarized in Table II.

4.1 Ultrafine Classification

In constructing his classificatory scheme, Sapir cautions at great length (pp.
103–105) that intermediate forms exist. They can be understood on the present
theory as lexemes that depart from the defaults in idiosyncratic ways that
must simply be listed in the lexicon.

On a theory in which varying sorts of morphological adjunctions take place
in varying components of the grammar (e.g., Anderson, 1982; Baker, 1985),

Table II Classification System for Lexemes, Refined

	Stem	Affixes			
		Inflectional	Derivational	Incorporating	Clitic
Syntax	X^0	—	—	$[_{Y1}X^{max}\_\_\_]$	$[_{Zn}X^{max}\_\_\_]$
Semantics	P or R	—	$F(X^{-0})$	$F(X^{max})$	$F(X^{max})$
Morphology	X^{-0}	$[_{x-1}\, X^{-0}\_\_\_]$	$[_{Y-0}\, X^{-0}\_\_\_]$	$[_{Y-0}\, X^{-0}\_\_\_]$	$[_{w-2}\, Y^{-1}\_\_\_]$

it is hard to imagine how indeterminate cases with some of the properties of clitics, and some of the properties of inflection, say, could be accommodated. From the present standpoint, however, according to which a notion like "clitic" or "inflectional affix" is a cluster of potentially independent features related to different modules of grammar, mixed cases are allowed.

But there is a cost. At every stage where there is a further departure from the expected clumping of properties, the grammar requires further parochial enhancement. Either the lexical entry is more complicated than that for a lexeme that follows the defaults, or additional rules must be postulated to handle deviant cases, or both.

We should thus expect that the more deviant a form, the rarer it is both among the languages of the world and within the lexicon of a particular language. I believe these expectations are entirely correct.

I have, for example, investigated in detail the more than 75 fully productive affixes of West Greenlandic that convert noun stems to verb stems. Almost all of them fall exactly in line with the incorporation principle E above: They attach morphologically to stems, syntactically to phrases, and the stems they attach to are the heads of the syntactic phrases they are combined with.

Five, however, differ from the norm established by principle E. Though they form stems, they do not always attach to stems, but rather to fully inflected words. They are therefore not introduced by any of the "normal" morphological rules M1–M4, but require a parochial rule of Eskimoic that demotes a full word to the status of a stem.

M5. $X[-0] = Y[-1]$ AF

The affixes in this group are *-it* 'to be' (added to a locative), *-kar* and *-liar* 'to go' (added to a dative), *-Vr* 'to travel' (added to a perlative), and *-Vr* 'to come' (added to an ablative). Since these affixes do attach to independent, inflected words, they meet the criteria of principle F and should attach to an adjacent word, rather than a head, which they do. Compare (26) with (33).

(33)   *Illumut   angisuumukarpoq.*
       house-dat big-dat-kar-indic/3sg
       'He is going to the big house.'

There are a number of aberrant morphemes that have come to my attention whose properties do not consign them precisely to one of the five categories in Table II. Space does not allow me to list them, let alone give a very full description of them here. Suffice it to say these constitute a collection of linguistic curiosities. Each has properties so infrequent as to constitute a singleton set in the rogues' gallery of grammatical miscreants. But they do exist and they must be describable in an adequate theory of human language. The theory sketched here allows them to be describable without making them normal.

References

Anderson, S.R. (1982). Where's Morphology? *Linguistic Inquiry* **13**, 572–612.

Baker, M. (1988). *Incorporation: A Theory of Grammatical Function Changing*. University of Chicago Press, Chicago.

Bloomfield, L. (1933). "Language." Holt, New York; reprinted, 1984, Univ. of Chicago Press, Chicago.

Borgida, A.T. (1983). Some formal results about stratificational grammars and their relevance to linguistics, *Mathematical Systems Theory* **16**, 29–56.

Bresnan, J., ed. (1982). "The Mental Representation of Grammatical Relations." MIT Press, Cambridge, MA.

Cresswell, M.J. (1973). "Logics and Languages." Methuen, London.

Gazdar, G., Klein, E., Pullum, G.K., and Sag, I.A. (1985). "Generalized Phrase Structure Grammar." Harvard Univ. Press, Cambridge, MA.

McCawley, J.D. (1981). "Everything that Linguists Have Always Wanted to Know about Logic, but Were Ashamed to Ask." Univ. of Chicago Press, Chicago.

Manaster-Ramer, A. (1983). The soft formal underbelly of theoretical syntax. *CLS* **19**, 256–62.

Pollard, C. and Sag, I.A. (1987). Information-Based *Syntax and Semantics, Volume I: Fundamentals*. Center for the Study of Language and Information, Stanford University, Stanford.

Pullum, G.K. (1982). Syncategorematicity and English infinitival *to*. *Glossa* **16**, 181–215.

Rischel, J. (1971). Some characteristics of noun phrases in West Greenlandic. *Acta Linguistica Hafniensia* **12**, 213–45.

Rischel, J. (1972). Derivation as a syntactic process in Greenlandic. *In* "Derivational Processes" (F. Kiefer, ed.), KVAL PM Ref. No. 729, 60–73. Stockholm.

Sadock, J.M. (1980). Noun incorporation in Greenlandic: A case of syntactic word-formation. *Language* **57**, 300–319.

Sadock, J.M. (1985). Autolexical syntax: A theory of noun incorporation and similar phenomena. *Natural Language and Linguistic Theory* **3**, 379–440.

Sadock, J.M. (1986). Some notes on noun incorporation. *Language* **62**, 19–31.

Sadock, J.M. (1987b). "Dutch as Two Formal Languages," MS.

Sapir, E. (1921). "Language: An Introduction to the Study of Speech." Harcourt, New York.

Chapter 16

On Anaphoric Islandhood

Richard Sproat

1. Introduction

Within the generative literature, it was Postal (1969) who first noticed facts like the following:

(1) a. *Drivers of trucks$_i$ fill them$_i$ up with diesel.*
     b. **Truck$_i$drivers fill them$_i$ up with diesel.*

What he noticed was that while it is in general possible to have coreference between words in a phrase, this possibility is removed when one (or both) of the words is contained within another word. Thus, words are ANAPHORIC ISLANDS, that is, they form inaccessible domains for anaphoric processes of various kinds.

More recently, this fact about words has been tied in with the more general claim that the internal structure of words is inaccessible to syntactic processes in general. One statement of this position (and one which we return to in the next section) is given by Simpson (1983) in the context of lexical functional grammar (LFG):

(2) REVISED LEXICAL INTEGRITY HYPOTHESIS (Simpson, 1983). Constituent-structure processes (which include annotation of functional information and indexing of anaphoric information) are blind to the internal structure of words.

The anaphoric islandhood of words seems to fit rather neatly with the common current view of morphology which claims that word formation is carried out in a separate component of the grammar. In particular, it is this separation of word formation from syntax which is often supposed to derive the "atomicity" of words.

In this chapter I present a different view of the matter. Elsewhere (Sproat, 1985) I have presented a view of the grammar in which word formation does *not* form a separate component; thus the well-formedness of words is checked by exactly the same principles as are used to check well-formedness in other parts of the grammar. I do not defend this position here, but it should be in any event immediately obvious that, in such a view, anaphoric islandhood cannot be construed as derivative of the separation of morphology from the rest of the grammar, syntax in particular; in such a view, no such separation exists. Some other mechanism must therefore derive anaphoric islandhood. I argue that anaphoric islandhood derives in an utterly trivial fashion from a principle which seems necessary in the grammar anyway; I argue that anaphoric islandhood is not evidence for separating morphology from syntax.

The chapter is organized as follows. In the next section I review Simpson's analysis of anaphoric islandhood as an example of what I am arguing against, showing that such a view is not entirely coherent. In Section 3 I present the anaphoric/pronominal argument indexing condition, which I argue to be necessary in the grammar and sufficient to derive the anaphoric islandhood of words given the assumption—apparently correct for English—that maximal projections do not occur within words. I also discuss a phenomenon which might look like a problem for the model proposed and present an example from Warlpiri which seems supportive of the model. I also show that the separation of morphology from syntax is not useful in explaining the nonoccurrence of maximal projections within words; if it were useful, it would mean that even if my solution to anaphoric islandhood is correct, I would still need to assume this separation. I then discuss how my analysis fits into lexical integrity more broadly. Finally, in an appendix, I look very briefly at some of the evidence from apparent exceptions to anaphoric islandhood, particularly those discussed in Lieber (1984).[1]

2. Simpson's Proposal: A Brief Note

As noted in the introduction, Simpson argues that the anaphoric islandhood of words is derivable from the lexical integrity hypothesis (LIH) as given in (2). Given such a statement, it follows trivially that such indexinngs as those in (3) are illicit:

---

[1] I shall assume for the greater part of the chapter that the contrast exemplified in examples like (1) is the relevant one, rather than assuming differing degrees of acceptability among anaphoric islandhood violations: I therefore do not assume "Peninsular dialects" as discussed in Corum (1973).

(3) a. *Truck$_i$drivers fill them$_i$ up with diesel.*
     b. *Wombat$_i$ meat is best from the young ones$_i$.*
     c. *Reagan$_i$ haters would never be seen standing next to him$_i$.*
     d. *Bill was a McCarthy$_i$ite and Fred was also a him$_i$ite.*

However, the LIH would appear to be stipulative, and it would appear desirable to try to reduce it to some independent principle of grammar, perhaps one related to the independence of morphology and syntax. Indeed, following Pesetsky (1979) and Mohanan (1982), Simpson suggests that the LIH is reducible to bracketing erasure, a principle of lexical phonology, which may be given as follows:

(4) BRACKETING ERASURE CONVENTION (BEC) (Kiparsky, 1983). Internal brackets are erased at the end of every level.

That is, at the end of every level (or stratum) of the morphology, the internal structure of words derived at the stratum is made invisible to subsequent strata by erasing the internal brackets which delimit the internal structure. Of course, bracketing erasure also takes place at the last stratum of the morphology, making the internal structure of words invisible to syntax. So, *truck driver* enters the syntax, under this view, as [*truckdriver*], with no internal structure; hence there is no internal subpart to index. We would therefore appear to have derived the LIH.

But this view, appealing as it might be, is conceptually flawed, I believe. Bracketing erasure, if it is motivated at all in lexical phonology, is almost exclusively motivated for phonological reasons. That is to say, for the purposes of the phonology, internal structure from one stratum to the next may become invisible, but this says nothing about the (morpho)syntactic structure of the word. Indeed, as argued in Marantz (1984) and also Sproat (1985), there is substantial evidence—from morphological bracketing paradoxes in particular—that we must recognize two levels of structure for a word, one phonological and one syntactic. Since it is a fair assumption that co-indexation is an operation over syntactic structures and not over phonological strings, the reduction of the LIH to the BEC does not seem appropriate.

In the model of morphology I am assuming, we do not have recourse to special principles of morphology because I assume that there are none; see, again, Sproat (1985). So we cannot appeal to such principles, or to the separation of morphology from syntax, in dealing with the anaphoric islandhood problem. Fortunately, as I show in the next section, we do not have to.

3. The Solution

3.1 The Anaphoric/Pronominal Argument Indexing Condition

Why are constructions of the following form bad?

(5)   *[a picture of itself$_i$]$_i$

Such forms are out because the anaphor cannot be coreferent with the containing NP; it has often been assumed that there is some grammatical condition such as the I-WITHIN-I CONDITION (Chomsky, 1981), or some condition on semantic interpretation, which rules them out. But why is the following not a possible co-indexing?

(6)   *[a picture$_i$ of itself$_i$]

Clearly we want to also rule this out, and additionally such co-indexings as (7), where it is the noun *man* alone which is co-indexed with *him*.

(7)   *The large man$_i$ had a hat with him$_i$.

The reason such co-indexings are bad is intuitively clear: In (6) *picture* is a noun, not an NP, and as such cannot have reference of its own. So we want to rule out co-indexings as exemplified by (6) and (7) in some way. I suggest the following condition, one which has certainly never been stated before, but has always been tacitly assumed, as far as I can tell:

(8)   ANAPHORIC/PRONOMINAL ARGUMENT INDEXING CONDITION. In a configuration...α...β...(linear order irrelevant) where α is the antecedent of β and β is an argument (i.e., maximal projection), α must also be an argument (i.e., maximal projection).

Why are NPs (i.e., arguments) the only referential nominal expressions? I assume (following Higginbotham, 1985) that a noun such as *dog* does not refer in that it does not pick out any particular dog or any particular set of dogs. Only NPs have this property [though see the discussion of (10a)]. Higginbotham's statement of this condition (his 33) is given in (9).

(9)   Every argument is saturated.

Given (8), the anaphoric islandhood of words follows trivially given also the observation that word formation deals in submaximal projections. So, in (10), each of the intended antecedents is submaximal, and by (8) cannot serve as antecedent.

(10)   a.   *John is a Reagan$_i$ite but I don't like him$_i$.*
        b.   *Truck$_i$drivers fill them$_i$ up with diesel.
        c.   *Aardvark$_i$ hunters rarely find them$_i$ on the veld.

It is interesting to note, in regard to (10a) that *Reagan,* which must be an X^0 since it is within the word *Reaganite,* still apparently refers to a particular individual. This is important in that apparently the indexing condition must be a syntactic restriction rather than a semantic one: Since the semantic reference of *Reagan* is clear, it must be simply the fact that the intended antecedent is an X^0, which is causing the ungrammaticality.

Furthermore, given the reasonable assumption that pronouns such as *he* and anaphors such as *himself* obligatorily subtend NPs, (11) is ruled out on purely syntactic grounds.

(11) a. **Fred is a Reagan$_i$ite but I am not a him$_i$ite.*
      b. **Edna is an aardvark$_i$ hunter but I am not a them$_i$ hunter.*
      c. ** Truck$_i$drivers are often hefty individuals and them$_i$ drivers are also quite often found in truckstops.*

So a construction such as **them driver* is ruled out for the trivial reason that *them* is an NP, whereas the left member of a compound cannot be a maximal projection.

One final set of data has to do with verbal anaphora with *do so,* also discussed by Postal (1969):

(12) a. **[Smoke]$_i$ers really shouldn't [do so]$_i$.*
      b. **People who hand[carve]$_i$ pipes compete with those who don't hand[do so]$_i$.*

Do so apparently refers to VP predicates, and, we might fairly assume, subtends a VP also:

(13) a. *John looked at Mary and Bill did so too.*
      b. **John looked at Mary and Bill did so at Sally.*
      c. *Eric hunts aardvarks and Hortense does so too.*
      d. **Eric hunts aardvarks and Hortense does so pigs.*

Since VP predicates (or predicates in general, in fact) do not occur within lexical forms such as compounds, it is therefore not surprising that *do so* is unable to refer back to a verb within a compound (and given that *do so* subtends a VP, it follows too that it cannot occur within a compound, since VPs are X^{max}s). This requires an extension of (8) to cover not just arguments but predicates as well:

(14) ANAPHORIC/PRONOMINAL ARGUMENT/PREDICATE INDEXING CONDITION (APAPIC). In a configuration...α...β...(linear order irrelevant) where α is the antecedent of β and β is an argument/predicate (i.e., maximal projection), α must also be an argument/predicate (i.e., maximal projection).

In this section I have argued that anaphoric islandhood can be reduced trivially to a condition which is arguably necessary in the grammar anyway so as to rule out arbitrary co-indexings of pronouns or anaphors with non-maximal antecedents.

3.2 An Apparent Problem

One class of cases which might appear problematic for the APAPIC are the familar cases of pro-drop in many languages. Here, at some level of abstraction we find structures such as (15).

(15) $[_{I''} [_{NP}pro]_i [_{I'} [_I \ldots AGR_i \ldots]]]$

AGR is the governor of the NP subject *pro*, since it is part of INFL, and it is also co-indexed with *pro*: Apparently, then, an NP pronoun can be co-indexed with a nonmaximal projection after all. The particular problem arises, of course, from the fact that in many languages AGR merges with the verb at some point in the syntax to form a word. Thus, co-indexation of a pronoun with an antecedent within a word is allowable.

But this kind of example is really irrelevant for the APAPIC, since the latter explicitly constrains cases of antecedent co-indexation of pronouns and anaphors and the AGR/*pro* co-indexation is surely not one of this kind. AGR is *not* the antecedent of *pro*. In fact, if it were, such constructions would be violations of Condition B of the binding theory, since a pronoun would be locally bound by an antecedent. Presumably, rather, AGR *licenses* the existence of *pro* under co-indexation. This, for example, is the position taken in McCloskey and Hale (1984), who suggest a condition such as (16).

(16)   *pro unless governed by AGR, where [αF] is some combination of
        | |
        [αF]   [αF]

        person–number features.

Clearly this is a condition on licensing rather than antecedence, which renders the case of AGR and *pro* irrelevant for the APAPIC.

3.3 Confirmatory Evidence from Warlpiri

Naturally, were a language to allow maximal projections within a word, we would expect, other things being equal, to allow coreference between pronouns and such maximal subparts of words. Such a case occurs in Warlpiri[2] as shown in (17).

---

[2] Thanks to Mary Laughren and Ken Hale for this example.

(17)   *Jampijinpa* [[*wawirri   yalumpu-wardingki*]$_i$ *pu*] *-ngu. ?Japaljarri*
        J.   kangaroo that   place   kill-er   J.
        [*nyanungu$_i$ pu*] *-ngu-yijala.*
        that   kill-er   also
        'Jampijinpa is a killer of [kangaroos in that place]$_i$. Japaljarri kills
        those$_i$ also.'

In Warlpiri, the construction [[[*wawirri yalumpu-wardingki*] *pu*] *ngu*] is
apparently, at least syntactically, a word; in particular, the nominalizing affix
-ngu is attached to the verbal construction [[*wawirri yalumpu-wardingki*] *pu*]
to form a noun. But this word contains a full NP (*wawirri yalumpu-wardingki*),
and the pronoun *nyanungu* 'that' in the next sentence is able to refer to it.
The question mark at the beginning of the second sentence indicates that the
Warlpiri example is a little odd only insofar as it is hard to interpret the left
member in the compound in the previous sentence as being specific in
reference; taking that point into account, however, the example is apparently
well formed. This evidence would appear to confirm the position of this
chapter, which claims that the basic reason for anaphoric islandhood effects
in English is that there are no maximal projections within words.

4. Final Thoughts: On the Separation of Morphology from Syntax and the General Problem of Lexical Integrity

In this section, I clear up a couple of conceptual issues, namely, how the
separation of morphology from syntax might still appear to aid in the analysis
of anaphoric islands, and the theoretical status of lexical integrity.

4.1 What the Separation of Morphology from Syntax Might Buy

The proposed solution to anaphoric islandhood depends crucially upon the
observation that maximal projections are unavailable as parts of words in
English. At first glance one might be tempted to suppose that this is precisely
the kind of situation one would expect if morphology were a separate domain
from syntax: Since maximal projections are crucially syntactic projections,
if words are built up in a different component of the grammar from where
sentences are built up, it would seem to follow that maximal projections could
not occur within words; thus, it might be argued, the separation of morphology
from syntax is useful for handling anaphoric islands after all.

However, this point of view seems empirically inadequate: clear (nonmaximal) phrasal entities do occur within compounds at least (see also discussions of this point in Fabb, 1984):

(18)   a.   [$_{N'}$ *brown dog*] *catcher*
        b.   [$_{N'}$ *one-eyed one-horned flying purple people*] *eater*
        c.   *one-eyed* [$_{N'}$ *one-horned flying purple people*] *eater*
        d.   *one-eyed one-horned* [$_{N'}$ *flying purple people*] *eater*
        e.   *one-eyed one-horned flying* [$_{N'}$ *purple people*] *eater*

Each of the examples in (18) contains a syntactic construction which one can reasonably assume is not X^0. So word formation does have access to phrasal constituents after all. To capture this within a framework such as lexical phonology and morphology (LPM), which advocates a strict separation of morphology from syntax, one has to appeal to a move such as that suggested by Kiparsky (1982) whereby there is "some limited recursion from phrase-level syntax back into the morphology anyway." This move—necessary given the data—weakens considerably the strong separation hypothesis advocated by theories such as LPM. In particular, since we now have access to the output of phrase-building operations in word formation, we now need to stipulate a limitation on the kind of material that can be funneled back into the lexicon from the syntax and insist that it be nonmaximal. It should be clear that this stipulation is equivalent to stating the observation that syntactic words of English do not contain maximal projections, which in turn means that separating the lexicon from the syntax buys us nothing in solving the problem of anaphoric islandhood. In terms of the framework I am assuming, the observation would be statable as a constraint such as (19), which disallows X^{max}s as a daughter of X^0.

(19)

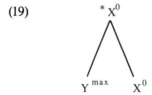

4.2 The Status of Lexical Integrity

What then is the status of lexical integrity? In fact, there are two parts of this principle, one which seems to describe a genuinely empirical fact about natural language and one which is less clearly an empirical issue at all. The first, empirically motivated, part is anaphoric islandhood, which I have shown to be trivially derivable from a constraint on co-indexing which surely must be operative in the grammar as a whole anyway. The second part of lexical integrity has to do with movement operations in and out of words. In particular, it is often assumed that allowing syntax to participate in the formation of words is a bad idea, and a principle such as lexical integrity is designed to rule such possibilities out. Nevertheless, it is fairly clear that this is not obviously an empirical point, but rather depends upon how one has constructed one's syntactic theory. In particular, recent work by Baker (1987) suggests that there is reason to think that syntactic movement (i.e., Move-α) is directly involved in the formation of words in languages which exhibit morphology which marks syntactic operations of various kinds such as passive, applied verb shift, and incorporation. An argument for this is that many of these operations obey the usual locality constraints imposed on Move-α elsewhere in the grammar. In such a theory, of course, lexical integrity is massively violated. Of course, this part of lexical integrity is making an empirical prediction of a sort: It claims that it is possible to construct theories of natural language without recourse to the kinds of word building operations which Baker allows. But it is not clear by a first-order description of the data from natural language whether lexical integrity is correct about this. This is quite a different situation from anaphoric islandhood, where even a first-order description would show it to be correct.

So lexical integrity as a hypothesis about natural language really breaks down into two parts, the first of which is correct but trivial, and the second of which is not obviously correct. It remains to be seen, therefore, whether the separation of morphology from syntax advocated by lexical integrity is either desirable or possible. Be that as it may, anaphoric islandhood does not seem to fuel the fire of strict separationism.

5. Appendix: A Short Note on Lieber (1984)

Since Postal presented his original work, it has been noted by a number of researchers—among them Lakoff and Ross (1972), Corum (1973), Browne (1974), and Lieber (1984)—that the prohibition on inward and outward pronominalization imposed by Postal does not account for the fact that there is a gradation of judgments within anaphoric islandhood violations. Lieber (1984) discusses data such as the following:

(20) a. *McCarthy$_i$ites are now puzzled by him$_i$.*
      b. *His$_i$ mother distrusts McCarthy$_i$ites.*
      c. **He$_i$ distrusts McCarthy$_i$ites.*

The judgments indicated here are Lieber's. I have, in contrast, assumed that all such examples are ill formed—a position which I believe to be correct— but Lieber (and the researchers who preceded her) is quite correct in pointing out that there is a difference between (20a–b) which, though marginal, are at least interpretable as indicated, and (20c), which is quite uninterpretable.

Lieber makes the interesting observation (also noted earlier by Lakoff and Ross (1972)) that the conditions under which such anaphoric islandhood violations are deemed marginal as opposed to completely uninterpretable are precisely those under which normal intrasentential coreference is possible as opposed to impossible; that is, the pronoun may not c-command its antecedent since that would mean that the antecedent, an R-expression, is bound in violation of Principle C of the binding theory (Chomsky, 1981). To see this, contrast (20a) with (20c), the relevant structures of which are given in (21).

(21)   a.   (= 20a)

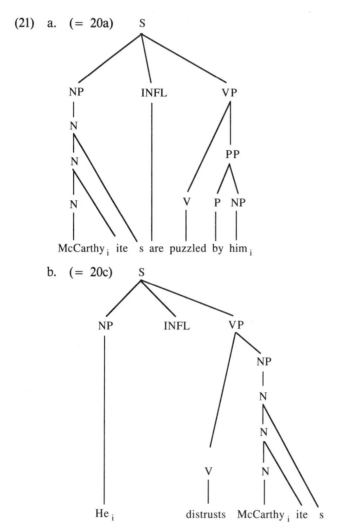

So, neither *McCarthy* nor *him* in (20a) c-command the other. In contrast, in (20c), *he* c-commands *McCarthy*. Thus the contrast is explained.

Within the proposal of this chapter, we can make sense of this observation in the following way. Let us first allow that all nonanaphor/nonpronominal elements are R-expressions, regardless of their X-bar status. Therefore, the binding theory, particularly Principle C, is relevant for co-indexings such as those in (20). Let us now assume that binding theory violations are absolute in that at no level of analysis may a proscription on co-indexing imposed by the binding theory be relaxed. This seems fairly reasonable, in that examples like *He$_i$ saw Bill$_i$* cannot be saved. So (20c) involves a co-indexing which violates Principle C. Of course, it also violates the APAPIC, as does the entire set in (20). Let us assume, however, that while not violating the APAPIC is a precondition for full grammaticality of an intended coreference relation, nevertheless the APAPIC is a weaker condition than the binding theory. That is, it can be relaxed at a later level of interpretation. If we make these assumptions, then we can at least explain why words do constitute anaphoric islands while still explaining why there is a gradation in grammaticality across examples. Naturally there is much more research to be done on this topic, and it will be interestinng to find out to what extent the behavior of the marginal examples such as (20) mirrors genuine syntactic coreference.[3]

References

Baker, M. (1987). "Incorporation: A Theory of Grammatical Function Changing." University of Chicago Press, Chicago.

Browne, W. (1974). On the topology of Anaphoric Peninsulas. *Linguistic Inquiry* 5, 619–20.

Chomsky, N. (1981). "Lectures on Government and Binding." Foris, Dordrecht.

Corum, C. (1973). *Anaphoric Peninsulas.* Papers from the Ninth Regional Meeting of the Chicago Linguistic Society.

Dressler, W.U. (1986). *Preferences vs. Strict Universals in Morphology.* Paper presented at the Milwaukee Morphology Meeting, University of Wisconsin, April.

Fabb, N. (1984). *Syntactic Affixation.* Unpublished Ph.D. dissertation, MIT.

Higginbotham, J. (1985). On semantics. *Linguistic Inquiry* 16, 547–593.

Kiparsky, P. (1982). Lexical phonology and morphology. *In* "Linguistics in the Morning Calm" (I.-S. Yang, ed.), pp. 3–91. Hanshin, Seoul.

Kiparsky, P. (1983). *Word Formation and the Lexicon.* Mid-America Linguistics Conferences.

Lakoff, G., and Ross, J.R. (1972). A Note on Anaphoric Islands and causatives. *Linguistic Inquiry* 3, 121–125.

Lieber, R. (1984). *Grammatical Rules and Sublexical Elements.* Papers from the Parasession on Lexical Semantics: Chicago Linguistic Society.

McCloskey, J., and Hale, K. (1984). On the syntax of person-number inflection in Modern Irish. *Natural Language and Linguistic Theory* 1, 487–533.

Marantz, A. (1984). *Tagalog Reduplication is Affixation, Too.* Paper presented at the LSA, Baltimore.

Mohanan, K.P. (1982). *Lexical Phonology.* MIT Ph.D. dissertation, published by IULC.

Pesetsky, D. (1979). *Russian Morphology and Lexical Theory.* Unpublished ms., MIT.

Postal, P. (1969). *Anaphoric Islands.* Papers from the Fifth Regional Meeting, Chicago Linguistic Society.

Simpson, J. (1983). *Aspects of Warlpiri Morphology and Syntax.* Unpublished Ph.D. dissertation, MIT.

Sproat, R. (1985). *On Deriving the Lexicon.* Unpublished Ph.D. dissertation, MIT.

Sproat, R., and Ward, G. (1987). *Pragmatic Considerations in Anaphoric Island Phenomena.* Papers from the 23rd Regional Meeting, Chicago Linguistic Society.

[3] Indeed, in Sproat and Ward (1987) we investigate the discourse conditioning of Anaphoric Islandhood in such cases, and also cases such as those raised by Dressler (1986) for German and Italian, which have counterparts in English like *The children will go **treasure** hunting. When they find it* (= *treasure*), *they will return.*

Part V

Morphophonology

Chapter 17

On the Nature of
Internal Reduplication

Stuart Davis

1. Introduction

Marantz (1982) proposes that reduplication is an instance of normal affixation onto the consonant-vowel tier. The reduplicative affix itself is viewed as
containing a specified CV-template left unspecified for any phonemic content.
The reduplicative affix (or template) acquires its phonemic content by a process
of phoneme copying (in which stem phonemes are copied) with one-to-one
association (between the copied phonemes and the reduplicative affix) subsequently applying. An example of this is shown in (1) for one type of perfect
reduplication in Sanskrit in which the reduplicative affix is a CV-prefix. (The
following abbreviations are used: AF, affixation; PC, phoneme copying; A,
association; and L-R, left to right.)

(1)   SANSKRIT PERFECT REDUPLICATION: *tud* ⟶ *tutud* 'strike'

$$
\begin{array}{llllll}
t\,u\,d & & t\,u\,d & & t\,u\,d & & t\,u\,d \\
|\;|\;| & \xrightarrow{\text{AF}} & |\;|\;| & \xrightarrow{\text{PC}} & |\;|\;| & \xrightarrow[\text{L-R}]{\text{A}} & |\;|\;| \quad = \textit{tutud} \\
\text{CVC} & & \text{CV + CVC} & & \text{CV + CVC} & & \text{CV + CVC} \\
& & & & & & |\;| \\
& & & & t\,u\,d & & t\,u\,d
\end{array}
$$

Generally, the association is from left to right if the reduplicative affix is a
prefix (as in the Sanskrit example), and from right to left if it is a suffix;
any phonemes left unassociated are deleted. Furthermore, according to
Marantz, association is phoneme driven. This means that the association starts
with the copied phonemes and they link up (one-to-one) with the appropriate

Theoretical Morphology   Copyright © 1988 by Academic Press, Inc.

CV slots of the reduplicative affix. Association does not start with the elements on the CV tier.

Steriade (1982) proposes that a reduplicative affix can sometimes acquire its phonemic content by autosegmental spreading (AS). When the reduplicative template acquires its phonemic content in this manner, no copying of phonemes occurs, rather the template is filled by AS from a phoneme in the stem. An example from Ancient Greek present reduplication is shown in (2). Here, the reduplicative template is a CV prefix with the V slot preassociated to /i/.

(2)   ANCIENT GREEK PRESENT REDUPLICATION: *dō* ⟶ *didōmi*

Steriade (1982) shows, on the basis of vowel-initial stems, that (2) must be handled by autosegmental spreading and not by phoneme copying. For example, consider the derivation in (3).

(3)   *akʰ* ⟶ *iakʰō* 'to cry'

In (3) the output is *iakʰō*. The phoneme /kʰ/ cannot spread to the empty C slot of the prefix, since such would violate the general principle against crossing association lines. This is shown in (4).

(4)

Further, the correct output cannot be derived by phoneme copying, as is shown in (5).

(5)

Thus, the reduplicative template of the Ancient Greek present acquires its phonemic content only by autosegmental spreading, while the Sanskrit reduplicative affix in (1) acquires its phonemic content by just phoneme copying (with subsequent one-to-one association).

The Marantzian analysis of reduplication as affixation onto the CV tier has been extended with minimal modification to cases of infixing (or internal) reduplication (IR) by Broselow and McCarthy (1983) (henceforth B&M). These two researchers divide IR into two types: true IR and apparent IR. True IR involves the infixing of the reduplicative template at a specified point along the CV tier, with the whole melody of the stem being copied; association subsequently occurs, stipulated (language specifically) as being left to right or right to left. Apparent IR involves the prefixing or suffixing of a reduplicative affix to a phonological constituent (normally, a syllable or a foot), with the entire phonemic melody of that constituent being copied and association subsequently taking place. In (6) an example of true IR from the Austronesian language Temiar is provided, and in (7) an example of apparent IR is shown from Samoan (I, infixation; R–L, right to left).

(6)   TEMIAR CONTINUATIVE REDUPLICATION: slɔg ⟶ *sglɔg* 'to lie down'

$$
\begin{array}{c}
s\,l\,\mathit{o}\,g \\
|\ |\ |\ | \\
CCVC
\end{array}
\overset{I}{\longrightarrow}
\begin{array}{c}
s \quad\quad l\,\mathit{o}\,g \\
| \quad\quad |\ |\ | \\
C\ +\ C\ +\ CVC
\end{array}
\overset{PC}{\longrightarrow}
\begin{array}{c}
s \quad\quad l\,\mathit{o}\,g \\
| \quad\quad |\ |\ | \\
C\ +\ C\ +\ CVC \\
slɔg
\end{array}
\overset{A}{\underset{R-L}{\longrightarrow}}
\begin{array}{c}
s \quad\quad l\,\mathit{o}\,g \\
| \quad\quad |\ |\ | \\
C\ +\ C\ +\ CVC \\
slɔg
\end{array}
= sglɔg
$$

(7)   SAMOAN REDUPLICATION: *alofa* ⟶ *alolofa* 'love'

$$
\begin{array}{c}
a\,l\,o\,f\,a \\
|\ |\ |\ |\ | \\
VCVCV
\end{array}
\overset{I}{\longrightarrow}
\begin{array}{c}
a \quad\quad l\,o\,f\,a \\
| \quad\quad |\ |\ |\ | \\
V\ +\ CV\ +\ CVCV
\end{array}
\overset{PC}{\longrightarrow}
\begin{array}{c}
a \quad\quad l\,o\,f\,a \\
| \quad\quad |\ |\ |\ | \\
V\ +\ CV\ +\ CVCV \\
lo
\end{array}
$$

$$
\overset{A}{\underset{L-R}{\longrightarrow}}
\begin{array}{c}
a \quad\quad l\,o\,f\,a \\
| \quad\quad |\ |\ |\ | \\
C\ +\ CV\ +\ CVCV \\
|\ | \\
l\,o
\end{array}
= alolofa
$$

The Marantzian theory of reduplication has recently been challenged by Clements (1985) who argues that the reduplicative template is not affixed onto the CV tier but is "parafixed" to it. That is, it is put on a tier parallel to the CV tier. The reduplicative affix then acquires its phonemic content by processes of association and transfer. In Clements's framework, the Sanskrit perfect example in (1) has the derivation in (8) and the Temiar continuative example (6) has the derivation in (9) (P, parafixation; A, association; T, transfer; S, sequence or linearization).

(8)

$$
\begin{array}{ccc}
\begin{array}{c} t\,u\,d \\ |\ |\ | \\ \text{CVC} \end{array} & \xrightarrow{P} &
\begin{array}{c} t\,u\,d \\ |\ |\ | \\ \text{CVC} \\ \\ \text{CV} \end{array} & \xrightarrow{A} &
\begin{array}{c} t\,u\,d \\ |\ |\ | \\ \text{CVC} \\ |\ | \\ \text{CV} \end{array} & \xrightarrow{T} &
\begin{array}{c} t\,u\,d \\ |\ |\ | \\ \text{CVC} \\ |\ | \\ \text{CV} \\ |\ | \\ t\,u \end{array} & \xrightarrow{S} &
\begin{array}{c} t\,u\,t\,u\,d \\ |\ |\ |\ |\ | \\ \text{CVCVC} \end{array}
\end{array}
$$

(9)

$$
\begin{array}{ccc}
\begin{array}{c} s\,l\,ɔ\,g \\ |\ |\ |\ | \\ \text{CCVC} \end{array} & \xrightarrow{P} &
\begin{array}{c} s\,l\,ɔ\,g \\ |\ |\ |\ | \\ \text{CCVC} \\ \\ \text{C} \end{array} & \xrightarrow{A} &
\begin{array}{c} s\,l\,ɔ\,g \\ |\ |\ |\ | \\ \text{CCVC} \\ | \\ \text{C} \end{array} & \xrightarrow{T} &
\begin{array}{c} s\,l\,ɔ\,g \\ |\ |\ |\ | \\ \text{CCVC} \\ | \\ \text{C} \\ | \\ g \end{array} & \xrightarrow{S} &
\begin{array}{c} s\,g\,l\,ɔ\,g \\ |\ |\ |\ |\ | \\ \text{CCCVC} \end{array}
\end{array}
$$

With reference to IR, Clements observes that his theory of reduplication can straightforwardly analyze several cases of IR that are problematic under a Marantzian account. Consider Lushootseed counting reduplication where the reduplicative affix is infixed after the second consonant of the stem; for example, *c'ukʷs* 'seven' reduplicates as *c'ukʷ-ukʷ-s* 'seven people.'[1] In (10) the derivation for *c'ukʷukʷs* is provided in Clements's framework. In (11) the derivation for the same form is shown in B&M's Marantzian framework.

(10)

$$
\begin{array}{ccc}
\begin{array}{c} c'\,u\,k^w\,s \\ |\ \ |\ |\ \ | \\ \text{C\ VC\ C} \end{array} & \xrightarrow{P} &
\begin{array}{c} c'\,u\,k^w\,s \\ |\ \ |\ |\ \ | \\ \text{C\ VC\ C} \\ \\ \text{VC} \end{array} & \xrightarrow{A} &
\begin{array}{c} c'\,u\,k^w\,s \\ |\ \ |\ |\ \ | \\ \text{C\ VC\ C} \\ |\ | \\ \text{VC} \end{array}
\end{array}
$$

$$
\xrightarrow{T}
\begin{array}{c} c'\,u\,k^w\,s \\ |\ \ |\ |\ \ | \\ \text{C\ VC\ C} \\ |\ | \\ \text{VC} \\ |\ | \\ u\,k^w \end{array}
\xrightarrow{S}
\begin{array}{c} c'\,u\,k^w\,u\,k^w\,s \\ |\ \ |\ |\ \ |\ |\ \ | \\ \text{C\ VC\ VC\ C} \end{array}
$$

(11)

$$
\begin{array}{ccc}
\begin{array}{c} c'\,u\,k^w\,s \\ |\ \ |\ |\ \ | \\ \text{C\ VC\ C} \end{array} & \xrightarrow{I} &
\begin{array}{c} c'\,u\,k^w \\ |\ \ |\ | \\ \text{C\ VC} \end{array} +\, \text{VC} +\,
\begin{array}{c} s \\ | \\ \text{C} \end{array} & \xrightarrow{PC} &
\begin{array}{c} c'\,u\,k^w \\ |\ \ |\ | \\ \text{C\ VC} \end{array} +\, \text{VC} +\,
\begin{array}{c} s \\ | \\ \text{C} \end{array}
\end{array}
$$

$$
c'\,u\,k^w\,s
$$

---

[1] B&M note that words which undergo VC infixing reduplication in Lushootseed are usually derived, at least historically, from a CVC root plus a consonantal suffix (e.g., *c'ukʷs* can be analyzed as consisting of the root *c'ukʷ* plus a lexical suffix -*s*). Hence it is tempting to analyze the Lushootseed reduplication as an instance of normal suffixing reduplication and not as an instance of IR. B&M point out, however, that this type of VC reduplication applies productively to borrowings from Chinook jargon which are not analyzable as bimorphemic. Thus, some way is still needed to account for the internal reduplication of VC.

$$\xrightarrow[\text{L-R}]{\text{A}} \quad \begin{array}{c} c'\,uk^w \\ |\ || \\ \text{C VC} \end{array} + \text{VC} + \begin{array}{c} s \\ | \\ \text{C} \end{array} \quad = \ *c'uk^wc's$$
$$\begin{array}{c} | \\ c'uk^w\ s \end{array}$$

The output in (11), $c'uk^wc's$, is incorrect. In the association in (11), the $/c'/$ of the copied phonemes links to the C slot of the reduplicative affix; the following $/u/$ is unable to link to the V slot of the affix lest the anti-crossing-lines constraint be violated. Further, if association in (11) were right to left instead of left to right, the output would be the incorrect $*c'uk^wuss$. In order to arrive at the correct form for (11), B&M are forced to posit an ad hoc stipulation that starts the association with the first vowel of the copied phonemes. Left-to-right association produces the correct $c'uk^wuk^ws$, as shown in (12).

(12)
$$\begin{array}{c} c'\,uk^w \\ |\ || \\ \text{C VC} \end{array} + \text{VC} + \begin{array}{c} s \\ | \\ \text{C} \end{array} \xrightarrow{\text{PC}} \begin{array}{c} c'\,uk^w \\ |\ || \\ \text{C VC} \end{array} + \text{VC} + \begin{array}{c} s \\ | \\ \text{C} \end{array} \xrightarrow[\text{L-R}]{\text{A}} \begin{array}{c} c'\,uk^w \\ |\ || \\ \text{C VC} \end{array} + \begin{array}{c} \text{VC} \\ || \\ \end{array} + \begin{array}{c} s \\ | \\ \text{C} \end{array} = c'uk^wuk^ws$$
$$\qquad\qquad\qquad c'uk^ws \qquad\qquad\qquad\qquad c' \quad u k^ws$$

Clements takes the fact that his theory of reduplication can handle Lushootseed IR (and other cases similar to it) without any ad hoc stipulations as evidence for the correctness of his account of IR.[2] In this chapter, however, I argue for the correctness of the Marantzian account of IR over that of Clements. In Section 2 I argue that, within the Marantzian framework, association in IR is always template driven (not phoneme driven); that is, the association for IR starts with the template slots of the reduplicative infix and not with the copied phonemes. This proposal alleviates the problematic nature of several cases of IR (such as Lushootseed) which B&M can handle only by positing various sorts of ad hoc stipulations. By incorporating the pro-posal made for template-driven association, the problematic cases of IR can be analyzed straightforwardly without any such stipulations just as in Clements's analysis of these cases of reduplication.

In Section 3 I argue that the Marantzian account of IR proposed here is, in fact, superior to Clements's account of internal reduplication. The argu-ment comes from a type of IR that can be handled quite easily in a Marant-zian framework but cannot be handled (or handled only with ad hoc stipulations) in Clements's framework. These are cases of IR where (in

[2]Clements's theory of IR, like that of B&M, must distinguish between true IR and apparent IR. In B&M's theory, the difference between them is in terms of phoneme copying: In true IR the entire phoneme melody is copied, while in apparent IR only the phonemes of a prosodic constituent are copied. In Clements's theory the difference between them is in terms of associa-tion: In true IR association begins with the leftmost (or rightmost) V slot the stem linking to the appropriate V slot of the reduplicative template, while in apparent IR association begins with the leftmost (or rightmost) V slot of a prosidic constituent linking to the appropriate V slot of the reduplicative template.

Marantzian terminology) the reduplicative template is filled partly by autosegmental spreading and partly by phoneme copying with subsequent association. Specifically, the analysis of plural reduplication in the Chadic language Hausa as well as in the Australian language Mangarayi are considered. That reduplication in these languages can be readily analyzed in a Marantzian framework but not in Clements's framework is taken as strong evidence for a Marantzian account of IR over that of Clements.

2. Template-Driven Association

B&M are forced to posit various language-specific stipulations in their (Marantzian) analysis of true IR for the languages of Washo, Lushootseed, and Takelma. Clements (1985) has taken the fact that his theory of reduplication can handle these cases of IR without any such stipulations as evidence for the correctness of his account of internal reduplication. In this section I propose that, within a Marantzian framework of reduplication, association for IR is, by convention, template driven (not phoneme driven).[3] As I show in the following subsections, template-driven association obviates the need for the various language-specific stipulations posited by B&M in their analysis of IR in Washo, Lushootseed, and Takelma. I hold off until Section 3 the comparison between Clements's account of IR and the Marantzian account of it that I propose here.

2.1 Washo

In Washo, a Hokan language, according to B&M, plurals are formed by infixing the reduplicative affix VCV after the first C slot of a stem; subsequently, the phonemes of the stem are copied and (phoneme-driven) association takes place between the copied phonemes and the VCV reduplicative affix. This analysis is illustrated in (13), in which *mokgo* has the reduplicated form *mogokgo* 'shoes.'

(13)

---

[3]Specifically, I propose this for true IR only. Henceforth, the term "IR" refers only to true internal reduplication unless specified otherwise. I leave for further research the applicability of template-driven association to apparent IR.

A later language-specific rule shortens the long vowel in *mogookgo.*

When this analysis of B&M is applied to Washo stems ending in consonants, however, the wrong output is produced. This is illustrated in (14) by the word *damal*, whose reduplicated form is *damamal* 'to hear (pl).'

(14)

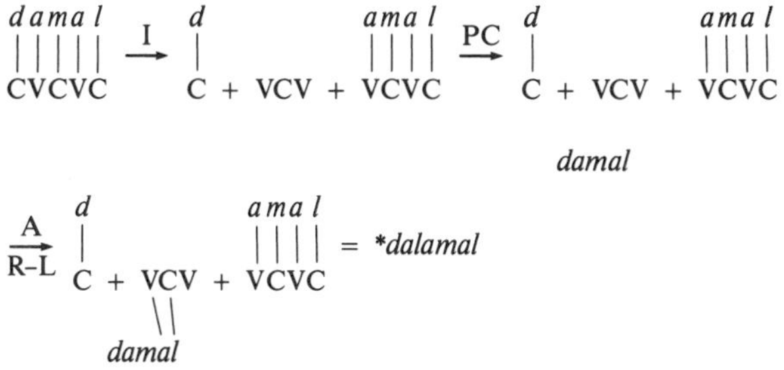
damal
CVCVC
I
d
C + VCV + VCVC
amal
PC
damal
A
R-L
= *dalamal

In the above derivation, after the reduplicative affix is infixed and the stem phonemes copied, right-to-left association occurs. Since association is phoneme-driven, the /l/ of the copied melody associates with the C slot of the reduplicative affix, and /a/ associates with the first V slot of the reduplicative affix. (The final V slot of the reduplicative affix is not associated with the other vowel from the copied melody tier lest the line-crossing constraint be violated.) This produces the incorrect **dalamal.* In order to obtain the correct form *damamal*, B&M suggest that the stem-final consonant in Washo is extrametrical and thus exempt from association. Though B&M do not discuss the potentially problematic consequences of extending the use of extrametricality beyond stress and tonal phenomena, the need for such a stipulation of extrametricality is obviated if association in IR is template driven and not melody driven. This is shown in (15) for the same pair: *damal–damamal.* (I indicate template-driven association by the presence of a dot under the CV slots of the reduplicative affix.)

(15)

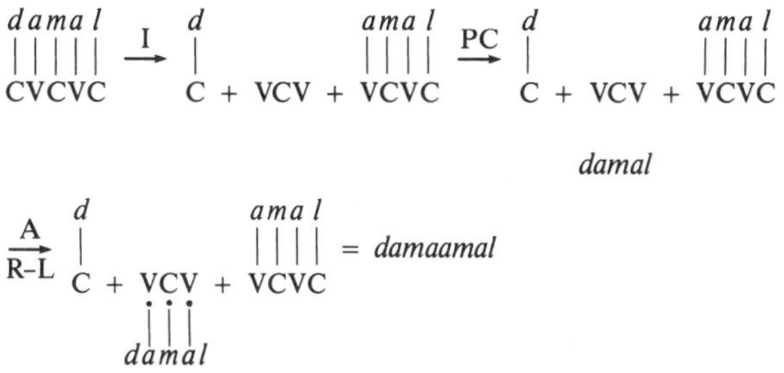
damal
CVCVC
I
d
C + VCV + VCVC
amal
PC
damal
A
R-L
= damaamal

(Again, a later rule shortens the long vowel of *damaamal*, as already motivated by B&M.) Further, template-driven association also produces the correct output for Washo forms having vowel-final stems. This can be seen from (13), repeated in part as (16):

(16)   m $o\ k\ g\ o$
        | $|\ |\ |\ |$ = *mogookgo*
        C + V CV + VCCV
              | ||
            $m\ o\ k\ g\ o$

Here, with template-driven association, the last V slot of the reduplicative affix links to the last /o/ of the copied melody, the C slot links to /g/, and the first V slot associates with the first /o/. In Washo IR, then, both template-driven association and phoneme-driven association produce the correct output for words in which the stem ends in a vowel. But it is only template-driven association that produces the correct linking for consonant-final stems. Thus, template-driven association obviates the need for a language-specific stipulation of extrametricality of final stem consonants.

2.2 Lushootseed

The above analysis of Washo IR also works for internal reduplication in the Salish language Lushootseed. This is another case cited as problematic by B&M. In Lushootseed, one of the functions of IR relates to counting. For example, *c'ukʷs* 'seven' has the reduplicated form *c'ukʷukʷs* 'seven people.' The reduplicative affix consists of a VC template infixed after the second consonant. B&M's analysis for the reduplication of *c'ukʷs* would be as in (11), repeated here as (17).

(17) $c'\ u\ kʷ\ s$ $c'\ u\ kʷ$ s $c'\ u\ kʷ$ s
        $|\ |\ |\ |$ I $|\ |\ |$ $|$ PC $|\ |\ |$ $|$
        C VC C   →   C VC + VC + C   →   C VC + VC + C

                                                              c'ukʷs

        A $c'\ u\ kʷ$ s
        —→ $|\ |\ |$ $|$ = **c'ukʷc's*
        L–R   C VC + VC + C
                        |
                     c'ukʷs

In (17), after infixing and phoneme copying have applied, /c'/ will link to the C slot of the reduplicative affix; the following /u/ is unable to associate with the V slot of the affix lest the line-crossing constraint be violated. The output produced is the incorrect **c'ukʷc's*. B&M are thus forced to posit a language-specific association rule that stipulates that the first vowel of the copied phoneme melody links to the first V slot. This is shown in (18).

(18) $c'\ u\ kʷ$ s
        $|\ |\ |$ $|$
        C VC + VC + C
                |
             c'ukʷs

The stipulation linking the first vowel of the copied melody with the first V slot of the reduplicative affix prevents the association of the first consonant of the melody with the C slot of the affix. Left-to-right association then produces the correct *c'uk^{w}uk^{w}s*. However, a language-specific stipulation of association is obviated if association is template-driven. This is illustrated in (19).

(19)

$$c'\ u\ k^w\ s \quad \xrightarrow{\ I\ } \quad c'\ u\ k^w \qquad s \quad \xrightarrow{\ PC\ } \quad c'\ u\ k^w \qquad s$$

$$C\ VC\ C \qquad\qquad C\ VC\ +\ VC\ +\ C \qquad\qquad C\ VC\ +\ VC\ +\ C$$

$$c'uk^w s$$

$$\xrightarrow[\text{L-R}]{\ A\ } \quad \begin{array}{c} c'\ u\ k^w \qquad s \\ |\ |\ |\ \qquad | \\ C\ VC\ +\ VC\ +\ C \\ |\ | \\ c'\ u\ k^w\ s \end{array} = c'uk^w uk^w s$$

In (19), after the reduplicative VC morpheme has been infixed and the phoneme melody copied, association takes place starting with the V slot of the reduplicative affix which links up to the /u/ of the copied melody; the following C slot links to /k^w/. No language-specific stipulation is needed.

2.3 Takelma

A third case in which template-driven association obviates the need for a language-specific stipulation is frequentive reduplication in the Penutian language Takelma. The frequentive form of a verb is formed by infixing a VC affix after the second C slot of the stem, with left-to-right association subsequently taking place between the copied melody and the VC affix. If association is melody driven, an incorrect output is produced. This can be seen in (20) where *hemg* 'take out' incorrectly reduplicates as **hemhg* instead of *hememg* 'take out (freq).'

(20)

$$h\ e\ m\ g \quad \xrightarrow{\ I\ } \quad h\ e\ m \qquad g \quad \xrightarrow{\ PC\ } \quad h\ e\ m \qquad g$$

$$CVCC \qquad\qquad CVC\ +\ VC\ +\ C \qquad\qquad CVC\ +\ VC\ +\ C$$

$$hemg$$

$$\xrightarrow[\text{L-R}]{\ A\ } \quad \begin{array}{c} h\ e\ m \qquad g \\ |\ |\ |\ \qquad | \\ CVC\ +\ VC\ +\ C \\ | \\ hemg \end{array} = {}^*hemhg$$

In the above example, when left-to-right (phoneme-driven) association takes place, the /h/ of the copied melody links to the C slot of the reduplicative affix. The vowel of the copied melody /e/ cannot associate due to the constraint against crossing association lines; thus, the output is the incorrect *hemhg*. Consequently, B&M, for their analysis of Takelma IR, are again forced (as with Lushootseed) to posit a language-specific stipulation that links the final vowel of the copied melody to the first V slot of the reduplicative affix, as seen in (21).

(21)
$$
\begin{array}{ccc}
h\,e\,m & & g \\
|\ |\ | & & | \\
\text{CVC} + & \text{VC} + & \text{C} \\
& | & \\
& hemg &
\end{array}
$$

Normal left-to-right association then produces the correct frequentive form *hememg*. If, though, association for IR is template driven, there is no need for a language-specific stipulation. This is illustrated in (22).

(22)
$$
\begin{array}{c}
h\,e\,m\,g \\
|\ |\ |\ | \\
\text{CVCC}
\end{array}
\xrightarrow{\text{I}}
\begin{array}{ccc}
h\,e\,m & & g \\
|\ |\ | & & | \\
\text{CVC} + & \text{VC} + & \text{C}
\end{array}
\xrightarrow{\text{PC}}
\begin{array}{ccc}
h\,e\,m & & g \\
|\ |\ | & & | \\
\text{CVC} + & \text{VC} + & \text{C}
\end{array}
$$

hemg

$$
\xrightarrow[\text{L-R}]{\text{A}}
\begin{array}{ccc}
h\,e\,m & & g \\
|\ |\ | & & | \\
\text{CVC} + & \text{VC} + & \text{C} \\
& |\ | & \\
& h\,e\,mg &
\end{array}
= hememg
$$

Again, we see that template-driven association for IR obviates the need for any language-specific stipulation.[4]

2.4 Conclusion

In the preceding subsections I have shown that the cases of IR from Washo, Lushootseed, and Takelma, which are problematic under B&M's analysis, are not at all problemtaic under the proposal made here that association for internal reduplication is template driven. Not only can template-driven reduplication handle the so-called problematic cases of IR, but it is also compatible with all other cases of IR considered by B&M, plus additional cases they did not consider. For example, B&M's Temiar IR example shown in (6) can just as well be analyzed with template-driven association as with phoneme-driven association. Additional cases of IR they did not discuss, though, can only be analyzed with template-driven association. Consider IR in Agta, a language of the Philippines. According to Healey (1960), Agta has a type of IR for

---

[4]Clements (1985) independently notes that, if Takelma reduplication is template driven, there would be no need for a language-specific stipulation on association.

diminutives where the first VC sequence of a word (in which the vowel is [+high]) reduplicates immediately following the VC sequence (with the reduplicated vowel being [−high]). Thus, for example, *hutug* 'bow' reduplicates as *hut-ot-ug*, and *gilat* 'barbed steel arrowhead' reduplicates as *gil-el-at*. We analyze these as in (23) and (24) with the V slot of the reduplicative affix being preassociated to the feature [−high], and, as proposed, with the use of template-driven association.

(23)

$$\begin{array}{ccccc} \underset{\text{CVCVC}}{h\,u\,t\,u\,g} & \xrightarrow{\text{I}} & \underset{\text{CVC}}{h\,u\,t} + \underset{\text{VC}}{\overset{-H}{u\,g}} + \underset{\text{VC}}{u\,g} & \xrightarrow{\text{PC}} & \underset{\text{CVC}}{h\,u\,t} + \underset{\text{VC}}{\overset{-H}{u\,g}} + \underset{\text{VC}}{u\,g} \end{array}$$

hutug

$$\xrightarrow[\text{L-R}]{\text{A}} \quad \underset{\text{CVC}}{h\,u\,t} + \underset{\text{VC}}{\overset{-H}{u\,g}} + \underset{\text{VC}}{u\,g} \;=\; \textit{hutotug}$$

$$hu\,t\,ug$$

(24)

$$\begin{array}{ccccc} \underset{\text{CVCVC}}{g\,i\,l\,a\,t} & \xrightarrow{\text{I}} & \underset{\text{CVC}}{g\,i\,l} + \underset{\text{VC}}{\overset{-H}{a\,t}} + \underset{\text{VC}}{a\,t} & \xrightarrow{\text{PC}} & \underset{\text{CVC}}{g\,i\,l} + \underset{\text{VC}}{\overset{-H}{a\,t}} + \underset{\text{VC}}{a\,t} \end{array}$$

gilat

$$\xrightarrow[\text{L-R}]{\text{A}} \quad \underset{\text{CVC}}{g\,i\,l} + \underset{\text{VC}}{\overset{-H}{a\,t}} + \underset{\text{VC}}{a\,t} \;=\; \textit{gilelat}$$

$$gi\,l\,at$$

Agta IR cannot be analyzed using phoneme-driven association unless some ad hoc stipulation is made such as in (25), where the correct *hut-ot-ug* is derived using phoneme-driven association by marking the first consonant extrametrical.

(25)

$$\begin{array}{ccccc} \underset{\text{C VCVC}}{(h)u\,t\,u\,g} & \xrightarrow{\text{I}} & \underset{\text{C VC}}{(h)u\,t} + \underset{\text{VC}}{\overset{-H}{u\,g}} + \underset{\text{VC}}{u\,g} & \xrightarrow{\text{PC}} & \underset{\text{C VC}}{(h)u\,t} + \underset{\text{VC}}{\overset{-H}{u\,g}} + \underset{\text{VC}}{u\,g} \end{array}$$

utug

$$\xrightarrow{\text{A}} \quad \underset{\text{C + VC}}{(h)} \; \underset{}{u\,t} + \underset{\text{VC}}{\overset{-H}{u\,g}} + \underset{\text{VC}}{u\,g} \;=\; \textit{hutotug}$$

$$u\,t\,ug$$

That only template-driven association readily derives all the cases of IR discussed by B&M as well as other cases not discussed by them (such as Agta) without the need for ad hoc stipulations constitutes strong evidence that association for IR is always template driven.

Additional evidence that association for IR is template driven comes from the observation that, in all cases of true IR cited by B&M as well as in all other cases known to the author, the C slots and V slots of the reduplicative affix are always associated with some element on the copied phoneme tier. In fact, B&M always propose language-specific stipulations when normal phoneme-driven association would leave a C slot or a V slot of the reduplicative affix unassociated. Thus, it seems that all C slots and V slots of reduplicative affixes in IR have to be associated. In prefixing and suffixing reduplication, on the other hand, it is not unknown for C slots and V slots of the reduplicative affix to be left unassociated (and subsequently deleted). The most reasonable explanation of why the C slots and V slots of the reduplicative affix are never left unassociated in IR is that association in IR is template driven.

3. An Argument for the Marantzian Account of IR

In Section 2, I showed that IR can be readily handled in a Marantzian framework under the proposal that association for IR is template-driven. Adopting this proposal makes the Marantzian account of IR equivalent to that of Clements's account (discussed in Section 1) in the sense that, for example, both can handle Lushootseed IR without positing ad hoc stipulations (compare Clements's derivation for $c'uk^wuk^ws$ in (10) with a Marantzian account of it in (19) which incorporates template-driven association).

In this section I argue that the Marantzian account of IR proposed in Section 2 is, in fact, superior to Clements's account of IR. The argument comes from a type of IR that can be handled quite easily in a Marantzian framework but cannot be handled (or only handled with ad hoc stipulations) in Clements's framework. These are cases of IR where (in Marantzian terminology) the reduplicative template is filled partly by autosegmental spreading and partly by phoneme copying with subsequent association. Specifically, the analysis of plural reduplication in the Chadic language Hausa as well as in the Australian language Mangarayi are considered. That reduplication in these languages can be readily analyzed in a Marantzian framework but not in Clements's framework is taken as strong evidence to prefer a Marantzian account of IR over that of Clements's.[5]

3.1 Hausa

Hausa, a Chadic language of West Africa, has many ways of forming plurals, one of which is by suffixing either *-unaa*, *-uwaa*, or *-ukaa* to the nominal root

---

[5] We leave for future research the scrutiny of Clements's other arguments (besides the IR argument) for his framework.

(Newman, 1972, shows that the choice is phonologically governed). These are referred to as Class 2 plurals by Kraft and Kraft (1973). Sample data (from Kraft and Kraft, 1973; Leben, 1977; Newman, 1972) are given in (26) (tones are not indicated; the nominal root is indicated in parentheses).

(26)   Hausa Class 2 plurals
      a. *baaki* (*bak*)   *baakunaa*   mouth
      b. *tuduu* (*tud*)   *tuddunaa*   high ground
      c. *kwaayaa* (*kway*)   *kwaayukaa*   kernel
      d. *hannuu* (*han*)   *hannuwaa*   arm

Some nouns that have Class 2 plurals also possess a reduplicative plural that is derived from the Class 2 plural. The location of the reduplicative affix is between the nominal stem and the plural suffix. In (27) I show the plurals of (26a) and (26b). The reduplicated part is in boldface.

(27)   a. *baakunaa* ⟶ *baaku**nk**unaa* mouths
      b. *tuddunaa* ⟶ *tudu**nd**unaa* high ground

As can be seen, what is reduplicated comes in part from the stem (*k* in (27a) and *d* in (27b)) and in part from the suffix *unaa*.

In addition to the Class 2 plurals like those in (27) that have optional variants, there are some Class 2 nouns that only have the reduplicative plural. These, though, are clearly derived from an intermediate form [similar to those on the right side in (26)]. Some examples are given in (28).

(28)   a. /jakunaa/ ⟶ *jaku**nk**unaa*   bags
      b. /batukaa/ ⟶ *batu**kt**ukaa* [*batu**tt**ukaa*] matter
      c. /garuwaa/ ⟶ *garu**wr**uwaa* [*garu**ur**uwaa*] towns

In the left column in (28) the underlying representations are shown. In the output the reduplicated part is in boldface. In (28b) *ukt* is reduplicated, but there is a general velar assimilation rule that assimilates velars to the following consonant; thus, it is realized phonetically as *utt*. In (28c) *uwr* is reduplicated, but the glide becomes a vowel between a vowel and a following consonant; phonetically, it is realized as *uur.*

The Hausa reduplicative affixes (in boldface in (27) and (28)) can best be understood as interfixes. Interfixes are empty morphemes placed between a stem and a suffix. Dressler (1985) has identified the following characteristics of interfixes: They do not add any meaning to the word; they usually begin with a vowel followed by one or two consonants (i.e., a rhyme plus an onset); they are often added to shorter stems; and their occurrences can be optional. The Hausa reduplicative affix has all the characteristics of an interfix. It does not add any meaning on its own (e.g., the two forms in (27a) have identical meanings). A VCC sequence occurs between the stem and the root. The stems that do have the reduplicative affix seem to be shorter (at least for Class 2 nouns): The nouns that show the reduplication have biconsonantal stems, but Class 2 nouns with triconsonantal stems do not seem to form plurals with the reduplicative affix. Finally, its occurrence is sometimes optional and sometimes mandatory. The fact that the Hausa reduplicative affix has the characteristics of an interfix militates against a possible analysis (of Class 2 plurals) whereby a CVC sequence is reduplicated before the final vowel (i.e., whereby the word in (27a), *baakunaa*, has the *kun* reduplicated before the final vowel). The Hausa reduplicative affix can only be understood as an interfix.[6]

Under the Marantzian view of IR proposed in Section 2 which incorporates template-driven association, the Hausa interfixes have a straightforward analysis that involves both phoneme copying and autosegmental spreading. This is shown in (29) for the derivation of *baakunkunaa* from *baakunaa* (in (27a)).[7]

(29)

$$
\begin{array}{llll}
b\ a\ kun\ a & b\ a\ k & un\ a & b\ a\ k \qquad un\ a \\
\text{CVVCVCVV} \xrightarrow{\text{inter-fixing}} \text{CVVC + VCC + VCVV} \xrightarrow{\text{AS}} \text{CVVC + VCC + VCVV}
\end{array}
$$

$$
\xrightarrow{\text{PC}} \begin{array}{ll} b\ a\ k & un\ a \\ \text{CVVC + VCC + VCVV} \end{array} \xrightarrow[\text{R-L}]{\text{A}} \begin{array}{ll} b\ a\ k & un\ a \\ \text{CVVC + VCC + VCVV} \end{array} = baakunkunaa
$$

$$
\underset{bakuna}{\qquad\qquad} \qquad \underset{bakuna}{\qquad\qquad}
$$

In Clements's model of reduplication there is apparently no straightforward way of handling Hausa interfixing reduplication. A partial analysis is shown in (30).

(30)

$$
\begin{array}{lll}
b\ a\ kun\ a & b\ a\ kun\ a & {}^{*}b\ a\ kun\ a \\
\text{CVVCVCVV} \xrightarrow{\text{P}} \text{CVVCVCVV} \xrightarrow{\text{A}} \text{C VVCVCVV} \\
& \underset{\text{VCC}}{\qquad} & \underset{\text{VCC}}{\qquad}
\end{array}
$$

In (30) the problem about how to associate the C slot of the *k* without crossing association lines arises. The problem can only be alleviated by brute force.

---

[6] Hodge (1947) describes Hausa reduplicative plurals using the term STEM EXTENSION. He shows that these occur with several types of plurals besides the Class 2 type. All of these involve some sort of reduplication (usually of a stem consonant). For example, when the suffix *ii* is added to a noun stem to form the plural, sometimes a stem extension (e.g., *a*CC) is added, placed between the stem and the plural suffix *ii*. The example *tooroo* 'bull' (nominal root [toor]) which has the plural *toorarrii* illustrates this. Here the consonant that is reduplicated as part of the stem extension is /r/, the last consonant of the stem. This and other examples of stem extension that Hodge discusses for plurals can be understood as interfixes. The interfix of Class 2 plurals is different only in that its phonemic content comes from both the stem and the plural suffix, whereas the phonemic content of the other plural interfixes (e.g., *a*CC in *toorarrii*) does not come from the suffix.

[7] The analysis of this type of reduplication as given in (29) is somewhat different from the analysis of it given by Halle and Vergnaud (1980). They did not frame their analysis in terms of interfixing. Also, they have reduplication applying when the stem and the plural suffix (*una*) are on separate tiers; in the account in (29), reduplication applies when they are on the same tier. Nothing crucial hinges on this latter difference.

For example, leave the second C slot of the reduplicative parafix unassociated [as in (31)]. Then, transfer the phonemes of the base to the associated portion of the parafix [as in (32)] and sequence only the associated portion of the parafix to the CV tier [as in (33)]. Finally, reapply association, transfer, and sequencing to take care of the stranded C slot of the parafix [as in (34)].

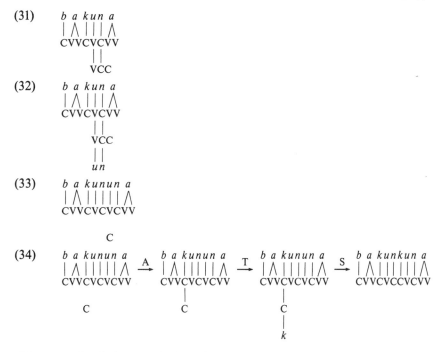

(31)
```
b a kun a
| ∧ | | | ∧
CVVCVCVV
   | |
   VCC
```

(32)
```
b a kun a
| ∧ | | | ∧
CVVCVCVV
   | |
   VCC
   | |
   u n
```

(33)
```
b a kunun a
| ∧ | | | | | ∧
CVVCVCVCVV
```

(34)
```
b a kunun a  A   b a kunun a  T   b a kunun a  S   b a kunkun a
| ∧ | | | | | ∧  →  | ∧ | | | | | ∧  →  | ∧ | | | | | ∧  →  | ∧ | | | | | ∧
CVVCVCVCVV      CVVCVCVCVV      CVVCVCVCVV      CVVCVCCVCVV
                    |               |
    C               C               C
                                    |
                                    k
```

This type of solution no doubt raises more problems than it solves. Other possible forced analyses can be thought up within Clements's framework, but these also would involve special stipulations. Note also that in (34) there is no principled reason why it is the C slot linked to the *k* that associates with the remaining C slot of the parafix. Any of the other C slots could link to the parafix as well. On the analysis of Hausa in the Marantzian account in (29), it is only the *k* that can spread. The other consonants cannot spread. The account in (29), then, is more restrictive than the one in Clements's framework. Thus, Hausa interfixing reduplication provides support for the Marantzian view of IR proposed in Section 2 over that of Clements.

3.2 Mangarayi

Mangarayi plural reduplication can only be analyzed in a Marantzian framework of reduplication that incorporates template-driven association for IR. Neither an analysis of it in Clements's framework nor in a Marantzian framework with only phoneme-driven association can account for the IR pattern of the Mangarayi plural.

According to Merlan (1982, p. 216) one of the plural reduplicative patterns in Mangarayi is the following:

> Nouns minimally of the shape CVCCV..., where the first syllable is closed, and the second not identical to the first, reduplicate by the formula:
>
> $$C_1V_1C_2C_3V_2 \longrightarrow C_1V_1C_2\text{-}C_3V_1C_2\text{-}C_3V_2$$
>
> The reduplicative segment consists of the first consonant after the initial closed syllable, and the vowel and the final consonant of the first syllable.[8]

Sample data are given in (35).

(35) | | | |
|---|---|---|
| *jimgan* | *jim-gim-gan* | knowledgeable people |
| *waŋgij* | *waŋ-gaŋ-gij* | children |
| *gambura* | *gam-bam-bura* | mother's brothers |
| *guryag* | *gur-yur-yag* | (having a lot of) lilies |

The Mangarayi plural reduplication pattern in (35) is readily analyzable in the Marantzian account of IR proposed in Section 2: The CVC reduplicative infix acquires its phonemic content by both autosegmental spreading and phoneme copying (with subsequent template-driven association). The analysis for *gur-yur-yag* is shown in (36).

(36)

Note that if association were phoneme driven instead of template driven, the incorrect **gurygyag* would be derived. This is shown in (37).

---

[8] It is possible to describe the reduplicative affix as $V_1C_2C_3$ infixed after C_3 (instead of $C_3V_1C_2$ infixed after C_2). However, Merlan (personal communication) states that the argument against this is that absolutely no morphemes of any type in Mangarayi begin with vowels, and moreover, the C_2C_3 sequence of a posited $V_1C_2C_3$ affix could be filled by consonants that otherwise do not co-occur in a morpheme-final cluster.

Mangarayi reduplication, as Merlan describes it, is a counterexample to Ter Mors's (1984) claim that in IR the reduplicative template is filled by phonemes that are either to the right of the reduplicative affix or to the left of it, but not by both. The Mangarayi reduplicative pattern is a counterexample because the reduplicative affix is filled by C_3 (to the right of the reduplicative affix) and by C_1C_2 (to the left of the reduplicative affix).

(37)

```
     gu r          y a g
     | | |      ⌐--¬| | |
     CVC + CVC + CVC  =  *gurygyag
            |
          guryag
```

Thus, only template-driven association produces the correct output.

Additionally, Clements's framework of reduplication is unable to account for the above pattern of Mangarayi reduplication. This is seen in (38), where the correct output *gur-yur-yag* can be produced only by illicitly crossing association lines.

(38)

```
guryag   P  guryag   A  guryag   T  guryag   S  guryuryag
||||||  →  ||||||  →  ||||||  →  ||||||  →  |||||||||
CVCCVC      CVCCVC      CVCCVC      CVCCVC      CVCCVCCVC
                        X           X
            CVC         CVC         CVC
                                    |||
                                    yu r
```

Other analyses of Mangarayi internal reduplication without crossing association lines are possible in Clements's framework, but they are complex. For example, the reduplication process can first apply to the VC sequence of the parafix as in (39) and then reapply to the remaining C slot of the parafix as in (40).

(39)

```
guryag   A  guryag   T  guryag   S  gururyag
||||||  →  ||||||  →  ||||||  →  ||||||||
CVCCVC      CVCCVC      CVCCVC      CVCVCCVC
            |||         ||
            CVC         CVC         C
                        ||
                        u r
```

(40)

```
gururyag   A  gururyag   T  gururyag   S  guryuryag
||||||||  →  ||||||||  →  ||||||||  →  |||||||||
CVCVCCVC      CVCVCCVC      CVCVCCVC      CVCCVCCVC
              |             |             |
C             C             C             C
                                          |
                                          y
```

As was in the case in Hausa in (31)–(34), this type of solution is problematic. For example, in (39)–(40) there are essentially two reduplications occurring. In (39), a VC template is parafixed and eventually sequenced at one place on the CV tier. In (40), a C slot template is parafixed and eventually sequenced at a different point along the CV tier. In the proposed Marantzian analysis in (36), there is only one instance of infixation and it occurs only at one point on the CV tier. Hence, the Marantzian account of IR as proposed in Section 2 can handle quite straightforwardly Mangarayi IR as well as the Hausa IR discussed in Section 3.1, while on Clements's account of IR these can be handled only by positing complex stipulations.

In summary, I have argued that the Marantzian theory of IR as proposed in Section 2 is superior to that of Clements. One of Clements's arguments for his theory was that a Marantzian account had to resort to language-specific stipulations on association to handle several cases of IR. However, as I discussed in Section 2, no such stipulations are necessary under the proposal that association for IR is template driven. Furthermore, I demonstrated that the Marantzian analysis of the IR cases in Hausa and Mangarayi are quite straightforward: They involve autosegmental spreading and phoneme copying (the two ways in which reduplicative affixes acquire their phonemic content). Clements's account of these reduplicative patterns must make use of various language-specific stipulations. That reduplication in these two languages has a straightforward analysis in the Marantzian framework of IR proposed here (incorporating template-driven association) but not in Clements's framework is taken as strong evidence for the Marantzian account of IR over that of Clements's.

Acknowledgments

I acknowledge the following people for discussion and comments on various aspects of this chapter: Diana Archangeli, Dawn Bates, Richard Demers, Morris Halle, Richard Janda, Alec Marantz, Francesca Merlan, and Donca Steriade. All errors are my own responsibility. This work was supported in part by NIH Training Grant NS-07134-09 to Indiana University at Bloomington.

References

Broselow, E., and McCarthy, J. (1983). A theory of internal reduplication. *The Linguistic Review* 3, 25–88.

Clements, G. (1985). The problem of transfer in nonlinear phonology. *Cornell Working Papers in Linguistics* 7, 1–36.

Dressler, W. (1985). On the predictiveness of natural morphology. *Journal of Linguistics* 21, 321–337.

Halle, M., and Vergnaud, J.R. (1980). Three dimensional phonology. *Journal of Linguistic Research* 1, 83–105.

Healey, P. (1960). "An Agta Grammar." The Summer Institute of Linguistics, Manila.

Hodge, C. (1947). An outline of Hausa grammar. *Language* 23, (suppl.), (Language Dissertation No. 41).

Kraft, C., and Kraft, M. (1973). "Introductory Hausa." Univ. of California Press, Berkeley.

Leben, W. (1977). Doubling and reduplication in Hausa plurals. *In* "Linguistic Studies Offered to Joseph Greenberg." (A. Juilland, ed.), pp. 419–431. Anma Libri, Saratoga.

Marantz, A. (1982). Re Reduplication. *Lingustic Inquiry* **13**, 435–482.

Merlan, F. (1982). "Mangarayi." North Holland Publ., Amsterdam.

Newman, P. (1972). Syllable weight as a phonological variable. *Studies in African Linguistics* **3**, 301–323.

Steriade, D. (1982). *Greek Prosodies and the Nature of Syllabification.* Unpublished Ph.D. dissertation, MIT, Cambridge, MA.

Ter Mors, C. (1984). Affix to X. *The Linguistic Review* **3**, 275–298.

Chapter 18

Blocking and
the Elsewhere Condition

Gregory K. Iverson & Deirdre W. Wheeler

1. Introduction

Defined on the relationship between morphological and phonological patterning, the theory of lexical phonology explicated by Kiparsky (1982, 1984, 1986) includes certain applicational principles and representational constraints which mirror functionally similar ones developed in earlier versions of generative theory. Thus, a seemingly systematic progression traces Kiparsky's influential alternation condition (1968) from its origins in the abstractness controversy through its generalization as the revised alternation condition (1973b) to, in cyclic and then in lexical phonology, its apparent elimination in favor of—actually, incorporation into—the strict cycle condition (Mascaró, 1976). Current varieties of lexical phonology further assume a special convention known as the Lexical Identity Rule, however, by which lexical entries may themselves constitute "rules." The primary function of this device is to enable exploitation of the elsewhere condition (Kiparsky, 1973a) in order to induce the familiar "blocking" effect among word-formation processes; but it is also construed to serve as a replacement for the strict cycle condition, and to so play a blocking role in the phonology as well by preventing certain rule applications.

We argue here that these moves are phonologically as well as morphologically mistaken. In phonology, retention of the earlier revised alternation condition turns out to be clearly preferable to having the ad hoc Lexical Identity Rule ride on the elsewhere condition, both for empirical and for formal reasons. Under a new, parsimonious interpretation of lexical insertion, moreover, absence of the Lexical Identity Rule in morphology results in no loss of generalization in word formation, either. In both components, the elsewhere condition is freed to function, not as an imposer of disjunction, but as a principle of applicational precedence assignment among rules in a proper inclusion relationship.

2. Phonological Preliminaries

The alternation condition Kiparsky advanced in 1968 placed a rather modest limitation on the abstractness of phonological representation. Doubt over the psychological validity associated with the diacritic use of phonological features called into question rules and analyses involving unrecoverable merger, or absolute neutralization, and the alternation condition eliminated these through the simple measure of prohibiting morphophonemically invariant morphemes from undergoing any rules of phonological neutralization. This resulted in essential identity between remote and superficial representation for such morphemes as English *right*, whose conservative spelling might suggest an underlying voiceless velar fricative but whose pronunciation is phonemically constant whatever the morphological context. Given the alternation condition, therefore, no /x/ could be posited to underlie *right* in present English—even if there is some indirect motivation for it (Chomsky and Halle, 1968)—because the segment's ultimate elimination would have to be accomplished via a prohibited context-free neutralization rule that deletes /x/ everywhere. Following Kiparsky (1982, p. 148), the alternation condition then can be defined as a negative constraint on rule application ("Obligatory neutralization rules cannot apply to all occurrences of a morpheme"), one "concretizing" effect of which is to prohibit rules of absolute neutralization.

In its 1973 revision (per Kiparsky, 1982, p. 152), the constraint is conversely formulated as a limitation on rule application to the effect that "Obligatory neutralization rules apply only in derived environments" (revised alternation condition (RAC)). Since a derived environment is one which satisfies a rule's structural description by virtue either of a relevant morphological operation or because of the crucial prior application of a phonological rule, the RAC also excludes (most) absolute neutralization analyses. In the derivation of *right* from /rixt/, for example, the environment in which obligatory neutralization of the underlying velar fricative with null would have to take place is not derived in any relevant sense because the source of the rule's input is lexically specified, that is, not created through morpheme combination or through any other phonological operations.

The revision thus imposes essentially the same restrictions on morphophonemic representation as did its predecessor. The RAC does display wider scope with respect to global rules (now largely overlooked, but actually the motivation behind Kiparsky's (1973b) refinement of the original alternation condition), and the earlier version still effects certain limitations (e.g., rejection of 'free rides,' whether in derived environments or not) that quite escape the RAC (Iverson, 1985). In all, however, the RAC basically still serves to preclude analyses incorporating synchronically irrecoverable phonological merger, and thus to limit in presumably psychologically realistic ways the remoteness of morphophonemic representation.

But with the advent of lexical phonology, the RAC was reinterpreted to govern phonological operations only within the individual strata affiliated with morphological operations. English Level 1 affixation, for example, includes familiar nominalizations with *-ity*, and these precipitate the phonological adjustment of Trisyllabic Shortening noted in derivatives like *divinity* (from *divine + ity*). Since Trisyllabic Shortening does not take place either in Level 2 derivation (*blindingly*) or in basic lexical entries (*nightingale*), affiliation of the rule with Level 1 morphological processes, and no others, expresses its appropriate domain. In lexical phonology, this association is made possible by adoption of the strict cycle condition (SCC), which restricts structure—changing, or neutralizing, applications of a rule just to forms which are derived in the level (cycle) to which the rule is assigned. The identification of Trisyllabic Shortening as a Level 1 rule thus correctly blocks its application both in underived lexical terms and in the products of the lower-order morphological strata.

The SCC is obviously RAC-like in preventing neutralizing rule application to lexically basic representations of the *nightingale* sort, but it is even more restrictive with respect to its exclusionary effects on the subsequent morphological strata which produce, without shortening, structures like *blindingly*. In such cases, where the phonologically neutralizing operation obtains only over a single morphological stratum, the RAC is simply redundant and, as has been argued (Mascaró, 1976; Kiparsky, 1982), could be replaced by the SCC. But this replacement would freely sanction unrestricted neutralization in the postlexical component, which is postcyclic and therefore immune to the SCC. These consequences are more fully explored by Iverson (1985), where it is argued that certain kinds of phonological rule application clearly call for retention of the RAC even within a theory employing the SCC.

One of these involves structure-changing rules, like English Velar Softening, which apply to the products of two or more morphological strata. Kiparsky (1982) and Halle and Mohanan (1985) maintain that such rules are not cyclic (i.e., are either postlexical or members of a noncyclic stratum), and hence are free to apply to both derived and basic structures. This relaxation permits Velar Softening to take place in Level 1 morphological configurations (*electricity*) as well as in Level 2 derivations (*criticize*), but it comes at the absurd price of tolerating underlying hard velars for the invariantly soft initials in *city, cent, cycle,* or even *sea, sin, seven,* while characterizing as lexically exceptional the masses of underived velars which actually are hard stops, as in *kitty, Kent, key, kin, chi.* Contra Kiparsky (1982, p. 153), such marginally /k/-like behavior as seen in the -*cede* fragment of *accede* (apparent place and manner assimilation in the prefix, cf. *afford*) is almost certainly synchronically irrelevant, and it remains an embarrassment to the theory of lexical phonology to have to either repeat or immunize against the SCC any rule operative in more than one morphological stratum.

However, a modification to the theory Kiparsky (1984) himself proposed—though designed to accomodate other phenomena—turns out to alleviate the particular problem with Velar Softening. Rather than organize phonological rules into strata paralleling those of the morphology, the modification instead groups all of the lexical phonological rules together (as in precyclic varieties of generative phonology), but subjects them to the strong domain hypothesis (SDH):

> The grammar may stipulate merely where a rule *ceases* to apply. According to this hypothesis all rules are potentially applicable at the first level of the lexicon, and apply there provided only that the principles of grammar permit it; at lower levels of the lexicon and in the postlexical phonology rules may be "turned off" but no new ones may be added. (p. 142)

The appropriate effect on Velar Softening, now included (as a lexical rule) in the new single stratum of lexical phonological rules, is to have it apply in Level 1 and Level 2 morphological configurations, but nowhere else. The SDH permits exactly this range of applicability for Velar Softening, provided it is identified as a lexical rule rather than, as above, a postlexical or otherwise noncyclic rule. This means that the rule is also subject to the SCC, of course, but with application restricted to derived forms irrespective of the level (1,2) on which they were produced. The necessary restrictions, it turns out, are also fully consistent with the RAC, which would have imposed them in the first place had it not been thought to have been replaced by the SCC.

Another kind of circumstance which advocates retention of the RAC consists in the existence of single rules with both neutralizing and allophonic consequences, but where the former take place only in derived environments while the latter occur accross-the-board. Iverson (1985) presents Korean palatalization as an illustration of such a rule, where /t/ merges with its affricated alveopalatal counterpart /c/ before /i/ in the next morpheme (/mat + i/ → /mac + i/ 'the eldest,' /tot + i/ → /toc + i/ '(sun)rise'), but **only** in the next morpheme (cf. monomorphemic /mati/ 'knot'/, /canti/ 'grass'); /s/, on the other hand, palatalizes to [ʃ] before /i/ both between (/os + i/ → [oʃi] 'cloth'-subj) and within morphemes (/si/ → [ʃi] 'poem'). The applicational difference here correlates exactly with the fact that Korean shows phonemic contrasts between /t/ and /c/, but has [ʃ] only as an allophone of /s/. With the RAC still governing all the rules of lexical phonology, including the postlexical ones, a single palatalization rule for Korean can be proposed whose neutralizing effects are automatically constrained to derived environments, but whose allophonic effects are correctly produced in all phonetically relevant structures. Without the RAC, though, this generalization would have to be split into two unrelated statements: a neutralizing, lexical rule for /t/ subject to the SCC, and an allophonic, postlexical rule for /s/ able to apply freely.

In principle, on the other hand, these facts could be made to hold even without the RAC, but at the expense of lexically specifying the features of palatalization (and of nonpalatalization) in just those environments where their values conflict with the ones imposed by the palatalization rule (e.g., both palatal /c/ and nonpalatal /t/ in /canti/). In other environments, as in those involving palatalization-consistent /. . .ci. . ./ or /. . .ta. . ./ sequences, and all involving /s/, the features of palatalization then would be lexically unspecified, their values to be filled in derivationally by the palatalization rule (/. . .ci. . ./, [. . .ʃi. . .]) or, in nonpalatalizing environments (/. . .ta. . ./, [. . .sa. . .]), as a consequence of unmarked, default, specification. Such judicious manipulation of the feature values, however, would have to be replicated on an ad hoc basis in each case (and in each language) where lexically operative phonological rules are also at play postlexically, a move which, by itself, quite conceals any principle that might govern the choice between complete and partial specification. The RAC, conversely, generalizes over all such cases as these, and therefore would seem to be clearly superior to, taken in isolation, the device of language-particular underspecification.

In contrast to Kiparsky's (1986) identification of postlexical activity among otherwise lexical rules—in which it is similarly proposed that a single rule may be assigned applicability to certain lexical strata as well as to the postlexical level (as perhaps governs the familiar neutralizing (lexical) and allophonic (postlexical) applications of transparent voice assimilation in Russian obstruent clusters)—Korean postlexical palatalization blocks just when its effect would be neutralizing (/t/ $\nrightarrow$ /c/), but applies without constraint otherwise (/s/ $\longrightarrow$ [ʃ]). The obvious restriction here is that, per the RAC, the rule applies freely, lexically and postlexically, up to the prohibited point of effecting neutralization in nonderived environments.

Thus, through the simple measure of retaining the RAC, lexical phonology makes possible unified descriptions of unitary phonological phenomena while still reflecting appropriate conditions on both lexical and postlexical neutralization, all without introducing the complexities of ad hoc underspecification in order to do so. With the extent of a lexical rule's applicability now determined by the SDH, moreover, and with the RAC instead imposing appropriate derived-form restrictions on lexical phonological rules, nothing at all is left for the SCC to do, since its effects are indistinguishable in the present model from those of the RAC. This would seem to hold even despite Kiparsky's (1986, p. 88) insistence

> with all possible emphasis that the SCC is essential to *any* cyclic phonology. . . in order to permit counterfeeding order among cyclic rules. Suppose that A, B are cyclic rules, where B could feed A but in fact does not. We can block feeding on the same cycle by ordering A before B, but only the SCC can prevent the output of B from undergoing A on the *next* cycle.

Aside from the prospect that counterfeeding (and all other) rule interactions might be determined by general principle rather than parochial stipulation (Iverson and Sanders, 1982), it is clear that, where cycle equates with level, the SDH can also induce these counterfeeding effects. Thus, if the above rules A and B are assigned to Level 1, and if A is then "turned off" with respect to all subsequent levels, B will also continue to fail to provide input to (counterfeed) A simply because the applicability of A—per the SDH—will have been terminated entirely. In other cases, of course, the RAC itself carries the function of blocking rule applications in all except crucially derived representations.

3. The Lexical Identity Rule and the Elsewhere Condition

Actually, Kiparsky's conception of lexical phonology (unlike that of Halle and Mohanan, 1985) does not axiomatize the SCC, but rather derives it as a special case of the ELSEWHERE CONDITION, which imposes disjunction on the application of any two rules in which the structural description of one constitutes a proper subset of the other, provided the structural changes of the two are distinct. This principle, or one like it, has figured prominently in phonological discussion for some time (see the detailed survey offered by Janda and Sandoval, 1984), but Kiparsky's innovation consists in exploiting it through assumption of the LEXICAL IDENTITY RULE (LIR) also to achieve the effect of the SCC. The LIR specifies that unmodified lexical entries are themselves rules, so that, in phonology, lexical entries interact with rules just as actual rules do. It is in this way that the SCC reduces to a special case of the elsewhere condition: Now lexically basic *nightingale* is exempted from Trisyllabic Shortening, not because the SCC precludes that cyclic rule from applying to underived forms, but because this particular trisyllabic lexical entry, qua rule, both properly includes the structural description of the general Trisyllabic Shortening rule and imposes a structural change (*nightingale* itself, with the long vowel) distinct from that of the Trisyllabic Shortening rule (short vowel). Of course, the reduction of the SCC to elsewhere condition cum LIR is entirely dependent on the necessity, and sufficiency, of both the elsewhere condition and the LIR. With regard to the latter, little can be said except to point out its clearly ad hoc character. The only function of the LIR is to create rules out of lexical entries so that the elsewhere condition can immunize these against the neutralizing effects of other, actual rules. The LIR is thus hardly independently motivated, but even this rather specific measure can be effective only if the elsewhere condition retains its nominal independent motivation as an imposer of disjunction among (true) rules.

Yet, beginning with Howard (1975), it has been noted that phonological support for the disjunction aspect of the elsewhere condition is virtually nonexistent. In segmental phonology, all of the persuasive cases suggest instead the validity of Sanders's (1974) PROPER INCLUSION PRECEDENCE principle (see also Koutsoudas *et al.*, 1974), which, under elsewhere condition circumstances, specifies applicational **sequence** such that the specific, properly including rule precedes the general, properly included rule. That rules in this kind of structural relationship typically do not both apply to the same representation then is often due just to their bleeding interaction rather than to imposition of disjunction. The few proper-inclusion related rules for which disjunction actually is appropriate, Howard pointed out, all involve "accent" rules, that is, segmental rules of stress assignment. With the advent of metrical phonology, of course, the dependence even of these on disjunctive application disappeared, along with the accent rules themselves, since stress assignment is now metrical.

Nonetheless, the two major metrical rules assigning stress in English still would seem to be constrained by the elsewhere condition's disjunction component. Kiparsky (1982) follows Hayes (1981) in discussion of the English Stress Rule (ESR) and the Strong Retraction Rule (SRR):

> The ESR applies at the right edge of the word, assigning maximally binary feet labeled S W, where W may not be a heavy syllable (not counting "extrametrical" material). The SRR applies iteratively from right to left, also assigning maximally binary feet labeled S W, but without restrictions as to syllable weight (p. 48).

The basic generalization here then is that stress falls on the penultimate syllable unless the final syllable is closed or contains a long vowel. (Apparent exceptions to this pattern are accounted for by assuming that final consonants are extrametrical in verbs and unsuffixed adjectives, and that final rhymes are extrametrical in nouns.)

Applicational precedence of the ESR over the SRR can be seen in the derivation of *illustrate*, the final heavy syllable of which satisfies the requirements of both rules (*F* represents the metrical foot):

(1)

illustrāte ⟶ (ESR) illustrāte ⟶ (SRR) illustrăte

At the right end of the word, where both rules are potentially applicable, invocation of the SRR—which is insensitive to syllable weight—would result in incorrect placement of primary stress on the penultimate syllable. The correct result with ultimate stress derives from application of the ESR instead, which is sensitive to syllable weight (and further restricted to the right edge of words, whereas the SRR freely applies to any string of syllables). Thus, the structural description of the ESR properly includes that of the SRR, and the elsewhere condition imposes disjunction on their mutual application while it assigns precedence to the more specific ESR.

Ultimately, however, Kiparsky (1982, p. 52) trivializes even this exploitation of the elsewhere condition as a determiner of disjunctive rule interaction, for he points out that the ESR and the SRR can be collapsed into a single, suprisingly simple rule (which we refer to as the REVISED ESR): 'Assign maximally binary S W feet from right to left, where W may not branch in environment ____]." If this straightforward interpretation of English stress assignment is adopted, then with it disappears the last relatively good phonological example of disjunctive application imposed by the elsewhere condition. In short, the original ESR is no "rule" at all, but simply a special condition on foot construction at the rightmost edge of the revised ESR's domain of application.

Of course, the elsewhere condition can still function to constrain the revised ESR's application in words with **preexisting** metrical structure, provided the LIR remains in force. Then the elsewhere condition will block structure-changing applications of stress assignment in such nonderived environments as *Attila, Kentucky, Mississippi*, and other irregular forms which cannot have been assigned stress by general rule. (We assume, with Kiparsky, that such apparent exceptions have metrical structure associated with them prior to the application of any regular rules.) The revised ESR could not apply to yield the incorrect antepenultimate stresses illustrated below, therefore, because application of this general rule is preempted by the disjunctive precedence assigned to the LIR (via the elsewhere condition).

(2)

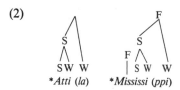

*Atti (la)   *Mississi (ppi)

In derived environments, conversely, the LIR does not come into play. This permits the revised ESR to apply even if it has the effect of changing metrical structure created in prior levels, as in Kiparsky's illustration of the lexical derivation of *paréntal* (Cf. *párent*).

(3)

$$
\begin{array}{ccc}
\overset{\text{F}}{\overset{\wedge}{\underset{\text{S W}}{}}} & \overset{\text{F}}{\overset{\wedge}{\underset{\text{S W}}{}}} & \overset{\text{F} \quad \text{F}}{\underset{\text{S} \quad \text{W}}{\mid \; \wedge}}
\end{array}
$$

parent ⟶ (ESR) *par*(*ent*) ⟶ *parent + al* ⟶ (ESR) *parent*(+ *al*)

But neither the elsewhere condition nor the LIR actually is required in order to achieve these results. The RAC alone, whether defined on structure-changing or on simple neutralizing rule applications, also suffices to permit modification of metrical structure in *paréntal* while preserving it in *Attila*. That is, structure-changing applications of the revised ESR, as with any other rule, are automatically restricted to derived environments under a theory which incorporates the RAC instead of the LIR, and this holds irrespective of the operation of the elsewhere condition. In the phonology, to summarize, retention of the more general RAC not only accomodates both lexical and postlexical phenomena (unlike the SCC), but it also quite invalidates the LIR, a peculiar device which in any case is derivationally distinguished as the only remaining "rule" to require the elsewhere condition's disjunction stipulation. With the RAC displacing both SCC and LIR, the elsewhere condition then reduces to a simple principle of application precedence assignment, as per the proper inclusion precedence principle of Sanders (1974).

4. Morphological Blocking and the Elsewhere Condition

But the elsewhere condition and LIR would seem to play a crucial role in lexical phonology's morphological component, where they are employed to block the derivation of various functionally equivalent forms. Absence of such "regular" words as **foots, *oxes, *keeped, *meeted*, according to Kiparsky (1982, p. 7), follows simply from the obligatoriness of the specific morphological rules which produce the irregular ones (*feet, oxen, kept, met*). Yet the model also must be prevented from generating doubly marked irregulars (**feets, *oxens, *kepted, *metted*), and it is for this purpose that the elsewhere condition and LIR are brought into play. We first sketch how the morphological component of lexical phonology depends on these devices, and then offer an alternative approach which does not.

Kiparsky (1982, p. 6) assumes that affixes (A) are introduced by rules of the form: "Insert A in environment $[Y\_Z]_X$" (where Y,Z correspond to the subcategorization frame of A and X corresponds to its inherent categorial specification). A further basic assumption of lexical theory is that derivational and inflectional processes are organized into a series of levels, the ordering of which correlates with the ordering of morphological processes in word formation, as schematized below (Kiparsky, 1982, p. 4). In English, irregular inflection and "+"-boundary derivation are Level 1 processes, "#"-boundary derivation and compounding take place at Level 2, and the more general or regular inflectional rules occur in Level 3.

(4)

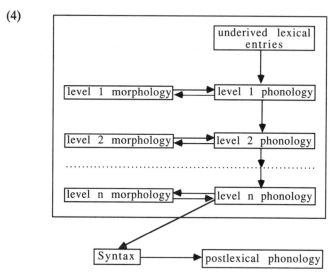

In this model shown in (4), for example, the specific rule deriving the plural *oxen* is an obligatory Level 1 rule: "Insert /en/ in the environment [ox__]$_{Noun,}$ $_{+pl}$." The general rule which accounts for regular plural formation is assigned to Level 3: "Insert /z/ in the environment [X__]$_{Noun, +pl}$." But, organized in this way, nothing prevents *oxen* (derived at Level 1) from serving as input to the regular plural rule to generate the incorrect, doubly marked **oxens*.

Kiparsky's explanation for the absence of forms such as these relies on the assumption that the output of each stage of word formation is itself a lexical item. So, at Level 3 when the regular plural rule applies, the relevant Level 1 output, namely "[oxen]$_{Noun, +pl}$," will be treated as a rule. Since the structural description of this instantiation of the LIR properly includes the structural description of the regular plural formation rule ("[X__]$_{Noun, +pl}$"), and the outputs [oxen] and [oxens] are distinct, the elsewhere condition imposes disjunction on their application and assigns precedence to the LIR, which blocks derivation of **oxens*. The same sort of account can be offered for why inherently plural nouns like *cattle* and *people* do not receive an overt affix, and why zero-derived deverbal nouns like *spy* and *guide* block application of the otherwise productive Level 3 rule which suffixes *-er* to verbs in derivation of ordinary agentives. In the case of *spy*, for example, the structural description of the LIR ([spy]$_{Noun, +agent}$) properly includes and is therefore disjunctive with respect to the general rule (inserting *er* in the environment [V__]$_{Noun, +agent}$).

In each of these instances, though, the generalization is simply that availability of a form with the appropriate syntactic (and/or semantic) features, either as a basic lexical entry or through derivation at an earlier level, blocks generation of any alternate form. Kiparsky indirectly achieves this result through the LIR and its disjunctive interaction with other rules imposed by the elsewhere condition. Yet the reason the derivation of words like *oxens*, *peoples*, and *spier* has to be blocked in the first place is just that the theory requires the output of an earlier level to pass through all subsequent levels of morphological derivation.

But what if lexical entries were not automatically cycled through all levels of the morphology, but rather allowed to feed into the syntax directly as they are formed? With the syntax sensitive to lexical-category specification anyway (including [transitive], [agent], [person], [number], as well as major class features), the process of lexical insertion would involve filling feature frames such as those in (5) with matching lexical items.

(5)   [ ]Noun, +pl   [ ]Noun, +agent   [ ]Verb, +transitive

The function of the morphology, on this view, is simply to derive appropriate forms not found among the set of basic lexical entries. Once a form is derived with the relevant category features, however, it becomes a candidate for lexical insertion. That is, word-formation rules apply only to the extent necessary in order to satisfy syntactic requirements, with the result that the lexicon may be exited either directly or from any of the morphological levels.

In deriving the plural of *ox*, for example, the Level 1 rule will apply to yield *oxen* since there is no corresponding basic lexical entry that matches the syntactic category features [Noun, +pl]. At this point, the derivation terminates, and lexical insertion may take place. With respect to the plural form of regular nouns (e.g., *dog*), on the other hand, both Level 1 and Level 2 rules are scanned, but it is not until Level 3 that a matching form ("[dogs]Nouns, +pl") is produced. Conversely, inherently plural nouns (*cattle*, *people*), which already have the feature [+pl], are available for lexical insertion directly.

A final question remains concerning the status of the representations which serve as input to the rules of morphology, since these must not be construed as lexical items themselves. For example, following Kiparsky (1982, p. 6), uninflected nouns are freely inserted into empty frames such as "[ ]Noun, +pl," which in turn condition the application of appropriate morphological rules to introduce plural affixes. But this means that inherently plural lexical entries such as "[cattle]Noun, +pl" will be formally indistinguishable from inserted input representations like "[ox]Noun, +pl," the first stage in the derivation of *oxen*. Thus, if the LIR is responsible for blocking *cattles* at Level 3, then it also would prevent application of the particular morphological rule pluralizing *ox* at Level 1, thereby inappropriately blocking the derivation of *oxen*.

Under the proposals advanced here (which do not assume the LIR in any case), problematic input representations like "[ox]$_{Noun, +pl}$" can be eliminated from the theory by the simple measure of introducing stems into morphological feature frames which already contain appropriate affixes. For example, the rule forming the plural of *ox* would be (6).

(6)   Insert [ox]$_{Noun}$ in the environment [__en]$_{Noun, +pl}$

This more straightforward kind of rule, which easily generalizes to other cases, vitiates the otherwise-unmotivated convention of introducing stems into empty inflection frames like "[   ]$_{Noun, +pl}$."

Within the derivational morphology, furthermore, the formulation of word-formation rules in the fashion proposed here clarifies how the application of specific processes blocks that of general ones when lexical insertion must take place relatively late. To return to the deverbal noun *spy*, for instance, the specific, Level 1 rule of zero-derivation would be (7).

(7)   Insert [spy]$_{Verb}$ in the environment [____]$_{Noun, +agent}$

The general, Level 2 rule for creation of ordinary agentive nouns, on the other hand, would take the form of (8).

(8)   Insert [. . .]$_{Verb}$ in the environment [____er]$_{Noun, +agent}$

Once [spy]$_{Noun, +agent}$ (via [[spy]$_{Verb}$]$_{Noun, +agent}$) is created at Level 1, of course, it becomes a candidate for direct lexical insertion in satisfaction of matching syntactic requirements. But if, as brought to our attention by Michael Hammond, the syntax instead requires the agentive noun it calls for to appear in the plural, even zero-derived *spy* must continue its morphological derivation through to the rules of inflection at Level 3. This means that it must also pass through the derivational processes of Level 2, where it would seem that *spy* derived at Level 1 should remain subject to the general agentive noun-formation process at Level 2 (producing intermediate *spier*), so as to result finally in the doubly marked plural *spiers*. That is, unless lexical exit is immediate for forms which undergo early, specific derivational processes, it would appear that nothing will prevent them from also passing through later levels which present much more general operations.

Nonetheless, "blocking" remains in effect for cases like these too, even without appeal to the elsewhere condition. This is because of the bleeding interaction that obtains between specific and general processes which serve the same morphological function. That is, conversion of the verb *spy* into the noun *spy* effectively blocks the further introduction of this term into the regular agentive noun-formation process, because that process requires a verb as its input and *spy* has already become a noun in this particular derivation. That the plural, then, is *spies* rather than *spiers* is due to the fact that, qua noun, *spy* at Level 2 does not satisfy the structural requirements of the rule affixing *-er* to verbs, and this precludes the production of intermediate **spier*. In fact, it will be the case generally in derivational morphology that the specific process blocks the general one simply by virtue of bleeding it. Whenever early lexical exit is not possible, in other words, the part-of-speech-changing function of prior derivational operations effects the blocking of subsequent ones when these stand in service of the same grammatical function.

5. Conclusion

Modification of the theory such that lexical insertion occurs just as syntactically appropriate forms are derived explains the absence of doubly marked forms in inflection—without appeal to the elsewhere condition or to the LIR—and the bleeding which characterizes the interaction of functionally equivalent derivational processes accounts for their mutual exclusivity when multiple levels are involved in a word's derivation. Morphological blocking, on this view, is a direct consequence of the natural assumption that word-formation rules apply only when producing structures in satisfaction of explicit syntactic requirements, and that they do so as parsimoniously as service of this function will allow. In a similar vein, phonological blocking derives neither from the elsewhere condition nor the LIR, but rather is a consequence of the RAC-imposed restriction of structure-changing rule applications to derived representations. The general preclusion of redundant morphological structures thus does not equate with the preemption of certain morpheme-internal phonological rule applications. Instead, following tradition, the blocking phenomenon per se is properly characterized as a feature of word formation alone.

References

Chomsky, N., and Halle, M. (1968). "The Sound Pattern of English." Harper, New York.

Halle, M., and Mohanan, K.P. (1985). Segmental phonology of Modern English. *Linguistic Inquiry* **16**, 57–116.

Hayes, B. (1981). *A Metrical Theory of Stress Rules*. Ph.D. dissertation, MIT (1980). Circulated by the Indiana University Linguistic Club, Bloomington.

Howard, I. (1975). Can the 'elsewhere condition' get anywhere? *Language* **51**, 109–127.

Iverson, G.K. (1985). *The Revised Alternation Condition in Lexical Phonology.* Paper presented at the 60th Annual Meeting of the Linguistic Society of America, Seattle, Washington.

Iverson, G., and Sanders, G.A. (1982). On the government of phonological rules by laws. *Studies in Language* **6**, 51–74.

Janda, R., and Sandoval, M. (1984). "'Elsewhere" in Morphology. Circulated by the Indiana University Linguistics Club, Bloomington.

Kiparsky, P. (1968). How Abstract is Phonology? Circulated by the Indiana Linguistics Club. Published as a section of "Phonological Representations" in "Three Dimensions of Linguistic Theory" (O. Fujimura, ed.), pp. 1–136. TEC, Tokyo.

Kiparsky, P. (1973a). 'Elsewhere' in Phonology. *In* "A Festschrift for Morris Halle" (S.R. Anderson and P. Kiparsky, eds.), pp. 93–106. Holt, New York.

Kiparsky, P. (1973b). Abstractness, Opacity, and Global Rules. Published as a section of "Phonological Representations" in "Three Dimensions of Linguistic Theory" (O. Fujimura, ed), pp. 1–136. TEC, Tokyo.

Kiparsky, P. (1982). From cyclic phonology to lexical phonology. *In* "The Structure of Phonological Representations" (H. van der Hulst and Norval Smith, eds.), Part 1, pp. 131–175. Foris, Dordrecht.

Kiparsky, P. (1984). On the lexical phonology of Icelandic. *In* "Nordic Prosody III. Papers from a Symposium" (C. Elert, ed.), pp. 135–164. Almqvist & Wiksell, Stockholm.

Kiparsky, P. (1986). Some consequences of lexical phonology. *Phonology Yearbook* **2**, 85–138.

Koutsoudas, A., Sanders, G., and Noll, C. (1974). The application of phonological rules. *Language* **50**, 1–28.

Mascaró, J. (1976). *Catalan Phonology.* Ph.D. dissertation, MIT. Circulated by the Indiana University Linguistics Club, Bloomington.

Sanders, G. (1974). Precedence relations in language. *Foundations of Language* **11**, 361–400.

Chapter 19

Bidirectional Foot Construction as a Window on Level Ordering

Juliette Levin

1. Introduction

In this chapter we examine several systems of stress assignment which appear to require rules of bidirectional foot construction, arguing that in some cases bidirectionality is a consequence of level ordering within a theory of lexical morphology and phonology (Pesetsky, 1979; Kiparsky, 1982, 1983a, b; Mohanan, 1982; Pulleyblank, 1983), while in others, bidirectional footing is a consequence of a constraint on noniterative footing. Such systems with bidirectional footing appear to necessitate enrichment of Hayes's (1981) original set of general parameters of metrical structure assignment, since at a single level, a foot-construction rule must be specified as going both from right to left, and from left to right. The claim made here is that, given independent motivation for level ordering, such enrichment is unnecessary, since we are able to show that bidirectional foot construction is a consequence of separate footing rules, each applicable at a different stratum or level. One consequence of this hypothesis is that in all cases of bidirectional foot construction, the first rule of foot construction feeds word-tree construction, since the output of each lexical level has word status. We attempt to extend this condition to the output of postlexical footing, where the claim is that the output of a postlexical metrical structure-building rule must be a phonological word as well. Finally, we note how such a condition might result in morphological transparency.

Theoretical Morphology   Copyright © 1988 by Academic Press, Inc.
All rights of reproduction in any form reserved.

2. Bidirectionality

2.1 Iterative Footing: Cahuilla Stress

First, we examine the metrical structure of the Desert and Mountain dialects of Cahuilla, a Uto-Aztecan language spoken in Southern California, within the framework of lexical phonology and morphology. All data are taken from Seiler (1965, 1970, 1977) and Fuchs (1970).

As noted by Seiler (1965), three levels of stress may be distinguished in Cahuilla: primary stress, secondary stress, and no stress. Primary stress falls regularly on the first syllable of the root, with few exceptions.[1] Secondary stress falls regularly on alternating moras both preceding and following the primary word stress, so that the surface stress pattern looks something like that shown in (1), where the boldface mora is the root-initial mora.

(1)

$$\ldots \quad \grave{m} \quad m \quad \grave{m} \quad m \quad \acute{\mathbf{m}} \quad m \quad \grave{m} \quad m \quad \grave{m} \quad \ldots$$

All rime-internal [−consonantal] segments have mora value in Cahuilla, with a maximum of two moras per syllable. That is, long vowels count as bimoraic sequences, as do VG and GV sequences, though a sequence of vowels or vowels and glides cannot count as more than two moras.

We interpret this constraint as an indication that mora count in Cahuilla is a function of nuclear-timing slots, with nuclei limited to at most two non-consonantal elements. That is, the stress-bearing unit in Cahuilla is a skeletal slot immediately dominated by N, the nucleus.[2] Stress-assignment algorithms, whether they involve tree construction or grid alignment, are anchored to skeletal slots immediately dominated by the syllable nucleus.

In (2) we see examples of the alternating stress pattern, where (2a–e) illustrate what appears to be simple left-to-right scansion, and (2f–i) show instances of bidirectional iteration of secondary stresses. The second glottal stop in (2e) is moraic, since it is nucleus internal. The general stress pattern is identical for nouns (2a–e) and verbs (2g–h). The stress pattern in (2i–k) are those generated by Seiler's algorithms, though these examples are taken from Seiler (1970), where only main stress is marked.[3]

(2) a. ná   father
     b. wélnet   mean one

---

[1] Roots with noninitial stress are assumed to have lexically accented syllables. Though such stems are rare, we do find a minimal pair in [néñukum] 'female cousins,' and the lexically accented [neñúkum] 'male cousins' (Seiler, 1965, p. 52).

[2] See Levin (1985) for discussion of the relationship between stress-bearing units, a theory of accent, and syllable structure. In related Southern Paiute, the stress-bearing unit is also the nuclear-timing slot, not the syllable.

[3] Precise glosses are not available for (2i–k).

c. náswetì   smoke tree (obj.)
d. tákalìcem   one-eyed ones
e. táxmu?à?tìh   song (obj.)
f. neyúwl   my younger brother
g. pàpentúleqàlevèh   where I was grinding it
h. cemèynú?inqàlet   he is our leader
i. ?axpè?yuníynèm   (Seiler,1970:43)
j. taxhèmcemáqinwèn   (Seiler,1970:61)
k. pà:mtèvaxáwen   (Seiler,1970:149)

To account for stress patterns in the examples above, we posit the preliminary set of stress rules shown in (3), where, as noted above, terminal elements of feet are not syllables, but rather those timing slots immediately dominated by the syllable nucleus.[4]

(3)   Stress rules   Domain
    A. Build L-dominant binary feet, LR.   Stem + suffixes
    B. Build L-dominant word tree.   Stem + suffixes
    C. Build L-dominant binary feet, RL.   Prefixes + stem + suffixes
    D. Destressing: Prefixes + stem + suffixes
    E. Stray adjunction (foot and word level)

With respect to the rule schema in (3), it is interesting to note that rules A and C are identical structure-building rules with different specifications for directionality. Derivations involving the rule schema in (3) are shown in (4).

(4)
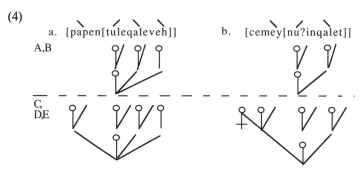

    a. [papen[tuleqaleveh]]   b. [cemey[nu?inqalet]]

Neither within the [stem + suffix] complex, nor at the prefixing level, is there any evidence of cyclic stress assignment. That is to say, regardless of the morphological constituency of strings of suffixes or prefixes, the stress

[4]Reference to tree-based metrical structure (Hayes, 1981; Hammond, 1984), as opposed to grid-based stress or the tree-grid composite of Halle and Vergnaud (1986), is not crucial to this analysis, although, as is seen below, it is more perspicuous in representing uniform headedness of metrical constituents throughout the derivation.

pattern shown in (1) remains constant. An example of ill-formed stress patterns derived from cyclic stress assignment is given in (5), where word-tree construction assigns main stress to the root-initial syllable, and the monosyllabic prefix is subject to destressing.[5]

(5)   hem—[[[[ʔew — lu] — ne] — wen] — eh]
  1st cycle   ʔéwlu
  2nd cycle   né
  3rd cycle   wén
  4th cycle   éh
  Output   *hemʔéwluʔnéwénéh
  Surface   hemʔéwluʔnèwenèh   'they initiated (girls)'

We note at this point that postlexical stress assignment will also fail to derive the correct surface-stress patterns in Cahuilla, since bracket erasure (or the autosegmental analogue, tier-conflation) will have eliminated all word-internal structure, making it impossible to identify the stem-initial mora.

It appears then that the stress rules in (3) are sensitive to particular morphological domains within the word, and that they are neither cyclic nor postlexical. The obvious hypothesis then is that stress rules (3A,B) apply noncyclically within a single lexical domain, call it Level 1, while rules (3C,D) apply noncyclically at the next level, say Level 2. We now turn to phonological and morphological evidence supporting this level-ordered hypothesis.

2.2 Evidence for Lexical domains

There are a number of phonological and morphological phenomena which point to a distinction between the [stem + suffix] domain and the domain of prefixes.

In the realm of phonological rules, Seiler (1977, p. 44) describes a process of vowel alternation, noting that such alternations occur between root or stem and inflectional or derivational suffixes, but never between root and prefix.[6]

Processes infixing or inserting glottal stops in Cahuilla also provide evidence for morphological structure. Infixed glottal stops are those which appear inside a morpheme, while inserted glottal stops appear at morpheme boundaries. These two types of glottal stops are in turn distinguished from "inherent glottal stops," which behave as underlying consonants and do not alternate with zero. Morphemes with underlying or inherent /ʔ/ include /taxmuʔa/ 'song' (2e), /ʔax−/ 'absolutive' (2i), and /ʔew/ 'blood' (5).

---

[5] There are various ways to define destressing in the suffixal cycle for these contrived environments, none of which generates all the correct surface forms. In particular, a form like [[mmm]mm] would never receive stress on the final mora within a cyclic analysis.

[6] Lack of examples is due to present unavailability of this source.

The rule termed GLOTTAL STOP INFIXATION by Seiler optionally inserts a glottal stop within a morpheme, and may only occur in the prefinal morpheme of a word, where this morpheme is within the [stem + suffix] domain. Examples of this are given in (6).

(6) a. [[[kul]vas]em]   *kulvacem* ~ *kulva?cem*
         'cooks'
     b. [[naswet]i]   *nasweti* ~ *naswe?ti*
         'smoke tree (obj)'

Glottalization is usually optional, as shown above, and in certain cases can also be morphologically conditioned. Hence, the objective case suffix /-ih/, the factual–absolute inflectional suffix /-i/, and the preterit /-eh/ regularly exhibit glottal infixation, while other suffixes such as the third person duratives /-qal, -wen/ may never co-occur with such glottal stops. That is, the rule, as formulated in (7), may have a morphological trigger.

The lexical idiosyncrasy of this rule admits to treatment as an early rule of the lexical phonology.[7] Furthermore, its regular limitation to the prefinal morpheme of the [stem + suffix] complex points to a noncyclic level-final application, where by level-final we mean following the application of all cyclic rules on a given level.

(7) GLOTTAL INFIXATION: Level 1; noncyclic (level-final)

$$\begin{array}{c} ? \\ | \\ \emptyset \rightarrow C/V \_\_ C] \ V \end{array}$$

Another process of glottalization is referred to as GLOTTAL INSERTION by Seiler. Insertion involves an optional glottal-stop/zero alternation either before the first suffixal morpheme or after the first prefix.[8] Some examples of this sort are given in (8); the rule of Glottal Insertion is formulated in (9).

(8) a. [pe[[[miisi]ne]qal]]   *pemiisineqal, pemiisi?neqal*
         'he is praying'
     b. [pa[[maylu]qaleve]]   *pamayluqaleve, pa?mayluqaleve*
         'where she was giving birth to'

(9) GLOTTAL INSERTION: Levels 1 and 2, noncyclic (level-initial)

$$\begin{array}{c} ? \\ | \\ \emptyset \rightarrow X/X \_\_ + X \end{array}$$

[7]The inserted glottal stop is meant to be represented on a separate tier to account for the apparent constraint which restricts inserted glottal stops to one per word. See discussion below.

[8]Seiler gives one case where insertion applies to a nonfinal suffix, but no ?/ø alternation is noted there, pointing to a possible additional lexical idiosyncrasy.

Stating this rule as level-initial means that it only has access to the first cycle input and is ordered before all cyclic rules.

While one might expect two or more derived glottal stops in a single word as the result of lexical glottal infixation, productive infixation, and insertion, there can never be more than a single inserted glottal stop per derivation. To account for this curious constraint, we propose that rules of glottal insertion (7) and (9) insert /ʔ/ on a unique tier, which we call the LARYNGEAL TIER. Multiple insertion will result in a violation of the segmental version of the obligatory contour principle (OCP) (see McCarthy, 1986), and is therefore blocked. This account is supported by the fact that vowel features spread over such derived glottal stops, pointing to their nonlinear sequencing with respect to the underlying segmental melody. (See Levin, 1982, for a phonological analysis of this process.)

One further remark is in order with respect to (9). We have used a left or right bracket to denote a morpheme boundary, but given a certain characterization of affixation in Cahuilla, we can assume that this rule applies noncyclically but still obeys the strict cycle condition (SSC), that is, only applies in derived environments. In this way, it will apply after the first instance of Level 1 morphology, and after the first instance of affixation at Level 2, but nowhere else. The SSC here could be a simple consequence of the structure of the lexicon: Forms enter the phonology only after affixation has occurred.[9] Having seen some phonological evidence for two lexical levels, we now turn to aspects of the morphology which point to suffix and prefix levels respectively.

Intensification in Cahuilla is a process affecting modifiers including adjectives and absolute qualities. It indicates an intensification of the quality in question. Of interest to us is the fact that it only affects root-initial sequences of the form CVCV or CVCCV. Intensification is illustrated in (10), and the rule of intensive formation is shown in (11).

(10) | | Nonintensive | | Intensive |
|---|---|---|---|
| | a. | *cexiwen* 'it is clear' | *cexxiwen* 'it is very clear' |
| | b. | *welnet* 'mean one' | *wellnet* 'very mean one' |

(11) INTENSIVE FORMATION (Level 1)

$\emptyset \rightarrow X/[CVC \underline{\quad} \ldots]_{\text{Intensive}}$

The rule in (11) involves infixation of an empty skeletal slot which is filled by spreading of the preceding nonvocalic segmental matrix. Intensive

---

[9]Note that this analysis suggests noncyclic rule application at the beginning and end of each level, level-initial for rule (9), and level-final for rule (7). This is somewhat different from Pulleyblank's (1985) analysis of Dahl's law as an instance of noncyclic rule application both prior and subsequent to affixation, since that rule did not obey the standard version of the SSC, applying in underived environments with effects of a morpheme structure constraint. Further data will most likely allow us to do away with this strange instance of rule application.

formation must precede prefixation in order to identify the correct infixation site.

Distributive formation must also precede prefixation for the same reason. The distributive morpheme involves reduplication of the first CV sequence of the stem. Several stems and their reduplicate forms are listed in (12).[10]

(12)   Stem   Reduplicate
- a. *pax*   *papax*
- b. *lepeqi*   *lelepeqi*
- c. *tumkaw*   *tutumkaw*
- d. *kutas*   *kuktas*   (*<kukutas*)
- e. *ʔiva*   *ʔiʔva*   (*<ʔiʔiva*)

(13) DISTRIBUTIVE FORMATION (Level 1)

     ø → CV/[CV __ ···]Distributive

Whether the underspecified CV distributive morpheme is analyzed as a prefix to the stem or as an infix like the intensive, it must identify the stem-initial morpheme boundary and hence must precede prefixation.

2.3 Synthesis and Hypothesis

Let us now look back at the preliminary set of stress-assignment rules in (3) in an attempt to incorporate them into a morphological model consistent with the facts noted above. Where Level 1 involves the morphological operations of suffixation, intensive formation, and reduplication, Level 2 includes all prefixation. Verbal prefixes include subject- and object-agreement morphemes as well as the absolutive /ʔax-/ and the stem joiner /pe-/. In nouns, possessive markers are prefixed, while case, number, and a variety of derivational morphemes are suffixed. Seiler (1965) does note that there are exceptions to regular stress assignment as observed above, and notes that their treatment "differs from one morphological category (noun) to another (verb)" (p. 52). However, we have found no evidence supporting a bifurcation of nominal and verbal morphology. Given such facts, we propose the revised footing schema in (14).

(14) Cahuilla: Revised footing rules
- A. Build L-dominant binary feet, LR. Level 1
- B. Build L-dominant word tree.   Level 1
- C. Build L-dominant binary feet, RL. Level 2
- D. Destressing
- E. Stray adjunction

With respect to the footing schema in (14), several tentative hypotheses are proposed. First, we suggest that the appearance of word-tree construction

---

[10](12d,e) are derived via syncope, another rule restricted to the root + suffix domain.

after Level 1 footing is a consequence of the assumption stated in (15).

(15)   The output of every cycle is a lexical item.

This assumption is critical to Kiparsky's (1983) derivation of the strict cycle condition, and makes explicit the intuitive notion of morphology as word-based. In Cahuilla, the iterative footing rule is noncyclic, but (15) implies that the output of every lexical level is also a lexical item. So, given a rule which says "construct an L-dominant word-tree," we propose that this rule is automatically ordered after Level 1 footing, since the output of Level 1 is a word, and words are defined (phonologically) by word-level stress. A concrete formalization of this condition follows:

(16)   LEXICAL CONSTRAINT ON WORD STRESS. If a language has word-tree construction, then the output of every lexical level must have word stress.

The second hypothesis, more tentative than the first, is that the lexical division of footing rules is a consequence of the fact that lexical footing must be iterative. Thus, at a given lexical level, a string will always be exhaustively footed, ruling out possible level-internal (or worse, cycle-internal) bidirectionality. We formulate this constraint as in (17).

(17)   LEXICAL CONSTRAINT ON ITERATIVE FOOTING. Noniterative footing is limited to the postlexical component. (Or, alternatively, all lexical footing is iterative.)

Together, (16) and (17) conspire to rule out bidirectional footing in the lexicon. While the existence of something like (16) follows as a natural consequence of (15), (17) is harder to justify. We turn now to evidence bearing on the validity and scope of (16) and (17).

3. Evidence for Lexical Constraints on Footing

3.1 The Lexical Constraint on Word-Stress

The lexical constraint on word stress (16) receives additional support from languages which do not exhibit bidirectional footing, but which do necessitate noncyclic level-ordered footing rules (see Halle and Vergnaud, 1986, for an analysis of cyclic assignment of main stress). In the two cases discussed, an analysis where Level 1 footing feeds word-tree construction is compatible with the surface-stress facts, while it cannot be the case that word-tree construction is absent at Level 1 and present at Level 2 and/or postlexically.

The first case concerns stress assignment in Berguener-Romansh, as analyzed by Kamprath (1986). Stress in this Raeto-Romansh dialect is limited to the last two syllables of the word, and is described as follows:

(18)   Stress Assignment in Berguener-Romansh
    a.   Stress the final syllable if it has a branching rime
    b.   Otherwise stress the penultimate syllable

Of interest to us is the fact that some words have two stressed syllables, while others have only one. For instance, the word [ómín] 'little man,' /om-in/, has stress on both the ultima and penult, while [buntÉt] 'goodness,' /bun-tEd/, has stress only on the ultima. (In words with two stressed syllables, relative prominence is not noted.) Kamprath argues convincingly that those words which have two stresses are just those words which have undergone Level 2 affixation, while those with single stresses are the output of Level 1 morphology, stress being assigned noncyclically level finally. In fact, the absence of cyclic lexical phonological rules, or any other level-ordered phenomenon leaves stress as the sole indicator of morphological levels. The model Kamprath proposes is outlined in Table I.

The stress-assignment algorithm in (18) receives the following representation:[11]

(19)   a.   Accent branching rimes
    b.   Make final (unaccented) rime extrametrical
    c.   Build a right-dominant word tree

Recall that in Cahuilla, word-tree construction did not reapply at Level 2, where only right-to-left foot construction took place. The significant difference between Cahuilla and Berguener-Romansh seems to be that (19c) is the only metrical-structure building rule in the latter, while the former has distinct foot and word-tree level rules. Kamprath's conclusion then that (19) applies at Level 1 and at Level 2 provides independent confirmation of (16), since, in this case, (16) plays no role in delimiting domains of (dissimilar) unidirectional foot construction.

Table I.   The Burguener-Romansh Lexical Component.

	Morphology	Phonology
Level 1	/-uws/ /-det/, /-tEd/, /-egv/, etc.	Stress
Level 2	/-in/, /-Et/, /-un/, /-Eca/, etc.	. . . Stress

[11] Another analysis is conceivable where (19b) is replaced by a foot-level rule: 'Build a single quantity sensitive left-dominant bounded foot at the right-edge'; however, this analysis would run counter to the hypothesis stated in (17). Unfortunately, data on the relative prominence of multiple word-stresses are unavailable.

In Wembawemba (Hercus, 1969), an aboriginal language of southeastern Australia, main stress falls on the first syllable of every word. The distribution of secondary stress is described as follows:[12]

(20) Secondary stress in Wembawemba
  a. In words of three or four syllables, the third syllable bears a secondary stress.
  b. In words of five or more syllables, the fourth syllable has a secondary stress, and again the sixth syllable, ...

From the description in (20), it would appear that two different stress rules are needed, each depending on the number of syllables in the word. This type of stress-assignment algorithm is just the kind made unavailable in a metrical theory of the type proposed by Hayes (1981).

Tomas (1986) shows that the available facts can be accounted for within the general Hayesian framework by assuming that morphological domains play a role in stress assignment. In particular, stress rules operate first on the root domain, and then on the suffix domain. The rules she suggests are as follows:

(21)   Wembawemba stress assignment
  a. Build an unbounded left-dominant foot   (root domain)
  b. Build left-dominant binary feet, L → R   (suffix domain)
  c. Build left-dominant word tree   (postlexical?)

Two representative derivations are given in (22).

(22)

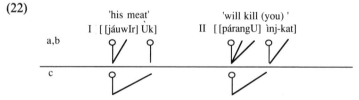

In the available data, no stem longer than three syllables is found, thus it is possible to account for what looks like a difference between initial binary and ternary feet by unbounded foot construction. Given the fact that without a constraint like (16), word-tree construction could be postlexical, this example is surely unconvincing. However, the challenge is to find a language with two levels of foot construction where it is the second level (and not the first) which must be seen as feeding word-tree construction. In other words, we bring up Wembawemba more as negative than positive evidence for (16): It is the absence of systems incompatible with such a hypothesis which is striking.

---

[12]Details of accented and extrametrical vowels have been omitted, as they do not bear on the proposed account. See Hercus (1969) for the full set of facts.

3.2 The Lexical Constraint on Iterative Footing

The constraint proposed to limit noniterative footing to the postlexical component, (17), is one which finds its roots in better-known cases of seeming bidirectional foot construction. Such languages include Piro-Arawakan (Halle and Vergnaud, 1986), Garawa (Hayes, 1981), and Lenakel verbs (Hammond, 1986). In (23) we see a description of Piro stress taken from Matteson (1965) and in (24) a metrical algorithm designed to account for such a stress pattern.

(23) Description of Piro stress

a. Primary stress occurs on the penultima
b. Secondary stress occurs on the initial syllable of all stress groups of four or more syllables.
c. Tertiary stress occurs on all stress groups of six or more syllables. It occurs on the odd syllables, counting from the initial syllable, except that in stress groups with an odd number of syllables, two unstressed syllables precede the primary stress.

(24) Piro stress assignment (postlexical)

a. Build binary L-dominant foot at R-edge (RL; noniterative)
b. Build R-dominant word tree
c. Build binary L-dominant feet L → R (iterative)
d. Build L-dominant cola
e. Destressing : 
f. Stray adjunction

An illustrative example of (24) is given below:

(25)

kàxru : kâkhimânatatkána
'They were joking together then, it is said.'

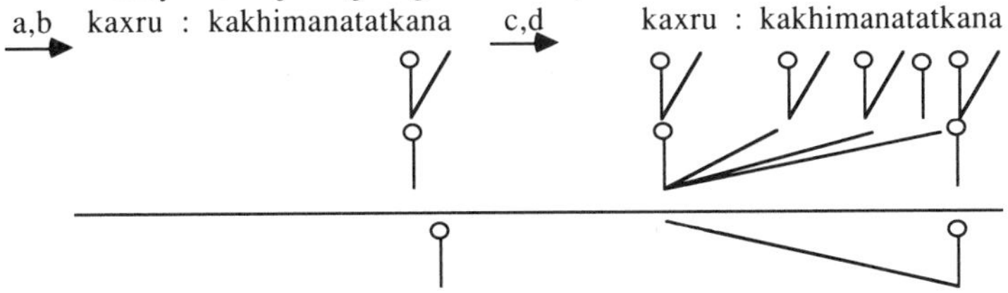

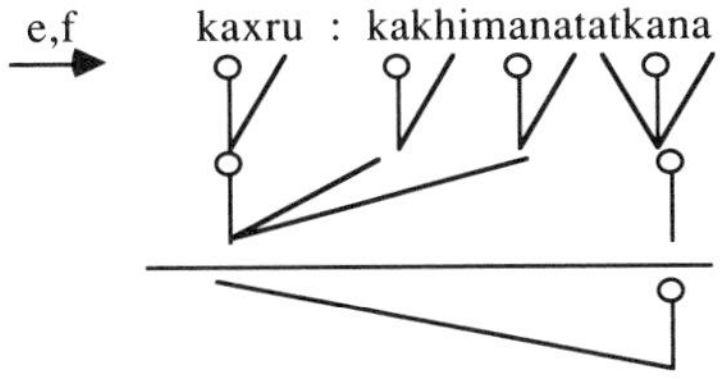

Evidence that footing in Piro is postlexical is of two sorts. First, Piro has both prefixes and suffixes, but prefixes are monoconsonantal and thus could never effect stress assignment. In addition, a set of suffixes regularly trigger a cyclic rule of syncope (Lin, 1986), and vowels deleted by syncope play no role in stress assignment. The earliest stress assignment could apply in the lexicon then would be cycle finally, following all suffixation/syncope. However, Matteson notes that monosyllables are frequently fused with a preceding or following word to form a single stress group. Examples of this process follow:

(26) a. *mámùnkakyanúplu* ~ *màmunkàkyanúplu*
          'in order that he should not tell it'
      b. *howúka yá* ~ *hòwukáya*
          'He went far away.'

The examples in (26) indicate that the footing rules in (24) can (optionally) span word boundaries, providing strong evidence that footing is a postlexical process.

The same argument can be made for stress in Lenakel verbs (Hammond, 1986), and words in Garawa (Furby, 1974). Postlexical stress assignment algorithms for these two languages are given in (27) and (28).[13]

(27) Lenakel verb stress (postlexical)
      a. (Quantity-sensitive OB feet) (see Hammond, 1986)
      b. Build a binary L-dominant foot at the R-edge
      c. Build a R-dominant word tree
      d. Build L-dominant binary feet $L \rightarrow R$
      e. Destressing
      f. Stray adjunction

(28) Garawa stress (postlexical)
      a. Build a binary L-dominant foot at the L-edge
      b. Build a L-dominant word tree
      c. Build L-dominant binary feet $R \rightarrow L$
      d. Destressing
      e. Stray adjunction

In Lenakel, we have further evidence of postlexical footing, similar in nature to the Piro data provided in (26). Lynch (1978, p. 20) notes that monosyllabic objects and possessors which immediately follow verbs and nouns respectively are destressed, with the immediately preceding syllable taking primary stress. Examples are provided in (29).

[13]Lenakel does have both prefixation and suffixation of full syllables, so that it is possible to show that stress assignment could not be either cyclic or level ordered, though see Halle and Vergnaud (1986) for a somewhat more complex account which concerns the details of accent assignment. The details do not alter the content of our proposal. Data on Garawa morphology are scarce, hence we follow others in assuming that the regular pattern described by Furby is generable only through postlexical stress assignment.

(29) a. /r-ám-kIn#nám/   →   /ramkÍnam/
         'He is eating fish.'
     b. /nélu#kÍl/   →   /nelúkIl/
         'the flying-fox's tooth'

Rather than propose an additional destressing rule (which, note, is not conditioned by adjacent stresses), we suggest that, postlexically, such monosyllablic elements form part of the postlexical domain of stress assignment.

Footing in Piro, Lenakel, and Garawa does not violate (17), since in each case noniterative footing occurs postlexically. Stress in these languages also suggests that (16) is truly a consequence of (15), since, even postlexically, the output of the first footing rule appears to feed word-tree construction. If we suppose that the output of every cycle is a word, and postlexically, that the output of every metrical structure-building rule is a "phonological word," then (16) can be revised as (30).

(30) LEXICAL CONSTRAINT ON WORD STRESS (revised). If a language has word-tree construction, then the output of every lexical and postlexical level must have word stress.

4. Concluding Remarks

Finally, several remarks are in order concerning the consequences of (16) and (17). To claim that bidirectional footing can provide a window on leveled ordering is to say that footing can in some cases be a transparent indication of lexical levels within the grammar. That is, if the language learner is exposed to secondary stress iterating out bidirectionally from main stress, then the learner will have the needed information to deduce level ordering within the grammar. Likewise, the existence of a noniterative footing rule, as evidenced by bidirectionality with consistent main stress on the initial or penultimate syllable in the languages exemplified here, would lead the learner to a single unambiguous hypothesis: Stress assignment is postlexical. While many investigations of possible acquisition strategies for monodirectional stress algorithms are underway (Dresher and Kaye, 1986), little work has been done on plausible acquisition strategies of level-ordered phonology and morphology. Clearly, this work is only a first attempt at allowing foot construction to provide a window on lexical organization. Nevertheless, given the relatively early acquisition of stress, and word stress as a salient cue to morphological constituency, this seems a reasonable place to start.

References

Dresher, E., and Kaye, J. (1986). "A Learning Theory for Metrical Phonology." University of Ottawa and University of Quebec at Montreal.

Dyk, W., and Hymes, D. (1956). Stress and accent in Wishram Chinook. *International Journal of American Linguistics* **22**, 3.

Fuchs, A. (1970). *Morphologie des Verbs im Cahuilla. Janua Linguarum, Series Practica* **87**.

Furby, C. (1974). Garawa phonology. *Pacific Linguistics, Series A* No. 37.

Halle, M., and Vergnaud, J.-R. (1986). "Stress and the Cycle." MIT and Tilburg University.

Hammond, M. (1984). *Constraining Metrical Theory: A Modular Theory of Rhythm and Destressing*. Doctoral dissertation, UCLA, revised version distributed by IULC.

Hammond, M. (1986). The obligatory branching parameter in metrical theory. *NLLT* **4**, 185–228.

Hayes, B. (1981). *A Metrical Theory of Stress Rules*. Doctoral dissertation, MIT, Cambridge; revised version distributed by IULC, Bloomington.

Hercus, L.A. (1969). *The Languages of Victoria. Australian Aboriginal Studies* No. 17, *Linguistic Series* No. 6. Australian Institute of Aboriginal Studies, Canberra.

Kamprath, C. (1986). *Syllables, Glides, Stress and the Lexicon in a Raeto-Romansh Dialect: A Case Study in Non-linear Phonology*. Doctoral dissertation, University of Texas at Austin.

Kiparsky, P. (1982). Lexical phonology and morphology. *In* "Linguistics in the Morning Calm." Hanshin, Seoul.

Kiparsky, P. (1983a). "Some Consequences of Lexical Phonology." MIT, Cambridge, MA.

Kiparsky, P. (1983b). On the lexical phonology of Icelandic. *In* "Nordic Prosody III" (C. Elert *et al.*, eds.). University of Umea.

Levin, J. (1982). "Metrical Structure in Cahuilla." MIT, Cambridge, MA.

Levin, J. (1985). *A Metrical Theory of Syllabicity*. Doctoral dissertation, MIT, Cambridge, MA.

Lin, Y.-H (1986). "Aspects of Piro Phonology and Morphology." University of Texas at Austin.

Lynch, J. (1974). Lenakel phonology. *University of Hawaii Working Papers in Linguistics*, **7**, 1.

Lynch, J. (1978). A Grammar of Lenakel. *Pacific Linguistics, Series B*, No. 55. Australian National University, Canberra.

McCarthy, J.J. (1986). "OCP Effects: Gemination and antigemination." *Linguistic Inquiry* **17**, 2:207–264.

Matteson, E. (1965). The Piro (Arawakan) language. *University of California Publications in Linguistics.*

Mohanan, K.P. (1982). *Lexical Phonology*. Doctoral dissertation, MIT, Cambridge, MA (reproduced by IULC, Bloomington).

Pesetsky, D. (1979). "Russian Morphology and Lexical Theory." MIT, Cambridge, MA.

Pulleyblank, D. (1983). *Tone in Lexical Phonology*. Doctoral dissertation, MIT, Cambridge, MA.

Pulleyblank, D. (1985). "Rule Application on a Non-Cyclic Stratum." University of Southern California.

Seiler, H.J. (1965). Accent and morphophonemics in Cahuilla and Uto-Aztecan. *IJAL* **31**, 1.

Seiler, H.J. (1967). Structure and reconstruction in some Uto-Aztecan languages. *IJAL* **33**, 2.

Seiler, H.J. (1970). Cahuilla texts with an introduction. *Language Science Monographs* **6**, *Indiana University Publications.*

Seiler, H.J. (1977). "Cahuilla Grammar." Malki Museum Press, Banning, California.

Tomas, I. (1986). "Stress Patterns in Wembawemba." University of Texas at Austin.

Chapter 20

Tone and the Morphemic Tier Hypothesis

Douglas Pulleyblank

1. Introduction

In McCarthy (1979, 1981, 1982, 1986), Prince (1987), Halle and Vergnaud (1987), and other works, it is proposed that features belonging to distinct morphemes are assigned to distinct autosegmental tiers at the point where morphological concatenation takes place. This proposal—which results in the same feature being assigned simultaneously to more than one tier—is motivated by several considerations. First, the type of morphology attested in a Semitic language like Arabic involves morphemes consisting of solely phonemic material (such as the root *ktb* 'write' and the perfective active marker *a* in (1)) as well as other morphemes consisting solely of skeletal material (such as the CVCCVC template indicating 'causative' in (1)) (subscripts in the example have no theoretical significance, permitting only the identification of morphemes):

(1) [kattab]
    `cause to write´

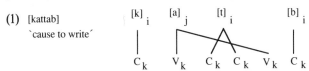

If features of distinct morphemes are represented on a single tier, then a representation such as (1) is required. But (1) is impossible because of the autosegmental crossing constraint (Goldsmith, 1976) which prohibits crossing of association lines:

(2) CROSSING CONSTRAINT: *[F] [G]

McCarthy therefore proposes the morphemic tier hypothesis (MTH), illustrated in (3), according to which the distinct morphemes of such a representation are assigned to distinct tiers, thereby alleviating the problem of crossed association lines:

(3)

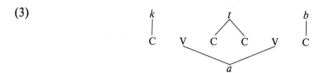

A second motivation for the MTH involves cases such as (4):

(4) [ktatab] $[k]_i$ $[t]_m$ $[a]_j$ $[t]_i$ $[b]_i$
    'write, be registered'

Apart from the fact that the crossing constraint would again be violated if all features appeared on a single tier, such a case poses an additional problem with respect to the correct association of features. The phoneme $[t]_m$ (of the reflexive morpheme) appears in the middle of the root morpheme $[ktb]_i$ as the result of a rule assigning the reflexive *t* to the second C slot in such a word.[1] Given the location of the reflexive *t*, it would be impossible for the root morpheme to be associated by autosegmental conventions if all features were to appear on a single tier, despite the fact that the attested root associations are predictable. If, however, the various morphemes appear on distinct tiers, then association of the root melody can proceed by simple left-to-right convention, skipping the slot occupied by the reflexive morpheme, as in (5):

(5)

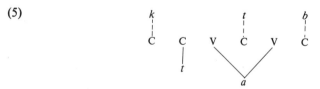

The MTH also solves a second problem involved in cases like (4). Imagine that the problem seen in (1) were solved by assigning the features required underlyingly for vowels to one tier, and the features required underlyingly

[1] A comparable problem is seen with the morpheme *a* in *kattab*. The case in (4) is somewhat different, however, because all phonemes involved are consonants, hence the problems in association could not be resolved by separating out consonants from vowels.

for consonants to another, that is, tiers would be established for phonological rather than morphological reasons [cf. Prince (1987)]. In a case like (4), this would result in (6).

(6)

$$
\begin{array}{ccccc}
k_i & t_m & & t_i & b_i \\
| & | & & | & | \\
C & C & V & C & V & C \\
\end{array}
$$
$$
\underset{a}{\vee}
$$

Such a representation involves at least two problems: (a) there is no straight-forward way of accomplishing associations without invoking rules of transformational power (e.g., of metathesis), and (b) such an approach allows violations of the obligatory contour principle (OCP) (Leben, 1973; Goldsmith, 1976; McCarthy, 1986): In (6), two identical autosegments t occur side-by-side. By assigning the morphemes involved to distinct tiers as in (5), association is straightforward and the OCP is not violated.

Since Goldsmith's original proposal in 1976, there has been abundant evidence in favor of autosegmental representations, that is, representations where phonological features are assigned to (semi-)independent tiers. Although many different types of features have figured in autosegmental discussions, the paradigm case has been tone. This is in marked contrast, however, to the types of features that have figured in discussions of the MTH which has, on the whole, dealt with segmental features. In this chapter, I argue that the MTH explains the behavior of certain tonal phenomena. Two types of arguments in favor of the MTH are presented. First, it is shown that certain properties of tone association follow automatically from the MTH; second, evidence in favor of the OCP is presented, where the MTH is required in order for the OCP analysis to be possible.

2. Initial Association: Evidence from Tiv

2.1 Floating L Tones as Downstep Triggers

Developing on work on Tiv by Arnott (1964, 1968), McCawley (1970), Leben (1973), and Goldsmith (1976), Pulleyblank (1983, 1986) argues that downsteps in Tiv are actually floating low (L) tones, that is, L tones present on the tonal tier but not associated to any vowel segment. Two of the basic arguments for this position are as follows (see Pulleyblank 1986 for additional arguments): First, lowering of high (H) tones by a downstep operator is of the same magnitude as the lowering triggered by a phonetically realized L tone (DOWNDRIFT) (Arnott, 1964). That is, the second H tone of (8b) is lowered by an interval comparable to the second H tone of (7b):

(7) a. *á vé gá*   [‾ ‾ ‾]   'He did not come (recently).'
    b. *á dzà gá*   [‾ _ ‾]   'He did not go.'
(8) a. *á vé*   [‾ ‾]   'He came recently.'
    b. *á ꞌvá*   [‾ ⁻]   'He came.'

Comparison of (7b) and (8b) with (7a) and (8a) shows that the lowering is indeed due to the presence of an L tone in (7b) or a grammatically induced downstep in (8b), since lowering of an H tone does not take place in either (7a) or (8a).

A second argument for analyzing downsteps as floating L tones comes from a consideration of cases where falling tones alternate with an H! pattern (Arnott, 1964, 1968): In phrase-final position, certain copulas are realized with a falling tone, (9a); the same copulas are realized as a H! sequence in nonfinal position (9b).

(9) a. *kásév mbâ*   'There are women.'
    b. *kásév mbáꞌ gá*   'There are not any women.'

The alternations in (9) are straightforwardly accounted for if tonal representations such as in (10) are assumed:

(10) a. kasev   mba
        \ /   ⌐‑‑
         H   H L

     b. kasev   mba   ga
        \ / | |
         H   H L H

To derive (9a), the L of *mba* must link to create a falling contour; to derive (9b), the L of *mba* must phonetically downstep the following H tone.

Additional cases showing alternations between a linked L and a floating L are produced by the application of a productive rule of H spread (Pulleyblank, 1983, 1986):

(11) H SPREAD: V   V
                  ⌐‑‑‑‑‑⌐
                 H   L

As one example of this rule, certain nouns appear in the singular with a L-tone noun-class prefix and in the plural with a H-tone prefix, producing alternations such as the following:

(12)   Singular   Plural
    a. *ikààndé*   *ákáàndé*   'type of shellfish'
    b. *igbìsé*   *ágbíꞌsé*   'type of tube.

In (12a), the application of H spread causes the H of the noun-class prefix to move one syllable to the right, displacing the L that previously occupied that position:[2]

(13)   akaande ⟶ akaande   [ákáàndé]
         │││╱ │   ││╱ │ │
         H L H   H L H

In (12b), the displacement of the L caused by H spread causes the previously linked L tone to float, thereby creating a downstep:

(14)   agbise ⟶ agbise   [ágbí'sé]
         │ ││   │╱ │
         H LH   H LH

2.2 Downstep Deletion

In a certain number of cases, the analysis sketched above generates floating L tones in configurations where no surface downstep results. Consider, for example, the application of H spread in recent past forms such as in (15). (As before, indexed brackets serve merely to identify morphemes for purposes of exposition; X_i, stem (segments + tone); X_j, recent past suffix (tone); X_k, third person plural subject (segments + tone):

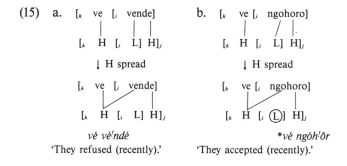

(15) a. [$_k$ ve [$_i$ vende]   b. [$_k$ ve [$_i$ ngohoro]
              │   │ │ │   │   │ ╱ │
          [$_k$ H [$_i$ L] H]$_j$ [$_k$ H [$_i$ L] H]$_j$

          ↓ H spread   ↓ H spread

          [$_k$ ve [$_i$ vende]   [$_k$ ve [$_i$ ngohoro]
                │   │   │ ╱   │
          [$_k$ H [$_i$ L] H]$_j$ [$_k$ H [$_i$ Ⓛ] H]$_j$

          vé vé'ndé   *vé ngóh'ôr
          'They refused (recently).'   'They accepted (recently).'

While H spread correctly generates a downstep in *vé vé'ndé*, it incorrectly generates a downstep in the form **vé ngóh'ôr* (the correct form being

---

[2]In Pulleyblank (1983, 1986) it is argued that the delinking of the L tone is an automatic result of constraints that hold of the lexical derivation of such items. Nothing in the present discussion hinges on this interpretation of H spread, however, and the rule would function correctly if reformulated to include delinking of the L in its structural change.

vé ngóhôr).[3] That is, the circled L tone must be deleted from (15b) to prevent the occurrence of a phonetic downstep.

In a related fashion, one can observe the overgeneration of a downstep in a morphologically triggered case like the following. The future tense marker is the prefix ⁱáⁱ. With a monomoraic verb like *vá* 'to come,' the expected future tense pattern ⁱáⁱ *vá* is attested (as in (16a)); but with a bimoraic (or trimoraic) stem like *úngwa* 'to hear,' the correct form for the future tense is ⁱá *úngwà* instead of the expected *ⁱáⁱ *úngwà* (as in (16b)). Just as in (15b), the circled L tone in (16b) must be deleted.

(16) a.

$$
\begin{array}{ccc}
[_J \quad a & \quad [_i \quad va] & \text{b.} \\
\quad | & \quad | \\
[_J \quad L \quad H \quad L & \quad [_i \quad H] \\
\end{array}
$$

ⁱáⁱ *vá*
'will come'

$$
\begin{array}{c}
[_J \quad a \quad\quad [_i \quad ungwa] \\
\quad | \\
[_J \quad L \quad H \quad Ⓛ \quad [_i \quad H] \\
\end{array}
$$

*ⁱáⁱ *úngwà*
'will hear'

Finally, in the habitual 1 tense, we observe that the initial downstep associated with monomoraic and bimoraic forms (as in (17a)) is absent in trimoraic forms (as in (17b)):

(17) a.

$$
\begin{array}{c}
[_i \quad ungwa] \\
\quad | \quad | \\
[_k L [_i H] \quad H]_J \\
\end{array}
$$

ⁱúngwá
'hear' (Habitual 1)

b.

$$
\begin{array}{c}
[_i \quad yevese] \\
\quad | \\
[_k Ⓛ [_i H] H]_J \\
\end{array}
$$

yévésè
'flee' (Habitual 1)

As with the two previous types of examples, the circled low tone must be deleted.

In Pulleyblank (1986), the deletion of such L tones is accounted for by the following obviously undesirable rule:

(18)   ⁱ-DELETION:
       (rime projection)

$$
Ⓛ \rightarrow \emptyset \ / \_\_\_ \ \begin{array}{c} V \\ | \\ H \end{array} \left(\begin{array}{c} V \\ | \\ H \end{array} \right) \ Ⓥ
$$

Apart from the generally ad hoc nature of this rule, it has the unfortunate feature of requiring specific reference in its structural description to a vowel

---

[3]The final vowel of /ngohoro/ is deleted by a productive postlexical rule that deletes the second vowel in a sequence

$$
\ldots V_i \quad C \quad V_i \ldots \\
\quad\quad [+son]
$$

The L tone set afloat by the application of this vowel-deletion rule then links up by another productive rule (see (9), (10)) to create a falling contour on the final syllable of *ngohor*. For a detailed discussion of both rules, see Pulleyblank (1986), and for an alternative not invoking deletion, see Pulleyblank (1988b).

unspecified for tone. This stipulation is required to prevent *!*-deletion from applying in a case like *!úngwân*, where the representation prior to *!*-deletion is as in (19).[4]

(19)

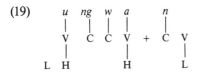

Rules of association and spreading commonly take as their targets only the class of slots that are unspecified for the feature involved. It is uncommon, however, for other sorts of rules to make such reference. That is, rules specifically requiring that segments in contextual positions not be associated with particular features (as (18)) do not commonly appear in the autosegmental literature. To account for the lack of such rules, Archangeli and Pulleyblank (1986) propose to rule out such reference to free slots entirely. It is proposed there that no phonological rule may refer to the absence of a specification, except where the segment concerned is the target of an assimilation or insertion rule. If such a proposal is correct, an alternative to (18) must be found.

2.3 The Morphemic Tier Account

It is shown in this section that the problems inherent in (18) do not arise in an approach adopting the MTH; in fact, under such an approach, no rule of *!*-deletion is required at all. Consider first the future tense cases seen in (16). Assuming both underspecification and the cycle (as argued for in detail in Pulleyblank (1986)), such cases would appear as follows on first the stem cycle and then the prefix cycle:

(20)   a.   b.

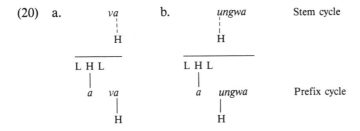

Of importance in such a case is the fact that the second L tone of the prefix is free (unassociated), as is the final vowel of the system. There is nothing

---

[4]As with the case of *ngohor* (footnote 3), the final vowel of the suffix deletes by a general rule of vowel deletion, thereby feeding a rule that creates a final contour. See Pulleyblank (1986) for details.

to prevent application of the universal association conventions, hence the L links up:

(21)

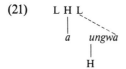

Under such a hypothesis, the "deletion" of the free L tone in the environment of a free-tone-bearing unit is actually the linking of the free tone to the free slot. By eliminating the rule of /-deletion, the need for a rule referring to a nontarget slot as being free is also eliminated.

Habitual 1 cases such as those seen in (17) behave in a comparable fashion. On the stem and suffix cycles, the association conventions assign tones from left to right. When the prefix of the habitual 1 is added, it is able to link in the trimoraic case but cannot link in the bimoraic case.

(22)   a.   b.   Stem and habitual suffix

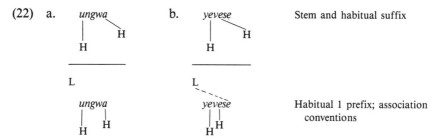

Note, however, that such examples raise a problem with respect to (22a). When all tones are conflated [prior to phonetic implementation, perhaps as a result of bracket erasure/tier conflation (McCarthy, 1986)], the cases in (20), (21), and (22b) are unambiguously represented as (23a–c).

(23)   a.   b.   c.

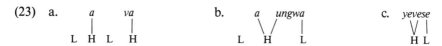

In the derivation of (23a) from (20a), the morpheme /á/ precedes the verb *vá*; consequently, all tones of /á/ precede all tones of *vá* straightforwardly after tier alignment. To derive (23b) from (21), two things must happen. First, the final L of the prefix (now linked to the final vowel of the verb) must follow the initial H of the verb in the post-alignment representation in order to avoid a violation of the Crossing Constraint. Second, the H of the prefix and the H of the verb fuse during alignment to prevent a violation of the Obligatory Contour Principle. I assume that both results are the automatic result of tier conflation. Finally, to derive (23c) from (22b), the L of the Habitual 1 prefix must follow all H-toned vowels again to prevent a Crossing Constraint violation after alignment, and the two H-tones must also fuse again to prevent a violation of the Obligatory Contour Principle. Hence for cases such as these, the order of tones in the post-conflation representation respects the morphosyntactic ordering of morphemes to the extent that neither the Obligatory Contour Principle nor the Crossing Constraint are violated.

Turning to the pre-conflation representation in (22a), however, we observe (1) that the floating L tone is not phonologically ordered with respect to any of the other tones present in the representation (recall that graphic order has no significance given that the relevant tones all appear on distinct tiers), and (2) that there are three possible post-conflation representations that are consistent with the Obligatory Contour Principle and the Crossing Constraint:

(24)   a.   *ungwa*   b.   *ungwa*   c.   *ungwa*
                ＼／   │ │   ＼／
            L   H   H L H   H   L

Note that the problem raised by such forms is a general one for the MTH; it is not specific to this analysis. In any case where affixal material is not associated by convention to skeletal slots, the problem arises as to how such material should be ordered with respect to previously existing material.

The problem can be resolved by adopting a proposal such as (25).

(25)   MORPHOSYNTACTIC ALIGNMENT PRINCIPLE: When the result of a morphosyntactic operation is an unordered tier α, α aligns itself with an existing tier in a manner that preserves the morphosyntactic relation between the morphological elements concerned.

I assume that a tier is unordered if no member of that tier is linked to a skeletal slot. Given the morphosyntactic status of the L tone in (22) as a prefix, the only representation in (24) that is consistent with the morphosyntactic alignment principle is (24a), the correct form.

Note parenthetically that within the framework of lexical phonology, the problem just discussed cannot be solved by simply "lengthening" the brackets of an input representation to keep autosegmental morphemes lined up, as in (26), unless such lengthening is intended as a notation simply for encoding a principle such as the morphosyntactic alignment principle. That is, lengthened boundaries could remind one that, all else being equal, an autosegment's alignment respects morpheme constituency.

(26)

Within a lexical framework, boundary symbols have no formal status. They serve only an expository function in representing on paper the morphological derivation of an item (Mohanan, 1986; Pulleyblank, 1986). As such, boundaries cannot prevent or determine the particular linking of autosegments, and it is noteworthy in this regard that linked autosegments easily cross morpheme "boundaries."

The final cases to be considered are those given in (15), where free L tones arise through the application of H spread. At the end of the stem and recent past cycles, the representation of such cases would be as in (27).

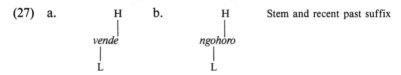

(27) a.   H   b.   H   Stem and recent past suffix

       vende   *ngohoro*

       L   L

The third person plural prefix would then be attached, its H tone linking by convention:

(28) a. H   b. H   Third plural subject prefix

       H   H

   vè   *vende*   *ve*   *ngohoro*

        L   L

Assuming that tiers align in order to meet the structural description of a rule (Schlindwein, 1986), H spread would delink the stem L tone in such forms, thereby making possible its relinking to the final vowel in the trisyllabic stem case as in (29).

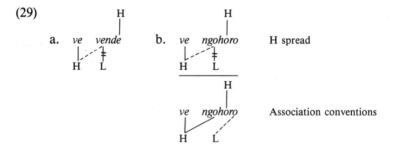

(29)   H   H

    a.   *ve*   *vende*   b.   *ve*   *ngohoro*   H spread

          H   L   H   L

                              H

                      ve   *ngohoro*   Association conventions

                       H   L

The crucial difference between the two types of cases is that the L tone set afloat in (27a) has nowhere to link, whereas the free L tone of (27b) can link to the final stem vowel, giving the appearance on the surface of deletion.

We see therefore that the MTH has had two results so far: (a) for Tiv, the rule of *!*-deletion can be eliminated, (b) more generally, it appears that one can restrict the ability of a rule to refer to a segment's being unspecified for [F] to the class of segments targeted by a rule assigning [F].

Before leaving Tiv, two problems need some discussion. First, a tense like the general past in Tiv is an exception to *!*-deletion (Pulleyblank, 1986). Such exceptionality can be accounted for within the MTH if we assume that the L tone of the general past (the sole marker of this tense) is not a morpheme per se, but is the result of a morphologically conditioned rule of phonological epenthesis. On the assumption that phonological rules operate on existing tiers (except in the case of an insertion rule where no tier yet exists), the L tone inserted by such a rule will be assigned to the existing tonal tier, as in (30) and will be unable to link to noninitial stem vowels because of the crossing constraint:

(30)   *yevese* ⟶ *yevese*
            | |
            H   L H

Such exceptionality would only be possible where the element involved consists of a single segment, given the general prohibition against the insertion of multiple segments by a phonological rule: *A ⟶ B C/P __ Q (Chomsky and Halle, 1968). Secondly, Ellen Livingston (personal communication) notes a problem concerning the tonal behavior of the first and second person singular prefixes. Such prefixes have the pattern H*!* and it would therefore be expected (incorrectly) that the floating L tone downstep marker should link up in stems of sufficient length. I tentatively assume that the correct tonal representation for these two prefixes is with a prelinked L with H spread applying to derive the H*!* pattern. The application of H spread is blocked lexically because of the strict cycle condition; its postlexical application is allowed, but applies after tier conflation/bracket erasure, deriving the fact that the floating L cannot link up, as shown in (31).

(31)

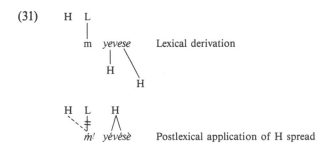

3. Antigemination Effects

Another type of argument in favor of the MTH concerns the OCP. McCarthy (1986) argues that the OCP holds at noninitial stages of phonological derivations, that is, the OCP is an active constraint on phonological processes. If the application of a rule would create an OCP violation, then application of the rule is blocked. For example, the rule of Afar syncope given in (32a) applies straightforwardly to the examples in (32b), but is blocked from applying to the cases in (32c) since its application would yield violations of the OCP.

(32) a. AFAR SYNCOPE: V   → ø/# CVC __ CV
                        [−stress]
      b. *xamíla*   *xaml-í*   'swampgrass (acc/nom-gen)'
         darágu   *darg-í*   'watered milk'
      c. *xarar-é*   'he burned'
         miḍaḍí   'fruit'

If the identical segments that would be brought together by syncope belong to different morphemes, however, then the rule is not blocked:

(33) a. *as-is-é-y-yo*   →   *asséyyo*   'I will cause to spend the day'
      b. *sas-is-é-tto*   →   *sassétto* 'You will cause (him) to hide.'

The above distribution of facts is accounted for by the MTH in conjunction with the OCP. Application of syncope is blocked in (34a), but permitted in (34b).

(34) a.

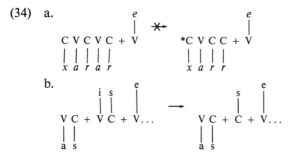

Returning to tone, it should first be noted that tonal properties provided the original motivation for the OCP (Leben, 1973). Although somewhat controversial (see for example Odden, 1986), it is clear that one of the most rampant cases of violations of the OCP consists of heteromorphemic sequences of identical tones. Such cases do not constitute violations, however, if the MTH is adopted. The argument that I make here is the following: If cases of tonal antigemination are observed, this indicates the active presence of the OCP (at least in the languages and domains where antigemination holds); if the OCP holds, then the MTH is required to prevent heteromorphemic sequences of identical tones from consituting violations.

3.1 Object Clitics in Yoruba

As a preliminary point, I assume here that the OCP can be relativized to the CV skeleton (or X skeleton). This means that two string-adjacent identical elements constitute an OCP violation only if they are linked to adjacent skeletal positions, where skeletal positions are adjacent if either string-adjacent or adjacent on the relevant projection.[5] For example, because the OCP is skeleton sensitive in Yoruba, sequences of identical tones are possible in examples like those in (35). (Following Yoruba orthography, a grave accent indicates L; an acute accent indicates H; absence of tone marking, M).

(35) a. *àlapà* 'type of food'
          | |
          L L

      b. *tíotó* 'grey hornbill'
          | |
          H H

Note that in such cases the surface M tone is underlyingly unspecified, receiving an M tone by a default rule.[6]

The tonal behavior of object clitics is completely predictable. I interpret this as meaning that tone is not specified underlyingly [the minimal redundancy condition of, for example, Kiparsky (1982) and Pulleyblank (1988a)] but is assigned by a redundancy rule. When the verbal host ends on a L tone (36a) or on a M tone (i.e., unspecified) (36b), then the clitic surfaces as H; when the verb ends on a H tone (36c), the clitic itself is M:

(36) a. *rà* *á* 'buy it'   *lù* *mí* 'beat me'
      b. *jẹ* *ẹ́* 'eat it'   *pa* *mí* 'kill me'
      c. *rí* *i* 'see it'   *rí* *mi* 'see me'

Given the function of the OCP as a blocker of rules (the antigemination effect), the above pattern follows straightforwardly from the rule stated in (37).

---

[5]For detailed discussion of the skeleton-sensitive OCP, see Archangeli (1986) and Archangeli and Pulleyblank (1986). In particular, Archangeli and Pulleyblank argue that skeleton sensitivity is derivative from general properties of rule application in conjunction with a hierarchical structure of distinctive features.

[6]For arguments in favor of M-tones being underlyingly unspecified in Yoruba, see Pulleyblank (1986) and Akinlabi (1984).

(37)   OBJECT CLITIC TONE ASSIGNMENT: $V \longrightarrow H/\underline{\quad\quad}]_{obj\ cl}$

Where the verb is either L toned or toneless, object clitic tone assignment proceeds without problem (38a,b); but on the assumption that phonological rules apply to already existing tiers (see Section 2.3), the rule is blocked by the (skeleton-sensitive) OCP where the verb is H toned (38c):

(38)   a.   *lu mi* ⟶   *lu mi*
         | | |
        L   L H

    b.   *pa mi* ⟶   *pa mi*
                     |
                    H

    c.   *ri mi* ⟶̶   **ri mi*
       | | |
       H   H H

This analysis also accounts for the one object clitic that behaves differently from those shown above. With the second person plural object V*yin*, object clitic tone assignment always applies, even if the verb is H. The reason for this is that V*yin* is the only bimoraic clitic. When an H tone is assigned by (37), the extra mora of the clitic prevents the output from constituting an OCP violation.[7]

(39)   *b u*   *y ī*   *b u*   *y ī*
      | | | | | | | |
      C V + V C V ⟶ C V + V C V
       | | |
       H   H   H

          bú uyín   *'abuse you (pl)'*

The tonal behavior of object clitics is automatically accounted for by the rule in (37) within a theory adopting the OCP; without the OCP, the cases involving H tone verbs would require an additional ad hoc rule, and the third person plural clitics would require an underlying tonal specification, unlike all other object clitics.

    [7]Note that while a general version of the OCP could account for the antigemination effect in (38), it would incorrectly fail to allow the insertion of a *H* in (39). The vowel quality of the first mora of the clitic V*yin* is accounted for by a left-to-right rule of spreading. This spreading rule also accounts for the quality of the third person singular forms in (31). For discussion, see Pulleyblank (1988a).

3.2 H-tone Linking and V Deletion

The second type of evidence for antigemination effects in Yoruba concerns a rule that inserts a H-toned mora at the end of a subject noun phrase in clauses of an appropriate tense and polarity (e.g., in the non future affirmative but not in the nonfuture negative) (see, e.g., Abraham, 1958; Bamgboṣe, 1966). The correct characterization of the syntactic conditions is not of importance here, hence I adopt for the purposes of exposition the labels "+nom(inative)" for subjecthood and "+t/p" for the appropriate tense/polarity properties. The rule can then be formulated as (40a), producing results such as those in (40b):

(40) a. H-TONE LINKING: ∅ ⟶ V /_]$_{NP, +nom, +t/p}$
             |
             H

     b. *bàtà*   *bàtàá wâ*   'shoes; there are shoes"

       ọmọ   *ọmọọ́ wâ*   'child; a child is there'

H-tone linking interacts with a rule of V deletion, which deletes the first in a sequence of two vowels. This rule is optional, but would normally apply in connected speech to derive *bàtă wâ* and *ọmọ́ wâ* from the forms in (40b). The rule can be formulated as in (41).[8]

(41)   V-DELETION: V ⟶ ∅/__ V (optional)

Noting as before that phonological rules assign features to existing tiers and assuming that H-tone linking is a (morphologically-conditioned) phonological rule, the derivations of the subject noun phrases in *bàtă wâ* and *ọmọ́ wâ* proceed as in (42).[9]

(42) a.

    b.

---

[8] For general discussion of this rule, see Courtenay (1969) and Oyelaran (1971). For arguments that it is always the first V slot that deletes, see Pulleyblank (1987).

[9] A regular rule of spreading derives the rising contour on the the final vowel of *bàtă*. Also, note that the quality of the inserted vowel is determined by the rule of spreading mentioned above in connection with object clitics.

Having established the basic pattern, there are two cases of interest with respect to antigemination, one case illustrating an antigemination effect with respect to H-tone linking (40) and another illustrating antigemination involving V deletion (41). Consider first the case involving H-tone linking. When a noun ends in an H tone, no lengthening takes place (Abraham, 1958; Bamgboṣe, 1966).

(43)	*Délé	*Déléé wâ*	'Dele; Dele is there'
	Délé wâ

This lack of lengthening is automatically accounted for by the OCP; were H-tone linking to apply in such a case, an OCP violation would result. Antigemination therefore correctly blocks application of the rule:

(44)
$$
\begin{array}{cccc}
d & e & l & e \\
| & | & | & | \\
C & V & C & V \\
\end{array}
\searrow\!\!\swarrow \quad \xrightarrow{\;\times\;} \quad
\begin{array}{ccccc}
{}^*d & e & l & e & \\
| & | & | & | & \\
C & V & C & V & V \quad \dots \\
\end{array}
$$
$$
\begin{array}{c}
\text{H}
\end{array}
\qquad\qquad
\begin{array}{cc}
\text{H} & \text{H}
\end{array}
$$

Concerning V deletion, Bamgboṣe (1966) observes that the lengthened vowel is obligatory when a final M tone is immediately preceded by an H tone:

(45)	*aláṣọ	aláṣọ́ọ́ wâ*	'cloth seller; a cloth seller is there'
	aláṣọ́ wâ

The failure of V deletion in such cases is again accounted for by the OCP. Application of V deletion would bring together two H tones; its application is therefore blocked by the OCP, another antigemination effect:[10]

(46)
$$
\begin{array}{ccccc}
a & l & a & ṣ & ọ \\
| & | & | & | & | \\
V & C & V & C & V \\
& & | & & \\
\end{array}
\longrightarrow
\begin{array}{cccccc}
a & l & a & ṣ & ọ & \\
| & | & | & | & | & \\
V & C & V & C & V & V \\
\end{array}
\xrightarrow{\;\times\;}
\begin{array}{cccccc}
{}^*a & l & a & ṣ & ọ & \\
| & | & | & | & | & \\
V & C & V & C & \varnothing & V \\
\end{array}
$$

3.3 The Morphemic Tier Hypothesis

Cases such as those in sections 3.1 and 3.2 show that the domain of the OCP in Yoruba includes stages of the derivation as late as the postlexical stratum, the stratum on which phrase-level rules like object clitic tone assignment, H-tone linking and V-deletion take place (see Akinlabi, 1984). This is of interest as far as the MTH is concerned, because morphological concatenation is not blocked by the OCP. Consider, for example, cases of partial reduplication

---

[10]Recall that the OCP in Yoruba is skeleton sensitive. This allows the application of H-tone linking in (46).

such as those in (47), where nominal forms are derived from verbs by the affixation of C*í*.

(47) a. *dùn*   *dídùn*   'sweet; sweetness'
       b. *ga*   *gíga*   'tall; tallness'
       c. *rí*   *rírí*   'see; seeing'

Despite the fact that a verb like *rí* bears an H tone, no antigemination effect is observed when affixation takes place. That is, no asymmetry between H-toned verbs and verbs with M or L tones is observed. This fact would be problematic if all tones were assigned to a single tier given the evidence for the OCP as an active principle in Yoruba. On the other hand, if the MTH is adopted, then such behavior is expected:

(48) a. H   b. H   c. H
          | | |
       di + dun   gi + ga   ri + ri
          | |
          L   H

4. Conclusion

In this chapter, evidence has been presented in favor of the MTH. Tonal evidence from Tiv shows that initial associations of tones in that language reflect the configurations assigned by such a hypothesis. In Yoruba, the occurrence of tonal antigemination in phonologically derived contexts but not in morphologically derived contexts is a pattern predicted by the morphemic tier hypothesis in conjunction with the obligatory contour principle.

Acknowledgments

Thanks to Diana Archangeli, Morris Halle, Mike Hammond, Larry Hyman, Ellen Livingston, Michael Noonan, Keren Rice, and Debbie Schlindwein for discussion of an earlier draft of this chapter. The work on Yoruba was supported by a grant from the Faculty Research and Innovation Fund of the University of Southern California.

References

Abraham, R.C. (1958). "Dictionary of Modern Yoruba." Hodder & Stoughton, London.
Akinlabi, A. (1984). *Tonal Underspecification and Yoruba Tone.* University of Ibadan, Ph.D dissertation.
Archangeli, D. (1986). The OCP and Nyangumarta Buffer Vowels. *Proceedings of NELS* 16, 34–46.
Archangeli, D. and Pulleyblank, D. (1986) "The Content and Structure of Phonological Representations." MIT Press, Cambridge, Massachusetts, in preparation.

Arnott, D.W. (1964). Downstep in the Tiv verbal system. *African Language Studies* 5, 34–51.

Arnott, D.W. (1968). 'Introduction' to R.C. Abraham (1940). "The Principles of Tiv." Gregg International, Farnborough, Hants.

Bamgboṣe, A. (1966). "A Grammar of Yoruba." Cambridge Univ. Press, Cambridge.

Chomsky, N., and Halle, M. (1968). "The Sound Pattern of English." Harper, New York.

Courtenay, K. (1969). *A Generative Phonology of Yoruba.* UCLA Ph.D dissertation.

Goldsmith, J. (1976). "Autosegmental Phonology." Indiana University Linguistics Club; Garland, New York, 1979.

Leben, W. (1973). "Suprasegmental Phonology." Indiana University Linguistics Club.

McCarthy, J. (1979). *Formal Problems in Semitic Phonology and Morphology.* MIT Ph.D dissertation.

McCarthy, J. (1981). A prosadic theory of nonconcatenative morphology. *Linguistic Inquiry* 12, 373–418.

McCarthy, J. (1982). Prosadic templates, morphemic templates, and morphemic tiers. *In* "The Structure of Phonological Representations I" (H. van der Hulst and N. Smith, eds.), 191–224. Foris, Dordrecht.

McCarthy, J. (1986). OCP effects: Gemination and antigemination. *Linguistic Inquiry* 17, 207–263.

McCawley, J. (1970) A note on tone in Tiv conjugation. *Studies in African Linguistics* l, 2, 123–129.

Monahan, K.P. (1986). "The Theory of Lexical Phonology." Reidel, Dordrecht.

Odden, D. (1986). On the role of the obligatory contour principle in phonological theory. *Language* 62, 353–383.

Oyelaran, O. (1971). *Yoruba Phonology.* Stanford University Ph.D dissertation.

Prince, Alan (1987). Planes and Coping. *Linguistic Inquiry* 18, 491–509.

Pulleyblank, D. (1983). Tiv and the association conventions. *Proceedings of ALNE 13/NELS 13, GLSA, Amherst* 211–228.

Pulleyblank, D. (1986). "Tone in Lexical Phonology." Reidel, Dordrecht.

Pulleyblank, Douglas (1987). Vowel deletion in Yoruba. *J. African Languages and Linguistics,* in press.

Pulleyblank, Douglas (1988a). Vocalic Underspecification in Yoruba. *Linguistic Inquiry* 19, 2, in press.

Pulleyblank, Douglas (1988b). The feature hierarchy and Tiv vowels. In preparation.

Schlindwein, D. (1986). Tier alignment in reduplication. *Proceedings of NELS* 16, 419–433.

Chapter 21

Continuant Voicing in Slave (Northern Athapaskan): The Cyclic Application of Default Rules

Keren Rice

In many Athapaskan languages, there are alternations between voiced and voiceless stem-initial continuants. It initially appears that information about the internal structure of words in the form of c-command is required to express the distribution of the voiced and voiceless continuants. If access to structural information of this type is necessary, morphological makeup of a word is greatly weakened. I demonstrate in this chapter that if independently motivated principles of nonlinear and lexical phonology are adopted, all voicing alternations can be accounted for without recourse to structural information, namely c-command, thus allowing the maintenance of the strong claim that rules have only highly constrained access to the internal structure of a word.

In this chapter, I draw all my data from Slave (pronounced [slevi]), specifically the dialect spoken in Fort Nelson, British Columbia, Canada. The facts are similar in other Slave dialects and also in many other Athapaskan languages, and the analysis proposed generalizes to these other dialects and languages.

In Section 1, I discuss the underlying inventory of Slave consonants with focus on the continuants. In Section 2, the mechanism required to account for the voicing alternations is formalized and justified. The environment in which alternations are found is examined in Section 3. Section 4 offers an account of the distribution of continuants.

Theoretical Morphology   Copyright © 1988 by Academic Press, Inc.

1. The Consonant Inventory

The inventory of stem-initial consonants in Slave, together with an underspecified feature matrix, is given in Table I.[1] The default for [spread glottis], a feature that is of relevance in the following discussion, is given in (1).

(1)   [ ] → [−SG]

In general the unspecified values in the table are filled in by default rules such as the one given in (1). However, the continuant consonants require some comment.

Phonetically there is a contrast in aspiration in the stops and affricates, with all stops and affricates being voiceless. Continuants, on the other hand, differ phonetically in terms of voicing. While the continuants differ phonetically from the stops and affricates in terms of laryngeal features, both features of aspiration ([spread glottis]) and voice are not necessary distinctively. With just one of these features as distinctive, the second can be derived. I assume that the distinctive feature required is that of [spread glottis].[2] As shown in (1), the value [+SG] is the marked value for this feature; the unmarked value [−SG] arises either by a default rule (as in (1)) or by insertion of a morpheme consisting of this feature, as discussed in Section 2. Later

Table I   Stem-initial consonants in Slave

	b	m	d	t	t'	n	dð	tθ	tθ'	ð	dz	ts	ts'	z	dl	tl	tl'	l	dž	tš	tš'	ž	g	k	k'	gh	?
SG[a]				+				+				+				+				+				+			
CG[b]					+				+				+				+				+				+		+
Anterior																			−	−	−	−	−	−	−		
Coronal	−	−																					−	−	−	−	
Distributed							+	+	+	+																	
Nasal		+				+																					
Lateral															+	+	+	+									
Continuant							Λ[c]	Λ	Λ	+	Λ	Λ	Λ	+	Λ	Λ	Λ	+	Λ	Λ	Λ	+				+	

[a]Spread glottis.
[b]Constricted glottis.
[c]Branching segment (affricate).

[1]I use the practical orthography adopted by the government of the Northwest Territories, Canada. The following correspondences should be noted: *th*, [θ]; dh, [ɤ]; sh, [š]; zh, [ž]; gh, [ɣ]; ch, [č]. C' is a glottalized consonant. *ee* is a mid front tense vowel [e] and *e* is its lax counterpart [ɛ]. The acute accent over a vowel represents high tone and a hook below a vowel is nasalization.

[2]The choice of [spread glottis] as a distinctive feature over [voice] is well motivated. The stops and affricates differ phonetically in Slave by the feature [spread glottis], suggesting that this is the relevant distinctive feature. The patterning of the morpheme known as the *d* classifier also suggests this. See Rice (1986b) for discussion of this morpheme.

redundancy rules add the redundant voice feature.[3] The rules shown in (2) are those required to introduce this feature. Rule (2a) makes all unaspirated continuants [+voice] while rule (2b) adds the feature [−voice] to other consonants in the inventory.

(2) a. [+continuant, −SG] → [+voice]
     b. [ ] → [−voice]

Most stem-initial continuants alternate between the [+SG] ([−voice]) and the [−SG] ([+voice]) forms, as in (3).[4] The relevant segments are in boldface. The hyphen preceding the noun in the second column indicates that this noun must be preceded by a possessor, either a possessive prefix or a noun. The suffix -é on the possessed forms is found with many nouns and indicates that the noun occurs in a branching construction.

(3) | Nonpossessed | Possessed | |
     |---|---|---|
     | *sah* | *-zazé* | bear |
     | *xay* | *-ghayé* | year |
     | *thę* | *-dhéné* | wart, star |
     | *ƚue* | *-lué* | fish |
     | *shíh* | *-yídhé* | mountain |

The alternating continuants are unmarked for the feature [SG], with the feature values filled in as discussed in Section 2. The voiceless ([+SG]) counterpart occurs initially and the voiced ([−SG]) when it is preceded by segmental material.

The alternations found in (3) are typical: Most continuants show both values phonetically depending on environment. However, there is a set of continuant-initial stems in which no alternations are found between the [−SG, +voice] and the [+SG, −voice] forms. These stems are invariable, always beginning with a [−SG] continuant. Some of these words are given in (4).

(4) | *la* | work |
     |---|---|
     | *zhah* | snow |
     | *zhú* | clothing |
     | *zǫ* | only |

These nonalternating continuants are opaquely [−SG], the unspecified value for this feature.

---

[3] I often refer to the value for the feature [voice] even though this feature is redundant. This is because [voice] is the distinctive feature traditionally used in the Athapaskan literature to capture the distinction between the continuants (see, e.g., Cook, 1984; Hargus, 1985; Howren, 1968; Kari, 1976; and Rice, 1988).

[4] All syllable-final nonsonorant consonants in Slave neutralize to [h]. The underlying representation of the word 'bear' is thus /SaS/, where 'S' represents a continuant unspecified for the feature spread glottis. When word initial, the value [+SG] is realized; syllable-finally, [+SG] is the only feature that remains.

To summarize, underlyingly the nonalternating continuants have the opaque value [−SG]. Most continuants show alternations, and these are unmarked for a value of the feature [SG].

2. The Alternations

In this section I am concerned with only the alternating continuants in order to determine how the alternations between the voiced and the voiceless counterparts arise. I first look at alternations in verb stems and then turn to other categories.

In verbs, alternations between the voiced and voiceless continuants are transparent: The voiced ([−SG]) member occurs following a segment that is [−SG] and the voiceless ([+SG]) counterpart following a segment that is [+SG].[5] Illustrative verbs are shown in (5). The capital letters indicate continuants that are unspecified for a value of the feature [spread glottis]. The alternating continuants are in boldface.

(5) a. stem *-Se*
        hehse   'I shout'
        *he**z**e*   's/he shouts'
     b. stem *-Lu*
        *heh**ł**u*   'I net'
        *he**l**u*   's/he nets'
     c. stem *-Xa*
        *heh**x**a*   'I lace snowshoe'
        *he**gh**a*   's/he laces snowshoe'
     d. stem *-THah*
        *deh**th**ah*   'I start to carry'
        *de**dh**ah*   's/he starts to carry'

In order to account for these alternations, I assume that representations are hierarchically structured, as proposed by Clements (1985), Archangeli and Pulleyblank (1986), and Sagey (1986), among others. The segment [h] is characterized as consisting of just the feature [+SG], with all other features unspecified. In order to produce the alternations found in (5), there is a phonological rule that spreads the feature [+SG] from left to right, associating it with a stem-initial continuant.[6] This rule is shown in (6).

[5] There is one set of exceptions to this, the set of verbs where the stem is preceded by the morpheme traditionally identified as the *l* classifier. These verbs contain a morpheme consisting of just the feature [−SG]. See Rice (1988) for some discussion.

[6] Only continuants show this alternation; thus the target of the rule must be specified as [+continuant]. The rule appears to be restricted to verbs; this need not be specified in the structural description of the rule because verbs offer the only environment in which the structural description of the rule is met.

(6)   [SG] SPREAD:

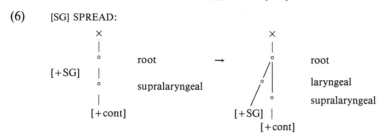

The feature [+SG] associates to the root node of a following segment that is continuant, providing the segment with its laryngeal features. By the process of node generation discussed by Archangeli and Pulleyblank (1986), the laryngeal node is automatically added to the continuant upon association of laryngeal features.[7]

When a continuant follows a segment that is not marked for the feature [+SG], the structural description for the rule in (6) is not met. The default rule that fills in [−SG] as the unmarked value, shown in (1), is able to apply. This is illustrated in (7).

(7)

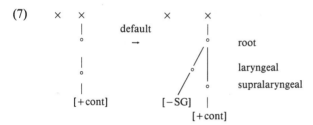

The rule of [SG] spread given in (6) and the rule adding the default value [−SG], illustrated in (7), are ordered (6) followed by (7) by the elsewhere condition, which orders a more specific rule before a more general one.

Having established the rule of [SG] spread, I now turn to an examination of continuant voicing alternations in nouns and postpositions. Here the situation is somewhat different from that in verbs. With nouns and postpositions, a stem-initial continuant is phonetically [−SG, +voice] whenever it follows segmental material, be it [+SG] or [−SG]. This is shown in the examples in (8) for possessed nouns. In these forms, as above, a hyphen before a possessed form indicates that the form must be preceded by a possessor, either a possessive prefix or a noun. In all cases, the initial consonant of the possessed noun is voiced. This noun is also shown in isolation to show that it is not underlyingly opaquely marked as [−SG], as the nouns in (4) are. Notice that the possessed stem begins with a voiced continuant whether it follows a vowel

---

[7]Node generation is defined by Archangeli and Pulleyblank (1986) as follows: A rule or convention assigning some feature or node *a* to some node *b* creates a path from *a* to *b*. Since the feature [SG] must be dominated by a laryngeal node, this node is automatically created when [SG] is associated.

(where the voiced form is found in verbs) or a [+SG] consonant (where the voiceless form is found in verbs). The former is illustrated in (8a) and the latter in (8b).

(8) Nonpossessed   Possessed
  a. *sa*   *-zaé*   sun
      sah   *-zazé*   bear
      łuh   *-luzé*   spoon
      łue   *-lué*   fish
      the   *-dheé*   belt
      tháhi   *-dháhé*   tent pole
      shi   *-yiné*   song
      sháh   *-yá*   knot
      shíh   *-yídhé*   mountain
      xay   *-ghayé*   year, winter
      xoh   *-ghozé*   thorn
      xeníh   *-gheníhé*   raft
  b. *shį*   *gah zhiné*   rabbit, rabbit's song
      łuh   *dezonah luzé*   child's spoon

In compounds the initial continuant of the second element is also voiced no matter what precedes. The continuants under discussion are in boldface. In these examples, the morphological makeup of the compound is shown on the second line. It can be seen that the stem in question begins with a voiceless continuant in isolation.

(9) *sahdhéh*   'bearskin'
       sah 'bear' + *theh* 'skin, hide'
     tthígha   'head hair'
       tthí 'head' + *xa* 'hair'
     tenihzélé   'pot handle'
       tenih 'pot' + *séł* 'hook' + *-é* possessive

In nouns with derivational prefixes, the initial continuant of the noun is voiced no matter what precedes.

(10)   *seh* 'hook'; *dahzeh* 'hook'
         dah' 'above' + *seh* 'hook'
       so 'frost'; *dahzo* 'frost on trees'

Finally, the initial continuant of a postposition is voiced no matter what precedes. Examples of the stem-initial continuant following a vowel are given in (11a) and examples with it following [h] in (11b).

(11) a. *seghá*   'next to me'
           se- first person singular + *xá* 'next to'
           seghǫ   'about me'
           sedhede   'before me'
           seghá   'for me'
           selǫ   'tip of me'
      b. *gah*   'rabbit'
              gah ghá   'for the rabbit'
           meeh   'knife'
              meeh lǫ   'tip of knife'

Clearly, the stem-initial continuants in the examples in (8) through (11) are not simply receiving their value for [SG] by the rules described for verbs; if they were, one would expect to find the [+SG, −voice] continuant following the [+SG] consonant [h]. However, the [−SG, +voice] counterpart is found. One would also expect the word-initial continuants to be voiced, given the default rule discussed for verbs.

The second problem, the fact that word initial continuants are voiceless, can be accounted for easily by simply adding to the grammar the rule given in (12).

(12)   [ ] → [+SG] / [_____
                         [+cont]

This rule leads to [−voice] stem-initial continuants when the continuant is initial in its domain. (See Section 4 for further discussion and definition of "domain.")

The first problem mentioned above involves the fact that when the continuant-initial element on a right branch is a noun or postposition, it must be phonetically [−SG, +voice] no matter what precedes it. Since the features needed to assign this value are not necessarily present in the representation of the first morpheme in a position adjacent to the stem-initial continuant, it appears that a feature must be introduced into the representation in the appropriate circumstances to give the correct value. I suggest that such a feature is introduced as a linking morpheme similar in nature to the Rendaku morpheme in Japanese discussed by Ito and Mester (1986). This morpheme in Slave is best characterized as consisting solely of the feature [−SG]. The morpheme is inserted into a structurally defined environment as given in (13).

(13)   Insert [−SG] in [__[ ]$_{N, P}$]

This morphological rule inserts the [−SG] morpheme when the second member of a branching construction is a noun or postposition, as in the constructions shown in (8) through (11). The morpheme associates to the initial

consonant of the following stem. It introduces the feature [−SG] for continuants, creating a specified value, the marked value for the feature [SG], for
continuants. It also introduces the default value [−SG] for other stem-initial
consonants. Since [+SG] is the lexically marked value, this morphological
insertion rule functions to fill in the default value, [−SG], leading to the
feature [SG] being specified for stem-initial consonants.

A derivation of *gahdhéh* 'rabbit skin' is shown in (14).

(14)

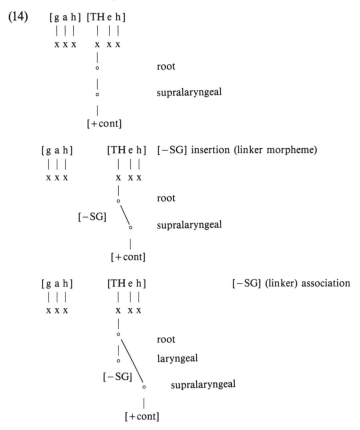

The voicing alternations found in Slave stem-initial continuants are thus
accounted for in the following way. In verbs, the feature [+SG] spreads from
a preceding morpheme ending in [+SG]. If spreading does not occur, the
default value [−SG] is assigned. In other major categories, the feature [−SG]
is introduced as a linking morpheme and associates to its right. In these categories, then, all right-branch continuants are phonetically [−SG, +voice].
Other rules introduce the appropriate values for [SG] in other environments
([+SG] stem initially and syllable finally).

3. The Environment

Having examined the mechanism needed to account for voicing alternations of stem-initial continuants in Slave, I now turn to the environment in which the voiced continuants occur. The environments in which they are found are summarized in (15) through (18). The relevant data are given in (8) through (11) and are not repeated here. Boldface signifies that an initial continuant is phonetically [−SG, +voice].

(15) possessed noun   In possessed nouns, the initial continuant of the possessed noun is voiced.

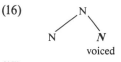

(16)   In compounds, the initial continuant of the second element is voiced.[8]

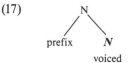

(17)   In nouns with derivational prefixes, the initial continuant of the noun is voiced.

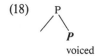

(18) P   The initial consonant of a postposition is voiced.

There are environments in which voiced continuants fail to occur. These environments, along with illustrative data, are given in (19) through (23). In each example, the nonpossessed and possessed compounds are shown on the first line. The second line illustrates the morphology of the compound. The third line shows the possessed and nonpossessed forms of the first word of the compound in order to demonstrate that the item in question shows voicing alternations.

---

[8]Possessed nouns (as in (15)) and compounds (as in (16)) have the same structure. There is a second compound type in Slave where the initial consonant of the second noun is voiceless, as in (i).

(i.)   *tth'atheh*   'moss bag'
       tth'a 'moss' + *theh* 'bag'
       dechįtuh   'wooden spoon'
       dechį 'wood' + *tuh* 'spoon'

See Rice (1985) for some discussion of the differences between the two compound types. The structure of this second compound type is discussed in Rice (1986a), where it is proposed that these compounds are reanalyzed phrasal structures.

(19) a. possessed noun   The initial continuant of a possessed compound

voiceless

is voiceless.

   b. Nonpossessed   Possessed
       sahdhéh   -*sahdhéh*   'bearskin'
       sah 'bear' + *theh* 'skin, hide'
       cf. *sah, -ʒaʒé* 'bear'
       sadzée   -*sadzée*   'watch, clock'
       sa 'month, sun' + *dzée* 'heart'
       cf. *sa, -ʒaé* 'month, sun'
       łétʼéh   -*łétʼéhé*   'bread'
       łé 'flour' + *tʼéh* 'charcoal'
       cf. *łé, -lézé* 'flour'
       tlitlʼulé   -*tlịtlʼulé*   'dog harness'[9]
       tlị 'dog' + *tlʼuł* 'rope' + -*é* possessive
       cf. *tlị, -lịé* 'dog'

(20) a. possessed noun   The initial consonant of a possessed deverbal
                              noun is voiceless.

   b. *tháts'eh²oni*   -*tháts'eh²oné*   'chewing tobacco'
       cf. *thá, -dháh* 'mouth'
       sǫ́ts'edę́yai   -*sǫ́ts'edę́yaé*   'necklace'

(21) a.   The initial consonant of the second member of
                             a compound is voiceless when it is a deverbal
                             noun.

   b. *²ehts'oisǫ́ts'edę́yau* 'beaded necklace'
       ²ehts'oi 'bead' + *sǫ́ts'edę́yai* 'necklace'

So far, I have shown that stem-initial continuants exhibit voicing alternations. Only stem-initial continuants display the voicing alternations, never those
that are prefix initial. This can be seen by examining the data in (22), where
voiceless prefix-initial continuants are found in environments where voiced continuants might be expected.[10] The relevant continuants are in boldface.

---

[9]The expected alternation is between [ł] and [l]. In the word 'dog,' there is an unexpected
affrication process so [l] alternates with [tl] rather than with [ł].

[10]The verb in Slave, as in other Athapaskan languages, has a complicated structure that is
only alluded to in this chapter. See Rice (1988) for detailed discussion of the intricacies of the
verb. In the first example in (22), the prefix *shine-*, glossed as 'sing,' is an incorporated stem
related to the independent noun *shị, -zhiné* 'song' and to the verb form *d·shị* 'sing.'

(22)   The initial continuant of a stem incorporated into
                                  the verb as a prefix is always voiceless.

 k'eshinededah 's/he walks around singing'
  k'e- 'around' + *shine* 'sing' + *de-* 'noise' + *dah* 'walk sg.'
  cf. *-zhiné* 'song' (possessed form)
 nísénįhtį 's/he placed me'
  ní- 'terminative' + *se-* first person sg. direct object + *nį-*
  aspectual prefixes + *htį* 'handle animate object'

Finally, voicing alternations are found only within a word. Stem-initial continuants are always voiceless when they are word initial, even when the continuant is preceded by other material within the phrase. This can be seen in the data in (23).

(23) *shíh gots'ęh sah* 'bear from the mountains'
  shíh 'mountain' + *gots'ęh* 'from area' + *sah* 'bear'
  dene thahne 'the lonely person'
  dene 'person' + *thahne* 'alone'

4. An Account of the Distribution of Continuants

The environments in which voiced continuants are found are summarized in (24), where boldface signifies that an initial continuant of the item is voiced.

(24) possessed noun, postposition left branch compound
   compound

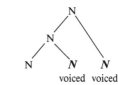

Those in which voiceless continuants occur are summarized in (25). Boldface here indicates voicelessness.

(25) possessed compound possessed deverbal noun

Given these environments, it is apparent that voiced continuants in Slave are found just in case X^0 c-commands the phonological material to its left within the word.[11] It is only in the cases that c-command does not hold that the voiceless consonant occurs. Thus in (24), the boldface item c-commands the item on its left. In (25), on the other hand, the boldface item does not c-command the material to its left since the first branching node that dominates it does not also dominate the item to the left. The voiceless continuant thus occurs.

While this c-command analysis is descriptively adequate, it raises an interesting problem. It has been proposed in the morphology literature that phonological and morphological rules have only limited access to the morphological makeup of a word (see, e.g., Allen, 1978; Siegel, 1977; Pesetsky, 1979; Mohanan, 1982; Kiparsky, 1982; Williams, 1981; Ito and Mester, 1986). Ito and Mester propose a generalized version of Williams's (1981) atom condition, stated in (26).

(26)   In lexical derivations from X, only features realized on X are accessible (Ito and Mester, 1986, p. 49).

This condition is equivalent to the strong version of the strict cycle condition, which prohibits access on a higher cycle to information contained wholly within a lower cycle. The c-command proposal violates this condition. To see this, consider the structure in (27).

(27)

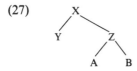

In order to know that a rule cannot affect A, it is necessary to know that Z branches. Given a principle of morphological inaccessibility, information about the internal structure of Z should not be available. Yet the c-command hypothesis requires just such information. It is therefore desirable to seek another explanation, one not requiring morphological access. The problematic forms are summarized in (28).

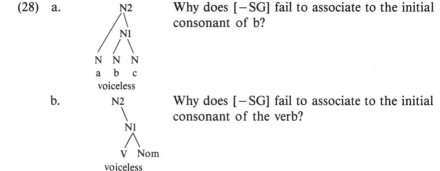

(28)   a.   N2   Why does [−SG] fail to associate to the initial consonant of b?

       b.   N2   Why does [−SG] fail to associate to the initial consonant of the verb?

---

[11]C-COMMAND is defined as follows: A node A c-commands a node B if the first branching node that dominates A also dominates B.

The solution that I propose relies on the cyclic filling in of default values. I employ three principles of lexical phonology: structure preservation, the strict cycle condition, and the strong domain hypothesis. The principle of structure preservation restricts rules that introduce nondistinctive features to the postlexical component of the grammar (Kiparsky, 1982). The strict cycle condition (Kiparsky, 1982, and elsewhere) states that nonstructure-building rules of the lexical phonology must apply in a cyclic manner. The strong domain hypothesis, also proposed by Kiparsky (1982), states that a rule will apply as soon as it is able to. While this proposal states that a rule will apply early if it can, it does not indicate just what "early" means. The strong domain hypothesis thus must be extended. I assume proposals made by Dresher (1985) and Archangeli and Pulleyblank (1986), that once reference is made to a feature value, its value must automatically be made active. This prevents ternary use of feature values, a desirable consequence, as argued by Stanley (1967), Kiparsky (1982), Pulleyblank (1986), Dresher (1985), and others.

The first issue is where in the derivation, in the lexical component or the postlexical component, the default value for the feature [SG] is filled in for continuants. Recall that while continuants in Slave are not generally distinct underlyingly for the feature [SG], a number of stem-initial continuants must be marked as opaquely [−SG] since they do not show alternations in voicing of continuants. Because there are opaque segments, [SG] is thus a distinctive feature for continuants. In addition, the rule of [SG] spread and the rule associating the linker morpheme [−SG] to continuants apply in the lexicon (see below for justification), again making [SG] a distinctive feature for continuants. Given this, the default rule required to fill in the unspecified value for this feature is not restricted to the postlexical component by the principle of structure preservation. The rule is predicted by the strong domain hypothesis to apply as early as possible.

The principle of structure preservation predicts that the default rule introducing the feature [SG] is not restricted to the postlexical component. In addition, the strict cycle condition allows this rule to apply in the lexicon. The rule of [SG] Spread and the rule associating the linker morpheme [−SG] to stem-initial continuants apply between morphemes and are sensitive to word-internal structure. The strict cycle condition thus allows the application of these rules in the lexicon. Once these rules have introduced the feature [SG] onto continuants, the default rule is predicted to apply immediately since both its values are active.

The second issue, given that the default rule for [SG] applies in the lexicon, concerns just what "as early as possible" means. As discussed above, once a feature value is made reference to, the redundancy rules assigning that feature value must automatically apply. The [SG] default rule therefore must apply as soon as reference is made to this feature, either by [+SG] association or by introduction of the linker morpheme. These rules, as argued above, apply cyclically. The default rule must immediately follow these rules and therefore it must apply before leaving the cycle. Thus at the end of a cycle, continuants are fully specified for the feature [SG]. On the next higher cycle, all continuants on the lower cycle are specified for a value of [SG]. Since the default rule is a feature-filling rule, it does not apply to continuants which are already specified for a value of this feature.

To illustrate the above analysis, consider now the derivations of the configurations in (28). In (28a), on the N1 cycle, the morpheme [−SG] is inserted by the morphological rule inserting the linking morpheme, given in (13). This feature associates to c, as in (29).

(29)
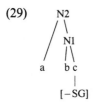

Once [−SG] associates to c, the default rule applies to fill in the [SG] values for other continuants on the N1 cycle. b thus receives the value [+SG] since it is initial. This is shown in (30).

(30)
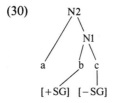

On the N2 cycle, b already has laryngeal features associated with it. The feature [−SG], the linking morpheme, does not associate to b since it already has a specified value for [SG].

In (28b), the structural description for the insertion of the linking morpheme [−SG] is not met on N1 because this morpheme is inserted when the right branch is a stem, not when it is an affix. The default rule filling in [+SG] applies on the N1 cycle, however. The resulting representation is given in (31) on the right side of the arrow. Even though the structural description for the insertion of [−SG] is met on N2, it fails to associate since the initial continuant of N1 is already specified for laryngeal features. The application of the default rule of N1 is illustrated in (31).

(31)

N2   N2
/ \   / \
/   N1   →   /   \ N1
/   / \   /   / \
a   b c   a   b   c
| |
[−SG]   [−SG]

[+SG] [−SG]

Now consider a left-branching structure, as in (32).

(32)

On the N1 cycle, the morpheme [−SG] is inserted, adding the feature [−SG] to b. Also on this cycle, a is specified [+SG] by the redundancy rule given in (12). On the N2 cycle, c has not yet been specified for a value of [SG]. The structural description is met for the morpheme [−SG] to be inserted and since c has not yet received a value for this feature, it can associate to c.

Given a constrained theory of underspecification and cyclic filling in of default values, an application independently predicted by principles of lexical phonology, the correct phonetic representations can be achieved.

An alternative analysis that suggests itself, given the similarity of Slave to Japanese Rendaku, is one relying on the obligatory contour principle (OCP) (Leben, 1973; McCarthy, 1986). It could be proposed that insertion of the morpheme [−SG] is blocked on the N2 cycle in the right-branching structures such as (28a) because OCP violations are created. Under the OCP analysis, in the structure in (28a) [−SG] is inserted before c on the N1 cycle. OCP blocks the insertion of [−SG] before b on the N2 cycle because adjacent occurrences of [SG] on the laryngeal tier arise. In (32), [−SG] is inserted before b on the N1 cycle. The insertion of [−SG] is blocked before c on N2. However, [SG] can spread from b to c by the rule given in (6), which allows either value of [SG] to spread.

There are reasons for rejecting the OCP analysis, however. First, the OCP solution is not a general one: The cyclic application of default rules is still required to account for the nominalizations (28b), assuming that the linker morpheme is inserted only before major category lexical items and not before affixes.

Second, the OCP solution is empirically inadequate even when the nominalizations are excluded from discussion. To see this, consider a structure such as (33), a compound composed of compounds or a possessive construction where the first noun is itself possessed. The relevant structure is given in (33a) and examples in (33b).

(33)   a.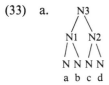

b. *sedené sahdhédhé* 'my husband's bearskin'
    se- 'my' + *dene* 'man' + *-é* possessive
    sah 'bear' + *thedh* 'skin, hide' + *-é* possessive
  sedezonáh sadzée 'my child's watch'
    se- 'my' + *dezonah* 'child' + *-´ possessive*
    sa 'sun' + *dzée* 'heart'
  sezazáh łét'éhé 'my bear cub's bread'
    se- 'my' + *sazáh* 'bear cub' (possessed form)
    łé 'flour' + *t'éh* 'charcoal' + *-é* possessive

The N1 and N2 cycles in this structure are independent of each other. Under the OCP analysis, on both of these cycles [−SG] can be inserted, before b and d respectively, creating [−SG, +voice]-initial segments of these morphemes, as expected. This is shown in the representation in (34).

(34)

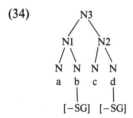

On the N3 cycle, c is in the environment for the insertion of the [−SG] linker. However, this structure is similar to that in (28a): OCP blocks the insertion of [−SG] before Nc.[12] However, as in the structure in (32), c is preceded by a noun with the feature [−SG]. On the laryngeal tier, this feature is adjacent to the initial consonant of c. Parallel to (28a), the spread glottis feature should spread, associating to c and yielding eventually a voiced continuant on c. As shown by the data in (33), this is not the correct form, since when c is a continuant it is always voiceless. This suggests that the OCP solution is not as general as the default ordering solution. The cyclic ordering of default rules predicts that default values are filled in on N2, and c is thus specified [+SG] on N2. When the N3 cycle is reached, c already has a specified value, which it retains.

5. Summary

Slave initially appears to present a counterexample to the claim that morphological structure is not accessible to the phonology. Specifically, it appears

---

[12]Another problem arises if the morphemic tier hypothesis (McCarthy, 1986) is assumed. The morpheme [−SG] would be introduced as a linker on its own tier; thus it would not be apparent that an OCP violation existed.

that access to the structural notion of c-command is required. However, a careful examination of the Slave data reveals that, given certain assumptions for the phonology, the need for access to morphological structure disappears. Reference is required to underspecification and the strong domain hypothesis with cyclic application of default rules. Default rules apply cyclically to fill in feature values. The apparent c-command facts follow from the nature of the cycle.

Given these assumptions, there is no need for access to morphological structure. In recent work on prosodic phonology, languages for which c-command has been claimed to hold of phonological rules (see, e.g., work by Kaisse (1985) and Manzini (1983)) have been reanalyzed. The environment for the rules that seem to apply in domains defined by c-command have been shown to follow from a highly constrained theory of prosodic domains, a theory that is more explanatory than that of c-command. See Selkirk (1987) for discussion. As Ito and Mester (1986) state for Japanese: "our explanation turns on the fact that prosodic structure itself carries forward the crucial information that later phonology depends on. We speculate that other putative counterevidence will fall to the same sort of analysis, when the relevant prosodic structures are properly understood" (p. 69). The Slave example proves to be just such a case.

References

Allen, M. (1978). *Morphological Investigations.* PhD dissertation, University of Connecticut.

Archangeli, D. (1984). *Underspecification in Yawelmani Phonology and Morphology.* PhD dissertation, MIT.

Archangeli, D., and Pulleyblank, D. (1986). *The Content and Structure of Phonological Representations.* Manuscript.

Clements, G.N. (1985). The geometry of phonological features. *Phonology Yearbook* **2**, 223–250.

Cook, E-D. (1984). "Sarcee Grammar." Univ. of British Columbia Press.

Dresher, E. (1985). Constraints on empty positions in tiered phonology. *Cahiers Linguistiques d'Ottawa.*

Hargus, S. (1985). *The Lexical Phonology of Sekani.* PhD dissertation, UCLA.

Howren, R. (1968). *Stem Phonology and Affix Phonology in Dogrib (Northern Athapaskan).* Papers from the 4th Regional Meeting of the Chicago Linguistic Society, pp. 120–129.

Ito, J., and Mester, R-A. (1986). The phonology of voicing in Japanese. *Linguistic Inquiry* **17**, 49–74.

Kaisse, E. (1985). "Connected Speech: The Interaction of Syntax and Phonology." Academic Press, New York.

Kari, J. (1976). "Navajo Verb Prefix Phonology." Garland, New York.

Kiparsky, P. (1982). Lexical morphology and phonology. *In* "Linguistics in the Morning Calm" (I.-S Yang, ed.). Hanshin, Seoul.

Leben, W. (1973). *Suprasegmental Phonology.* PhD dissertation, MIT.

McCarthy, J. (1986). OCP effects: Gemination and antigemination. *Linguistic Inquiry* **17**, 207–263.

Manzini, R. (1983). Syntactic conditions on phonological rules. *MIT Working Papers in Linguistics* **5**, 1–9.

Mohanan, K.P. (1982). *Lexical Phonology.* PhD dissertation, MIT.

Pesetsky, D. (1979). Russian Morphology and Lexical Theory. MIT ms.

Pulleyblank, D. (1986). "Tone in lexical phonology." *Studies in Natural Language and Linguistics Series*.

Rice, K. (1985). Noun compounds in Dene. *Journal of the Atlantic Provinces Linguistic Association* **6/7**, 55–72.

Rice, K. (1986a). *The Structure of Slave Compounds*. Paper presented at the Canadian Linguistics Association Meeting, May.

Rice, K. (1986b). *The Function of Structure Preservation: Derived Environments*. Paper presented at NELS, November.

Rice, K. (1988). "A Grammar of Slave (Dene)." Gruyter, Berlin, in press.

Sagey, E. (1986). *The Representation of Features and Relations in Nonlinear Phonology*. PhD dissertation, MIT.

Selkirk, E.O. (1987). On derived domains in sentence phonology. *Phonology Yearbook* **3**.

Siegel, D. (1977). The adjacency condition and the theory of morphology. *NELS* **8**.

Stanley, R. (1967). Redundancy rules in phonology. *Language* **43**, 393–436.

Williams, E. (1981). On the notions 'lexically related' and 'head of a word.' *Linguistic Inquiry* **12**, 245–274.

Subject Index

Language Index